THE ILLUMINATED HEART

THE ILLUMINATED

HEART

*Perspectives on East-West
Psychology and Thought*

Jock McKeen *&* Bennet Wong

THE HAVEN INSTITUTE PRESS

240 Davis Rd
Gabriola Island, BC
VOR 1X1 Canada

www.haven.ca

ISBN 978-0-9784618-0-5

Designed and typeset by Toby Macklin
www.tobymacklin.com

To Carl Jung & Confucius

Voices from the past,
you represent the lineage
of those who came before.

To Jennifer Bement Sass

Your lifetime of learning
in loving relationships
is an inspiration.

To Katrina Marlise Wong

You are
our personal connection
to the possible futures.

Contents

Part III • Chinese Philosophy

Part IV • Chinese Medicine

Part V • Integration

Foreword

For more than four decades we have been a team, working together with people in the area of health, wellness, life style and relationships. We have investigated approaches in Western medicine and psychiatry, and have added theories, practices and techniques from Eastern philosophy and medicine. Although we have worked primarily in North America, where we founded The Haven, a school for human development, we have also travelled and taught extensively in Asia, as well as in Latin America, Russia, Europe, Africa, and the Middle East. People have often asked us, "What do you call what you do?" and "Where did you learn to do that?" We want to share what we have synthesized from our eclectic investigations and practices.

This book has been a long time gestating. Our ideas have been steadily growing and changing, emerging from our personal and professional association over the past 40-plus years. We have described this odyssey elsewhere.[1] Others have also written about our approach.[2]

We both trained in Canada in medicine. Ben then studied psychiatry in the US and became a practising adolescent psychiatrist in the 1960s in Vancouver. Jock studied classical Chinese acupuncture in England after graduating from medical school, and practised East-West medicine after a stint in emergency medicine in Vancouver. In the early 1970s, we practised in adjacent offices with a common waiting room. We met every day to discuss our approaches with our clients, in order to deepen our understanding of our professional practices. We believed in a bodymind approach, seeing mind, body and spirit as one. Thus our approaches to medicine and psychology were the same – we attempted to deal with the whole person.

In the 1970s, we were both involved in the energy approaches of the human potential movement and were teaching seminars in personal development. We were very enthusiastic about the great gains in life and life style that our clients were able to make in residential experiential growth groups. In 1975, we left our medical practices to devote our time to teaching in group contexts. This ultimately led to our establishing a school, The Haven Institute, where we ran groups and trained others to work with people in a humanistic way. We utilized ideas from Western psychology, psychiatry, philosophy and medicine; we synthesized these ideas with what we had learned from classical Chinese philosophy and medicine. Incorporating a here-and-now existentialist perspective and a humanism that was part of the ethos of the 1970s, we have built a personal philosophy. We live by these teachings ourselves, and they have given meaning and perspective to our lives, both individually and together. This philosophical and professional approach involves a synthesis of Western and Eastern ideas. It is woven into all that we have taught, and the programs we have developed, and the training we have done with other professionals.

We read and searched and questioned, not only in our own fields, but also in literature, philosophy and theology. We learned from our clients and friends. We met many groundbreaking authors and thinkers; we are grateful for their readiness to engage and investigate with us, and our lives are richer for our friendships with them. In our personal as well as our professional lives, we have travelled a long way. Our aim now is to share what we have learned, and to try to make sometimes complex and confusing ideas more accessible. We are writing from a personal point of view; our intention is to translate these ideas into palatable forms while retaining academic rigour.

In our work, we have focused on people learning to find their own way. The reader need not agree with what we say; instead, we hope that our style of study, self-reflection and self-discovery might be useful in itself. Our teaching approach is heuristic – enabling people to discover for themselves – rather than didactic. We have written this book in a spirit of investigation and challenge rather than as a pat series of answers. We include principles that have stood the test of time, addressing topics that have come up repeatedly with clients and in our own personal search.

We have studied and worked with people from diverse backgrounds, and have taught in other continents. We have been in the humbling position of teaching Chinese medicine to Chinese people in their own country. We first went to Asia to learn more, and discovered that Asian people are hungry for what we have to teach. Indeed, the initial impetus to write this book came from a request from our Chinese-speaking associates after we conducted an extended seminar in China. They told us that they learned a great deal from seeing the relevance of classical Chinese ideas to Western psychological notions. This has stirred us to look further at the key issues that pertain to very different cultures – we find that beneath the differences there is much commonality amongst people. We hope that this book will be relevant for people of many persuasions.

Frequently, misunderstandings have occurred in the process of translating Chinese material into English. Similarly, there are misconceptions amongst Asian people about Western approaches. Our goal is integration and enhanced understanding between the cultures. The West has disregarded some of the richest material from its own heritage.

The same has occurred in China: many classical notions are currently in disrepute in the country where they originated. We wish to regain some balance, so that past, present and future can be encouraged into deeper harmony.

In our blending of notions from philosophy, psychology and medicine, we have aimed to make this book practical and clear without being reductionistic or oversimplified. There are many publications that offer quick and trite answers to earnest and serious questions; if we manage to offer our opinions without prescriptions or easy answers, we will have accomplished what we set out to do.

Bennet Wong and Jock McKeen
Nanaimo, BC, Canada
January 2012

Acknowledgments

Many people have shared their lives with us, telling us their insights, their stories and their perspectives. The theories and ideas we put forth have been tested in the laboratories of many relationships. Thanks to you all. Out of all these people, we pull out one name to mention specifically – Jennifer Sass. Jennifer was always a staunch supporter of The Haven and "Ben and Jock" and responded with immediacy when funds were required to move this project toward completion.

Thanks to our many friends in Asia who have helped us learn so much by their generous and caring assistance every time we have had a question. Sean Feng has been a diligent and patient scholar of East-West translation. Donna Lee has helped in both scholarly ways and by connecting us with others with whom we can collaborate. And a special thanks to Yafang, who for years has pushed us to teach around the world, refusing to let us retire until we complete our mission of spreading the message of communication, and the integration of East and West. We are grateful to you all.

As well, we are grateful to Leanne Mcintosh and Linda Larkey for their long hours of reading of the first draft. Their comments, suggestions and criticisms helped us clarify our presentation. Thanks too to Judy Hancock for her proofreading of the final text.

We are deeply grateful to Toby Macklin for his editing talents, which he applied to this task with dedication and precision. Toby is an intelligent and formidable collaborator. He never once backed down when we had disagreements over language or ideas; yet he also never closed his ears or his heart as we worked through the many impasses which inevitably arose in the refinement of the work. His standards of excellence have prompted us to really say what we mean. And his insistence on the integrity of the book, and the flow of ideas, has taken us deeper into subjects we previously thought we knew well. More than once he helped us convert something "punctilious and prosaic" into "poetic and pertinent." He read the manuscript thinking always of the readers to come; yet he also was respectful and responsive to our ideas at all times. We value our friendship and professional association with him greatly.

The Structure of the Book

This book is in five sections, corresponding with the Chinese *wu xing*, the Five Stages of Change (Water, Wood, Fire, Earth, and Metal). You can read more about the Five Stages in Part IV. The cycle is based on what the ancient Chinese observed in the progress of the seasons: that each stage prepares for and becomes the next, and that though the cycle returns and repeats, its manifestation each year is never quite the same. The cycle can be applied to many things, including learning, communication, relationships … and books!

> PART I (BEGINNINGS) corresponds to the Water stage of change in the Chinese cycle and provides some preliminary context for the book, a gestation of ideas. In particular, we present for the first time in writing our Dynamic Empathy Model.

> PART II (THE WEST) corresponds to Wood; here we launch into discussing various idea systems from Western psychology and philosophy, from Freud through Existentialism to Dialogical Psychology.

> PART III (CHINESE PHILOSOPHY) corresponds to Fire. In these chapters, we look at the intricate conversation amongst the *Book of Changes* and the three "great doctrines" of the Chinese: Confucianism, Daoism, and Buddhism.

> PART IV (CHINESE MEDICINE) corresponds to Earth and digs into the rich soil of this practical and spiritual system.

> PART V (INTEGRATION) corresponds to Metal. Here we consider themes that speak to both East and West and draw this work to a close. Because this is a cycle, we intend that this ending is also a time for reflection, renewed investigation, and action.

Other Streams and the Imagined Dialogues

Within this overall structure, there are different streams of thought. Besides the main chapters, we have included other forms of writing. There are poems and some prose stories that speak to our East-West experiences. In addition, we have written a series of imagined dialogues that occur periodically through the book. Some readers will want to jump from one dialogue to the next, and gloss over the detailed chapters; others will find the more poetic presentations to be less important than the meaty text portions.

The imagined dialogues feature ourselves in conversation with two outstanding individuals, one Chinese and one Western, who to some degree speak for their respective cultures. For the West, we have invited Carl Jung, and for China, Confucius (Kong Zi). We have selected them because, for us, they both have a style of thought and an approach to humanity that is comprehensive, inclusive and true to their own heritage while remaining open to ideas from other sources.

Confucius expounded his theories in ancient China, and probably never met anyone from outside Asia. Jung was deeply interested in other cultures and travelled extensively; nevertheless, his European heritage undoubtedly configured his thought structures. Both men exemplify basic qualities of earnest seeking and personal development in their respective cultures. They both asked deep questions about the nature of human individuals and society. Although we refer to many other writers and thinkers from both East and West, bringing these two men into the foreground helps us make our questions more personal. As Jung speaks for the West and Confucius speaks for the East, we, in the middle, try to fill our cup and pass the contents on to you. We hope to stir up timely issues for us all to consider. In the turmoil of today's world, we need a new framework to consider topics that affect people around the globe.

A Note about Chinese Romanization and Translation
In our own rendering of Chinese words in this book, we use the Pinyin system of romanization. Pinyin is widely used and provides a good representation of Chinese sounds.

Many of the texts we quote, however, use different forms of romanization. For example, the word meaning "life force" is written in Pinyin as *qi*, whereas in earlier forms it was written *ch'i*. Another common example is Pinyin *dao*, which has also commonly been written *Tao*. You will see other variants in the texts we quote.

The tones in the Chinese language provide a formidable challenge for Westerners. In Mandarin Chinese, which has four tones, the same sound can have at least four different meanings, depending upon the tone. In our text we do not include these tones. The interested reader can consult the Glossary of Chinese Terms on page 410, where we note not only the tones, but also the original Chinese characters.

In translation, we have tried to render the original Chinese words into accessible and meaningful English, avoiding both "Chinglish" reductions and the stiff literal translations that frequently appear. In researching this book, we have compared different translations to arrive at the richest understanding of texts that we can. We have quoted a number of different translations, and occasionally have offered our own variants on these.

PART I

Beginnings

Water

Water is the stillness that underlies the activity of the universe. Water is beyond life and death. It is the dark cold depths of the ocean, and the flowing nature that integrates all of life. Water is associated with the winter season, a time of rest and quiet for the seeds of the future. It is the time of contemplation and spiritual rejuvenation. Water is depth, coldness, stillness, meditation, death and resurrection, and the mystery of the holy mountain. Water is both the end of one cycle, and the resting place from which a new cycle is born.

1.1 Introduction

East is East, and West is West, and never the twain shall meet.[1]

This line, written by Rudyard Kipling about 1895, is often thought to express a common view of his time – namely, that the gap between the Orient and the West was simply too great to bridge. But it is worth reading on:

> Oh, East is East and West is West, and never the twain shall meet,
> Till Earth and Sky stand presently at God's great Judgment Seat;
> But there is neither East nor West, Border, nor Breed, nor Birth,
> When two strong men stand face to face, though they come from the ends of the earth!

We think that Kipling anticipated the possibility of a meeting between East and West, if obstacles could be overcome. Now, more than a century later, the gap has indeed narrowed remarkably. There are still many misunderstandings to be sure, but with travel and the exchange of goods and ideas, a new understanding and a more global perspective have emerged. There is still much work to be done, but much has been accomplished.

We have found in working with people around the world – not only in Asia, but also in Europe, Latin America, the Middle East and North America – that humans are more alike than different when it comes to fundamental concerns. We are both Canadians who have travelled and worked in China extensively, and to a lesser extent in other countries. We write from this viewpoint, comparing our experiences of Canada and China. However, we think that much of what we have seen in China is also pertinent to other Asian cultures, and our Canadian background gives us a feel for the issues in North America, Europe, and, to some degree, in Latin America. Thus, when we write of the "East" we mostly draw on Chinese examples; when we write of the "West" we mean North America and its European heritage.

East and West have a lot to learn from one another. So, we hope to clarify differences in such a way that people can access unfamiliar material. We also want to see where people are actually talking about the same things in different languages, in different metaphors.

Richard Wilhelm wrote in the 1920s that for Confucius there were four basic dimensions of human concern: the individual, the family, the state and humankind.[2] Confucius' classic the *Great Learning (Da Xue)* contains thoughts on self-cultivation, family regulation, state governing and world peace; all these factors were involved in an individual's moral cultivation. Even today, these Confucian thoughts have a profound influence on Chinese people's thinking, and the same topics are equally important for Westerners. To a large degree, the divergences in East and West come down to a difference in emphasis. In Asian civilization the focus has been on the family and humankind, while the West has emphasized the individual and the state. What is foreground in one culture's history has been less emphasized in the other. The challenge now is to bring forth what has been previously hidden. The East has the chance to learn about individual concerns, and the West can learn a great deal about the tradition of the ancestors, and about becoming citizens of the planet, and indeed, of the universe. In her 1979 introduction to Wilhelm's *Lectures on the I Ching*, Irene Eber wrote, "Since traditional China considered itself the world, Chinese considered themselves responsible for humankind rather than for the state." She continues, "China, of course, was neither the world nor all humankind, and, wrote Wilhelm, … China now no longer holds this illusion." She summarizes, "The fact is, however, that society continues to be thought of as a large human organism, the strength of which lies in the family."[3]

Aims of this Book

The world is now in a time of global crisis. Violence and dehumanization abound. Greed, selfishness, and pride limit the growth of the world community into what we could be – a family of responsible citizens of the cosmos. We have compromised the natural resources of the planet so that critical ecosystems, and indeed life on the globe, are in deep peril. We, the authors, celebrate the world leaders who are now reaching out over past divides, extending hands of cooperation and listening to each other with new ears, letting go of past prejudices. Humanity as a species is still in its childhood, yet current threats urgently require that we become adult and mature. The time is ripe for a new global vision – of humanity, cooperation, friendship and love. Our survival depends upon our growing up quickly, because we have arrested in our development as a race. If we delay, we might not survive.

In this volume, we will set out a distillation of ideas we have found important in our years of working with people. We hope to contribute to an unfolding consciousness of humanity's place in the cosmos, by summarizing our assumptions to date and offering what we can to a vision of people growing and becoming increasingly related, loving, and kind. In our work, we have always focused on individual human development in harmonious relationships with family, friends, community and the world at large. We propose a vision of each human being responsible and related; this view embraces singularity without selfishness, a sense of participation with other humans and with the universe.

Although the cultures of East and West are different in so many ways, we have found that people around the world face similar issues, albeit in their own contexts. There are many similar patterns in the ways that people from different places handle the issues of their lives. Superficial appearances are often different, but the pattern is the same; the concept of *isomorphism* (literally "same pattern") has helped us understand this. We deal with this in more depth in Chapter I.5, with the goal of elucidating these common patterns and themes.

We want to clear up misunderstandings and prejudicial views between East and West. But, as we shall see, this clarification is only a first step in a much more complex process of integration. We are focusing on East and West because this is our heritage and experience, but there are many other separations between different cultures that beg attention – for example, lack of understanding between peoples of different races, sexual orientation, gender, religion, colour, and age groups. This book is our contribution to the process of integration.

In comparing cultures, concepts that appear dissimilar on the surface because of cultural and linguistic differences are sometimes, at base, the same notion. Joseph Campbell often referred to the early-nineteenth-century German anthropologist Adolf Bastian's notion of "elementary ideas" that are expressed differently in each culture as "ethnic or folk ideas."[4]

> Bastian ... was the first to note that, with very few exceptions, there are themes that occur in all the mythologies and all the religions of the world. He called these elementary ideas. Where do they come from? They don't come from the fact-world; they come from the psyche, just as fairy tales do.[5]

We want to get beneath ethnic expressions into the depth of ideas about human beings, where we can stand on common ground. Our intention in this work has been to be practical, historically accurate, yet artistically inspiring. We have set out to integrate, and make more accessible, some complex notions developed over time in two diverse cultures. We touch upon theories and idea systems from various disciplines, including art, science, literature, philosophy, theology, psychology and medicine. After so much mistrust and misunderstanding and internecine struggle, our goal is to bring the highest and best of two cultures into dialogue. Our aim is that this book can be comprehensive and current, yet relevant beyond this limited time, since the ideas on which it is based address timeless issues.

Preserving for the Generations

The past should remain relevant to today and the unfolding future. We wish to incorporate the past into the living present, retaining the highest and the best, informing current life with an understanding of the finest of our heritage. In this way we believe that our development as a species can unfold and prosper.

In families, it often falls to the grown children to deal with a lifetime of accumulated material and memories when a parent becomes ill or passes on. In 2007, Jock and his sister helped their mother move into a retirement home. Jock reports:

> As we closed up our mother's large house, we were faced with the daunting task of dealing with its contents. As we sorted through papers, photographs and furniture, we were constantly faced with questions. "Is this important for someone to have?" "Is there an important memory that this picture or letter represents?" We had history in our hands, and we were deciding what to keep, what to pass on, and what to throw away. We frequently came across photographs of people we did not know, or articles whose history we did not recognize. These represented a lifetime of collection, of memories, of significance, of importance. Fortunately, our mother could fill in some of the blanks for us, and tell us who the unknown faces in the photographs were, either from her own family albums, or from the collections of our deceased father. We were entrusted to find the proper home for the ongoing memory of two family lines, our father's and our mother's, which came together in the nuclear family created by their marriage and life together. Much of the memory had been passed on orally, and seemed only loosely attached to the photos and papers in front of us. So, as we prepared these articles for their next home, we were charged with the urgency to somehow find a way to attach the oral memories to these items. We interviewed our mother. "Who were these people?" "What did they do?" "What were their dreams and goals and values?" "How did you feel about them?" We wanted to keep the best of the previous generation, and pass it to our children and friends and community, keeping the meaning intact. We did this in the hope that our children will continue this process, and do this for us, to keep the memory and the meaning alive and growing and evolving. We are here to witness each other.

As we write this book, we are faced with a similar dilemma. We want to keep the best of the memories alive from two distinct cultures,

Chinese and Western. We authors are intellectual/spiritual children of both of these cultures (they are our two "parents"), and we are trying to preserve the essentials from these two cultures for our extended family and for future generations. We have papers, photographs and diagrams from two parent cultures, which have lived separate existences for millennia, only touching and intersecting from time to time in limited ways. The task of sorting through this material is daunting. What do we keep? What do we highlight? What do we not understand? What can one lineage offer to the other?

In the English language literature, there have been a number of high quality books that have provided introductions and scholarly outlines of classical Chinese views of the world. And of course, there are countless books about Western psychology and philosophy. We have set out not simply to cannibalize these books, or render yet another volume of material that has already been covered, but to offer something new. In our careers, we have concentrated on interpersonal relationships, believing that health, healing and quality of life are associated with the nature of one's relationships. In this book as well, our ultimate focus is on relationship.

1.2　On the Bridge

I am standing in the middle of a bridge
Between two worlds
　　　　One ancient, the other modern
Awaiting the arrival of two dead men
　　　　Well, others tell me they are dead
But to me, after years of study of their life and works,
　　　　they are alive, familiar, old friends

Now, without ceremony, they appear, each from his side
One is tall, whitehaired, gnarled as an ancient pine tree, eyes shining
The other moves with Asian grace, a soft wind rustling his flowing robe
I feel a deep stirring, my heart opens
　　　　as they slowly approach, towards the centre
Where we can meet and embrace and share

This meeting is not only for us,
　　　　It is also for you, and for those
　　　　　　　　who will come later
These wise men afford me the privilege
　　　　to set down for others
What they wish to pass on

I am eager to listen
　　　　and report to you
What I am told
　　　　　　– Jock McKeen

1.3 A Meeting of Minds

KZ = Confucius (Kong Zi), CJ = Carl Jung, BW = Ben Wong, JM = Jock McKeen

Ben and Jock are sitting together, awaiting the arrival of their two guests. Jock will conduct the interview, and Ben will be one of the interviewees, along with Confucius and Carl Jung.

BW (smiling warmly): I am astonished by your audacity at setting up this event. You are indeed bold to invite these two venerable men to talk with us about our little book project.

JM (a little defensively): Well, I didn't know how else to get to this. As you know, I respect you and your acquired wisdom much more than you seem to; to you, your life is what it is, and you don't look upon yourself as anything special. But for me, you are my touchstone. I have learned so much in living and being with you, and I would like to see how these iconic men respond to your heartfelt proposals for humankind.

BW: Well, OK. I do think the whole thing is brash and rather far-fetched. But whatever you want, I will cooperate. I love you, and I see what you are trying to do. I just think it's verging on the absurd.

JM: But worth a try. I hear them coming.

Confucius and Carl Jung enter, greet the other two graciously, and settle comfortably in their chairs. The atmosphere is quiet, and the two famous men are relaxed and informal.

Ben's gentle manner matches well with the demeanor of their guests. He greets them with a warm smile, his open hands extended in welcome.

Jung is much taller than Jock expected, with craggy facial features and bright shining eyes; with his huge gnarled hands and rugged stature, his solemn presence is like a giant ancient tree. His eyes twinkle with humour.

Confucius is surprisingly short, and very quiet and unassuming; however, his presence is vast, and sweet, delicate, like the fragrance of an orchid garden. His eyes are dark, and he gestures gracefully with his soft hands as he speaks quietly.

Jock is the unusual, more youthful energy in the room, eager, moving quickly, talking louder and more excitedly; he sits forward in his chair and enthusiastically begins the interview.

JM (addressing the others): This is such an honour to be with you all, and to be able to ask you questions that stir my mind. Thank you. The idea of this interview came to me as I struggled to write about your lives and works. I kept thinking, "I wish I could talk to them, as men, as scholars, and have a personal conversation that could help me translate their thoughts into a context for a modern reader." Dr. Jung, I met Ira Progoff, who studied with you and wrote about you and your work; I learned about his technique utilizing a written dialogue with buried aspects of the self, and thought maybe I could do something from this technique. As I was contemplating this, I suddenly thought of this interview. So on one level, all of this is a product of my limited imagination.

CJ (smiling with amusement): I like this idea. When I was doing my automatic writing exercises to explore the unconscious in about 1915, I was attempting something similar. I was using a technique to try to get my ego out of the way, so that the unconscious could speak to me, and through me.

JM: I do see the similarity between this "fantasy" and your automatic writing. For me, in a very fundamental way, this is not so much a "fantasy" as an earnest desire to get deeper into the consciousness of humans.

CJ: Yes, I agree with your association.

KZ: This is similar to the mental approach I took to the *Yi Jing*, the *Book of Changes*. The book and the casting of the coins was not in itself anything exceptional; they represented a ritualistic approach to uncovering something that was hidden by everyday consciousness. What I tried to bring to my questions of the *Yi Jing* was an open mind and an open heart, with a willingness to listen to what the universe had to tell me. So for me, this exercise is fine.

BW: For me, I have not pursued such things in this way. I have relied upon my intuition to tell me which direction to take. But my approach has not been so scholarly; it's more from my heart.

JM: My first question is for you all, about the past. Master Kong, I have read that you do not believe that you actually came up with your views of life, but rather you were enunciating a philosophy that had been created by ancient beings in China. Is this so?

KZ: Yes, this is so. The ancient ones were so wise. They were not distracted by modern concerns, and could see clearly the place for human beings in the cosmic order. I was humbled and privileged to try to bring their ideas forward again after centuries of disregard.

JM: This is similar to what Ben and I are trying to do in writing this book. There is much wisdom from ancient times that we should consider in attempting to articulate a comprehensive viewpoint for the modern era.

CJ: Well, I would take exception there. The wisdom is not really "from ancient times" ... the wisdom is a pattern of thought and understanding that is expressed in time, but it is not itself something from the past.

JM: This is your notion of the archetypes. They are not things, and they are not bound into time and space. They are eternal patterns or principles.

CJ: Yes.

JM: Master Kong, do you agree?

KZ: Yes, I do agree with Dr. Jung. The main issue is one of pattern. His idea of archetypes (ancient patterns) describes well what I attempted to teach. The *ba gua* (the eight primordial images) are the elemental patterns of the universe, which are not things, and are not bound into time and space. They are spaceless, timeless, and are the fundamentals upon which time/space things manifest. This is the idea of *dao*, of a pattern of the universe. When one is in touch with this pattern, and remains in harmony with it, one expresses one's full participation with the universe, and things will go as smoothly as possible.

JM: But you yourself had many years where your life was not easy. You were exiled, and no one listened to your ideas.

KZ: Yes, this is so. And then, when people began to listen, they only heard through their filtered perspective. People have reduced what I wanted to say.

CJ: My experience too. As an old man, I finally gave up, and decided to let people take what they could from what I had discovered. I lost my urgency to teach, and relaxed and accepted that I had contributed what I could.

BW: I am coming to something similar. I have been discouraged at the limitations that people impose on life with their prejudices and filters.

JM: I am trying to learn this lesson.

BW, CJ, KZ (in unison): You are still a young man, and are only beginning to listen.

JM: I humbly acknowledge what your choir is singing!

BW (ironically, with warmth to the two sages): He does seem to be listening!

JM (warmed with their teasing good humour and keen interest): Another question. Dr. Jung, you were very interested in ancient Chinese wisdom for much of your career.

CJ: Yes, ever since I met the Sinologist Richard Wilhelm, and discovered that his findings were so much in agreement with what I had found in my psychological research.

JM: So, you had a respect for Master Kong and his traditions.

CJ: Yes, of course. I used the *Yi Jing* frequently, and much of the commentary in this rich book had come from Master Kong. (Bowing to Confucius). Sir, I honour you.

KZ: Thank you. I have a high regard for you, and your efforts to bring the wisdom of ancient China to the West. For my own part, I lived in a time when we did not know that Europe or North America existed. So, the idea of "East" and "West" did not have any form in my thoughts. I thought the issues were for Chinese, and non-Chinese. I now see that modern human beings have developed their cultures in a rich and varied way. And this brings new challenges that we did not see in my day. The basic issues are the same, but the situation seems much more complex, and in some ways, more urgent.

JM: Why?

KZ: Because the world is so fast, and so superficially connected, through all the electronic media. In my years, we would take weeks to travel quite short distances. Now physical distances are much less relevant. But for some reason, the distance between two human hearts now seems to be growing, without people realizing. They think because they can communicate electronically that they are experiencing connection. What they are actually doing is linking symbolic systems, but their hearts are not involved.

CJ: Yes, I concur. In my day we were aware of China, and it was for most people only a place of mystery and strangeness. For me, the Chinese ideas were a confirmation of deeper truths. But as I observe the modern world from this privileged vantage point, I see that people are largely lost, and they don't realize the trap they are in.

JM: Trap?

CJ: Yes. People live on the surface, rebounding in reaction to external events, without an inner rudder, without a spiritual connection to the depth of life.

KZ: I concur completely. This was also the issue in my day. Not much has changed.

BW: This has been my life's work. I saw very early on that people wanted to connect – indeed, they were connected – but were defended against experiencing this connection. I tried to help them open up, to remove their defences. Then a natural process of connecting could show. I used to say, "If people let go, they will slide naturally into intimacy." My life has been an experiment in seeing how close people can be, and this has been my friendship and loving partnership with Jock.

JM: You three are men that I have respected and revered for your careful considerations about humanity. What would you say were your dark sides, your underbellies, your failures?

CJ: I was not personal enough. I had my close friendships and relationships. But I was basically an isolate, especially in my later years. I was an affectionate and jovial associate for many, and I had a few "friendships of the mind" with people like Wilhelm. Dr. Wong, you have pursued a very different path, and I respect what you have done. We would do well to address the question of objectification, and help people to learn more about intimacy.

KZ: I had no notion of personal friendship in the way that Dr. Wong expresses. I was myself caught in the biases of my time, and as a teacher, I was isolated from my students. I was role-bound in my family, as were the others of my time. We did not have the modern approach to "self" that has come with Western psychology and religion. I was scholarly and cordial, but not intimate in many ways. I was very caring, one could say loving, with my students, but this was not "intimate" in that they did not know me. I could learn a lot from you.

BW: I am humbled by what you say. I respect both of you gentlemen for your vast contributions. I am such a small town boy. My work has been "up close and personal" and lacks the vastness of your approaches.

KZ: Sir, you do yourself a disservice. Up close and personal is what is required for this time and era.

CJ: I completely agree.

BW: Thank you both. Recently, my grown son asked us a difficult question. With all the objectification and violence in the world, evidenced in the news reports daily, he asked us, "Are you still hopeful about humanity?" Jock replied quickly, "I'm sober, but I don't want to succumb to hopelessness."

My answer came to me without much reflection. "I'm basically hopeless," I said.

JM: When Ben acknowledged his lack of hope, I pondered my quick response, and modified it with Kevin. "I could easily be hopeless, but if I give in to this, I won't write this book."

KZ: You gentlemen afford us too much importance. We contributed in our day, in our way. But you are men of the modern world. You encounter issues we did not anticipate. We support your idea of seeking integration, building on the old, and wedding it with the new to deepen our under-standing. Perhaps someone in centuries to come will summon you for an interview and an update. Carry on writing, and we can meet from time to time to discuss the progress.

CJ: I look forward to this. There are so many topics that call for integration.

BW: I'm very interested too. What seemed at first like an outlandish idea actually brings out many key issues. This whole endeavour is like a jig-saw puzzle, and I think this method can help us to assemble the pieces. I think our conversation would make a very interesting dramatic play. Perhaps I shall write it some time.

JM: Thank you, gentlemen. We will meet again as the book progresses!

1.4 Return of the Flower

A beautiful flower grew in the rich soil of ancient China. For centuries it developed, becoming ever more lovely, more varied, more strong. Then the climate in China changed, and the flower became rare. Its survival was threatened by many forces.

Its beauty was in danger of being lost forever. Remarkably, at this same time the threatened flower was carried to foreign lands, where it was transplanted. The hardy plant took readily to the new soil, and thrived in its adopted home, establishing deep roots and hearty blooms. Many people appreciated its mysterious beauty and helped it to grow. Now, years later, people who love this flower want to bring it back to the land of its origin, China.

The "flower" in this story represents Classical Chinese Medicine and philosophy, which have the qualities of beauty, grace, strength, fragrance, delicacy, sophistication, perhaps exoticism. Classical Chinese Medicine grew for many centuries, and then was endangered by cultural forces. Before it disappeared in China, it was transplanted to foreign soil. Now, the time is ripe to return a lost treasure from ancient times.

The Story of Chinese Medicine

For many centuries, Classical Chinese Medicine (CCM) existed in China, passed on from master to student. The system of CCM was made up of different parts – acupuncture, herbalism, moxibustion, diet, exercise, massage, and other therapeutic approaches. Western scientific medicine, on the other hand, which grew in Europe and North America, was first introduced into China about 1650, and gradually become more prevalent. In the 1800s, the Western system gained strength in China, spread by traders and missionaries.[1] Acupuncture, which was part of the Chinese medical system, was gradually transplanted to foreign lands through these same missionaries and traders. It had first appeared in Japan in AD 562, and reached Europe in the 1600s, spreading to Germany, Holland, France, Italy, and England. In the 18th, 19th and 20th centuries it continued to develop in these countries.[2]

Chinese Medicine in Europe has focused primarily on acupuncture. The thought systems accompanying European acupuncture have included both *wu xing* (Five Stages of Change) and, less prominently, *ba gang* (Eight Principles). European scholars worked on translations of classical Chinese acupuncture and philosophy texts and these ideas became available in French, German, Italian and English. The study of Chinese medicine, especially Five Element Acupuncture, flourished alongside an interest in *dao* and *Yi Jing.*

Meanwhile in China, Classical Chinese Medicine did not fare so well. In 1822, the Grand Medical College ordered that acupuncture and mox-ibustion practice be stopped. The reasons given included the cultural notion that the naked body was disgraceful. In its place, herbal medi-cine became the official method permitted. In 1929, there was an official attempt to abolish acupuncture theory altogether. Acupuncture went "underground" in China. Practitioners still worked in secret, but risked penalties from the authorities of the day.[3]

In 1949, the Peoples' Republic of China was established. The new leadership encouraged a form of treatment known as Traditional Chi-nese Medicine (TCM), rather than Classical Chinese Medicine. The goal was to provide health care to millions. The approach was primar-ily a practical one, and was less concerned with philosophical ideas. In this process TCM began to merge with Western scientific ideas. Signifi-cantly it did not include many of the ideas that had been transplanted to Europe, in particular the classical notions of *wu xing* (Five Stages of Change), *Yi Jing* and *dao, which* had been studied and developed for sev-eral centuries in Europe. For this reason, we distinguish in our writing between TCM (Traditional Chinese Medicine), which did not include the 'European' (classical) features, and CCM (Classical Chinese Med-icine), the earlier system that was transplanted into Europe. Our own interest is primarily in the ideas of Classical Chinese Medicine.

Acupuncture was introduced to North America in the late 1800s and continued quietly during the early 20th century; it was not in popular use in a culture dominated by Western medical approaches. In the 1970s, however, North Americans began looking to the East for ancient wis-dom. Teachers of Eastern ideas came to North America and Western students went to Asia to explore and study. In this context, the Euro-pean schools of acupuncture had many students from North America, and, in 1972, Jock became one of them, traveling to England to study. Upon his return to Canada, Jock established a medical practice focusing on energy medicine and acupuncture. It was at this time that we began to see the importance of integrating old and new ideas from East and West, with Jock practicing acupuncture, and both of us using the con-cepts of Wilhelm Reich in our work with people. We have written of this elsewhere, in particular in our book *Health and Happiness.*[4]

Ancient Wisdom: Teaching and Learning

For all the North American interest in things Eastern in the 1970s and 80s, the medical establishment and most lay people remained unconvinced. We quickly became accustomed to ancient Asian ideas being rejected in North America as quaint, or antiquated, or flat wrong. We thought things would be different in China. When we first went there in 1987 to attend an acupuncture congress, our intention was to learn more about this ancient culture, and especially about Daoism, Confucianism and acupuncture. To our surprise, we discovered that what we had learned in Europe and North America about classical Chinese ideas was far more detailed than the modern Asian teachings. We gradually learned that this was the result of 150 years' suppression of the ideas in Asia. We found ourselves in the ironic position of having come as students, and being invited instead to be the teachers. The previous generation of Chinese doctors was suspicious, and at the conference most of them held back defensively, regarding us with evident suspicion and concern. But the young people, themselves medical students and scholars, swarmed to the podium to ask us about ideas they had only dimly heard of before.

In the two decades that followed, we travelled to Asia numerous times to teach about Eastern and Western ideas, mostly, until 2006, in Hong Kong and Taiwan. Although we did not conduct seminars for lay people in mainland China until this current century, we did present at professional meetings and did some private consulting in the decades preceding. We realized that there was a growing hunger for classical Chinese ideas, which had until then been rejected as superstition. We were known as the "masters," who knew what the Chinese people did not. Even more ironically, the "master" of Chinese culture was Jock, the Caucasian, while Ben, the one with Asian blood, held the fort for the Western approaches. Since Ben was so deeply steeped in the ways of the West, he was seen as inwardly a white man, while Jock was regarded as having a Chinese interior. We were known affectionately as "the banana and the egg."

On an early trip to China in 1988, we took an excursion to visit some ancient sites. An odd situation arose during a tour of Xi'an. Jock, the ever diligent student, was taking notes as the guide spoke about the Chinese dynasties. As we walked about, Jock noted the vestiges of Confucian design and Daoist symbols in the architecture and layout of this once temple, now museum. One of our party noticed that the guide was surreptitiously taking notes every time Jock spoke about what he knew. Who was teaching whom? We say more about this experience at the beginning of Part III.

In China, we saw over and over again the same rejection of ancient Chinese thought we had experienced in Canada – in both cultures such ideas were generally regarded as quaint superstitions. Then, as China opened to the West, we thought that the response to our ideas would become more positive; this was when we began to consider teaching in mainland China. We had already been conducting seminars in Hong Kong and Taiwan for almost two decades by the time we conducted our first seminar for lay people in mainland China in 2006.

In 2006 and 2007, we were invited to Beijing to present ideas from both Western and Eastern medicine and philosophy in a two-part seminar entitled *Harmony: East-West Integration*. When we began this project, we thought we were returning a valuable possession to China, old ideas we had been caretaking until the time was right for China to reintroduce them – and, given the more open attitude of the 'new China', we thought that time was now. As we prepared for the seminar, we thought our task would be straightforward – to carry a thriving plant back to China, so that after the two programs, we would be done.

But we did not anticipate the atmosphere of the group. In our dialogue with the participants, we were surprised at the continuing rejection of the Chinese ideas, and the over-zealous embracing of Western ideas (including ideas that we thought somewhat suspect). So we were challenged in the teaching, and often found ourselves advocates for the ancient Chinese way. The experience was strange, humbling. But we persevered, and the participants stayed with us as we proceeded.

We came to realize that the ancient notions of *qi*, *dao*, meridians and other ideas, which had been suppressed in China for so long, have been slowly reintroduced, *stripped of their original spiritual associations*. And it seems that the Chinese people do not realize what has happened. They think they are receiving these concepts in a *modern* fashion; it seems to us that they are receiving reduced versions that lack the wealth of associations so splendidly maintained in Europe along with the Chinese ideas.

In the West, secondary schools have largely discontinued the teaching of classical languages such as Latin and Greek, from which many of our languages have arisen; as a result, the average student has less access to the roots of the language and the rich cultural background that underlies many concepts. A similar process has occurred in mainland China, where classical complex Chinese writing has been simplified in an endeavour to make the language more available to more people. In both East and West, the associations with ancient times have become more distant.

New Perspectives

We are accustomed to having our ideas about medicine, growth and learning questioned or outright rejected in the West. We have for decades found that Western medicine has been slow to adopt ideas from other cultures; in particular, it has been arrogant about ancient Chinese ideas. Also, our scientific colleagues have questioned us about our strong interest in humanistic ideas, which put the human experience at the centre; we have been criticized as not objective, "too involved" and "strange."

And, stranger still, as invited teachers, we often found that our seminar participants wanted one thing, and we wanted to provide another. The same dilemma confronts us as we write this book. Many readers will want a "how-to" book that outlines the practical application of ideas. We do give some suggestions about this, but we are staunch in our commitment not to reduce the elegance of ideas from either culture in the service of getting some "modern" popular approach.

We are also resistant to the idea that we can tell people "how it is." Such an expectation generally comes from Asian participants as an amalgam of transference and a tendency to elevate the teacher to a master status too easily, at the expense of their own critical thinking. When students in the West have asked us for answers, it seems to be the same thing. We are more concerned with clarifying the idea systems and the questions they raise, so that readers can craft a philosophical perspective of their own, pertinent to their own lives and activities.

In our recent visits to China we learned lessons from unexpected sources. We had thought we were transplanting a flower back to its original home; in fact we are discovering new perspectives on our own legacy of thought. We are being challenged to revisit our assumptions about history and culture and thought and medicine, and work towards a deeper synthesis.

1.5 Key Concepts

In this chapter, we are introducing some key notions that recur throughout the book. A basic understanding of these concepts will help you navigate what is to come. We have added some further comments on these topics in Appendix 1 so that you can investigate these issues in more depth whenever you wish. For now, we provide brief introductions to these key concepts.

Power and Strength

We have written about power and strength at length in other books.[1] Since these are often misunderstood, and are so important in human experience, we offer this summary here. Keep them in mind as you proceed. Here is a definition synthesized from our previous writing:

> Power is the use of the will to dominate or control, self or other; strength is the use of the will for self-expression.

Power involves the exertion of control over people or things. One can certainly exert power over oneself; but the main focus is generally in controlling the outside world. Strength is mainly in reference to oneself, not to the external world. Strength occurs when one embraces any situation without resistance. Strength involves the capacity to accept oneself. We put it this way:

> Power is the energy I use up to control others; strength is the energy I *am* in asserting myself.

To summarize, strength involves the use of the will *for* the expression of the self. Power involves the use of the will *against* self or other.

Dichotomies and Foreground/Background

When two dissimilar notions are presented, people often have the inclination to choose one over the other as better or more relevant. Yet, two different things can co-exist without cancelling each other. This is an important issue that comes up frequently in this book. The term dichotomy refers to a duality, seeing two different things as separate; people often see them as contradictory, or mutually exclusive, but this need not be so. A trite example involves the two condiments common on a restaurant table, salt and pepper. When there are only two seasonings offered, this is a dichotomy. But it is not necessary to choose only one or the other. One can select one, or both, or neither.

An important and related concept is that of foreground and background.

Whatever has one's focus or attention is foreground in one's awareness, and what is disregarded or forgotten is put into the background. In the example of salt and pepper, if one uses the salt liberally, and only a light dusting of pepper, the salty taste would be more foreground and the peppery taste would be more subtle, in the background.

When we propose ideas from the East and the West, we urge the reader to avoid the trap of choosing one over the other as the more important or "correct" aspect of the dichotomy. Instead, we recommend seeing East-West comparisons as issues of foreground and background. In this way, what sometimes seem like irreconcilable opposites actually co-exist on a continuum, with the emphasis constantly shifting.

Yellow River and Blue Sea Philosophies

We have written at length about this in another book; so, here a brief introduction will suffice.[2] The ancient Greeks developed their civilization near the Aegean Sea; their 'Blue Sea' approach has been the structuring principle for Western thought and development. In this perspective, reality resides in "things" (physical objects), and energy is seen to be derived from the physical reality. Western science has evolved as a comprehensive system to study the physical universe, and understand how "it" works. This has given rise to cause and effect logic and investigative science and a materialistic view of development and acquisition. The physical world, or *substance*, is primary, and energy is secondary, a manifestation of the behaviour of the physical objects.

The Yellow River philosophy emerges from ancient China in the northeast, where the famous Yellow River flows. This perspective evolved through a number of philosophical schools, including Daoism, Confucianism and Chinese Zen, all of which we discuss in Part III. The basic notion is that the universe ultimately is energy, not things. Energy, or *process*, is primary, and things are secondary, derivative manifestations.

These are two very different styles of thinking. They operate from distinct points of view, and underlie the great manifest differences between China and the West. But they need not be in competition; they can also be mutually informative and useful. As we have said, there is value in thinking of such dichotomies in terms of foreground and background.

Too Much or Too Little: Finding Balance

We have observed that people from both the East and the West often skew idea systems in two different ways – by *over-romanticizing* or by *pre-emptive dismissal*. Carl Jung, for example, has been vilified by some, and romanticized by others. In China, Confucius has at times been a cornerstone of Chinese politics; at other times, he has been dismissed as merely a dogmatic "rule guy." This is an issue of morality – when people judge the ideas as "good," they tend to romanticize them as true. If the ideas are judged "bad," they become wrong or false. This orientation to right/wrong and true/false skews one's viewpoint away from a balanced perspective. Idea systems have their use and limitations; if we avoid the temptation to make them right or wrong, we can use them in a neutral way.

In this book we investigate a range of theories and concepts, looking for nuggets of usefulness that are often lost by over-zealous dedication to the ideas, or dogmatic dismissal. We are looking to find balance between Eastern and Western approaches, and, indeed, to find equilibrium between over-reverence and curt rejection of ideas and theories.

The Notion of Psychology

Until recently, most Chinese universities did not have a department of psychology; instead, psychology was traditionally seen academically in China as a part of philosophy. In the 1980s, there were only five psychology departments in the entire country! This situation has been changing rapidly in recent decades, and the focus on psychology as a distinct field has been introduced into more academic institutions. Nevertheless, the historical blending of psychology and philosophy undoubtedly remains in the minds of many scholars.[3] Furthermore, the number of training programs is relatively small, and thus psychological services are often unavailable in face of the vast numbers of Chinese citizens.

Whereas in the West psychology has focused on the individual, in Asia more attention has been given to structures of conduct in social groups, beginning with the family; this has been more the domain of philosophy and anthropology than psychology. Now that Chinese universities have departments of psychology, we wonder what the focus will become. How will they adopt psychology, which in the West has emphasized individual development, into the Asian context where family is such a strong focus? We probably should not expect Chinese psychology to be the same as Western psychology.

Psychologists, counsellors and therapists now working in China have been mostly trained by Westerners; they have imported Western approaches, assuming they apply directly to Chinese culture.[4] But it might not be an easy fit. In many ways, Chinese culture utilizes a "copy and reproduce" principle. In our experience, the Chinese seem to believe (in a Confucian way) that the key to learning is to see the structure. Thus, when they are learning a new subject, they are able to grasp the whole structure of the system if the teacher shows them, and use the terms and elements appropriately after a very quick study. They are generally less able to see the structure by investigating the individual elements. If the teacher points out the forest, they can easily appreciate each tree; Western students more readily extrapolate from the behaviour of the individual trees to arrive at the structure (the Socratic way). For example, when we were teaching Freud's theories of development, the Chinese class questioned the overall system; once they knew the structure of psychodynamics, they learned the nomenclature and could apply it to their lives and experience within a few hours. In a similar class in the West, the students would have taken much longer to acquire the language.

In the West, we assume that an "enmeshed" family is a dysfunctional family, and Westerners working with Chinese people will often try to help them individuate beyond their enmeshment, to get past their so-called dysfunctional relationships. But this notion of "dysfunctional" comes from Western assumptions that do not necessarily apply in the East. Enmeshment in Chinese culture is not abnormal or dysfunctional per se: it is *indigenous to the culture*. For example, it is common for Chinese children to sleep with their parents and grandparents for a much longer time than in the West. Western family counsellors will urge parents to teach their children to sleep the night alone in their own beds, reflecting their well-intentioned confidence in the importance of self-soothing and self-reliance. When they encounter Chinese children sleeping in their parents' beds, they are inclined to label this as "dysfunctional." But this behaviour is occurring in the cultural context of the East, where it is seen as the norm.

Now that psychology is being introduced into China, cultural differences will highlight many misconceptions that need clarification, and many challenges will arise on the way to making a psychology that is appropriate for Chinese culture in the modern day.

Isomorphism
Isomorphism is a little understood and very important concept that will recur throughout the book. The word isomorph literally means "same shape" or "same pattern." In personal terms, this means that every aspect of your life is an expression of the same pattern; thus "you" are "you" in every minute of your life, in all your activities and roles. You might appear different (more conservative in your business life, more funloving in your home life); but the basic pattern is the same. The various expressions of you are isomorphs; they demonstrate the same structure.

Although your cells in your body are continually being replaced, and all the atoms in your physical structure will have changed within seven years, you continue to keep a consistent "look." You might be a little older, but someone who knew you 20 years ago will still recognize it is "you." Another way of saying this is that even though your physical structure has undergone some modification through aging, it is still an expression of your elemental unique pattern. So, you at age 60 and you at age 20 are isomorphic: the pattern is the same. Note that the pattern is not "like" or similar"; the pattern is the *same*.

For example, a child shows his hockey playing skills as a youngster, and years later when he is a professional athlete, the same "style" is still in evidence, but much more highly developed. The child showed the talent of the adult, but with less clarity; as a youngster, there was more promise than actual development. Nevertheless, the hockey playing of the child and the adult are isomorphic with each other.

In therapy and education, knowing these isomorphic patterns can be helpful. Commonly, people tend to relate to their environment in a habituated way that began early in life. For example, an abused, fearful child might develop the habit of sitting with her back against a wall to protect herself; years later as an adult, even though she seems very self-assured, she still chooses her location in a room with this fixated pattern. The pattern shows itself in various aspects of that person's life; she is cautious in investing and hesitant to trust her financial advisor (back against the wall, facing the door); she is reluctant to open up in her relationship with her partner; she chooses the same foods when eating out, rather than experimenting. Her childhood defence is isomorphic with her adult choices. Commonly, when people enter new situations as an adult, they tend to employ fixated behaviours to replicate the psychological/emotional substrate of earlier experiences. The adult behaviour is isomorphic with the child's process. In psychotherapy, this has been described as people continually reconstructing and projecting their imagined pasts. This fixation can be altered through reflection, feedback, and dialogue; but it takes will and imagination and clear decisions.

This idea is far-reaching, yet difficult to grasp. We hope that by introducing this early, you will become more and more familiar with this important and useful perspective as you proceed through this book.

Guru and Master Styles

For people to mature into full responsibility, their development requires a progress from dependency, through independence, to an amalgam of interdependence and autonomy. In both China and the West, education systems and family habits have promoted childhood dependence upon parents and authorities, without a comprehensive or effective means to pass through and beyond this childhood stage. Children look to parents and teachers for answers, and remain dependent so long as they are not stimulated to develop their inner resources to finding their own solutions. There are two styles to parenting, teaching and leadership, which we have dubbed the *guru style* and the *master style*.

GURU STYLE

The guru style is common in many human organization, beginning in the family. This point of view emphasizes morality (right and wrong), and authority is placed outside of the individual. Someone bigger or more important "knows" what is best and true. This is often seen in Asian religious systems; but, beyond this, we find it to be pervasive in both East and West.

MASTER STYLE

The master style is less common, because it requires individual maturity. Authority rests in the individual, and the individual chooses actions based upon personal ethics and information. There is no objective truth to follow, but rather the instructions of one's conscience. External authorities are respected, but not revered. Individual decision making is highly valued.

The master style promotes the growth and individuation of each person. There is more insecurity for everyone, because there is no absolute external authority that dictates action; but there is also more freedom. In a master system, people can participate in social systems without abandoning personal responsibility. In "mastery medicine" the patient is the decision maker; the doctor provides information. In "mastery education" individual learning and viewpoints are encouraged from both students and teachers, and there is no set dogma that cannot be questioned or revised. There is no ultimate "truth" – only individual perspectives to discover. The individual conscience is the final authority, with consequences for every decision and action taken.

COMPARING GURU AND MASTER STYLES

The guru style promotes an immature populace. People remain limited in their psychological development, and irresponsible in their lives and actions. They are fixated in a world of power, dependence, and brittle independence. The master style promotes more mature, responsible people who grow in their individuation and strength. For many, this is a frightening prospect, because the individual is the ultimate authority, and must bear the uncertainty of living beyond a pat morality, struggling to develop a personal ethical approach to life and relationships.

Decide What Fits for You

This book contains many ideas. In the turmoil of so many different mental conceptions, you are challenged to find what is relevant to your own experience. For us, this is an engaging and fulfilling project; we hope you find it the same. Good luck!

I.6   Helping

KZ = Confucius (Kong Zi), CJ = Carl Jung, BW = Ben Wong, JM = Jock McKeen

JM: Gentlemen, I would like to discuss the ideas about guru and master with you. Ben and I distinguish between guru systems and master systems to address the issue of personal responsibility.

BW: To us, a modern day guru is a power-based teacher who insists that students follow directives without question. We are aware that traditionally, guru teachers in the East were dedicated to helping their students to find their own way, and not insisting on blind obedience. But in many places, this system has broken down, and unfortunately, many teachers and students succumb to the temptation for one to know and the other to follow.

KZ: Yes, the guru system in classical times was not like this. The guru was a caring facilitator, inviting the student to do his own work towards self-realization. But this system has been prone to much abuse.

JM: We have observed this frequently. So, when we distinguish between guru and master, it is to get at this difference between power-based instruction and strength-oriented education. In terms of power and strength, the guru system is one of power; the master system is one of strength. Power involves exerting control over another or oneself. Strength involves integrity that comes with honest self-expression in vulnerability, which is the antithesis of control.

BW: A master teacher would be someone who caringly expects the student to practice and discover for himself or herself. The teacher is at times a guide, while holding the student responsible. A guru teacher often uses power and control and obedience and guilt; a master teacher sees that the student is not inferior, and encourages the natural learning process.

KZ: This dichotomy was already in evidence in my day. Emperors would start out with a harmonious relationship with heaven and would have the good of the people in their heart; and gradually, over time, this would erode into a power organization. The history of the Chinese dynasties shows this process over and over.

BW: They would start out as masters, and end up as gurus.

CJ: I notice the growing trend of the cult of "experts" who claim to know what is best for everyone. This has been so evident in the politics of both

East and West. Unfortunately, this power-based guru approach has often occurred in the churches of the world too.

BW: Throughout history, master style leaders have not lasted long before they are replaced by guru-style leaders. In my youth, this was a source of deep disillusionment for me; I thought that humans wanted to be free and were willing to be responsible. But I have seen over and over that people prefer a powerful figure to tell them what to do. They would rather have a leader to follow than be fully responsible themselves.

JM: From time to time, the followers rise up and pull down the leader, only to replace them with another power figure. Their desire for freedom is lost when they succumb to blame and victimhood.

CJ: Nietzsche wrote of the "man of resentment" as being a prototype of this irresponsible stance.

JM: I recall Dostoevsky's *The Brothers Karamazov,* in which the character of the Grand Inquisitor states that human beings don't want to be free. They are like sheep and only want miracles, mystery and authority.

KZ: This was my experience too. Over the centuries since my death, I have watched for evidence of people wanting to take responsibility. The inclination to accountability has emerged in the occasional individual. Sometimes such people have gathered in small groups. But in the history of humankind, no one has yet succeeded in establishing a society based upon personal responsibility. It was my dream that this could be.

BW: In my early career, I was concerned about this issue in my work with adolescents. The young rebels wanted to have freedom, and I tried to help them see that freedom came with the price of tremendous responsibility. If they became free, they would have to become leaders themselves in order to teach others. They generally wanted to rebel against the system, but were not willing to enter the system, engage with it, and change it from within. So the system remained powerful, and the rebels gradually weakened themselves in their rebellions. I was sad to see this.

CJ: This is an important subject, that of individual responsibility. This is the burden of individuation and freedom. In my work with patients, this was an important issue, to help them move into more accountability, to engage fully with their lives.

KZ: We four have this in common – we have all pursued a life of learning. Yet, what we have distilled to teach has been misunderstood by many.

JM: Please say more.

KZ: We four all believe that people are responsible for themselves, and their lives.

BW: I have often said that you can't control the hand of cards that is dealt to you, but we each decide how to play the cards we are given.

CJ: My sentiments exactly.

KZ: People do not understand this ... I think because they don't want the burden that comes with acknowledging this.

CJ: Master Kong, I want to return to your vision for an advanced society. I myself was not political. I was interested in my own development. Perhaps in this way I was too self-centred, but it was so. Later, I extended this interest to helping the individuals I met. But I never aspired to a change in the overall community. Dr. Adler hoped for more of this, with his notion of "community interest." He said that the roots of neurosis and illness in humans can be traced to selfishness.

Jock sees the opportunity to talk about a vision for therapy and education.

JM: Well, here we are now. What could we do if we put our minds to it?

BW (laughing): Here comes the world saviour again! Jock, you know what I think – it's not up to us, it's up to each individual. That fervent revolutionary strain still lives strong in you – you want to change the world!

JM (persistently): Well I was a child of the 1960s. At least we could discuss it. If we could offer the world something, what would it be?

KZ: The problem that Dr. Wong well knows is that if we were to try to do something, we would be engaged in power, and this would have the roots of its own demise in our operation. So we can feel for the world and be ready ourselves to connect and communicate. But we can't devise a plan to change things. We must stay within the boundaries of our own consciousness.

JM: But Dr. Jung, you believe that the individual consciousness is an expression of the universal consciousness. I understood that the individual structure is the "self" (with a little "s"), which is isomorphic with the universal Self (with a big "S").

CJ: Yes, I do believe this ... but I do bow to Master Kong ... the individual consciousness operates within its own field, and can only transform what is immediately in its purview. You're still relatively young, although you do qualify as a neophyte elder. You still have the enthusiasm of youth, and the desire to change things.

JM (a little sadly): So I must give up this desire to change things, and allow them to be, including everyone's readiness to harm themselves and each other and the mother earth.

CJ: Regrettably, yes.

KZ: I was like you too. Zhuang Zi was more ready to accept the fates of the universe; I always wanted to try to accomplish something, even when it seemed impossible. Gradually I learned that this was simply my personality, and was not wrong. I could only be what I was. I admire you for your zeal, even though it is likely not to go anywhere – or at least not beyond keeping your spirit vibrant!

Kong Zi's face is transfigured into a most benevolent and warm and holy smile.

BW (his eyes tearing): Jock, I am so touched by your childlike desire to help and heal. Yet the dark forces of indolence are so strong, we have to learn to accept them, and find sunny days when we can.

JM (protesting): There has to be more than this!

Kong Zi and Ben regard the younger man with gentle eyes, and knowing glances at each other.

KZ: This is your torment. You want to help, and you see you cannot. But you will not let go. It's admirable how you want to struggle for something better. But – it's inevitable – you will eventually learn to relax and let go. But in the meantime, I feel tenderly toward you for your ardour.

BW: Thank you Master Kong. I sense your feelings for Jock in your comment. My heart connects with yours.

JM (tearfully): Why? What can we do? Is it hopeless?

KZ: Yes, in that way, it's hopeless.

BW: Yes, I'm afraid so.

Jock is flooded with a mixture of experiences – disappointment, warmth from the loving attention of the others, and an intuition that something very important is to be learned.

CJ: Jock, you struggle so hard to be an existentialist, when all along, you have such a faith and a fervour for people, and a childlike desire to help. You, my dear boy, are such an essentialist, your faith in God and the fates is so deep. You are indeed a passionate man.

BW: You succumb to the trap of hope, which is the flip side of despair. In your hope is a presumption that things could be, should be, different. As we have often discussed, this is the one basic sin ... the sin of presumption. We cannot make life different. Hope tries to do that.

CJ: I myself had such feelings when I was younger. I struggled to find a God that was compassionate, and became disillusioned. But I persisted, and I am now at peace with what I have found.

Jock is aware of the kindness and mental acuity that is surrounding him.

JM: I appreciate the feelings and insights you are all offering to me. There is much for me to learn.

1.7

The Dynamic Empathy Model

> To be fully alive is to be committed to continually evolving, to end-lessly changing. – James Bugental[1]

Human beings have a great capacity to grow and develop throughout their entire lives. Along the way, however, there are many obstacles, and often people get stuck, limiting further possibilities. But it is never too late to recommence the growth process toward becoming fully human. This is a basic premise of what we have taught at The Haven and in our travels to China and elsewhere. It is also the essential context for the ideas we present in this book. In our work with people, we assume that human beings are capable of vastly greater development, and are usually limited by their restrictive attitudes.

Psychologically, this process of growth and learning involves moving from the symbiotic world of the newborn, through a world of objectification and control systems, into the possibilities of becoming an empathetic, caring individual, and ultimately being able to inclusively think of others in one's living and activity. The process involves a cycle of five interrelated and overlapping stages; these stages are *fusion, objectification/isolation, contact, resonance,* and *inclusion.* Crucially, this is not a one-time-only linear development. Rather, it is a cyclic process that iterates and modifies throughout one's life. All five facets of this process are involved in an adult's life; certain features will be foreground at certain times, and will be less emphasized at others.

With encouragement and good modelling, the early childhood experience that begins with the *fusion* of infant with mother develops into a subsequent stage that occupies much of the early years of life, a process of *objectification/isolation.* In a nutritive environment, this stage can naturally proceed to *contact* and then to *resonance* and *inclusion.*[2] Most people do not fully accomplish this progression; along the way, fixations and limitations inhibit the full expression of the possible self. However, people can address these limitations at any stage in their lives, and reopen a growth process where previous defensive postures had closed possibility. Furthermore, this development is a life-long process, a cycle of interrelated aspects, not a sequence to be achieved and surpassed. In times of stress, people are prone to regress to less integrated functioning; this is part of the cycle.

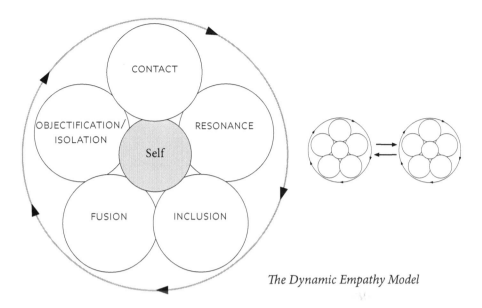

The Dynamic Empathy Model

The diagram above illustrates the Dynamic Empathy Model, with the self in the centre as the integrating function for the process. Note that the circles overlap each other, indicating that these are dynamic interrelationships rather than discrete elements. The two small instances of the cycle to the right with the arrows between illustrate that this does not operate in isolation but in the interactions between people. In a relationship, one person might be at one stage while the other is at a different one; this can bring challenges and turbulence at times, but also allows for growth and development.

There is currently much emphasis in the fields of education and personal growth on the importance of *empathy*. In popular discussions and in the psychological literature, empathy is defined in a wide and sometimes confusing range of ways. For us, the experience of empathy in its fullest sense includes all three stages of contact, resonance and inclusion. Indeed, it also requires a knowledge and acceptance of the capacity, in one's self and others, for fusion and objectification. These too are vital aspects of the cycle.

Many people from both West and East have contributed to our understanding of this process, including Freud, Jung, Adler, the existential writers, Daoist sages, the gestaltists and the dialogical psychologists. We discuss many of their views in the course of this book. In particular, we consider two other developmental cycles that have similar features. In Chapter II.14 we address the cycle of contact and withdrawal in gestalt therapy; in Chapter IV.2 we explore the ancient Chinese notion of the Five Stages of Change. We have also addressed the concept of interrelated developmental stages in relationships and in communication in our previous books.[3] Now we address the topic of growth, learning and the development of empathy in the context of a similar five-stage model.

FUSION

Infants do not distinguish self and other. Their experience is of a global merging, without any distinct awareness of the separate others in the field. This is the early symbiotic stage of *fusion*. Human beings are in this way relational from the beginning; the human infant is related to its mother, in touch and in communication even in utero. Once children are born, this connection, now increasingly psychological, remains strong and important for months and years to come. But distinct interpersonal relationship is not yet possible, because the infant remains merged psychologically with the mother, even after physical separation at birth. In adults, the remnants of fusion are seen in the gestaltists' notion of "confluence," where inadequate boundaries result in co-dependence.

OBJECTIFICATION/ISOLATION

As the child accumulates language and motor and perceptual skills develop, a world of objects "out there" becomes apparent and increasingly intricate. The child learns to name "things" and take actions on them. This is the process of *objectification*. As the child names "Mommy" and "Daddy" and a favourite toy, the assignment of labels solidifies a psychological framework of operating from "inside" onto a world of objects "out there." As the child becomes more established in her own identity, and can name herself and her actions and feelings, the language she uses is objectifying. She has accomplished a lot of development in getting this far. She is no longer so enmeshed with parents; she is able to communicate with a world of objects, and sees herself as one of these objects within this field. She is developing as a distinct entity. This is the existential project of standing forth in solitariness to embrace the world of objects around; with it comes a sense of aloneness, and the capacity for individual decisions and actions and personal responsibility.

This solitariness or *isolation* is a feature of becoming located as a separate self and being. It is necessary so that an individual identity with distinct boundaries can be established and maintained. As this separate identity develops, so too does the capacity for contact and relationships. At the same time, children remain very attached to their parents and caregivers, especially in the early years, and are dependent upon them for learning the lessons that will take them beyond their sense of psychological isolation into a connection with others in relationships.

CONTACT

To establish interpersonal relationships, one must convert the objectifying view into a more personal one that includes awareness and then sharing of the feelings, impressions and perspectives that are vital aspects of one's own uniqueness. When a person experiences feelings in response to another person, the possibility of *contact* arises. Establishing contact will require the sharing of these feelings and is deepened by curiosity and an acceptance of oneself and the other. When a person has feelings *in association* with another, she is no longer isolated; she is in contact and communication with the other, who while still seen as separate, is now relate-able.

Contact becomes possible when one becomes present and responsible. As we have often pointed out, breathing can help one experience one's body and feelings. My feeling experience is based upon my context, perceptions and interpretations of you, but I cannot know for certain your experience. I must use my own experience to imagine what your experience is. Since I cannot get inside your skin and see things through your eyes, at base I am only guessing. You might agree with my guess, but this does not mean that I am "right" or that I have come up with the correct, "accurate" assessment; it only means we agree on this. This is a central consideration in our Communication Model.[4] We have contact in sharing our individual points of view with each other.

We assert that one cannot actually feel another's feelings; what one feels are one's own feelings in response to another, based on one's perceptions and interpretations. This is all self-contained.[5] I don't even have to feel the same kind of feeling as you; I might feel happy when you are sad, perhaps recognizing that you have let go into a grief you had been withholding. It's all based on my interpretations and the meanings I assign to what I experience. The more I share my experience, however, the deeper the relationship that is possible between us.

Experiencing feelings in response to another does not require sophisticated mental adroitness. Children learn it quite naturally. Animals can share feelings too; for example, your dog can feel sad along with you. This ability to feel in response to another is important as a means to move past the isolation of objectification, but to go further involves a willingness to make contact through sharing. This opens up the possibility of experiencing resonance and inclusion.

RESONANCE

Whereas contact is self-contained, *resonance* involves participation in an energy field that includes both self and other. Two people can resonate together, even when separated. We describe the process of resonance in our other books, devoting an entire chapter to this topic in *The New Manual For Life*[6] and another chapter in *The Relationship Garden*.[7] Participants in personal growth groups at The Haven frequently report how they are enlivened when an individual in the group shares deeply personal experiences; they often report feeling moved and sometimes they are overtly emotional themselves in response.

Resonance, however, is not limited to the feeling level; indeed, one can resonate without being emotional at all. Resonance can be experienced as a sense of heat or bodily excitement; it can include emotion, but can also be experienced primarily mentally. An audience at a symphony concert can experience a sense of oneness and participation with the musicians and the maestro that is based on vibrational resonance; sometimes this is emotional, and sometimes it is not. Resonance can also occur at a lecture when the audience is very involved, engaged with the ideas the speaker is presenting; this is the resonance of open-minded attendees with an open-minded presenter. Partners in a relationship who are exploring the kind of contact we describe above are increasingly likely to experience this resonance with one another.

INCLUSION

Inclusion is a mature psychological capacity wherein one can imagine the thoughts, feelings, attitudes and perspectives of another person. In inclusion, one can adopt the viewpoint of the other, to be able to see and experience the world as the other sees and experiences it. When this faculty is developed, relationships take on a previously unimagined richness and suppleness; furthermore, the individual who can be inclusive calls upon the wealth of a deeply integrated personality, being profoundly aware of his or her own experience and distinguishing it clearly from the experience of the other. Friedman writes,

> Only inclusion, or imagining the real, can confirm another; for only it really grasps the other in his or her otherness and brings that other into relationship to oneself.[8]

These five stages comprise an iterative growth process, with all the stages having different emphasis at different times and situations. Individuals can become increasingly aware of their capacity for relating to the world and others in these interrelated ways. With awareness comes choice about what aspect will be foreground at any given time. In adult relationships, all these five facets can be made available; by the same token, one can get stuck in any one of them, including the places where they overlap. For example, when couples get fixated in blame, they are stuck in the objectification/isolation aspect. Helpers who have difficulty maintaining personal boundaries in eager attempts to empathize with patients can be seen as stuck around the contact stage. Sometimes, members of an angry mob get stuck in the resonance aspect and lose perspective. And in ecstatic states, one can become lost in the fusion of loss of ego boundaries. Inclusion integrates the other aspects, taking account of oneself and the other, swinging back and forth between the two. It is possible to become stuck in inclusion too; we need discrimination to choose in what circumstances and relationships we practice this ability. It is also possible to lose oneself in the movement back and forth between self and other; as personal boundaries become unclear or lost, inclusion can devolve into fusion. Again, people can be aware and choose the situations and relationships where they wish to experience these various stages. Problems arise in people's growth when they become stuck in specific parts of this cycle; when this occurs, the dynamic movement of development is inhibited by the fixation on the particular part. Courage is required to move the cycle forward; fear inhibits the unfolding of the process.

Getting Unstuck: The Courage to Face Anxiety

Everyone has "blocks" or fixations, places they are stuck; these limit their full expression. When they severely inhibit regular life, that person is said to be suffering from a neurosis. A basic tenet of Freudian psychoanalysis is that an earlier psychological trauma usually underlies a person's development of neurotic limitations. Later in life, that individual can show the symptoms of neurotic behaviour (for example, irrational fears or anxieties) that manifest the limitation in the personality structure.

Freud's work in the early part of the 20th century focused on psychological development and the neurotic problems that ensue from traumatic experience. Wilhelm Reich extended Freud's work into the physical/physiological domain, maintaining that the blockages that occur psychologically also occur in the physical structure of the body, making up the "character armour." Freud focused on releasing the bound, fixated psychological energy; Reich aimed at freeing both psychological and physiological fixations through breathing and other approaches. In China, Confucius' focus was on the development of a full person. Lao Zi's emphasis was on the misunderstandings that limit consciousness. Zhuang Zi was interested in mental viewpoints that facilitate full participation in life and society. We address the contributions of these various thinkers in chapters to come.

We ourselves are very interested in development, and what can be done to rectify situations of impeded growth. When adults attend growth groups and readdress lessons that have not been learned, they often face big hurdles. As they look into themselves and investigate their patterns of life and relating, they frequently encounter extraordinary defences in themselves. Denial and rationalizations maintain habituated attitudes and stances. A common and very potent defence involves morality, the notion of right and wrong. For example, males often have difficulty accessing their feelings, believing that men should be powerful, and that it is wrong for them to let go and cry. Frequently when people are invited to try something new, they find an excuse for not doing it such as "That's stupid" or "I feel silly." Underlying this comment is usually a moral limitation that deems the activity unacceptable. One of the biggest obstacles to self-learning involves the thought "I shouldn't do this, it's not right." If people decide to try something new anyway, they often find they are very anxious, fearing that they have done something "wrong." People are prone to invoke morality in subtle ways and to use moral defences even in commonplace, seemingly trivial situations. Right and wrong are everywhere.

Theologian Paul Tillich proposes that people's fervent adherence to a notion of good or bad is profoundly anchored in their unconscious avoidance of basic existential givens. The human experience is one of being "thrown" into existence by forces beyond one's control. Individuals have no say in the setup, and must make their way as best they can through a forest of confusing and threatening circumstances. Adopting a moral stance of "right" and "wrong" is the conventional approach to handling these basic human dilemmas. Little children try to please their parents, to be "good" in order to avoid the parents' displeasure, thus evading the ultimate terror of abandonment (which would leave them susceptible to the inimical and threatening forces of the universe). Thus, they live in a world of good and bad and stay stuck in this matrix, denying the basic condition of isolation and insecurity. Their later relationships continue in this same "good" and "bad" context, as they try to please others in order to avoid being alone with the horrible responsibility and threat of existence.

Throughout history, the notion of good/bad has permeated thought systems in both Eastern and Western culture. People want to "get it right" and are desperate in this. According to the existentialists, this is because if they do not occupy their days with issues of right and wrong, they will face the enormity of the cosmos, alone. The irresponsible neurotic options include self-denial, self-punishment, guilt, and blame. A life-affirming attitude would require the courage to face the existential uncertainty and live with it; this is an uncommon approach. Most people choose the neurotic options.

Can we move through and past this? We believe so, and we want to show you the tools and approaches we have learned. In personal growth seminars, people can investigate new ways of relating by facing their defences and anxieties, which often inhibit open communication. Thus, when people accept their anxiety they can learn about their habitual defences and gain more freedom of interaction. Acceptance of anxiety permits moving beyond the moral defence, which constitutes the primary interruption in moving around the cycle of the Dynamic Empathy Model we have outlined, to experience all the stages from fusion to inclusion. The reward is more freedom; what is required is the courage to face anxiety.

The thornbush is the old obstacle in the road. It must catch fire if you want to go further. – Franz Kafka[9]

1.8 Professional Puzzles: Ben's Perspective

The year was 1973. I had been practising adolescent psychiatry for a dozen years, following a decade of professional training. But my interest in psychology went back to days long before I attended university. I very early on developed a keen interest in people. As a teenager growing up in a small prairie town, one of my main amusements was to go to the local library and read. I set upon reading all the mythology books, and revelled in their lustrous stories. Then one day, I came to the end of the books on mythology. So I looked at the next shelf, and found an entire section devoted to psychology. I devoured the books, and my interest in human beings and their issues deepened with every read. I then studied medicine, and later psychiatry. So by this time in 1973, I had been thinking about psychological issues for almost thirty years.

During my training, I saw the gap between theory and practice. I tried hard to learn the theories that were taught, in my endeavour to have as many tools as I could to assist people. But I realized quickly that the ideas were not really that helpful; what seemed to work was just to be present and open and caring with the patients. So, honestly, when I was doing therapy sessions in my training, I often would abandon the theories I was supposed to practice and just converse with my patients in a curious and caring atmosphere. They seemed to get better when we could have a connection.

When I entered practice in 1961, I continued to study other approaches. I was especially interested in the energy and breath theories of Wilhelm Reich. I was accompanied in this investigation of body-mind approaches by my partner, Jock, who had joined me in my practice after his training in Western medicine in Canada, and acupuncture in England. Jock practised acupuncture in the office next to mine. I found the Chinese medical theory fascinating but strange. I would tease Jock about his unconventional and unscientific approach, especially about the charts of acupuncture points that Jock displayed on the walls of his office.

A 14-year-old boy (I'll call him David) had been referred to me for a severe case of stuttering. Before he came to me, he had been seen by at least a half dozen other doctors who had been unsuccessful in bringing any alleviation of the symptoms. I tried everything I knew from my professional experience, and after weeks of effort I had to acknowledge to David that I was not helping him at all. Realizing that I had nothing further to offer, I had a final appointment to say good-bye. I felt such a sense of failure and dejection. I really liked David and I wanted to help him, but I was out of tools. I told him about my feelings, and said "I want to do something for you, and I have been studying massage. So, how about I give you a neck and face and shoulder massage as a good-bye gift?" David agreed, and I began to work on his face, while encouraging him to breathe deeply and fully. As I worked on points over the cheeks, I asked David how he felt. "It feels good," said David. "I feel relaxed, and I really like it." I was stunned as it hit me that he had said this with no stammer. I said to him, "Do you realize your speech is clear?" The boy replied, "Yes, it's amazing!" David was speaking smoothly without a stutter! Shocked, I continued to explore, and gradually mapped a series of points that seemed to relieve the stammer.

I rushed to Jock's office, waving my handmade diagram of the facial points that would cure stuttering. Jock glanced at the drawing and then motioned to the charts on his wall. "You didn't have to go to all that trouble – you have discovered the acupuncture points, and your ancestors mapped them for us many centuries ago!" As we held up my drawing, the correspondence was exact! Since that time, I have been more of a believer, and began to have deeper interest in my ancient Chinese medical roots. I had stumbled into something that acupuncture energy theory covered in detail. I thought to myself, "This crap really works!"

Jock and I set out to teach each other what we knew and explore together what we did not know – Jock read widely in the psychiatric literature and I used more and more approaches from energy theories. We met every day to discuss our experiences with our patients. We worked on our personal relationship with each other, to overcome the defences that would interfere with our interpersonal connection and our professional learning. We studied Reichian breathing techniques which were designed to stimulate the body's natural energy flow and overcome tissue blocks that inhibit full expression of life. We practised on each other to learn the effects of this breathing practice first-hand – we were determined only to use a technique on our patients after we had experienced it ourselves.

At the core of our investigation was a search for connection, with ourselves, with each other, and then extending this to our family, friends, and clients. The 1970s was a decade of social change; people questioned the status quo, and were interested in personal development and new ways of living meaningfully. In the spirit of these times, we began to conduct residential growth groups; we were amazed to discover how rapidly and effectively people could make changes in their lives in the process of a group. We devoted more and more of our time to group work, and in 1975 we closed our practices and dedicated our full time professionally to working with people in groups. People came to the centre where we worked, and lived in community for up to three months at a time. As our practice continued, we took our work "on the road" and conducted personal growth seminars in other locations. This led eventually to our working in foreign countries, especially in Asia. At the centre we developed in Canada, we created a school for personal and professional development; some participants came for personal growth and investigation, while others entered the training program. Eventually we had a full-fledged school, training professionals in the skills of group dynamics and relationship and individual counselling.

We searched for explanations to help us deepen our understanding of our experiences with people. We read, we discussed, we studied, and we attended seminars and conferences. We were looking for perspectives that would make us better at what we were doing. We studied idea systems, lots of them. We kept on our quest to find theories that helped explain the remarkable growth and change that people were finding. But we remained clear that theory is only a set of ideas that helps to explain experience; experience is something else, and cannot be contained within any theoretical framework. When we found ideas that related to our work, we pursued them and synthesized them with other related notions. We sought explanations in the literature of East and West, psychology, medicine, the arts, theology, and psychology, as well as a host of other disciplines.

We often found that oddly disparate sources could help us to get clarity on puzzling issues. Sometimes when a psychological explanation did not bring us to understanding, we would find the missing piece in a poem, or in an Asian source. Everything we read and experienced in seminars and conferences was filtered to test if it was relevant to human caring and relatedness. We discarded what didn't fit, and used what did. When we did find ideas that held up, we taught them to our trainees, to assist them in their insights and skills. We remained centred on our focus of relationship and personal growth and wellness. In this book, we are sharing with you the theories we have found most useful. So this is a home-grown array of theories we have synthesized to help us understand ourselves, each other, and our clients and friends and family.

When you go through your closets to do a spring cleaning, you are trying to find order and practical usefulness. You take everything out and display all the articles to have a good look. As you go through the pile of clothes, you decide how often you will wear each piece. Then you put the most important pieces back into your main closet. You tuck away non-seasonal wear in the back of upstairs closets, and less used things are folded and kept in trunks. You know where they all are, and their availability is determined by their usefulness. What you don't want, you give to recycling for others to use. And some things become rags or are thrown away.

We are bringing to you the results of the spring cleaning of our professional careers. After all our years of study, we have several libraries crammed with books, numerous filing cabinets bursting with notes, and computers full of documents. We have patiently gone through them to do a spring cleaning of ideas. We have brought the most useful and used theories to the front of our closet, and this is what we share with you here. We hope you find them useful in your own life and searching.

> There is a process of spiritual reality that moves beneath and beyond all the doctrines like a flowing underground stream ... It is left to us, as individuals, however, to find by our own experience the deeper truth that lies between the lines of any book. – Ira Progoff[1]

PART II

The West

Wood

Wood is associated with spring, when life stirs and awakens; the new year is reborn from the stillness of winter. This is the time of new beginnings. In this phase, the emphasis is on potentialities, planning, and possibilities. Psychologically, Wood is the domain of the imagination and forethought, with considerations of possible future goals and the decisions to move towards those goals.

II.1 Sigmund Freud: Controversial Pioneer

In a letter to a friend in 1900, Sigmund Freud wrote:

> You often estimate me too highly ... I am not really a man of science, not an observer, not an experimenter, not a thinker. I am nothing but by temperament ... an adventurer ... with the curiosity, the boldness, the tenacity that belongs to that type of being. Such people are apt to be treasured if they succeed, if they have really discovered something; otherwise they are thrown aside. And that is not altogether unjust.[1]

This was a prophetic insight. Man of science or not – and more often Freud insisted he was – there is no doubt that he was an adventurer and a pioneer in the investigation of the unconscious. Even those who disagree with Freud find they must address the ideas generated by this prolific and monumental figure.

Sigmund Freud (1856–1939), the founder of psychoanalysis, is a giant in the development of Western psychology and psychiatry. For us, he has been a touchstone, a fundamental viewpoint against which other theories can be assessed. Ben was trained in a psychoanalytically oriented school of psychiatry where he encountered many proponents of the analytic approach. In our view, Freud raised many interesting and important questions; one need not agree with his theories or his conclusions to benefit from his panoramic and penetrating mind.

Freud's Deterministic View

Freud's early work was in zoological research; he and his co-workers were dedicated to the idea, then not widely accepted, that all vital processes could ultimately be explained in terms of the natural sciences of physics and chemistry, thus eliminating religious and vitalist concepts from biology. Freud adopted this perspective as a young researcher and remained a determinist throughout his career. He maintained that all vital phenomena, including psychological activity like thoughts, feelings, and imaginings, are governed by biological determinants operating under the principle of cause and effect.[2]

Sigmund Freud saw human beings as evolved animals driven by instincts, with no spiritual or religious purpose. In Becker's words, he "had no illusions about man's basic *creatureliness.*"[3] He believed that many questions that others thought unrelated would be answered as scientific research uncovered the mysteries of the human nervous system. To some degree, the expansion of knowledge in neuroscience in the past century has supported his assertion. But Freud's own scientific methods were not stringent. He was prone to imaginative speculation, often extrapolating clinical observations into far-reaching theory that extended into anthropology and other disciplines. His investigations were not rigorous by the standards of today's science. Richard Webster, for example, calls psychoanalysis "perhaps the most complex and successful" pseudoscience in history.[4] We take a more moderate view of Freud, appreciating much of what he contributed and leaving aside what we don't find useful.

Freud was a compelling writer, engaging and persuasive. Whether you agree with him or not, he is rarely boring. And although his methods and logic are certainly open to criticism, the questions he raises are deeply germane to the world today.

Freud was a theory maker, whose goal was to formulate a comprehensive system that could explain human psychology. Although he himself continued to reassess and transform his theory, he was insistent that those who followed him accept the dogma that he pronounced. He had an unswerving conviction in his own rightness. Indeed, he had a mission to develop psychoanalysis as a movement, and was more interested in adherence to its tenets than he was in intellectual debate. He was decidedly intolerant of disagreement, which he tended to see as betrayal; this led to a series of defections in psychoanalytic history. Joseph Breuer, an early collaborator, was the first in a line of colleagues who became estranged. We will discuss Jung, Reich, Adler and Perls in this regard. Recognizing that Freud was postulating his theories based on a small sampling of people, Breuer said:

> Freud is a man given to absolute and exclusive formulations ... this is a psychical need which, in my opinion, leads to excessive generalization.[5]

While Freud brooked no disagreement from his colleagues, he was very accepting of the foibles and idiosyncrasies of his patients, who reported feeling comforted by his acceptance. This acceptance also appeared in his writings as an invitation to tolerance in society's attitudes towards neurosis, sexual variations, and emotional maladaptations.

Freud and the Unconscious

Freud is probably best known for his exploration of the human unconscious. Contemporaries of Freud were already hypothesizing about a hidden aspect to the psyche that was not immediately available to everyday view and it was when Freud, as a young doctor, observed Charcot's results with hypnotised subjects that he realized that the understanding of neuroses could come from psychology. He still hoped for a neurological explanation at some future time; meanwhile, his emphasis shifted to the recovery of unconscious material. He utilized hypnosis for a time with his patients, and later dream analysis and free association. In an early paper with Joseph Breuer, the two men wrote:

> We found, to our great surprise at first, that each individual hysterical symptom immediately and permanently disappeared when we had succeeded in bringing clearly to light the memory of the event by which it was provoked and in arousing the accompanying affect.[6]

This work with Breuer established some basic principles. Freud proposed that memories were subject to repression, and could be brought to consciousness again through therapeutic intervention. Symptoms could be cured by bringing repressed memories to light, and catharting the emotions associated.

For Freud, many aspects of human behaviour are unconscious or subconscious. Just as an iceberg is mostly hidden below the water line, most of the psyche is hidden below the level of consciousness, accessible with the appropriate investigation, but out of sight in day-to-day life. People's memories are packaged and put away much like one does with winter clothing at the coming of spring. The garments are placed carefully away in the basement, available for retrieval, but not at a moment's notice; in the same way, memories of past experiences are filed away in the basement of the unconscious, possible to retrieve, but not in one's everyday mind. We have found this notion of "bringing the unconscious to consciousness" useful in helping people gain awareness of the patterns in their lives and of their choices in how to respond.

Freud conceived that the contents of the unconscious are repressed material that the individual does not wish to face. So in his view, the unconscious is full of memories, unresolved conflicts and disowned affect that originate in the external reality of one's life. Freud believed that many symptoms, both psychological and physical, express repressed unresolved conflicts. Anthony Storr summarizes Freud's doctrine:

> Past emotions are the cause of present problems ... [and] such emotions are invariably shameful or painful or frightening.[7]

Disowned affect that is not expressed directly, but rather repressed, gives rise to the neurotic symptoms. The cure, as Freud saw it, is to investigate repressed material, and release the psychic pressure by revealing the hidden memories. Freud described this repressed material with the physical metaphor of an abscess, which grows beneath the surface when it cannot discharge its toxic material. Freud saw the psychoanalytic method in a surgical frame, believing that the disowned affect that induced neurotic symptoms could be excised as one would a foreign body.

Freud also investigated the meaning of the symptoms that arose from the repression. Constriction in the throat, for example, might express an inability to swallow an insult, or pain in the region of the heart might signify that the heart had been metaphorically broken or wounded.

The fundamental aim of psychoanalysis was to "unrepress the repressed" so incomplete issues could be resolved. This notion has been oversimplified by many, who suggest that all current issues have their root in the past, and that the individual has to "go back" to the past to fix up issues that have not been resolved. In our view, this is not always so; nevertheless, we do agree that people tend to carry with them attitudes and inclinations that they first developed in their attempts to deal with earlier experiences through various forms of repression.

Because of the prominence in childhood of bodily sensations, Freud hypothesized that many adult neurotic issues stem from unresolved sexual conflicts dating back to childhood. He thought he had found "the source of the Nile" when he arrived at his theory of the cause of psychological disturbances:

> I therefore put forward the thesis that at the bottom of every case of hysteria there are one or more occurrences of premature sexual experience, occurrences which belong to the earliest years of childhood ...[8]

At first, he thought that in most cases there had been an experience of seduction by an adult; this was the period of Freud's "seduction theory." Later, he relinquished the universality of the seduction hypothesis, believing that occurrences of adult seduction of children simply could not account for every case of neurosis he was seeing. He began to theorize that experience and fantasy in early childhood are blurred to a degree where it is impossible to tell what actually occurred in revisiting past experiences years later. In his own self-analysis, he became aware of sexual feelings he himself had experienced towards his mother. He concluded that memories of childhood sexual experiences could be the result of infantile sexual desire that gave rise to a fantasy, which later was difficult to distinguish from an actual event. When his patients would recall memories of sexual experiences, he gradually took the position that they were, in many instances, recalling childhood fantasies, rather than actual events. In 1910, he wrote:

> Quite unlike conscious memories from the time of maturity, they

[childhood memories] are not fixed at the moment of being experienced and afterwards repeated, but are only elicited at a later age when childhood is already past; in the process they are altered and falsified, and are put into the service of later trends, so that generally speaking they cannot be sharply distinguished from phantasies.[9]

While recovered memories did not necessarily describe actual events, they nevertheless had a psychic reality, even if it was imaginative. Anthony Storr notes that Freud's abandonment of the seduction theory brought a new perspective for psychoanalysis:

From this time onward, psychoanalysis changed from being an attempt to disclose a causal series of events culminating in the outbreak of a neurosis to an exploration of the patient's imaginative world, especially as that world manifested itself in the early years of childhood. The medical model of neurosis had almost disappeared.

At this stage in Freud's theorizing, infantile sexuality was seen to be at the root of all neurosis, whether though experience or imagination. Freud further developed this notion into his conceptualization of the stages of psychosexual development, which were to be a focus of much of his career. In his later years, he became less attached to the idea that all issues have a sexual basis and recognized that other influences impinged on a developing psyche. As we have seen, he certainly moved past the fixed notion that every memory recovered in the analytic process necessarily related to an actual event. He gradually came to the view that it was not any specific event that brought on psychological disturbance, but rather the individual's response:

Thus, it was no longer a question of what sexual experiences a particular individual had had in his childhood, but rather of his reaction to those experiences – of whether he had reacted to them by 'repression' or not.[10]

The Authors' Experiences with Repression and Memories

We, like Freud, believe that people commonly utilize repression to keep internal conflicts away from consciousness. When experiences, thoughts and feelings are repressed, this compensation leaves "incomplete gestalts," unfinished business that can be brought to light and resolved. Freud utilized dreams and free associations as the "royal road to the unconscious." We ourselves have not emphasized either of these approaches in our work with people; instead we focus more on the here and now, utilizing other methods of accessing unconscious material, such as such as guided fantasy, gestalt, journalling, and communication processes.

In our early work with clients, we utilized perspectives from Ben's training in psychoanalytic psychiatry, focusing on past wounds that were unresolved. Jock's training in both Western medicine and acupuncture supported this approach. In this view, people are victims of their past, and the counsellor/therapist can act as a guide to help them overcome their fixations. We did not rest easily with these assumptions ourselves, and continued to seek other explanations. After a number of years of encouraging people to recover lost memories so that they could move on from past fixations, we began to doubt the central tenet of memory recovery and healing. Although people seemed to experience temporary relief when memories were retrieved, we distrusted the accuracy of the memories and questioned the analytic theory that maintained that insight would heal. People would be momentarily relieved, and yet their lives would not change.

As we have seen, Freud himself struggled with the question of whether memories recovered in analysis were of real events or were products of a person's imaginative world. We were distressed in the 1990s by an emphasis on so-called retrieved memories, and the quick and easy trend in psychology to consider all recovered memories as factual accounts of events that had for certain occurred. We ourselves recognize that memories are easily altered, and sometimes have no root in factual events. We wrote at length about this in our book *The New Manual for Life* in the chapter entitled "Memories of Abuse – A Call for a Balanced Perspective."[11] For our thoughts on this issue, we refer you to that book.

We often contrast this fixation on memories with the Asian perspective that the past is an illusion, to which people remain attached as a means of having stability and predictability in their lives. We propose that *memories always occur in the present* and are, at best, stories about what possibly happened in the past. One can never be sure about these memories. We encourage people to embrace their memories, but not be slaves to them. To us, the important issue is connecting and relating, which supersedes the retrieval of memories and de-emphasizes ideas about healing through insight. We move through fixations not simply by uncovering them, but through acknowledging them to others as they arise and making choices to relate in the present.

Pleasure, Aggression, and Reality

A core concept in Freudian theory involves pleasure and reality. Humans are driven to maximize pleasure in face of the often unpleasant demands of reality. The human infant seems to be driven by a pressure to satisfy and express all needs, desires and impulses with a minimum of pain. This is the "pleasure principle." Reality impinges upon this when the desire to satisfy impulses is thwarted or interrupted. This is the "reality principle," the necessity for restraints to be placed on the expression of pleasure and pain in the service of social harmony. These two principles are in action in the operations of the psyche of the individual. Pleasure is neurologically related to the body's erogenous zones, as we shall see below in our discussion of Freud's psychosexual stages; these zones are areas of intense innervation, allowing for sensations of satisfaction and enjoyment.

In his later writings, Freud devoted more attention to ideas about the "aggressive instinct." Psychic energy, he came to believe, has two aspects: one life enhancing (libido, associated with the pleasure principle) and the other life-inhibiting (destrudo, which manifests in the aggressive instinct). He eventually advanced the idea that human civilization itself was the result of, and at the mercy of, the struggle between these two forces.

Freud postulated that the aggressive instinct arises in the id (we discuss id, ego, and superego further below) and is initially directed outwards as aggression and control. It is the task of the superego to limit this acting out, redirecting the aggressive impulse inward against the individual through the agency of guilt and engendering self-reproach, self-punishment, and self-hatred. Freud wrote:

> Civilization, therefore, obtains mastery over the individual's dangerous desire for aggression by weakening and disarming it and by setting up an agency within him to watch over it, like a garrison in a conquered city.[12]

As we have written elsewhere, this gives rise to a multitude of symptoms that express this self-hatred, which are addressed in the Selves Model that we teach at The Haven.[13]

Stages of Psychosexual Development

Children grow and learn and are influenced by their experiences, both positive and negative. Freud believed that the psyche matures as neurophysiology matures, in sequential stages of psychosexual development (oral, anal, phallic, latency, genital). With the exception of the latency stage, Freud's view of the developing psyche focused on parts of the body rather than cognition, learning or attachment (all approaches that were adopted after Freud). He proposed that different regions of the body have heightened focus at different ages. During the first year, the mouth is the focus in the *oral stage*. Between one and three years of age, the anus is the focus in the *anal stage*. This is followed by a *phallic stage* when the penis or clitoris become an area of libidinal intensity and masturbatory exploration. The *latency stage* is a period where the energetic turmoil in the preceding stages becomes quiet, as the psychological matters associated with them are repressed; in this "cooling of the engine" time, the young person has energy free to pursue interests, to study and to explore, without the distractions of the inner psychic conflicts that characterize the earlier phases. The latency period is a time of ego adaptation and growth, where the young person establishes friendships and relationship to the larger community beyond the family. Freud proposed a later *genital stage*, which only comes into fullness when an individual is capable of satisfying sexual relations. Traces of previous stages of libidinal development persist into adult life, according to Freud. Fixations at a specific stage will manifest in the personality structure, and symptoms of neurotic behaviour can be traced back to limitations in the development of one or more psychosexual stages. For example, a fixation at the oral stage shows as an infantile dependency, and a predilection for oral activities (eating, drinking, sucking); these fixations will also contribute to specific sexual interests. As another example, fixation at the anal stage gives rise to symptoms related to fastidiousness (or absence thereof); psychologically, the anally fixated individual tends to excessive neatness and order (holding back, rather than letting go); anally fixated people are prone to a different range of sexual interests from those who are orally fixated.

Freud's concept of the Oedipus complex maintained that children have sexual interest in the parent of the opposite sex, which is repressed. This complex develops in association with the stages of development mentioned above; it reaches an intensity in the phallic stage, and is resolved in the latency period as the child learns to identify with the parent of the same sex. Although we, the authors, have not found this concept particularly compelling or relevant, we mention it here because it was one of the key features of Freud's doctrine at an early stage of his theorizing, and a point of major disagreement between Freud and Jung, who did not subscribe to the Oedipal theory. The Oedipal theory in regard to young girls is even more controversial and complicated; we will not go into this here, other than to mention it. Nor do we address Freud's notions of penis envy and castration anxiety; these concepts have not been useful in our work.

Underlying these various theories is Freud's conviction that sexuality is a prime mover in human behaviour and development. Although the details of Freud's focus on sexuality are now largely disregarded, many have found the general roadmap to be of practical use. We ourselves have found the concept of stages of psychological development that parallel physical maturation to be useful. That there are stages of development linking psychology and the physical being seems apparent; but, we, like many others, question the importance of sexuality in this. We see that many difficulties in life, relationships and intimacy stem from early insecurities that are not related to sex.

The Structure of the Psyche: Id, Ego and Superego

Freud's theory was a dynamic one, with a concept of psychic energy with two components (a constructive force named *libido* and a limiting force called *destrudo*). His notion of the architecture of the psyche includes raw unfettered psychic energy in the *id*, which requires progressive control to help the child to cope; the agent of the control is the *superego*, which pushes back against the eruption of the id. In the middle, arbitrating between the id forces and the superego restrictions and controls is the *ego*, the psychic structure for integration and relating to the external world (reality). The three mental divisions interact with each other. The id is the source of energy, and is unrestrained force that impinges on the ego, and expresses itself into the external world (reality). The ego receives stimulation from both the id and the superego, and also interacts with reality. The superego interacts with reality and the ego. So, there is a dynamic ebb and flow as the demands from each zone impinges on the other. The ego is the integrating factor that attempts to balance the demands of the superego, the insistence of the id, and the reality of the external world. Each person makes compromises between drive forces, ego defences, superego demands and environmental influences.

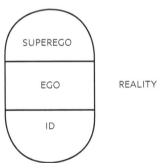

This notion of erupting force and control and an integrating function is very compatible with the classical Chinese medicine idea – which we discuss later in this book – of *qi* energy and the two cycles (the *sheng* cycle for expansion of *qi*, and *ke* cycle for control of *qi*). It also relates to the Selves Model we described in *The New Manual For Life*, wherein we outline the tension between striving and goal setting on the one hand, and self-acceptance and mastery on the other.[14] Freud's model of the psychic apparatus is an allegory, a story of how the psyche operates. We have found it to be a useful dynamic map, helpful in understanding human behaviour.

THE ID

The id is the reservoir of instinctual energy, including libido and destrudo. Freud saw the id as the oldest part of the mind, from which the other structures are derived. The id is chaotic and functions with primary process thinking (prelogical thought). Freud described it this way:

> It contains everything that is inherited, that is present at birth, that is laid down in the constitution – above all, therefore, the instincts which originate from the somatic organization and which find a first psychical expression here in forms unknown to us.[15]

THE EGO

The word "ego" has been used in many ways, both in writing and in everyday speech; as a result, the term is often more confusing than useful. Freud used the word in very specific ways in his exposition of psychoanalytic theory. Freud saw the ego as a "special organization" connected with the organs of perception, whose goal is self-preservation. The ego develops in response to external stimuli that are detected by the senses. The ego mediates between the person and reality. Freud said, "The ego is first and foremost a bodily ego,"[16] meaning that it is inextricably linked with the perceptual system, which is a function of the physical body and its structure. Ira Progoff summarizes Freud's view of ego and id:

> The ego, he said, begins to form itself at the outer edges of the psyche where it meets its environment, while the id has its source in the inner depths; and somewhere in between, they meet and intermingle.[17]

He elaborates:

> The ego, Freud said, has as "its nucleus the Perceptual system"; it is based on the individual's conscious contacts with the world around him. The id, on the other hand, is derived from the vast forces of instinct. Its roots are in the deepest recesses of the unconscious, so deep that they are inherently inaccessible to the conscious mind. The id contains the tremendous untamed power of the psyche, and everything that is unconscious is ultimately encompassed by it.[18]

Unlike the id, which is chaotic and unpredictable, the ego is organized and can generate coordinated action. It is derived from the raw energy of the id, but functions with secondary process thinking (logical thought), with the capacity to delay immediate responses to external stimuli or to internal instinctive promptings. The ego is responsible for maintaining homeostasis (balance) of the demands of the id, the super-ego and reality. The threat of impending imbalance sets off the alarm reaction of "anxiety."

THE SUPEREGO

Freud postulated the superego as a third aspect of mind that is dedicated to self-observation. The superego contains the data bank of the values of reality (the external world) that have been swallowed whole (intro-jected) or digested (assimilated). It controls through praise (reward) and punishment (guilt). It arises by internalizing parental and societal injunctions and prescriptions. Whenever the superego notes a discrep-ancy between the ego ideal and the ego's activity, the voice of conscience operates to urge the individual to conform. The superego is described by Freud:

> The long period of childhood, during which the growing human being lives in dependence on his parents, leaves behind it as a precipitate the formation in his ego of a special agency in which this parental influ-ence is prolonged. It has received the name of super-ego. In so far as this super-ego is differentiated from the ego or is opposed to it, it con-stitutes a third power which the ego must take into account.[19]

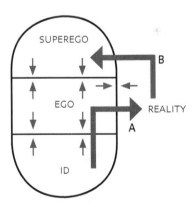

In the diagram above, the large arrow "A" from the id through the ego out to reality indicates the aggressive impulses from the id. For Freud, the superego is primarily created by the introjected aggressive impulses (large arrow "B" back from reality to the superego). This intro-jection results in feelings of guilt, low self-esteem, and inferiority, or sometimes more broadly as depression.

Intrapsychic Conflict and Homeostatic Balance

The Freudian conception of the psyche thus has three divisions that are often in conflict. The ego is an integrating function, balancing forces from the external world, the id and the superego, each of which might be urging different action. As the ego struggles with its task, a person may experience indecision or even become completely arrested for a time.

Conflict, however, is not necessarily negative; rather it relates to the tension between the different aspects, and can bring strength to the psychic system. Sometimes people associate peace with health and conflict with illness; our view, however, is that conflict can promote development, even though the process is sometimes painful.

In psychoanalytic theory, it is the task of the ego to create a state of homeostasis or balance by addressing the often conflicting demands of the id, the superego and reality. The ego can respond or react to these demands in two basic ways: through developing *ego adaptive skills*, which promote growth, or by using *ego defensive mechanisms*, which in an effort to overcome threats to internal balance tend to inhibit growth, promoting fixations and neurosis. Ego adaptive skills include thought, judgment, communication and creativity; examples of ego defensive mechanisms are delusion, denial, projection, acting out, intellectualization, and moralization.

To be successful, the ego must develop a healthy range of ego adaptive skills. If it becomes overly reliant on defensive mechanisms it will not be able to create balance. When the tensions become fixated, there will be rigidification into particular personality structures. The diagrams below illustrate some examples, some more successful than others:

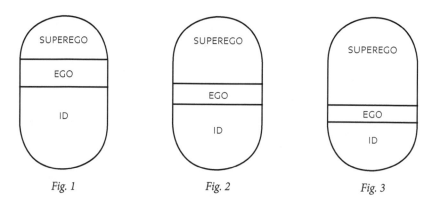

Fig. 1   Fig. 2   Fig. 3

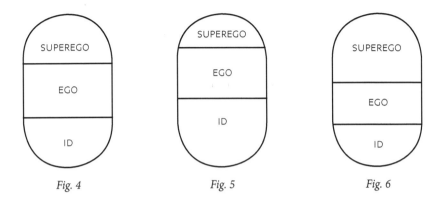

Fig. 4   Fig. 5   Fig. 6

Fig. 1 represents an individual with an id force that is too strong for the undeveloped ego to subdue. The superego acts to further reduce the size of the ego. This individual will be prone to acting out when the id impulses overwhelm the superego constraints. Impulsive behaviour would be exacerbated when the superego influence is lessened, for example, when the person is inebriated.

Fig. 2 shows a larger superego that keeps the id in check, but at the expense of ego development. The ego is sandwiched in between the forces of the id and the repressive forces of the superego. This individual will experience inner tension and will be prone to depression.

Fig. 3 shows a superego that has grown huge, and accomplishes the restraining of the id. This individual will be less energetic, and will be prone to depression. The ego has no strength to balance these intense forces.

Fig. 4 illustrates a well developed ego, which permits more flow and balance between the impinging forces from the superego and id.

Fig. 5 shows a person who is well integrated in a situation of play; a mature adult playing with a grandchild would be an example.

Fig. 6 shows a relatively integrated ego, but coping with very strong self-restrictive forces from the superego. Such a situation occurs with moralistic adults, struggling to respond in a human fashion to the demands from the other regions of the psyche and from the external reality, but with deeply ingrained moralistic injunctions from the superego. There is a relative subduing of the id, but some of this comes from the excessive superego, and such an individual will be prone to more symptoms of self-hatred, including depression.

Relationship Dynamics, Cathexis and Decathexis

Freud did not address relationship dynamics per se; he was more focused on the notion of *cathexis* and *decathexis* to explain how people make each other important. We ourselves have applied his ideas of id, ego and superego to relationships, and we discuss this below. First, though, we offer some thoughts on cathexis and decathexis.

Cathexis is the attachment of psychic energy to persons, objects, body parts, or ideas. In this process, one invests emotional energy in the cathected object or person. Cathecting another human makes that person very important. In a similar way, one can cathect an idea, and become an adherent of a religion or a political belief, or a particular life style. The eager adoption of a favourite football team is an example of cathexis, and people can use this to bond to a group or an activity. In *decathexis*, people detach psychic energy from persons, objects, body parts, or ideas, withdrawing emotional energy from the person or object. This is part of the process of grieving and coming to peace with a departed loved one – through decathexis, the focused person is relegated to the background, and thus "laid to rest." This is similar to the Buddhist notion of non-attachment.

Our own interests have prompted us to consider how the balance of superego, ego and id in each person in a relationship will determine the kind of relationship they have. When the ego is well developed, there is more possibility for growth in each partner; when the superego is excessive, a control relationship can be the result. Thus we distinguish between two styles of relationship, one for control, and the other for growth.

CONTROL RELATIONSHIP The ego does not grow so readily in a control relationship. The partners tend to relate from rule-bound moralistic behaviours (superego) rather than from dynamic interpersonal human considerations that would require more strength from the ego. Ego growth and development would come through the agencies of the ego adaptive mechanisms.

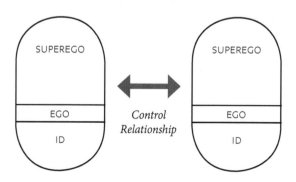

GROWTH RELATIONSHIP This is a pairing where each partner has well developed ego strength. They are less prone to interact from prejudice and reaction, and can relate to each other in a situational, human way. This is the picture of a couple in the Integration Phase of relationship. For more details about the Integration Phase, see our book *The Relationship Garden*.[20]

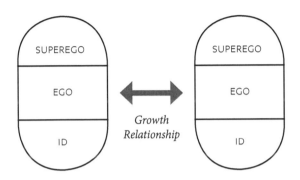

Growth Relationship

The Individual and Society

Freud extended his ideas about the psychic make-up of the individual into a theory of the relationship of the individual to society in his late book *Civilization and its Discontents*, first published in 1930. He wrote of the tension between the desires of the individual for freedom and pleasure and the demands of society for order and predictability, to give security for everyone. As a result, individuals have to deny themselves, restrict and modify ("sublimate") their innate impulses, and accommodate to the demands of society in order to belong. As a way of coping with pains and disappointments in life, people search for powerful deflections, substitutive satisfactions or intoxicating substances. Nevertheless, even with these compensations, humans are always threatened with suffering from three sources – their own bodies, nature, and their relations to other people (which Freud suggested was probably the most severe of sufferings). In this context, Freud describes the ego adaptive and ego defensive mechanisms we have already discussed, which are responses and reactions to this inescapable dilemma. In particular he discusses the defences of isolation, intoxication and addictions, and repression. In the extreme, people can cope by participating in delusions; for Freud, investment in religion constitutes a delusion.[21] On the more adaptive side, one can participate in society and find meaning as a member of the group; also, people invest in loving and being loved, with the accompanying fear of loss of the loved one. Other approaches include the attempt to overcome nature through science, or harvesting nature's resources, and the pursuit of art and aesthetics.[22] Written in the ominous period between two world wars, *Civilization and Its Discontents* is a serious and pessimistic work that confronts the human predicament head on.

Transference and Projection

Janet Malcolm captures the essential pessimism of Freud's perspective on human relationships in her discussion of transference and projection:

> The phenomenon of transference – how we all invent each other according to early blueprints – was Freud's most original and radical discovery ... Personal relations ... [are] actually a messy jangle of misapprehensions, at best an uneasy truce between powerful solitary fantasy systems. Even (or especially) romantic love is fundamentally solitary, and has at its core a profound impersonality.[23]

Transference, as originally conceived by Freud, is a particular form that occurs in psychotherapy between patient and analyst of the more general phenomenon of projection. Projection is a psychological defence mechanism in which one imputes one's own thoughts, motivation, desires or feelings onto another, without taking ownership oneself. This is a very common phenomenon that occurs in most everyone; indeed, whenever I do not check out an interpretation I have of you, there is the real possibility that this is projection, rather than something that pertains to you. As Janet Malcolm points out, the implications of Freud's discovery extend beyond the therapeutic situation into the fabric of our everyday lives.

As Freud first described it, transference is the patient's attribution to the analyst of attitudes and ideas that originated with previous figures in the patient's life; he later extended this idea to include the total emotional attitude of the patient towards the analyst. Freud maintained a psychological distance from his patients and refused to become personally involved; he believed this promoted the phenomenon of transference, which could be observed, analysed, and utilized to provide insight for the patient. Therapeutic relationships are special kinds of interpersonal relationships in which the activity is directed towards helping the client. The nature of that help depends upon the therapist's orientation; it ranges from attempting to cure to attempting to educate. For some therapists, transference is used to control the client's behaviour, as a parent would do with a child. Others object to using transference in that way, seeing it as a means of fostering a dependency upon the therapist and therapy; they may prefer to help the person to "individuate."

Furthermore, transference is a two-way street. In a therapeutic relationship, the therapist's propensity to do so is referred to as "counter-transference." The client's transference can be complicated by the therapist's counter-transference, especially when it is not clearly understood. Therapists who have an inner need to be needed will tend to cultivate their clients' dependency, and this interferes with their process of individuation. However, as we have said, in some therapies, individuation is not a goal.

Although the term "transference" properly refers only to the psychotherapeutic situation, it points at the general human tendency to project onto others. Through this process, people create the psychological/emotional environment in which they live and develop. For example, if a person's earliest years are dominated by rejecting and hostile parents, this person might be inclined to transfer these expectations upon all future authority figures and – to the extent that they are seen as parental – on future intimate partners. If the early parent-child transactions are primarily loving, that expectation (transference) will be placed upon future relationships.

In interpersonal relationships, this propensity towards projection ("ghosting" or "placing hats" upon the other person) produces a difficulty in getting to know others as they really are, instead seeing them through the screen of projection. Generally, it is this very screen that underlies attractions and repulsions with others. It motivates selection of partners and friends, upon whom individuals can most easily place needs and expectations. These attractions and repulsions play a huge part in determining the nature and quality of interpersonal relationships.

Projections will almost always occur in human interactions, especially in the early stages of a relationship. This is a prominent feature of the stage of objectification/isolation that we described in our Dynamic Empathy Model. In our experience, if these projections are recognized and acknowledged, people can move past them into more genuine contact. Through recognition and acknowledgment of projections, both parties involved will have the information necessary to make informed choices around feelings and behaviour. Instead of being driven by unconscious forces, individuals can take charge of their own lives. This has been a focus of much of our work in our own lives and with our clients.

Freud's Influence on Psychotherapy

The majority of contemporary psychoanalysts believe that neurosis is not so much a matter of inhibited or underdeveloped sexuality as of a wider failure to make satisfying human relationships on equal terms. Interpretation of transference, therefore, depends upon the psychoanalyst detecting and commenting upon the way in which the patient is relating to him in the present ... to do this effectively requires that the psychoanalyst is not concerned solely with the events of early childhood, but also recognizes that there is a real relationship in the here and now.[24]

Freud's approach utilized free association, dream interpretation, and interpreting transference and countertransference. Today, psychoanalysis in particular, and therapy in general, rarely follow all Freud's recommendations. Nevertheless much of therapy and counselling in modern times owes a great debt to Freud's original approach.

Classical psychoanalysis has now given over to more object relations approaches, with more emphasis on the importance of bonding and interpersonal dynamics. The analysis of the transference now focuses on developing a healthy, open adult relationship with the therapist, and then learning to extend this into one's life. As clients become more confident in a sharing relationship with the therapist, they can more readily confide in others in their personal lives and become more capable of loving and fulfilling relationships.

Furthermore, the people coming to seek counselling and therapy today are different from those who consulted Freud. Storr says, "Whereas Freud's patients sought help for clear-cut hysterical or obsessional symptoms, today's patients often consult the analyst for what Szasz has called 'problems in living', difficulties in interpersonal relationships, or generalized dissatisfaction with life."[25] For us, what is useful from Freud is the perspective – of a personal unconscious, of a psyche with dynamic intersecting forces, of repressed memories and material, of a developmental schema of the unfolding of the psyche, of the architecture and terrain of the personal mind. Freud's notions pointed towards a mind-body perspective; for him, mind was primary and influenced the body, but he did believe in a mind-body relationship. His theory included a notion of psychic energy, which we find useful in conceiving of dynamic approaches with clients. We have always encouraged our students and interns to read some of Freud's writings – not just commentaries on Freud, but Freud himself – and we make the same recommendation to you. Not for truth, but for perspective and inspiration. As Storr notes:

Anyone can give 'good advice' to people in distress. It was Freud who taught us to listen.[26]

II.2   Ego Dynamics: Growth and Defence

Growth and Defence: A Biological Basis for Behaviour

In the late 1990s, we came across the work of cell biologist Bruce Lipton and found an interesting new perspective on ideas we had been exploring. Lipton notes that all living cells have two processes available: growth or defence. The same occurs in cell clusters and in multicellular organisms of all levels of complexity. So, this applies to the human being, a vastly complex multicellular creature.

> Growth processes require an open exchange between an organism and its environment. For example, food is taken in and waste products are excreted. However, protection requires a closing down of the system to wall the organism off from the perceived threat.[1]

Lipton has related his work with cells to personal growth and development. Humans, he says, behave like single cells – in any circumstance, a person can either grow or defend. Lipton notes that these growth/protection behaviours are essential for survival. However, he adds, "the longer you stay in protection, the more you compromise your growth."[2]

In our work, we have focused on strength and power as a dichotomy in human interaction (see Chapter I.5). We associate strength with a quality of openness and vulnerability that matches Lipton's conception of "growth" in his biological model; when we speak of power, there is considerable overlap with Lipton's term "defence." We emphasize that these dichotomies should be viewed in terms of foreground and background rather than absolutes of either-or. Life processes are in continuous states of modification and evolution. So, we would not say "grow or defend"; instead, we would look for how much growth and how much defence a person experiences in any situation.

Physiologists have long been interested in the equilibrium of the human body systems. Claude Bernard's notion of the "milieu intérieur" was extended in the late 1920s by Cannon's definition of "homeostasis," a property of a system that regulates the interior environment to maintain stability. As Freud himself believed, this notion of internal balance can also apply to psychological phenomena. Both growth and defence are necessary for health; we think, however, that most people tend to defend more than is good for them.[3]

Ego Defence and Adaptation

The so-called ego psychologists, notably Freud's daughter Anna Freud (1895–1982), extended psychoanalytic thought by elaborating on the *ego defence mechanisms*. These are psychological control systems that maintain stability by counterbalancing threats to internal balance; they protect individuals against dangers arising from their impulses or affects. Anna Freud lists the following ego defence mechanisms: regression, repression, reaction-formation, isolation, undoing, projection, introjection, turning against the self, and reversal or sublimation (displacement of instinctual aims).[4] To this list we would add these: suppression, denial, rationalization, somatization, substitution, intellectualization, obsession, compulsions, and identification. Note that these are not inherently negative. They are limiting, in that they function through control in the system. But they have positive uses (for example, holding back from speaking impulsively in a heated debate). The defence mechanisms act as a restraint to unfettered development and probably stimulate resilience by challenging the dynamics of the psychic system, much in the same way that muscles grow by lifting increasingly heavier weights.

Other ego psychologists, such as Heinz Hartmann (1894–1970), emphasized *ego adaptation* as playing a strong role in health. This was addressed in "adjustment" or "adaptation" theory in Karl Menninger's *The Vital Balance*. In this context, *ego adaptive mechanisms* can offset the limitations of ego defences.[5] For our purposes, we use the term *ego adaptive* to mean operations of the psyche that are inclined to growth and meaningful contact with the environment. The ego adaptive mechanisms include thinking, judgment, reality testing, memory, language, movement, creativity, exercise and athletics, logic, music, art, problem solving, goal setting, creative competition, social contact and intimacy.

The ego adaptive mechanisms work in concert with the ego defence system to maintain balance and stability in the psyche. They are analogous to the accelerator and brakes on an automobile, which must operate together to maintain a continuously shifting balance of movement and inhibition. Synthesis of the activities of the defence mechanisms and the adaptive mechanisms maintains psychological homeostasis

Sometimes defences which were beneficial at an earlier stage outlive their usefulness and need to be updated. What was previously helpful can later be a hindrance. In the same way, messages that are incorporated into defensive positions may be appropriate at the time. For example, "Don't run out into traffic!" protects a child from dangerous action; but later, when one is an adult, this message needs to be updated, since one might want to do just that to protect a dog loose on a highway.

Both defences and adaptations are necessary. The control implicit in the defence system is not a problem in itself; indeed, this limiting can be life-sustaining. But difficulties can arise when one becomes stuck. *The problem is not control, but fixation.* When the ego defence mechanisms become rigidified (i.e. "blocked"), there is less fluidity, flexibility and balance in the personality; the ego adaptive mechanisms can be helpful in getting past such a fixation. These blockages in extreme can also limit a person's development and can even make one sick.

Everyone acquires some degree of fixation in the evolution of their character structure. We all carry some "scars," which can become challenges later in life. These impediments (blocks, arrests) are in part what make up the idiosyncrasies and uniqueness of an individual personality. Although often disruptive, they are not immutable: they can be overcome through patient, diligent self-examination and choice. So, *blocks are normal.* Fixations are not bad; they are simply challenges that can be fodder for later growth and development.

These blocks arise in the process of establishing the controls and habits that make people socially acceptable and effective; they become a problem if they are so fixated that the individual becomes neurotically maladapted or physically ill. One is always able to work with these limitations to move through and past them. Sometimes professional assistance is useful in this project, and helping people learn to do this has been the focus of our medical/psychological careers. Personal development is like training in any discipline; it is possible to overcome limitations and unhelpful habits and make further progress into becoming a master of one's life.

Correspondences with Chinese Medicine
We discuss Chinese medicine in some detail later in this book. For now, a few notes may be useful. Classical Chinese medicine embraces an energy theory of balance and harmony, which is similar to the notions of adaptation and homeostatic balance. From this perspective, underlying all illnesses (whether psychological or physical) are "energy blocks" that inhibit the free flow of the life force, *qi.* Blocks and imbalances arise in a variety of ways, and all people have them. When the blockages become fixated, they can contribute to the evolution of progressive disease states, with symptoms on the physical, emotional, mental and spiritual dimensions. In this way, the work of the ego psychologists and psychoanalysts in the West parallels the ideas of the ancient Chinese medical practitioners. Health is associated with balance and harmony.

The ancient Chinese also had a concept of two interrelated processes of life (*sheng*, generativity, and *ke*, limitation) that are similar to the ideas of growth and defence. The model of the Five Stages of Change (*wu xing*) is based on two aspects of the life force (*qi*): there is a creative or unfolding aspect to the cycle (*sheng* cycle = generative cycle) and a balancing aspect (*ke* cycle = control or limiting cycle). This model, which sees expansion and limitation as dual aspects of a dynamic process, is similar to our notion of strength and power (see below, Power and Strength Principles), where growth and limitation are the respective aspects in this dynamic process. The Chinese have a saying: *xiang sheng xiang ke* ("generativity and limitation mutually support each other"); by this they mean that a balancing function from the *ke* control system restrains the expansive process of the generative *sheng* cycle. The interaction between control and generativity brings harmony and health.

The Harvard Longitudinal Study

Psychiatrist George Vaillant was for years the director of Harvard's comprehensive longitudinal Study of Adult Development, which followed the lives of 268 men who entered Harvard in the late 1930s (the "Grant Study"), and also followed 456 socially disadvantaged men from the inner city and 90 middle-class, gifted women. The complete study involved questionnaires every couple of years, physical examinations every five years, and standardized interviews every 15 years. Based on the study's findings, Vaillant formulated ideas of development based on adaptation and defence and noted the value for mental and physical health that comes from relationships and behaviours that we identify as strength-based.[6,7] Defence mechanisms are value neutral; to Vaillant, how they are used is what is most important:

> "Much of what is labeled mental illness," Vaillant writes, "simply reflects our 'unwise' deployment of defense mechanisms. If we use defenses well, we are deemed mentally healthy, conscientious, funny, creative, and altruistic. If we use them badly, the psychiatrist diagnoses us ill, our neighbors label us unpleasant, and society brands us immoral."[8]

Vaillant emphasized adaptive mechanisms as a key to health. Joshua Shenk reports,

> In contrast to Anna Freud, who located the origins of defenses in the sexual conflicts of a child, Vaillant sees adaptations as arising organically from the pain of experience and playing out through the whole lifespan.[9]

Vaillant's is a long-range view. He notes that diseases and people have a "natural history." For example, his statistics show that immature adaptations of late childhood (such as acting out and projection) often fade as the child matures. The tendency with passing decades is for his subjects to show increasing use of mature defences such as altruism and humour (ego adaptive mechanisms in ego psychology terms), and this process continues into old age.

Vaillant identified seven major factors that predict healthy aging, both physically and psychologically. They included education, stable marriage, not smoking, not abusing alcohol, some exercise, and healthy weight. The last factor was employing "mature adaptations" that involved an attitude of forgiveness, gratitude and joy; rather than be despondent over what they didn't have, people who aged in a healthy way were happy for what they had. Regular exercise in college predicted late-life mental health, and mental attitude was found to be a key to physical health:

> Pessimists seemed to suffer physically in comparison with optimists, perhaps because they're less likely to connect with others or care for themselves.[10]

Vaillant was very interested in the potency of relationships. He said, "It is social aptitude, not intellectual brilliance or parental social class, that leads to successful aging."[11] He also said, "... the only thing that really matters in life are your relationships to other people."

As part of this emphasis on relationship, Shenk writes of Vaillant's strength and vulnerability orientation to health:

> Only with patience and tenderness might a person surrender his barbed armor for a softer shield. Perhaps in this, I thought, lies the key to the good life – not rules to follow, nor problems to avoid, but an engaged humility, an earnest acceptance of life's pains and promises.[12]

Vaillant' positive report about ego adaptive behaviours shows the value of openness and vulnerability; these are aspects of strength, which we will now discuss.

Power and Strength Principles

We wrote of the dichotomies of power and strength in previous books.[13,] We mentioned this briefly in Chapter I.5; we return to this topic now to make the connections between our work and the other principles in this chapter. We maintain that psychological growth, health and well-being are enhanced through the strength attributes of openness, vulnerability and respectful responsiveness. When one reverts to power (closed, controlled and reactive), the self shrinks into the prison of objectification, blame and self-criticism. Some degree of control is necessary in order to maintain homeostatic balance, but it is all too easy for the power orientation to become fixated. In terms of Lipton's growth and defence duality, power operates for control and defence; strength encourages growth.

In reference to ego psychology, the ego defensive mechanisms are power and control based; the ego adaptive mechanisms are more associated with strength.

Most people are prone to become fixated in power orientations in some aspects of their lives, while in other areas they may be closer to strength. For example, a couple might have a harmonious relationship of strength with each other, and yet have an embattled power struggle with one of their children. The path to moving from the limiting fixated power stance towards strength is through vulnerability and openness. In the cultures of East and West, vulnerability is often viewed with suspicion or disregarded as "weak." In our view, however, true organic personal strength can only be experienced by someone who is open and vulnerable; if a person is closed and defended, they will not experience the resilience necessary for an integrated response to life's situations. Becoming vulnerable can be profoundly unsettling, but one can learn to celebrate this anxiety as a harbinger of doors opening to further possibilities. For the popular saying "No pain, no gain," we would substitute "No anxiety and vulnerability, no growth." Being vulnerable is a strength, and supports the ego adaptive mechanisms.

The cultures of both East and West reward people for power activity and discourage strength in many subtle ways. This is deeply embedded cultural programming, which impinges upon everyone. So it is neither right nor wrong to be caught in right and wrong; the issue is to become aware of one's fixations and work through and past them. For us, this notion of power and strength has been a cornerstone of our own personal and professional development, and has aided us immeasurably both in working on ourselves and in helping others.

> Where love rules, there is no will to power; and where power predominates, there love is lacking. The one is the shadow of the other. – C.G. Jung[14]

II.3　Object Relations:
The Developmental Continuum

Within each of us is a flame that seeks to grow. – James Bugental [1]

The Separation-Individuation Project

According to Margaret Mahler (1897–1985), every human infant goes through a developmental process, moving from an undifferentiated psychological fusion with its environment, through increasing discrimination of self and other, towards an experience as an autonomous and unique being. She called this the "separation-individuation theory" of child development. We briefly outlined this process in *The New Manual For Life*.[2] Now we wish to elaborate upon this object relations view of child development.[3]

Mahler saw child development as requiring a psychological separation from the mother and a growing autonomy into individuation.[4] Although individuation is the same term Jung used in his Analytical Psychology, the meaning for Mahler is specific to the early child development. In her scheme, early childhood involves a series of developmental phases, each with its own set of tasks, and each one depending upon the previous steps. The overall movement is from fusion, through separation, to individuation. The process Mahler outlines is necessary for the development of empathy, which we discuss in our Dynamic Empathy Model in Part I. One needs a sense of psychological autonomy (which Mahler calls individuation) in order to establish the human to human contact that is involved in our model's stages of contact, resonance and inclusion.

At birth the infant is fresh and psychologically unformed. Like a bud that will eventually become a flower, the potential for the mature self is in the newborn. In the early years of life, the individual person gradually emerges in an interaction of mutuality with the parent figure(s). At first, another person is regarded only as an object, an "it"; gradually, the infant manages to internalize a memory of the other, which becomes increasingly constant. As the little person grows toward more internal object constancy, the sense of the self becomes more established. This is accomplished through the "separation-individuation project" which every child (and every parent) experiences.

Mahler's Stages of Infant Development

Mahler proposed three early phases of infantile development: *absolute autism, symbiosis* and *separation-individuation*.[5] The separation-individuation phase comprises three subphases: *different, practicing* and *rapprochement*. Successful completion of these stages leads to a period called *object constancy*. This development is illustrated in the diagram below.[6]

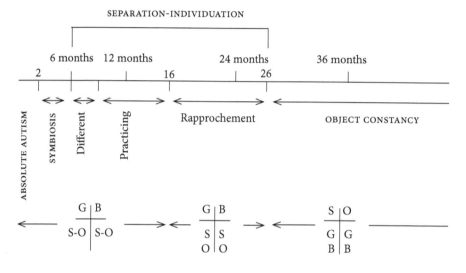

ABSOLUTE AUTISM (FIRST MONTH)

The initial phase, *absolute autism*, occurs in the first month after birth and involves basic life-sustaining reflex activities and responses that are not accompanied by mental representations. Experience is limited to basic needs such as hunger, temperature and comfort and the infant makes no distinction between self and environment. In the diagram, this fusion of self and other in the infant domain is represented as S-O. Within this unity, the infant is either content (fed, warm, dry) or unhappy (hungry, cold, wet); this dichotomy is represented by G for good and B for bad. The infant experiences this as an either-or, although in fact there is movement along a continuum. Sometimes G is foreground, and the child feels mostly comfortable. Sometimes B is foreground, and the child experiences discomfort. At this stage, comfort or discomfort are raw experiences, since the child has not yet developed abstract symbols to represent the experience mentally. She reacts instinctively, without thought. Later, as the child develops language, the words "good" and "bad" refer to the basic experiences of pleasure or discomfort.

To reiterate, the early days of life are as S-O fused, sometimes experienced as G, sometimes experienced as B. The basic dichotomy is between G and B, with the fused S-O as a subset. This is the meaning of the section in the diagram:

$$\frac{G \mid B}{\text{S-O} \mid \text{S-O}}$$

SYMBIOSIS (2–6 MONTHS)

The second phase, *symbiosis*, occurs between the second and the sixth postnatal months. During this time, the child's "good-bad" perceptual dichotomy becomes increasingly organized in relation to the primary caregiver (the mother or mother surrogate). Although the child gradually experiences some primitive acknowledgment of the mother, the mother is not yet distinct as a separate object. Rather, she is an extension of the child, a possession that is subject to the child's whim and desire. Even the breast of the mother is experienced as inseparable from the infant. Self and other are still basically fused in a mutuality which is now called "symbiosis." This primitive self-other concept (S-O) is organized within the basic dichotomy of good and bad. So there is a "good self-other" and a "bad self-other." When mother performs the child's bidding, S-O is good; when the child is hungry or unattended, S-O is bad.

SEPARATION-INDIVIDUATION (6–26 MONTHS)

The third stage, *separation-individuation*, commences at about six months of age and passes through three subphases (different, practicing, rapprochement). The infant now begins to "hatch" from the symbiotic unity of mother-child. Children begin to develop a sense of themselves, pay attention to the environment, and gradually begin to explore the world using their own feelings and sensations.

As the infant's perceptual system matures, she learns to focus and distinguish objects "out there." She discovers that her hands belong to her, and that when she cries, a large cooing face comes and provides nourishment. She gradually distinguishes that this is "Mommy," which she creates as a mental object that is separate from herself. As the child pokes at the mother's face, she progressively learns to attach language, providing names for "nose," "eyes," and "mouth," all belonging to "Mommy." The development of nouns that apply to the world out there facilitates the child's establishment of stable objects. She is learning to separate S and O, self and other. The basic dichotomy is still between G and B, but now S and O are becoming separated. This is the meaning of the section depicted in the diagram as:

$$\frac{G \mid B}{\begin{matrix} S & S \\ O & O \end{matrix}}$$

She learns that Mommy comes when she cries, and learns to communicate with Mommy (the first O). This process involves control; the child owns the other and wants to establish domination over this other from the beginning, because this O provides relief from the discomforts of B and helps to maintain G. This is the beginning of the control dynamic that characterizes the power orientation to life, in contrast to the strength orientation. In power, the child wants to control the parent (the O), who provides and protects. In strength, the child gradually learns to tolerate the discomforts and to self-soothe, and accept her situation; to the extent that she can do this, her S becomes strong and she is less bound to try to control the O. This is a delicate balance; at first, the infant is so helpless that the parents must do absolutely everything. But even in the first few days, a wise parent will learn to delay responding to the infant's every cry, watching to see if the child can learn to tolerate the anxiety and discomfort and attend to the situation herself, thus becoming stronger (relying on herself), rather than more powerful (controlling the other).

DIFFERENT AND PRACTICING SUBPHASES (6–16 MONTHS)
At about six months, babies show increasingly sustained attentiveness to their environment, as they learn that the environment is separate and can be learned. This is the *different* subphase. The ten months that follow (6-16 months) are marked by rapid and extensive development of the infant's sensory-perceptual and motor coordinative skills.

Youngsters gradually begin to assert individuality by crawling away from mother and exploring the world independently. This process begins with small forays away and quick scampers back to mother's protection. The distance of the crawling excursion and the time period tolerated away from mother's protection increase steadily. This is the *practicing* subphase, where the child builds up a repertoire of experience led by a growing independent will and activity. The child will keep looking back at mother to check that she is there. As youngsters become more confident of the lengthening psychological tether between themselves and mother, they begin to develop confidence in exploring the environment from their own perspective.

At this phase, children are psychologically internalizing a memory of the image of mother, to be utilized as a security reference as they crawl away. In their excursions away from mother, children will turn around to check to see that their internal mother image is consistent with the actual mother. As this "practicing" increases, the youngster is getting ready to differentiate from mother; the project is to internalize an image of mother (internalized object), to which the child can relate when mother is not immediately available. Towards the end of this phase, a child will be able to play unattended while mother is in the next room; the child will periodically speak to the mother, to hear the sound of her voice, in order to continually check the consistency of the internalized image with outer reality.

The infant is still operating within a basic matrix of good and bad (G/B). However, what was a fusion of self and other as S-O is now transforming into separate S and O. This does not occur all at once; rather the link between S and O gradually fades as the separation occurs. Nevertheless, during the early exploratory phases, S and O are still linked. When the child is pleased, the S-O is good; when the child is displeased, the S-O (linked by a longer psychological cord) is bad. Sometimes difficulties can occur at this phase, which can be carried forward as restrictions or psychological skewing. If the child looks back at mother and sees her as overly concerned, or if the mother follows the child and is overly attentive, the child might get the message that all is not safe in the environment, and hence may not dare to leave. Children who look back and see that the mother is not paying attention may get the idea that leaving will result in abandonment. The task for the mother is to provide "good-enough mothering," paying enough attention without excessive concern or premature lack of interest.

If all goes well, the child who proceeds along this developmental continuum will be able to tolerate Mommy's absence for longer and longer periods, secure in the "stable internal object" (an internal mental representation of the actual Mommy who always returns).

The child is learning to separate from parents, and to develop some independence. But, being tied to the parent for protection and security, she is not autonomous as a being; her little S is in a state of G when Mommy (O) does as she desires, and B when Mommy (O) does not.

RAPPROCHEMENT SUBPHASE (16–26 MONTHS)
At about the 16th month, toddlers enter the last subphase, *rapprochement*, which develops for roughly the next ten months (16-26 months). During this phase, children gradually develop a sense of self distinct from the mother (other). Since this is still within a context of G/B, mother can be all good when the child experiences pleasure with her, and all bad when the child is displeased with her. In the same fashion, youngsters

also see themselves as all good or all bad; they might slap themselves to bring self-punishment for a judgment that they are all bad. To this point, youngsters are defining themselves with *walls*, which function in the all good/all bad fashion. *Boundaries* begin to appear as children develop an increasing sense of self. If development continues, children can achieve a stable internal image of the parent, and thus retain a picture of mother to relate to at all times. The stabilizing of this internal picture involves the recognition that mother is not all good or all bad; rather, the mother is herself an individual, who is sometimes good and sometimes bad. This relativistic view is a harbinger of a completely revised perspective. Instead of a dualism of good/bad, *one begins to see the world in terms of self/other*. At this stage a distinct self is emerging, which is capable of sensitivity to the boundaries of other selves, and capable of setting boundaries for oneself.

The rapprochement subphase includes a number of ambivalent and sometimes regressive behaviours that indicate children's dawning awareness that they are separate and distinct from mother. Children's gradual recognition that they have an identity separate from mother brings forth the behaviours often associated with the "terrible twos." This is a time of testing of will, when youngsters are prone to loud outbursts, willful demands, stubbornness, and attempts to control others. The shift from a world organized by "all good" and "all bad" occurs gradually over the third year, as the child's internal self-representations (S) and object-representations (O) become more differentiated.

OBJECT CONSTANCY

With "good enough mothering" youngsters can proceed into the next phase, that of *object constancy*, in which the self-representation and the object-representation become stabilized and dependable. At that point, if they have successfully navigated the challenging turbulence of the previous phase, the internal world organization has undergone a major shift; the child's primary mental representations transform from all good and all bad, replaced by a context of self (S) and other (O). Within this, the internal stable self-representation and internal stable object-representation are sometimes good, sometimes bad, allowing for flexibility and fluidity instead of the "all-or-none" reactivity of the earlier phases. The child at 36 months is capable of maintaining a stable personality.

Once a stable internal object is present, it is possible to shift to a world-orientation of self and other, seen in the diagram as:

$$\begin{array}{c|c} S & O \\ \hline G & G \\ B & B \end{array}$$

This shift can be accomplished only once the child has a stable internal object of the parent figure, and has enough security to tolerate some anxiety of separation and discomfort, having experienced these tensions in her growth.

In this new framework, the basic dichotomy is self and other. Both S and O are mixtures of G and B; sometimes S is mostly G and sometimes S is mostly B; sometimes O is mostly B (Mommy is bad), and sometimes O is mostly G (Mommy is good). It is not clear how a developing consciousness becomes morally tinged with "right" and "wrong"; nevertheless, as language and attitudes develop, a steadily increasing reliance on moral systems is evident. Youngsters show evidence that their decisions, attitudes and actions are cast in the light of what is right and wrong. This "right and wrong" shifts from moment to moment, usually not as either-or, but as foreground-background shadings. Situation ethics – deciding upon actions in a sensitive specific manner without relying upon preset rules – can come into play only after a self emerges.

Approaches to Separation-Individuation Problems

We appreciate this developmental continuum model for its usefulness in identifying where individuals have become stuck. Often the personalities of adults show the fixations of incomplete individuation. We do not use diagnostic labels with our clients, but recognize the insights of much psychological literature that does use these terms. Rinsley, in his 1980 article from which we draw much of this material, describes how borderline and narcissistic personality structures can arise when "good-enough" mothering is not provided and children get "stuck" in the process of development described by Mahler.

According to Rinsley, the borderline personality develops from the dynamics of a mother who rewards dependent, clinging behaviour in the child and threatens rejection or abandonment when the infant makes efforts to become independent of her. This youngster develops an inner conviction that growth and autonomy lead only to abandonment; accompanying this is the belief that remaining symbiotically dependent guarantees support and nurturing. This explains the extreme dimensions of dependency seen in some adults.[7] This can express itself in a tendency both to placate and to blame others, often switching rapidly back and forth between the two attitudes; in such people, frustration tolerance is low and they tend to see situations and people in infantile fashion as "all good" or "all bad." For these individuals, others are valued for what they give and reward, or take and withhold. Accompanying this perspective is often a buried self-representation as "all bad" which is sometimes split off from consciousness, showing in the symptoms of low energy or depression. In terms of the Dynamic Empathy Model, these people show evidence of fixation in later aspects of the fusion phase, and in the early process of objectification/isolation, and thus have difficulty developing skills for empathetic relating with others.

The narcissistic personality arises from maternal rewards and reinforcement of the child's growth to separation-individuation, but only in relation to the mother's view of how the child should be. The youngster is rewarded for independence, yet remains dependent upon reward for appropriate behaviours. This personality is more developed than that of the borderline and has a more stable self-object, but is prone to regressive fragmentation if the self-image is somehow not maintained by others' approval, as occurs in so-called narcissistic wounding. "Thus," says Rinsley, "the latter appears more internally coherent and capable of sustained, genuine achievement than does ... the borderline, albeit on the basis of a still partly fused, undifferentiated, mother-infant self-object which robs him of any real capacity to invest himself significantly in, and relate meaningfully to, others."[8] Although such people have developed a little further than the previously mentioned borderline personality, the crucial transformation in orientation from good/bad to self and other has not been completed; they remain tied to the approval of others, seeing them not as real people but as objects whose function is to provide them with some sense of self. They cannot experience a full-fledged sense of self as a core from which to relate to others in a caring fashion. Such a person is stuck in the objectification/isolation stage of the Empathy Model.

The developmental continuum is useful in assessing how to help people who have been stuck in their personality development. People struggling with borderline issues can come to realize that there are people "out there" who care for them (this can happen in individual counselling or therapy, in groups, and in friendships) and can make headway in their individuation process; their task is to discover and affirm their own inner resources in relationship with others and learn some appreciation of the "grey" areas of their own and others' personalities, rather than seeing these as either black or white, good or bad. Those individuals with narcissistic issues are challenged to appreciate the human qualities in others beyond the restrictions of objectification, and thus to develop relationships based on respect for self and other. We have found that the honestly expressed, human responses of people in groups we have led at The Haven are often especially helpful to people dealing with both borderline and narcissistic issues. The task for everyone is to move from fusion and objectification/isolation into the stages of contact, resonance and inclusion.

Individuate or Individualize

For many children, development is interrupted before the stage of object constancy. The youngster continues to grow physically, yet he or she remains psychologically stuck in a basic dichotomy of good/bad and relates in a field-dependent fashion. If development does not reach the stage of object constancy, the child will *individualize* instead of individuating. Individualizing is a limited development wherein the person seems mature, and yet underneath is still caught in objectification and lacks the skills for dialogical engagement; such people appear to be more advanced than they actually are. In contrast, the *individuating* person has qualities of engagement and humility that accompany a developed capacity for self-acceptance and empathy; these are only possible after the stage of object constancy. Of course, this is not all-or-none. Most people are a mixture of processes of individuating and individualizing. The challenge is to emphasize the former and diminish the latter. This is the work of taking down fixated walls, establishing personal boundaries, and moving from a good-bad view of oneself and others towards a more compassionate and empathetic stance.

We emphasize that *personal growth is an ongoing process*. The strength orientation can come to fruition only if individuals develop sufficient ego adaptive mechanisms to tolerate the anxiety of separation and aloneness; only then can people learn to make truly autonomous decisions and be open to spontaneous feelings for self and other. As we have said, this is rare. Nevertheless, this is the key to cooperative human development, and to health and happiness.

Fortunately, it is never too late to address fixated issues, and make restitution for previous lacks in development. We believe that a task for all adults is to convert power oriented attitudes and actions into caring and empathetic interactive ones, moving through the Dynamic Empathy cycle towards more growth, fulfillment and relationships.

II.4   An Impossible Book?

KZ = Confucius (Kong Zi), CJ = Carl Jung, BW = Ben Wong, JM = Jock McKeen

JM: Well, those last few chapters were pretty heady stuff!

BW: Yes, we covered a lot of ground. Some of the ideas can be hard to grasp.

JM: How do you think we're doing?

BW: Well Jock, I've said this before – I think this book is actually impossible to write the way we would really like to. We cannot fully express what we want to say – because we want to include the primary process, eternity, in the equation.

JM: Yes ... it's not easy to hear, but please say more.

BW: So much of what we want to express, and what you and I experience, is in a nonlogical language of the primary process. This entire book project is an exercise in the expression of the secondary process. Primary process can probably be better expressed in dance or music or painting or drama. But you don't have those media available to the readers of this book.

KZ: I would like to hear more about the difference between primary process and secondary process.

BW: Of course, Master Kong. It was Freud who first made the distinction. Primary process is the elemental thinking process that is pre-rational. The language of the primary process is symbols, not words. Do you agree, Dr. Jung?

CJ: Yes, the collective unconscious is structured in archetypal patterns, whose language informs myths and dreams. The language is indeed that of symbols.

BW: The secondary process is developed as the child acquires human language, and is involved in naming objects in the surrounding world and being able to express his or her relationship to that external world. Freud called this the "world of reality," which is external. So the language of the secondary process is words.

JM: Freud thought the mature human had a well-developed secondary process. Do you agree, Dr Jung?

CJ: Certainly. The secondary process involves logic and analysis and is exemplified in our ability to control and manipulate the world around us. Humans could not build bridges or automobiles or aircraft without secondary process thinking. We influence the world of objects through secondary process thinking. Furthermore, we relate to each other in secondary process, not only through verbal and written communication, but also in our naming of each other and our memories of each other. These are held in secondary process. Our human value system and our individuality are configured and maintained using secondary process thinking. Without this, we would be mere animals.

KZ: I see. And perhaps this emphasis on secondary process means that we have lost our ability to commune with nature, to be a part of the whole.

CJ: Yes, Master Kong, this is the dilemma.

BW: Freud thought primary process was "primitive." He dismissed the expansive experience of oneness that some have had; he called this an "oceanic feeling." He believed this feeling was common in infants, as a symptom of not having separated from the mother and nature. Freud thought that when the oceanic feeling occurred in an adult, this was always a symptom of regression to an infantile state. He further said that people seek out religion and worship gods to satisfy the desire to return to this oceanic feeling of infancy. To Freud, people should grow up, and let go of such infantile yearnings.

CJ: On this basis, Freud rejected my idea of the collective unconscious as being infantile or primitive. And he believed that any religious or spiritual yearning was a symptom of regression too. He and I disagreed on many aspects of this, and ultimately we broke off our relationship.

JM: But for you, the "primary process" is primordial, not necessarily primitive.

CJ: Yes, exactly. It is so that "primitive people" are more in touch with this primordial patterned aspect and are more responsive to the symbols of the collective unconscious. They are less obstructed by civilized encumbrances. They are more in touch.

JM: So there is a difference between primitive, primordial, and elemental?

CJ: Yes, the primary archetype (which is the Self) is elemental, meaning "basic." It is neither "primitive" nor "infantile." But it is primordial, meaning "having been there from the beginning."

JM: Yes. I discuss some of this in our chapter about your work, Dr Jung.

CJ: I'm glad to hear it!

BW: The language of primary process is myth and dream, and probably music; it involves participation (not object-making) and is pre-scientific. The language of secondary process is logic, analysis, mathematics, and involves object-making and science.

CJ: Excellent summary, Dr. Wong!

JM: So, the nonlogical primordial world of primary process is not "less," only different ...

CJ: This is my belief.

BW: I see I have been deeply invested in the scientific model, with its language of logic and secondary process thought. I have been drawn to intuitive experiences, but I have sought to explain them with my secondary logic.

CJ: This was my struggle too.

KZ: This is very interesting. I myself left the understanding of the nonlogical to the ancients, and tried to express my understandings through what you call secondary process.

JM: This does explain my lifelong dilemma. I have always had an artistic nature and easily respond to feelings and moods and music. But I have struggled to be a good scientist, to understand the world through logic, and to articulate what I find. But I find the intuitive feelings very appealing, and natural to me.

CJ: The dichotomy you describe led to my assertion that I had two personalities, one that lives in the world of time and space, and one that is in touch with eternity.

JM: So, Dr Jung, do you understand why Ben thinks this book is impossible to write?

CJ: I had the same dilemma in trying to write what I discovered in my exploration of the unconscious. In the *Red Book*, which was my private journal, I used drawings, especially mandalas, to try to express what I found in colour and shapes and patterns. But it was insufficient as a tool to communicate myself to others.

KZ: My students urged me to write down what I was teaching. But I was aware that words could not fully capture the meanings of the universe. For that reason, I also believe that book learning can only go so far.

JM (a little dejected): Gentlemen, I understand your considerations all too well. But I will stubbornly push on and see where words can take us.

BW: This is such an interesting discussion. Perhaps the feelings we have with each other can somehow come through.

CJ (laughing): We are limited, but undaunted!

JM: The next main chapter in the book is about Wilhelm Reich and other people who worked with breath and the body. I think they were interested in this primary process understanding. And our friend Paul Reps certainly was, so we're including some words from him too!

II.5   A Reps Interlude

Reps, the Zen master, lived with us for the last years of his life. His simple, poignant and incisive writing perhaps can shock our system into a different framework for the next chapter. Breathe as you read these two poems!

All over completely at ease,
Be *you*.
Impose
no impulse
through your nerve network.

Dare you be you?[1]

COME TO LIFE

There seems to be some
confusion
about where all of us are
going.
We are here.

Our atoms and our cells are
those of
great nature and ever will be,
transformingly.

I am you
and you are me
spontaneously.

To return here
simply enter your rhythm
you come and go with.
Let breath breathe naturally
without imposing any
thought,
feel, impulse on it.

"That's too easy."

We make it hard
unnecessarily.

Press fingers
very slightly
with outbreathflow
and release
with inbreathflow.

In a few presses –
in our true nature.[2]

11.6   Wilhelm Reich and Approaches to the Body

> There is a unity between body and mind. I followed this track and I found that you reach out with your life energy when you feel well and loving, and that you retract it to the center of your body when you are afraid.– Wilhelm Reich [1]

Freud and most of his contemporaries saw psychotherapy fundamentally as a mental process involving verbal communication and imagery. Almost no attention was paid to the body, except when it produced physical symptoms that might be relieved by addressing the psychological level. Even today, "talk therapy" of one form or another (in addition to drug therapy) continues to be the norm.

However, body-oriented approaches also developed during the 20th century. We ourselves have been most influenced by the work of Wilhelm Reich, Alexander Lowen and Ida Rolf. These approaches to the body have added a rich dimension to counselling, therapy and education (and, indeed, to the training of actors, dancers, and musicians). These pioneering theories have shown a clear link between mind and body, overcoming the historical separation that has influenced Western thinking for centuries. Alexander Lowen writes:

> The body is not simply a vehicle for the mind, with the mind a separate force acting upon it. Instead, spirit is inherent in the living tissue.[2]

Some practitioners go so far as to focus primarily on the body, and take a very straightforward approach to enhancing self-awareness of the physical dimension of being, with a unified bodymind concept. Stanley Keleman, for example, writes:

> What I am trying to do is bring each person into more intimate contact with himself – with his own body. I do this by working directly with the body. You are your body, period. That is my working principle.[3]

Authors' Perspective
From our earliest professional days, we have studied many styles of growth and therapy that were definitely not in the mainstream, including body approaches. Our investigation has included sessions in Reichian breathing, both as trainees and as clients of Reichian practitioners.

We both had a series of Rolfing, which involves very deep (and often painful) tissue manipulation, so that we could have the first-hand experience of this controversial approach. We attended seminars and workshops in psychodrama, gestalt, dream work, psychosynthesis, tai ji, yoga, massage and a host of other approaches that involve the body. We practised on each other to learn the effects of these unusual techniques from both sides, practitioner and client. We were especially impressed with the potency of breath approaches, and began to utilize them in our practices. We developed a technique set which we called "body work" – an amalgam of approaches from acupressure, Reichian breathing, Rolfing and other styles – and were gratified to find that our clients made rapid progress.

The goals of conventional psychotherapy are often limited to addressing various emotional blockages and family-of-origin issues. We think this is usually only a beginning, and further work involves learning about creativity and self-expression. Thus the programs we developed have included diverse methods, including writing, music, body awareness, dance, expressive movement, yoga, and tai ji.

We have also integrated energy approaches from Chinese medicine into our work. Western medicine is grounded in the assumption that the physical reality is fundamental, and energy is a byproduct of this basic physical reality. Classical Chinese medicine functions from a radically different perspective – energy is primary, and all other dimensions of reality (including the physical) are expressions of this basic energy. We discuss this more thoroughly in later chapters.

Body work can help a person have a new experience of life in the physical being, to become present and vital and connected. But we caution people not to see body work as an end in itself. To us, it is an important tool for helping people to get in touch with themselves deeply and significantly. But ultimately, the change that needs to occur is not just release or enhanced vitality. People need to reorient themselves from a defensive, self-centred perspective into a more relational and social attitude, becoming citizens of their community and, ultimately, the world. Thus our work integrates body approaches with interpersonal communications, dialogue, and self-expression.

Wilhelm Reich

Wilhelm Reich (1897–1957) was an Austrian-American psychiatrist and psychoanalyst who created his own system of body and energy release, which he called vegetotherapy. He studied neuropsychiatry at the University of Vienna, had a short training analysis in the 1920s, and joined Freud's Vienna Psychoanalytic Society. He became a prominent member of the psychoanalytic community, but his relationship with Freud cooled in the late 1920s and they broke contact in the early 1930s.

In 1933, he began to teach and experiment at the University of Oslo. There, he claimed the discovery of energy vesicles called "bions," which he maintained were the transition from lifeless to living matter. This was also the period in which he published some influential ideas about character analysis and 'character armour', which we discuss below. In 1939 he moved to the United States, where he taught at the New School for Social Research in New York. In 1942, he established a facility in Maine, where he conducted research on *orgone*, his term for life energy. Around this time, his thought became more and more difficult to comprehend, even to friends and associates. In the 1950s, Reich wrote about DOR (Deadly Orgone Energy) as a cause of illness. He attempted to counteract DOR using "orgone accumulators," boxes he constructed to concentrate the beneficial orgone energy.

Reich was investigated by federal authorities, who ordered him to stop shipping orgone accumulators, on the grounds that he was making false and misleading claims about their potential health benefits. He was sentenced in 1956 to two years in prison, and died while incarcerated. That year, several tons of his publications were burned by the FDA.

Reich was a controversial and compelling figure. Some see him as a visionary, a genius before his time; others dismiss him as a lunatic. His work influenced a generation of intellectuals, and was incorporated into Fritz Perls' Gestalt therapy and Alexander Lowen's Bioenergetic Analysis.[4] With the resurgence of interest in the 1970s especially, his books gradually became available again.[5] One biographer, Colin Wilson, wrote:

> In short, what kept drawing me back again and again to Reich was the fascination of the strange no-man's-land between genius and insanity, greatness and paranoia, self-belief and self-deception.[6]

Reich was prone to dogmatism and forcefulness when he believed he was right (which was often). However, his "scientific" work would not stand up to the scrutiny of modern science. Charles Rycroft notes that "no scientist of any standing or merit has ever taken the slightest notice of Reich's researches" and that "his enemies dismissed his orgone theory as a paranoid delusional system."[7] But, he says, "if one is capable of surmounting these various obstacles to taking Reich seriously, his account of vegetotherapy is not without interest and the technique is not as foolish as its theoretical trimmings."[8] He even proposes this perspective on Reich's later career:

> There is ... a more interesting and also more charitable way of

approaching the system of ideas developed by Reich in his later years. This is to regard it not, as Reich himself claimed, as a scientific theory based on experimental researches, but as a philosophy of life ... perhaps even a cosmology or theology.[9]

Many have disregarded Reich completely. We ourselves find some insightful ideas in the elaborate theories that he stated as scientific facts. Some of his ideas are eminently useful and should not be ignored, regardless of how one might judge his scientific methods. Though his theoretical explanations were often suspect, he nevertheless had a genius for practical approaches to releasing energy in a client quickly, with strong effect. We ourselves have used, with benefit, Reich's methods, but certainly not all of his theory.

Reichian Theory and Therapeutic Practice

Central to Reichian ideas is the concept of body-mind unity. Alexander Lowen, who underwent analysis and studied with Reich, wrote that for Reich, body and mind were two aspects of a unitary process, like the two faces of a coin. Whatever ones does with the coin, he said, affects both sides simultaneously.[10] Lowen describes Reich's energy theory:

> Reich saw the energy process as a pulsation (expansion and contraction, as in the beating of the heart) and the propagation of waves of excitation that can be experienced as streamings in the body.[11]

Reich's ideas about life-force energy are central to his understanding. He called this energy *orgone energy*, which he proposed is a cosmic energy that flows through all organisms. His ideas about orgone have many parallels with the ancient Chinese idea of *qi*.

Reich, like Freud, initially believed that the repression of sexual energy is a root cause of neurosis. Reich came to believe that the goal of therapy should be to restore the natural energy flow of the body so that the individual has the freedom to alternately build up an energy charge and then release it completely. Reich believed that the natural energy flow is inhibited by persistent defences, manifesting in chronic tension in the muscular system, making up what he called a "character armour." Reich described character armour this way:

> It is as if the affective personality put on an armor, a rigid shell on which the knocks from the outer world as well as the inner demand rebound. This armor makes the individual less sensitive to unpleasure, but it also reduces his libidinal and aggressive mobility and, with that, his capacity for pleasure and achievement.[12]

Reich derived his ideas about defences from his early analytic training. Rycroft writes:

Just as Reich's ideas on life-energy derive from Freud's ideas on mental energy and libido, so too his ideas on 'character' can be traced back to Freud's concepts of 'defence.'[13]

Freud understood these defences to be primarily psychological. Reich added the idea of bodily tension that physicalizes these defences into character armour. This thinking led the way into the new territory of body-oriented psychotherapy. Reich would read bodies as a way of analyzing a person's defences and character structure. He maintained that resistance is revealed not only by *what* is said, but also by *how* it is expressed in the body, revealing the person's character.

Reich believed that the chronic withholding of life-force energy would ultimately result in diseases, both psychological and physical. If the flow of life force could be reestablished, the illnesses could be overcome. He said:

> Now when the natural streaming of the bioenergy is dammed up, it ... spills over, resulting in irrationality, perversions, neuroses, and so on. What do you have to do to correct this? You must get the stream back into its normal bed and let it flow naturally again.[14]

Whereas Freud saw defences as originating from early childhood experiences in the family of origin, Reich believed that repressive cultural attitudes were the cause of the individual's limitations and miseries. For this reason, Reich tried to link political solutions with therapeutic ones. He suggested that society should provide conditions that allow the freest and safest growth for children, with a minimum of inhibitions and a maximum of freedom. He believed that the frustration of primary drives (love, motility, and sexuality) gives rise to destructive secondary drives of anger, hatred, sadism, masochism, spite and dependency.

Neuroscience teaches that the human autonomic nervous system (vegetative nervous system) balances the internal environment. There are two aspects to this system, the *sympathetic* system, and the *parasympathetic* system. These two operate in concert, balancing each other. The sympathetic system comes into play when there are dangers or extra demands on the body. The parasympathetic system is more of a maintenance system allowing pleasure and relaxation. With increased sympathetic tone comes a redirection of blood flow from the interior of the body to the external musculature, increased heart rate, raised blood pressure, dilated pupils and increased breathing (the so-called "fight-fright-flight" response). Increased parasympathetic tone, on the other hand, brings blood flow to the internal organs, facilitating digestion and relaxation.

Reichian theory conceives of character armouring in terms of the autonomic nervous system. The daily stresses of living bring a gradual accumulation of a biolectric charge (enhanced sympathetic tone), which can be released through orgasm or breathing exercises. Reich maintained that the chronic tension in character armouring inhibits complete release of the charge; he believed that people usually do not fully let go in sexuality, with a gradual accumulation of chronic tension which does not get released. Thus, in popular terminology, people are "up tight," and this tension increases through a life of defences. The end result is illness, both physical and psychological.

Release of chronic tension can occur in sexual orgasm. But to Reich, the orgasm is not just an ejaculation or a climax, but rather a total body response manifested in rhythmic convulsive movements. This same kind of movement is frequently observed in body work sessions without any distinct sexual connotation. To Reich, the orgasm regulates the bio-energy by discharging the accumulated tension, bringing a sense of well-being and pleasure. When a complete orgasm is not achieved (either in sexuality, or in breathing practice), the system fails to return the organism to a state of full relaxation. This situation of "energy stasis" interferes with a full appreciation of the senses. The armoured individual in stasis becomes numb, has less sense of aliveness and pleasure, and loses touch with feelings of connection and love.

In Reichian therapy, chronic tensions are released by directing the person's attention to them, by breathing techniques, and by direct manipulations of the physical structure. Relaxing of the character armour results in bodily vibrations, tremors, and feelings of "streamings" in the body, often accompanied by spontaneous expression of emotions, sometimes with associated memories. Reich first named this "Character Analysis" (when he was more associated with psychoanalysis) and, then later, "Vegetotherapy" (as he progressed with his understanding of life-force energy), and ultimately, "Orgone Therapy." As the individual relinquishes chronic tension, the body armour gradually dissolves, bringing forth feelings of relaxation, well-being and pleasure. In addition, the relaxed state facilitates a sense of connection with one's surroundings and with other people. This approach is what we studied in the early 1970s and incorporated into our work with people. In the programs we designed, breathing exercises are a frequent activity, and participants are encouraged to explore their own breathing, by themselves and with others. We described a method of exploratory breathing in a previous book.[15]

Alexander Lowen and Bioenergetic Analysis

Bioenergetic Analysis (often just called Bioenergetics) is an offshoot of Reichian therapy developed by New York psychiatrist Alexander Lowen (1910–2008), who was in therapy with Reich in the 1940s and subsequently studied Reichian therapy himself. The aim of Bioenergetic therapy is to let go of inhibitions, blocks and tensions that interfere with self-awareness and self-expression. Similar to Reichian therapy, this method utilizes focused awareness on areas of body holdings, and deep breathing. As the deep breathing progresses, the individual experiences a build-up of "charge," which is experienced as feelings of numbness, tingling, and spontaneous vibrations in the body. The goal is to build up this charge sufficiently for a breakthrough to occur, with release of tension and emotion.

Bioenergetics is characterized by the use of many different postures to facilitate breakthroughs. By placing the body into positions where some muscle groups come under tension, the vibration is elicited more readily. For example, a common posture is to bend forward from the waist, letting the head hang loosely, with the tension along the backs of the legs exaggerated by the position. As the person breathes deeply in this stance for some minutes, vibrations tend to develop in the tension area along the backs of the legs and gradually spread through the body, facilitating the eventual breakthrough. Lowen practised the techniques himself every day; we witnessed him at a conference when he was in his eighties, stripped down to shorts, breathing deeply before an assembled audience of fully dressed professionals.

To Lowen, breathing is the key to vitality, to a fuller embodied life. Lowen describes modern man:

> Having dissociated himself from his body, he no longer thinks in bodily terms. He ignores the simple truth that to be alive one must breathe and that the better one breathes, the more alive one is.[16]

There are many similarities between Bioenergetics and Reichian Therapy. Both assume body-mind unity and the presence of a human energy system. Both depend upon reading the personality from the body, though Bioenergetics places greater emphasis on working through personality problems analytically. Bioenergetics also makes use of a greater variety of body techniques (Lowen's books show dozens of different positions to facilitate the work). Other differences are in evidence:

> What differentiates Bioenergetics from its parent system is its less systematic approach to loosening the armor, besides a downplaying of Reich's concept of the orgone and its minimizing of cause-and-effect relationships between social or political issues and our inner blocks.[17]

We have found Bioenergetics to be practical and useful. The exercises certainly help people become embodied and can easily be taught to groups. People can work in pairs, learn the methods, and then practice at home. In longer programs at The Haven, there is usually an informal breathing group which participants attend in pairs, to explore breathing and bioenergetics.

Rolfing

A third influence on our own approach to body work was Ida Rolf (1896-1979), an American biochemist who created Structural Integration, also known as "Rolfing." Rolf traced problems in physical alignment to chronic habits of fixation within the body. But unlike others who proposed that body fixations are centred in the musculature, Rolf said the difficulties arise in the fixations in the *fascia*, the connective tissue envelope that holds the structures of the body together, and links muscles to bones:

> Fascia is the organ of posture. Nobody ever says this; all the talk is about muscles ... we must understand both the anatomy and physiology ... of fascia.[18]

Rolfing involves awareness, observation, and soft tissue manipulation. Rolf conceived of the body as a whole, integrated by a "web" of fascia:

> The body is a web of fascia. A spiderweb is in a plane; this web is in a sphere. We can trace the lines of that web to get an understanding of how what we see in a body works. For example, why, when we work with the superficial fascia, does this change the tone of the fascia as a whole?[19]

Rolf's concept was to align the body with the natural flow of gravity; she believed the body could heal itself when it was in proper alignment. She said,

> This is the gospel of Rolfing. When the body gets working appropriately, the force of gravity can flow through. Then, spontaneously, the body heals itself.[20]

This approach shares some assumptions with classical ballet training, which describes efficient stance and centring in its notion of "placement." In ballet there are optimal stances and positions where the body is free to utilize full power and flexibility. Early in his ballet training, Jock was plagued with a chronically painful knee that seemed like an ongoing strain or inflammation. When he showed this to his teacher, she dismissed it as unimportant, saying, "That will disappear when you learn to stand properly, with your weight over your feet." She was correct; after some time in the discipline of ballet practice, Jock no longer had any knee problems, and still does not, over a decade later.

The Rolf approach is about gravity and verticality. Rolf said,

> Forget anatomy and take on art and you'll look at a body as a something around a line, a vertical line.[21]

Rolf urged her students to allow a natural process to do the work. Even though she would accept very deep manipulation as a reasonable approach at times, she was definite that any touch, light or strong, should be done only after reading the body, and being aware of the body's receptivity:

> Don't force things. If you've done your preparation right you don't have to force things. There's a steadiness, a gradual straightening that organizes the body.[22]

She taught her students that theorizing is of limited use. To her, what was most important was a developing sensitivity to the body and its alignment:

> Our job is to learn to contact reality as the reality exists in the human body. Not to contact names, not to know the names, not to know abstract patterns.[23]

"All this metaphysics is fine," she said, "but be mighty sure you've got physics under the metaphysics."[24] She was not particularly interested in emotional content and discouraged her students from following the emotional releases of their clients, emphasizing instead that gravity would take care of everything without psychological intervention. We ourselves were Rolfed early in our careers and utilized some of the soft tissue manipulations from this approach in the body and breath work we did with clients. In particular, we see that there are common physical points of stress in most people, and we generally would start a breathing session by investigating these areas. Unlike Rolf, we often focused on the emotional content that was released in this process, and found much benefit for people in dealing with their expression of feeling and content.

We noted that the release points that Rolf taught are similar to acupressure and acupuncture points. For example, most people do not breathe fully into the chest, and we would focus on deeper breathing in the Reichian fashion, assisted by soft tissue manipulation of points on the upper chest, shoulders and neck, using Rolfing style techniques. Other common places of holding that we usually addressed include the jaw and the neck. We also note that most people hold in the pelvis, and we would devote attention to points in this area, although usually not in the first session, since this often is a particularly sensitive region. Like Rolf, we have always cautioned our trainees to use sensitivity, to invite the client to come to meet the touch rather than insensitively "plunge in." When a practitioner brings this sensitivity to a body work session, it is possible to work with the full cooperation of the client to do very deep tissue manipulation. When pain occurs, this is evidence that the client is retreating from the touch; this is a signal to back off and invite the client to breathe and come forward again. From the outside, deeper touch can seem aggressive or insensitive, but when properly done, the work is thoroughly respectful of the client's boundaries and limits, and can bring remarkable breakthroughs.

Body Language and Reading

People's bodies often speak what they are not saying verbally. We have all observed someone with slumped shoulders and a downcast look on their face, and known that the person is feeling low.

People do this all the time with their partners and children. The communication is both ways; people are "reading" the nonverbal cues from their partners, and they are being read by the partner too. With training in the body approaches, a practitioner can hone these intuitive skills to communicate with the client.[25]

Ben used to teach medical students this approach by taking them from the classroom and sitting on the lawn with them on the university campus. The topic of the day was for the students to "guess" the life stories of the unknown students they could observe around them. After the medical students got past their initial resistance, they found their imagination was ignited, and they would probe more deeply into the lives of the people they witnessed. To Ben, this was excellent training to develop a deep imagining of the life of the other, a step on the way to empathy and inclusion. This same kind of "educated guesswork" can be used to imagine an unknown person's medical history.

In training programs at The Haven, Ben would ask interns to read a volunteer's life story from watching as that individual walked into the room. Objectively, all the intern had to go on was the facial expression, stance, speed and manner of walk, and so on. But, remarkably, the readings were often very subtle, touching on a person's tentativeness or brashness, grace or awkwardness, confidence or self-defeat. When the intern would "guess" at past events, the volunteer would frequently respond with surprise and amazement at how accurate these guesses could be.

Return to the Body

We close this chapter on a poetic note. Robert Bly suggests that the emphasis on masculinity in Western culture has led us to acquisitiveness, power orientation, and inadequacy of social contact. This same patriarchal attitude has kept human beings disassociated from physical being and our bodies. In a radical and thought provoking conversation, he proposes a translation for the Lord's Prayer from an arcane Slavonic manuscript, which places the feminine into the centre, inviting us into the body. We offer it here for your consideration.[26]

Mother's Prayer

Our Mother who art in earth,
    your name was always holy.
Your Kingdom has already arrived here
    in the body.
May we sense what the whole universe wants to be,
    both in the body and in the spirit.
May we make our own bread, every day,
    and may we forgive everyone,
even those who have not transgressed against us.
    Do not lead us into sickness,
and save us from the longing we have to damage ourselves.
    For the body is yours,
and delight, and ecstasy,
    forever and ever,

              AMEN

II.7 What is Normal?

KZ = Confucius (Kong Zi), CJ = Carl Jung, BW = Ben Wong, JM = Jock McKeen

Having met a few times, the men are more relaxed, informal, and personally more connected and clear. There is more humour and teasing. BW and KZ obviously have an affinity. They are quietly wise and noninvested in getting their way, yet curious and interested to learn. It is also apparent that CJ and JM are very similar in their personality structures. CJ is a strong sharp presence, an older version of JM in many ways. JM is self-assured, but perhaps too egotistical – CJ shows evidence of this too, but he hides it well. CJ and JM are both men who are well aware of the effect they have on others; they are self-conscious actors, but with earnest intentions.

JM: Gentleman, the last chapter about Wilhem Reich has set me thinking about what is normal. A lot of people thought Reich was crazy.

KZ: I think "normal" is a word that applies to a specific civilization, and relates to the definitions of that culture. So in China it is normal to use chopsticks to eat. In the West, a knife and fork are normal. Normal means "what is common." Reich's idea were certainly not common in his culture ... though some of them might seem less odd to us Chinese!

JM: I agree about that! And we use the word normal in many different contexts. In Western medicine, for example, "normal" is a word to mean "not pathological." In medical school, I was trained to determine if a person's situation was within normal limits or was in a pathological range.

CJ: Yes, this is the medical approach, which was first applied to physical symptoms and findings. Then it was applied to psychological situations too. Certain behaviours were judged "normal" and others were called "pathological." During my early days in psychiatric training at the beginning of the 20th century, we were struggling to find a way to talk about what we were treating.

BW: This was distressing to me during my psychiatric training in the 1950s. I would see special people who were labeled as abnormal simply because they did not have the same outlook as others.

CJ: My experience too. Psychiatric diagnosis uses the medical model and applies this idea to human behaviour and attitudes. Thus, certain psychological situations become labeled as pathological when they might only be artistic, or distinctive, or unique. I dislike any diagnosis that labels people, tries to slot them into some category so that they can be dealt with in a medical way.

KZ: As a nonmedical person, I did not have this perspective. My relation to this concept was political, not medical. Politically, when people do not fit the expected structure, they are labeled too – but the label is "dissident" or "defector" or "disloyal" or "enemy of the state." This is how "normal" is used in politics and government.

BW: When I was in psychiatric practice, I had to provide a diagnosis so that the medical provider would pay the patient's bill. My solution was to give the exact same diagnosis to every person I saw.

JM: What was that diagnosis?

BW: I found something that did not say anything, and was within the scope of the diagnostic schema. It was something like "adjustment reaction." That way, I could avoid words like "psychotic," "neurotic" ... "crazy."

JM: Let's talk about those words. What does medicine and psychiatry mean by them traditionally?

CJ: Well, honestly, we were trying to find words to replace the cultural habit of calling special people "crazy." To Freud's credit, he saw the uniqueness of different people's situation, and his attempt was to categorize people's disturbances without using this dismissive term. Thus we had the habit of talking of neurotics and psychotics.

BW: As I learned it, there was so-called normal behaviour, which fell within the cultural expectations. Then there were people who were having difficulty adapting, who were disturbed and not living fully happy and successful lives. We applied the label "neurotic" to people who could still function, hold a job, raise a family, live in community. But they were neurotic because their adjustment was at the cost of a psychological illness. Neurotics are in touch with reality; they are struggling to adapt to the reality with which they are in touch.

JM: So, they aren't "crazy" ... just screwed up?

BW: That's a rather crude way of putting it.

CJ: But appropriate. Under the surface gloss of psychiatric language is this issue of who is crazy. In my day, when someone was very far from the usual we called them "psychotic" – meaning that they were out of touch with reality.

JM: So this labeling is just to help doctors determine what range of malad-aptation people are experiencing.

BW: Yes. Neurotic means dysfunctional but in touch with reality; psy-chotic means dysfunctional and out of touch with reality. But I never liked this labeling and I resisted using it.

JM: How would you categorize people's experience if it weren't in these terms?

BW: I recognize that people's problems intensify when they are isolated and constricted. So my work has always been to help people establish and maintain contact, and then deal with their defence systems so that they could get more freedom to live and learn. I would encourage people to expand their container of experience so that they could encompass a larger range.

KZ: I like this. Every person is unique, and can learn to open up to possibilities.

CJ: But there are certainly problems trying to apply physical medicine ideas to psychiatric conditions. Freud believed that this was going to be an integrative path, to see all situations as physiological malfunctions that need correcting, returning people to normal.

BW: There is still a strong trend in modern psychiatry to do the same.

JM: Was this part of your separating from Freud?

CJ: Sadly, yes. I wanted to dialogue with Freud about special people, and not just label them and dismiss them as patients who needed treatment. He judged their experiences as abnormal, all the while trying to help them. He did not believe in psychic phenomena, and he did not believe in God.

JM: The next chapter in the book is about Alfred Adler, whom I believe you knew, Dr Jung. I think he would have agreed with you, Ben, when you talked about helping people establish and maintain contact. And with you too, Master Kong, when you mentioned opening up to possibilities.

II.8 Alfred Adler: Unacknowledged Originator

> I have taken forty years to make my psychology simple. I might make
> it still more simple. I might say 'all neurosis is vanity'–but this also
> might not be understood.– Alfred Adler[1]

Alfred Adler (1870–1937) was a Viennese physician and psychotherapist
who founded an approach he called Individual Psychology. He collaborated with Freud from 1902 to 1911, and was an early member of the
Vienna Psychoanalytic Society. Psychoanalysis was certainly affected by
Adler's thought; he was a critic of the primacy of sexuality and voiced
numerous other objections to the central tenets of analysis. He split
from Freud in 1911 and went on to make a major contribution to psychotherapy and education. In particular he had a profound influence on the
neo-Freudian shift towards ego psychology and on the development of
humanist and existentialist psychotherapy.

Adler represents a bridge from the objectifying approaches of medicine and psychoanalysis to a more egalitarian view that engages people in their own healing. The former view sees patients as damaged and
needing to be fixed by a doctor. In contrast, Adler involved his clients as
co-participants in the healing enterprise; this approach is very appealing to us and has been a cornerstone in our own professional evolution.
The influence of Adler is often underestimated, eclipsed as he tends to
be by the dynamic personalities of Freud and Jung. He is rarely quoted
or acknowledged as the originator of many ideas that now have common currency – ideas such as the 'inferiority complex', the notion of 'life
style', and the influence of birth order. Nevertheless, he has been a very
significant figure in the evolution of psychology, medicine and education in the West. One writer put it this way:

> I realize that most observations and ideas of Alfred Adler have sub-
> tly and quietly permeated modern psychological thinking to such a
> degree that the proper question is not whether one is Adlerian, but
> how much of an Adlerian one is.[2]

Early Life and Career

Adler never accepted the suggestion that he was a student of Freud;
rather, he came to psychoanalysis with his own already well formed
ideas about social medicine, education, and in particular the role of

what was referred to as organ inferiority (more on this below). In contrast to Freud, whose university career was central to his professional life, Adler worked in the community as a general practitioner, advocating for the creation of social medicine. Whereas Freud's patients were often well-to-do, Adler's were mostly lower or middle class; social concerns remained foreground for him throughout his career. Although he ultimately became very famous himself, he remained involved with the less affluent population in whose midst he had spent his childhood.

Afflicted with rickets as a child, young Adler could not run and play with other children; he struggled hard to overcome his physical limitations, and his own personal experiences contributed to his developing a psychological theory that people strive to overcome a "basic organ inferiority" and can use their will to move beyond limits. He was deeply intuitive, and could quickly assemble an accurate view of a client's condition and circumstances with only a few questions. Ellenberger says he was gifted in his ability to establish connection with any person, "including rebellious children, psychotics and criminals."[3] Further,

> He felt a genuine interest for all human beings and compassion for their sufferings, but ... he would immediately detect the part of play-acting and mendacity on the part of his patients.[4]

Adler believed in the equality of women and men, and urged both sexes to find their place of significance. In *Cooperation Between the Sexes*, he wrote

> The exaggerated ideal of masculinity represents a demand, a continuous incentive, a permanent unrest, which results in nothing but demands of vanity, self-enrichment, and privileged position, which contradict the natural conditions of humans living together.[5]

Principles of Individual Psychology

"To be a human being," Adler wrote, "means the possession of a feeling of inferiority that is constantly pressing on towards its own conquest."[6]

The *inferiority-superiority dynamic* is the cornerstone of Adlerian psychology. Ira Progoff says, "Weakness was, to Adler, the starting point for all achievement."[7] Adler was optimistic about human nature, believing the essence of humanity includes a *drive to self-perfection*. He saw individuals as self-determining, with free will; each person is an initiator of actions for which he is responsible. Through striving for success, perfection, security, completion, self-mastery, one moves from feelings of inferiority to superiority. Adler called this the "law of overcoming." One can achieve a superior level of adjustment in overcoming the "inferiority complex" – thus weakness can be the beginning of high achievement.[8]

Adler expounded on the contemporary medical theory of *organ infe-riority*. He proposed that each person is born with inclinations to ill-ness in particular regions of the body, determined by organ weakness believed to originate in fetal development. Thus, the localization of ill-nesses in a patient results not so much from chance as from the interplay of basic organ inferiority and the influences of the environment. Early childhood experiences, such as sibling competition and the position of the child in the sibling row, can influence the manifestation of illness, which tends to occur in the weaker organs.

The principle of *goal-striving* is central to Adler's ideas. He believed that all life forms move in the direction of growth and expansion. Thus, from the beginning, he disputed the psychoanalytic idea of early life trauma; he believed that psychological issues can be resolved with clear decisions and use of the will to execute them. Whereas Freud's psycho-analysis emphasized *cause*, Adler's principle of dynamism emphasized *aim*, the intentionality of the psychic process. His question was not "whence?" but "whither?" Implicit in this approach is each individual's freedom to choose. Adler wrote,

> We do not suffer from the shock of our experiences – the so-called *trauma* – but we make out of them just what suits our purposes. We are *self-determined* by the meaning we give to our experiences ... mean-ings are not determined by situations, but we determine ourselves by the meanings we give to situations.[9]

He assumed that the components of the mind will spontaneously organize and equilibrate according to the life goal – make a clear decision, he said, and the psyche will spontaneously organize. Adler maintained that the child's personality is shaped by psychological com-pensations for physical weakness; the family is the context in which choices must be made and this balancing can occur.[10]

Adler's drive to self-perfection is not the same as Nietzsche's "will to power," though the same phrase is often used to describe them both. Adler did indeed entertain Nietzsche's idea early in his career; but his ideas evolved and by 1908 (more than a decade before Freud wrote *Beyond the Pleasure Principle*), he was writing about an "aggressive instinct" to contradict Freud's insistence on the primacy of the sex-ual instinct. His focus on the aggressive instinct changed again, how-ever, when he postulated the notion of striving for superiority. He also increasingly saw the importance of "social concern" working in associa-tion with the drive to self-perfection. In his later writings, striving for mastery is coupled with sensitivity and responsiveness to the environ-ment.[11] Ellenberger comments:

Adler ... did not consider the striving for personal power as a primary drive, but as the result of a false guiding ideal that could be replaced by that of community feeling.[12]

Adler postulated that *social feeling* is a fundamental trait in human beings, which is developed through family influences in child raising, and through education. The German term rendered as 'social feeling' implies an intimate connection with the community that is intrinsic and important to human beings.

Adler put great emphasis on appropriate child raising in order to bring forth the capabilities of each individual. Pampered children remain self-centred, receiving without giving; they do not readily develop their capacity for social feeling. A neglected child will also be less prone to engage, expecting others to be cold and unavailable. Adler believed that the child should learn enhanced social concern and achieve satisfaction from joining with others. The attitude of the mother is very important in this development, to give the child the most complete experience of human fellowship and then to widen it into a life-attitude towards others. This social attitude develops in the family with appropriate child raising and is furthered in school. Much of its development occurs with peers, under the direction of adults.

Whereas Freud emphasized the relationship with parents as the most important to the child, Adler attributed more significance to the position of the child in the sibling line. He wrote, "... no two children, even those born in the same family, grow up in the same situation."[13] Each child in the sequence has different circumstances and challenges. The eldest child is the trail blazer who initially gets all the attention, whereas the second child is always in a race against the elder. The youngest child is in a favourable position, since he or she can never be dethroned. Adler believed this contributed to different personality characteristics.[14] He was clear, however, that "predictions based on the position of children are expressed in the form of tendencies; there is no necessity about them."[15]

Adler had a holistic outlook, and subscribed to a theory of mind-body unity. He regarded all aspects of the person as working in concert, with the individual as a part of a larger system involving relationships with the self, the earth, and the community. According to his "principle of cosmic influences," each individual is related to the universe. As individuals develop community feeling, they also find a felt sense of participation in the greater order. This is notably similar to ancient Chinese thought, in which the individual participates in interconnected systems of family, society and the cosmos.

Life style, as understood by Adler, is the unity within each individual, involving thinking, feeling, and acting in both the conscious and unconscious. One's goals depend upon the meaning one gives to life. From his work in the children's clinics in Vienna, Adler concluded that

> ... by the time the fifth year of life has been reached, the child has formed character traits and an approach to his environment, a "style of life," that is more or less permanently fixed.[16]

Each individual adopts a unique "law of movement" which is an aspect of the "style of life" formed during childhood, and retained as a distinct personality pattern throughout life. Individuals develop a characteristic way of carrying and presenting themselves, a particular "psychic gait" that can be seen in attitudes and activities, both psychological and somatic. Adler also extended this into the notion of body language, which he called "organ dialect." Progoff summarizes:

> Adler ... claimed that because the body and psyche are encompassed by a larger organismic unity, the man who understands the body's language can understand the depths of the psyche as well.[17]

Adlerian Therapy and Education

Adler opposed Freud's tendency to reduce neurosis to sexual explanations. He did not diminish sexuality as an issue in the development of personality, but he believed that Freud did not grasp the larger perspective and did not consider the person as a whole. Each individual has a unique point of view, from which he or she interprets life events and circumstances; specific factors are given personal meaning in what Adler called the "style of life." To fully evaluate an individual's personality involves assessment of organ inferiorities, early interpersonal relationships, family dynamics, the degrees of natural physical and mental energy, one's free choices, and one's courage.

Adler, like Jung, criticized Freud and psychoanalysis for the focus on investigating past events. Progoff writes:

> To turn back self-consciously to the events of the past encourages the tendency to retreat from life that has already become a pattern for the patient and is the hallmark of his illness.[18]

The allure of investigating the past can be counterproductive if it does not accomplish Adler's primary therapeutic goal, namely, to help the patient deal with the present. Progoff states the Adlerian view:

> Such [past] probings may be exceedingly interesting in the psychic material they produce, and also in the self-knowledge they bring both

to the patient and to the therapist; but they do not meet the primary requirement of healing the person sufficiently to help him meet the pressing problems of his existence.[19]

For Adler neurosis originates in avoidance. The neurotic is unwilling or unable to face the problems of daily life, retreating into unreal fantasy or becoming physically ill. What brings the patient to the doctor's office is the problem of the present moment that is too difficult to face. Writing about Adlerian therapy, Progoff says,

> The job of the therapist is, then, so to strengthen the individual that he will be able to look his present situation squarely in the eye and come to grips with it.[20]

Mental illness to Adler involves "a mistaken life style" or "fictitious life goal" – he identified a 'ruling type', a 'getting type', and an 'avoiding type' – and, commensurate with it, an underdeveloped social interest. These "mistaken life styles" are, through their lack of social concern, forms of vanity: hence the dictum with which we began this chapter, that "all neurosis is vanity." With this alternative emphasis, Adler's framework tends to disregard traditional distinctions of mental illness (such as hysteria, phobias, obsessions, and psychoses). For him, the psychotherapeutic task was to transform the egocentric, neurotic personality by helping the client to restore social feeling. He maintained that human beings have a natural healing process available to them; when people discover their goals and direct their lives meaningfully towards them while participating in community, they can find their original wholeness.

Adlerian therapy takes a much shorter time than traditional psychoanalysis – usually less than a year. It is practical and oriented towards problem solving, aiming to get the patient involved in a personal development process, in harmony with social concern. The first stage is for the therapist to understand the client; Adler was known for the swiftness with which he could grasp a client's situation. The second stage is to help the patient gradually become aware of his or her situation, including the "fictitious life goal and life style." Once this has been clarified, the patient must decide what choices he wishes to make concerning his life goal and life style. The goal of therapy is for the patient to recover the ability to fulfill three main tasks in life: *occupation*, *love*, and *relationships* with family and community.

Adler was very egalitarian in his approach with patients, and more dialogical than Freud. He sat facing his patients on chairs of equal size, thus diminishing the occurrence of transference phenomena that arose in the traditional psychoanalytic setting, where the patient reclined while the therapist sat behind, out of view. Friedman writes, "Adler's approach to therapy was ... closer to 'healing through meeting'."[21]

Adler's emphasis on the equality of practitioner and client opened the way for a style of practice that is still embraced in therapy and family medicine today: the doctor is an expert consultant and helps patients to make informed decisions about themselves, their illnesses and health, and their life styles. He was also one of the first to clarify the relationships between illnesses, life style and social factors. This recognition, in combination with his concept of mind-body unity, helped promote an attitude of personal responsibility in relating to illness process. He recognized that illness can be a way of handling life situations. A question he frequently asked patients was, "Supposing that you would not have this ailment, what would you do?"[22]

The patient's answer indicated what issue was being avoided; for example, if the patient replied that he would look for work if he did not have a sore back, the Adlerian approach would be to help the patient face up to the problem and consequences of seeking work.

Adler's work also influenced the development of community psychiatry and social psychiatry. He helped to extend psychotherapy beyond the individual appointment between client and practitioner, bringing it into the community to interface with other individuals and agencies. He was an early experimenter with group process.

Adler gradually moved from a medical-therapeutic model to an educational approach. He believed the main thrust of therapeutic education should be towards teachers, not families. He wrote,

> A mistaken style of life often escapes unrecognized at home, but it comes out in school ... The school thus becomes a place where we can really educate, and not merely give instruction.[23]

Hence, much of Adlerian psychology has found its way into educational systems. Adler writes,

> Teachers, by the very nature of their social function, are better equipped to correct the mistakes of children ... The school is the prolonged hand of the family, and it is there that the character of the child is formed to a great extent, and that he is taught to face the problems of life.[24]

Adler was optimistic that schools could have a strong influence in the development of healthy and cooperative people:

> In the future, schools will surely be run more along the lines of Individual Psychology, for the true purpose of a school is to build character.[25]

Adler proposed a simplified psychology, believing that more people could then partake of its principles. In this way, wrote Ira Progoff, Adler thought the task could be accomplished of "transforming the egocentric neurotic personality and of restoring 'social feeling' to the emotionally isolated human beings of modern times."[26]

Adler, Power and Strength, and The Haven

Some have disregarded Adlerian concepts as being too elementary; to us, they are practical, relevant, and worthy of consideration. While the principles may be simple, living them is a challenge that requires courage and dedication.

In our estimation, though his terms were different, Adler saw clearly the relationship between power and strength that we ourselves have explored; he advocated a style of life that emphasizes the latter through the development of social concern. As in Adler's "mistaken life styles," we acknowledge that people often become fixated on domination of others in a power attitude. For Adler, social concern was the key to living what we would call a more strength oriented life:

> As long as a person strives for superiority and tempers it with social interest, he is on the useful side of life and can accomplish good. But if he lacks social interest, he is not really prepared for the solution of the problems of life.[27]

Adler acknowledged that feelings of inferiority in young children are often handled by attempts to "directly seek superiority over others" and in this character development, they will exhibit "ambition, arrogance, jealousy and hatred."[28] Adler believed this often was the result of poor child rearing, usually involving either pampering or neglect.

Progoff writes, "In the family, as in our civilization, the greatest emphasis is placed upon the individual who is greater, and better, and more glorious than all the others in his environment."[29] Adler called this the psychology of the pampered child, who is raised to be selfish and self-interested, lacking social feeling and concern for others. For us, these are attitudes of power, rather than strength. In terms of our Dynamic Empathy Model, they betray an arrest at the objectification/isolation phase, where others are seen largely as objects to satisfy one's desires, rather than as genuine human beings with whom one can dialogue. Adler thought that this called for changes in education and parenting in order to develop deeper roots of social concern by encouraging children to have more sensitivity and caring for others.

Adler's response to the First World War (in which he served as a soldier) was that "civilization was about to destroy itself because of its lack of social feeling."[30] He believed that ego centred struggles for power could only be overcome by the deepening of social feelings. We recognize that the urge to dominate, the exercise of power rather than strength, is prevalent in people and underlies many of the social and psychological ills of our day. We agree with Adler that this can, and should, be addressed through an educational process that can assist individuals and humanity in general into deeper feelings of communion and caring. We feel some affinity with Adler in our own professional evolution. Like him, we transitioned from originally being private practitioners, moving into group therapy, and then into developing educational approaches. In our case, we co-founded a school, The Haven Institute. We acknowledge our change in paradigm from a therapeutic model to an educational one, a change that is paralleled in his career.

As we have studied spiritual approaches in both China and the West, we find this idea of social participation to be common between them. We agree with Adler's assertion that people remain limited to the degree they are selfish and uncaring. Families and schools and counselling can facilitate healthy living by encouraging social interest and social concern. Health (psychological and physical) occurs through family and education and groups that encourage communicating and connecting. We can thus open to our deep nature, which is a community spirit. The Communication Model that is taught at The Haven is structured to invite open dialogue and the development of empathy as we outline in our Dynamic Empathy Model. We think these models reflect an interest in 'social feeling' and the human spirit that we share with Adler.

II.9　The Unconscious Speaks in Many Ways

KZ = Confucius (Kong Zi), CJ = Carl Jung, BW = Ben Wong, JM = Jock McKeen

JM: Ben and I have not been much interested in dreams. We have found little use of them, either in ourselves, or with our clients. Occasionally we have used some dream techniques we learned from gestalt therapy. But Dr. Jung, you used dreams a great deal. We have wondered if there is something we have been missing.

CJ: You are different personality types from me. I was always informed by my dreams, from a very young age. But the unconscious reveals its secrets in different ways to different people.

JM: Please elaborate. I'd like to hear something about your ideas on personality types, as that is something we decided to leave out of our chapter on your thinking ... there is so much else to cover!

CJ: Well, I am a thinking intuitive type. I emphasize thoughts rather than feelings, and I am informed from inside (that's the intuitive aspect). Ben, you and I share the intuitive aspect, being informed from within. But you are a more feeling type I think.

BW: Yes, I feel things ... and I don't have the words to speak about them.

JM: Ben seems to be deeply in touch with music in a very universal way.

CJ: Probably the unconscious speaks to you in music.

JM: I share your mental tendency, Dr. Jung. I am a thinking type. But unlike you, I am more in response to the outside world as a sensation type.

CJ: So you are probably prone to mental images that are stimulated by your responses to the outside world. You would be poetic, or an artist.

JM: I relate to this.

KZ: For me, this is a puzzle. I definitely have a mental orientation. So I am probably more the thinking type. That means Ben is the only feeling type amongst us.

CJ: Well, everyone has all four aspects, and they are quite well developed in all of us assembled here. So this is a matter of inclination, of emphasis, not either-or.

KZ: Given this description, I would probably fit into the sensation type too. I am like Jock in that way ... emphasizing thinking and words in relation to what I observe in the world.

CJ: The two planes of thinking-feeling and sensation-intuition are useful as an approximation. But the main issue is that each of us is informed differently. For me, dreams were important (and Dr. Freud too). But for you, dreams lack significance, because you get your messages other ways.

JM: So the unconscious can be revealed in music, in the arts, in religious feeling, in dreams, in fantasy, in dance.

CJ: Yes.

JM: Then I rest easily. We have always found much importance in guided imagery and the use of art, drama, music, poetry, and creative writing.

BW: Jock and I have used body readings a lot in our work. We believe that the personality is revealed in a person's movement, speech patterns and energy states. We found Reich's work with body and energy very interesting.

KZ: In ancient China, we were very attuned to nuances of movements and gestures to read a person's intentions and true feelings. So in that way, I was a body reader too.

BW (with humour): Yes! Once again, you were ahead of your time!

CJ: The collective unconscious speaks in many ways, and over many millennia! Dreams are not necessary.

JM: Well, Dr Jung, the next chapter is about you! I am a little daunted ... you covered so much in your work, and we have only a few pages to discuss some of the topics that have most interested Ben and me. For myself, I have been fascinated with your ideas – I feel quite an affinity with you, and I am especially delighted that we share an interest in Chinese philosophy.

CJ: I am grateful for your interest in my work, and equally I have high regard for what you gentlemen are doing.

II.10 Carl Jung: Search for the Soul

The decisive question for man is: Is he related to something infinite or not? That is the telling question of his life. Only if we know that the thing which truly matters is the infinite can we avoid fixing our interest upon futilities, and upon all kinds of goals which are not of real importance. – C.G. Jung[1]

Psychoanalytic theory as presented by Freud has been useful to us, providing a dynamic model of the psyche that facilitates understanding ourselves and our clients. Yet, there was always for us a bleak limitation in Freud's pessimistic view of people as somewhat machine-like. Certainly, Freud's emphasis on childhood experience and family of origin has been helpful. Furthermore, we agree with Freud's view that humans can be very self-deceptive; his exploration of the personal unconscious has helped people uncover the depth of their psychological lives. Freud also addressed some difficult subjects, including the sources of human aggression. So we have learned a lot from studying Freud, and we have used some of his theory and models in our own thinking. But Freud's philosophy has not been so helpful to us with issues of relationships, meaning and spirituality.

Carl Gustav Jung (1875–1961) was a Swiss psychiatrist who pioneered a new vision for psychiatry and personal development. Jung founded his own type of psychology, which he called Analytical Psychology. Through his emphasis on spirituality and connection, Jung places human beings into a larger context, beyond the mechanics of biological considerations. For Freud, people are physiological mechanisms; to Jung, each individual life is significant, with hidden connections to a larger whole that can be discovered through exploration and uncovering. Instead of the psyche being a machine that might malfunction or need a tune-up, to Jung the psyche is a theatre of cosmic adventure.

Jung had a profound affinity with the philosophies of Asia, though he never abandoned his European Christian heritage. Hence, his explorations have helped us to integrate our own investigations into crosscultural issues of meaning and spirituality, and into Chinese medicine and philosophy in particular.

By the age of 30, Jung held a position at the University of Zurich, was senior physician at the psychiatric clinic, and was publishing in the psychiatric literature. He had begun to correspond with Freud, who took an immediate interest in this bright young psychiatrist. The two men's professional relationship intensified, and Jung soon became one of Freud's favourites; by 1911, he was the editor of the *Psychoanalytic Journal* and president of the Psychoanalytical Association. But Jung had his own ideas, and strongly disagreed with Freud in a number of key areas. Freud was intolerant of disagreement, even from his bright young star, and after a number of attempts at resolution, the two men had a gentlemanly separation that persisted for the rest of their lives. Their close professional association lasted only six intense years.

On the surface, the separation centred on their disagreement over the issue of the primacy of sexuality underlying human experience and the relevance of the so-called Oedipal attachment that Freud proposed. However, their differences were deeper and more far-reaching, based on many factors. Freud was determined to expound a physiological and physical basis for human behaviour, while Jung had a strong motivation to comprehend the religious and spiritual issues that Freud disregarded as superstitions. Anthony Storr summarizes:

> The men were products of very different backgrounds. Freud, an urban Jew, doted on as a child by a young and beautiful mother, was educated in a progressive tradition that led him naturally into science; while Jung, a rural Protestant, insecurely bonded to a depressed, sometimes absent, mother, was steeped in theology and Romantic idealism. Consequently, it is not surprising that Freud should be a sceptical empiricist and that he should believe in the universal significance of the Oedipus complex, while Jung retained a commitment to the life of the spirit and held that the Oedipus complex had no universal validity.[2]

For Jung the primary energy of human beings is not libidinal, as Freud thought, but psychic. He believed that a primary human desire is to experience a spiritual rebirth, a transformation in consciousness. Modern people, he thought, had "lost their soul" and needed to make a journey in life to rediscover their deep nature. Psychological healing comes through the process of bringing the unconscious into consciousness (he called this "progression"), and adjusting to the external world. He named the opposite process "regression," when unresolved conflicts are repressed from the conscious into unconsciousness.

Jung's Journey into the Unconscious
By 1913, Jung had broken his ties with the university, Freud and the Psychoanalytical Association. He withdrew from public life and devoted much of the next four years to a personal journey into the unconscious. This

was a period of intense self-investigation, during which he wrote down his dreams and his fantasies. He experienced himself entering a deep subterranean world, full of other beings that communicated with him. Ellenberger describes this period as a "creative illness" and likens it to processes that occurred in Freud, Nietzsche, and others. He notes that a shaman in primitive cultures commonly underwent psychological challenges in order to be reborn with a new vision; creative writers and philosophers also have undergone this transformational process, a kind of trial by fire.

As Jung explored this psychological territory he was often out of touch with ordinary reality. He anchored his life in the routine of family life and his patients. Then, for a portion of each day, he withdrew into solitude, and using various techniques, including automatic writing and mandala drawing, he attempted to get deeper into his own psyche. The recently published *Red Book* contains his private journals from this period. To his amazement and shock, he began to encounter other beings in his psyche, and developed a conversational rapport with them. He privately feared that he was becoming psychotic; nevertheless, as a staunch scientist, he continued to address and document the information he was encountering. During these sessions, he met a bearded old man called Philemon and a beautiful young woman named Salome. He later came to see these as the embodiment of two archetypes, the eternal feminine and the wise old man. His conversations with these figures supported his growing view that things happen in the psyche that are not produced by conscious intention; rather, they have a life of their own.

From this investigation came his theory of the archetypes. He later likened his experience to Ulysses' *nekyia*, or journey to the underworld, as described in Homer's *Odyssey*. Commonly, such an experience is accompanied by a profound transformation of personality and a conviction that one has discovered a great truth.[3] Ellenberger describes Jung following this period:

> Those who have known Jung remember the tone of absolute conviction with which he spoke of the anima, the self, the archetypes, and the collective unconscious. For him they were psychological realities that existed as certainly as did the material world around him.[4]

Jung emerged from his creative illness with a growing vision of humanity's place in the cosmos. His concept placed the individual at the centre of a growth process, in relationship with nature and the rest of the universe. He would devote the rest of his life to refining and expanding what he had discovered in this exploratory period.

He rejected the conventional approach to psychiatry, which diagnoses unusual mental events as necessarily pathological. He recognized that hallucinations could be the sign of an unbalanced psyche, but he also believed that the unbalances could be set right:

> My aim was to show that delusions and hallucinations were not just specific symptoms of mental disease but also had a human meaning.[5]

In an article published in December 1916, Jung outlined different possibilities for coping with the unconscious.[6] He noted that one can repress it or exhaust it through analysis, or one can be overwhelmed by it, as happens with schizophrenia. For Jung, the preferred solution is the "hero's journey" to encounter the contents of the unconscious in order to subdue them; this is dangerous but potentially very rewarding. In myths of many cultures, the hero fights a monster, and the reward is a treasure or a magic talisman. Jung's reward was a new psychology of human development that centred on personal development, a project he called individuation.

Jung's Model of the Psyche

Anthony Stevens offers an excellent diagrammatic representation of Jung's model of the psyche, intending it to be visualized three dimensionally as a sphere made up of three layers. We are modifying his original diagram somewhat, for the purposes of clarification. We like his conception of the three-dimensional sphere, and agree with much of his topography. The conscious mind is represented by a thin layer at the outer region; this is the domain of ego, the conscious notion of one's individuality. Beneath this layer is the personal unconscious, and deeper than this is the area of the collective unconscious, with Self at its centre and permeating the entire system. Within the personal unconscious are *complexes,* which are informed by life experiences, and by the *archetypes* which are within the collective unconscious.[7]

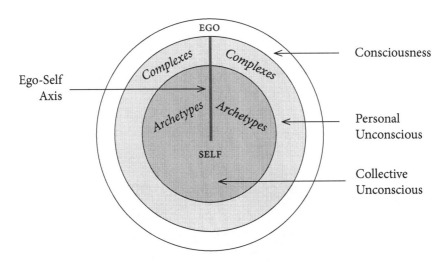

Personal and Collective Unconscious

Freud believed that the unconscious is entirely personal, derived completely from an individual's life experience and family dynamics. It is thus created *from without*, in interaction with the outside world, what Freud called *reality*. Jung did not disagree with the idea of a personal unconscious containing repressed material the individual had not addressed, but he thought this was only a small part of the picture.

Jung's modeling of the psyche therefore includes *two* domains of unconsciousness. The *personal unconscious* is similar to the Freudian notion, containing the repressed material from an individual's experience. The second domain is the *collective unconscious*, which includes psychological memories and patterns for all of humanity. The collective unconscious is the realm of the archetypes and the operations of biological instincts.

In this view, each individual has connection (and potential access) to the entire history of humankind. This is a particular aspect of being human, to be an individual point of consciousness, also connected to the universal. Jung summarizes:

> The collective unconscious contains the whole spiritual heritage of mankind's evolution, born anew in the brain structure of every individual. His conscious mind is an ephemeral phenomenon that accomplishes all provisional adaptations and orientations ... the unconscious, on the other hand, is the source of the instinctual forces of the psyche and of the forms or categories that regulate them, namely the archetypes.[8]

Much of the unconscious, Jung suggested, is not derived from personal experiences. Instead, each individual psyche is strongly informed and influenced *from within* by the archetypes, primordial formations that have been within humans throughout history. Each individual participates in the collective unconsciousness of humankind. Individuals are unique, and at the same time, they are a part of the whole. In Jung's own words:

> Looked at from without, the psyche appears to us to be essentially a reflection of external happenings – to be not only occasioned by them, but to have its origin in them. And it also seems to us that the unconscious can be understood only from without and from the side of consciousness. It is well known that Freud has attempted an explanation from this side – an undertaking which could only succeed if the unconscious were actually something which came into being with the existence and consciousness of the individual.[9]

... But the truth is that the unconscious is always there beforehand as a potential system of psychic functioning handed down by generations of man. Consciousness is a late-born descendant of the unconscious psyche.[10]

Individual consciousness is in this way permeated by the collective unconscious and the history of mankind. We suggest the image of a rum ball, a sweet candy soaked in liquor which penetrates into every part of the candy. Whether you taste a small fragment or take a big bite, the taste of the rum is manifestly present on your tongue. Jung writes,

> Just as the human body shows a common anatomy over and above all racial differences, so, too, the human psyche possesses a common substratum transcending all differences in culture and consciousness. I have called this substratum the collective unconscious.[11]

Jung used the image of the rhizome to further elaborate his theory of the individual in the context of the universal. Rhizomes are plants that have a horizontal underground stem. What seem to be many separate plants above the surface are actually all shoots from one plant system, connected underground. Bamboo and irises are examples. Jung said human consciousness is like a rhizome – we seem to be separate beings in our social life, but we are actually all joined in the collective unconscious:

> Life has always seemed to me like a plant that lives on its rhizome. Its true life is invisible, hidden in the rhizome. The part that appears above the ground lasts only a single summer. Then it withers away – an ephemeral apparition. When we think of the unending growth and decay of life and civilizations, we cannot escape the impression of absolute nullity. Yet I have never lost the sense of something that lives and endures beneath the eternal flux. What we see is the blossom, which passes. The rhizome remains.[12]

Jung believed that we live in two domains, a time-space world of human interaction, and a realm that transcends time and space. We are eternal beings in a mortal context:

> The psyche is not of today; its ancestry goes back many millions of years. Individual consciousness is only the flower and the fruit of a season, sprung from the perennial rhizome beneath the earth; and it would find itself in better accord with the truth if it took the existence of the rhizome into its calculations. For the root matter is the mother of all things.[13]

Complexes

In his early psychiatric career, Jung worked with a word association test as a diagnostic instrument; he believed that a person's responses to the words provided were not random but indicated the presence of subconscious "complexes," organizations of thoughts and feelings around core themes. Jung came to believe that complexes contain contents of the unconscious that have been split off from awareness and proposed that cure comes by assimilating these split off complexes to make a whole. Jung's relationship with Freud began when he sent him his *Studies in Word Association*, realising that this work offered support for Freud's theory of repression. Complexes, however, were later to take on new significance for Jung as the personification of archetypes, the means through which archetypes manifest themselves in the individual psyche. Thus, for example, an individual's "mother complex" is likely that person's amalgam of personal experience with the actual mother and the universal mother archetype. The complexes are within the personal unconscious section of Jung's topography, and are generated from life experiences and from archetypal symbols from the collective unconscious.

Archetypes

The archetypes of the collective unconscious are, for Jung, a priori forms that underlie the structuring of reality. The word archetype means "ancient pattern" and Jung's archetypes are constellated supra-human patterns that manifest in human lives. As we have seen, an individual can develop a personal "mother complex" which is a manifestation, an actualization, of the universal, archetypal mother in association with experiences with the actual mother. It is vital that this happen (and that a mother actualize in herself the archetype of the child) so that the two can form the bond that is necessary for the life cycle to continue.

For Jung, archetypes are dynamic and purposeful, seeking their actualization in the personality of an individual. They are, he says "born anew with every generation [and] have an enormous influence on individual as well as collective life."[14] From a holistic viewpoint, the *Self* is the central unity and primary archetype; all other archetypes are reflections, or isomorphs, of it.

> The conscious mind does not embrace the totality of a man, for this totality consists only partly of his conscious contents ... In this totality the conscious mind is contained like a smaller circle within a larger one.[15]

Normally unconscious, the Self manifests in projected forms in the outer world, or through the emergence of archetypal figures in dreams and fantasy and works of art.

Animus and Anima, Archetypes of the Soul

For Jung, gender identity and relations between the sexes rest on an archetypal foundation characterized by the so-called archetypes of the soul, *animus* and *anima*. They are archetypes of the opposite sex that seek expression, and are most often repressed, in the individual's personality. For men, there is an internal anima, a feminine pattern that is the largely repressed femininity of that man; to the degree that this femininity is unacknowledged it is projected out onto women in the environment, and this forms the basis of sexual attraction. A man is attracted to a woman who posseses qualities of his own denied feminine nature. For women, there is an internal animus, a masculine pattern which when repressed is is projected out onto men. Thus, when people fall in love, they often are responding to the projected images from their animus or anima. When men and women get into conflict, it is often because they are not relating to each other as persons but objects; they are dealing with their projected animus or anima, using defences such as blame and guilt.

As people become more aware, they gradually incorporate their awareness of their own inner masculine and feminine aspects, and are less prone to project these qualities onto others. Jung was intrigued with the medieval notion of the androgyne, a mythological figure that possesses both male and female characteristics (for example, having both a penis and breasts). He utilized the concept of androgyny to explain his idea of integrating split-off elements in the psyche. For most men, their internal feminine is out of reach; the majority of women seek masculine characteristics in their partners, rather than embrace them within themselves. Through personal development, the masculine and feminine aspects of one's nature can be made conscious and integrated into the personality.

When this happens, the individual is no longer a slave to the image projections that occur from the repressed animus or anima; one does not have to blindly follow another who exhibits the characteristics that one denies in oneself. This mature state of individuation brings personal freedom from illusions, and more substantial human relationships become possible, based on self-awareness and self-responsibility. Often difficult, sometimes painful, the task of becoming self-responsible has been a central theme in our work with people.

Ego, Persona, Shadow

The theme of integrating conscious and unconscious aspects of oneself, as seen in the concept of animus and anima, is foundational to Jung. In the diagram on page 127, such integration occurs along the ego-Self axis in a process Jung called individuation.

The *ego* is the centre of the conscious mind. It is what one refers to in saying "I" or "me." Through the ego, individuals maintain their sense of consistent identity throughout life. The ego is the executive agent of the Self, the universal consciousness.

The *persona* is the "mask" of the conscious personality; in Asian culture, this is the "face." It gets its name from the masks used in ancient Greek theatre, where the actors could depict a specific character and hide their own personality by donning the mask. Much of our personality, says Jung, is hidden by the social mask of the persona. Jung noted that the persona is actually a "mask of the collective psyche, a mask that feigns individuality, making others and oneself believe that one is an individual, whereas one is simply acting a role through which the collective psyche speaks."[16] The persona is thus a pseudo-individual.

Much of the real individual remains hidden in the layers of the unconscious, unless it is brought into awareness. This is the *shadow*, containing the repressed elements in the personality. Note that the shadow is not inherently negative. A person whose persona is kind will have cruelty in the shadow; someone whose persona is mean will have generosity in the shadow. To *individuate*, one must address one's shadow and bring the unconscious elements into consciousness in order to integrate them into a whole personality.

In the first half of life, people need to develop strong egos in order to deal with the tasks before them, such as separating from parents, establishing a career, and raising a family. In the second half of life, the ego gradually can recognize its subordinate status to the Self, and proceed on the project of *individuation* by strengthening connection along the ego-Self axis.

Individuation

Jung saw individuation as the developmental process in which people become themselves. He maintained that the individuation process occurs naturally, and is usually unconscious. As a calf becomes a cow, a human being will become himself or herself. In Jung's words,

> Individuation is an expression of that biological process – simple or complicated as the case may be – by which every living thing becomes what it was destined to become from the beginning.[17]

His therapy was to help clients engage in a process of learning, to actively take part in the organic unfolding by becoming more aware. As awareness grows, the authentic nature is revealed and integrated. This perspective is one that is central to our philosophy and work.

Individuation is a process, not an end point. As the unconscious and conscious are increasingly united, the individual personality stands forth as an integrated being. Such people become more aware and responsible for all their actions and thoughts and intentions. An individuated person stands forth in strength and is revealed.

> Individuation, therefore, can only mean a process of psychological development that fulfils the individual qualities given; in other words, it is a process by which a man becomes the definite, unique being he in fact is. In so doing he does not become "selfish" in the ordinary sense of the word, but is merely fulfilling the peculiarity of his nature, and this, as we have said, is vastly different from egotism or individualism.[18]

As one individuates, identification is less with the trappings of the external world, and more with the timeless melody of the universe. Jung suggests that an individuated being is self-responsible, not swayed by illusions or instincts:

> The aim of individuation is nothing less than to divest the self of the false wrappings of the persona on the one hand, and of the suggestive power of primordial images on the other.[19]

The individuating person thus acquires a balanced view of life. We are aligned with this attitude; we believe that an individual life is meaningful in relationship to others and to the universal context in which we live. Jung describes a sense of participation in a wider world:

> The more we become conscious of ourselves through self-knowledge, and act accordingly, the more the layer of the personal unconscious that is superimposed on the collective unconscious will be diminished. In this way there arises a consciousness which is no longer imprisoned in the petty, oversensitive, personal world of the ego, but participates freely in the wider world of objective interests ... bringing the individual into absolute, binding, and indissoluble communion with the world at large.[20]

One cannot simply sink into identification with the wholeness, for that, says Jung, would be a "melting away of the individual in the collective."[21] The task is to become a full and whole human being, unique and distinct, yet participating with others in the symphony of life.

Dreams and Symbols

For Jung, dreams are expressions of the unconscious psyche. Both Freud and Jung believed that dreams give messages that can show us what we are ignoring in daily life. But for Jung dreams are much more than the expression of repressed content:

The view that dreams are merely the imaginary fulfilments of repressed wishes [cf. Freud] is hopelessly out of date. There are, it is true, dreams which manifestly represent wishes or fears, but what about all the other things? Dreams may contain ineluctable truths, philosophical pronouncements, illusions, wild fantasies, memories, plans, anticipations, irrational experiences, even telepathic visions, and heaven knows what besides.[22]

This difference between Jung and Freud in the understanding of dreams reflects a distinction between *symbols*, on the one hand, and *signs*, on the other. *Symbols* for Jung are spontaneous products of the archetypal psyche. They are living organic entities, representing the unknown and what is possible. They express the hidden, invisible patterns that direct manifestations in the world of phenomena; they appear in dreams, fantasies, creative art and myths. Symbols involve the "meaning" of our life and experience, and are the structuring principle of the human soul.

Signs, in contrast, are tokens of meaning standing for a known entity; thus language is a system of signs, not symbols. A sign is an agreed-upon commonality, and is not living. Symbols to Jung are alive. Whereas a symbol conveys living, subjective meaning, a sign communicates abstract objective meaning. For Jung, Freud's dream analysis dealt mostly with signs, not symbols.

While we ourselves have had little involvement with dream analysis, we have incorporated Jungian ideas into our programs through the use of music, poetry, art and guided imagery to invoke the impulses of individual imagination, meaning seeking, and inspiration. Visualizations we offer, for example, may include references to archetypal symbols such as the wise old man, identified by Jung as archetypes of the spirit. Jung, especially later in his life, demonstrated an openness to other forms of expression from the archaic psyche such as those we have explored.

Jungian Psychotherapy

The purpose of Jungian psychotherapy is to bring the unconscious into consciousness and assist in the process of individuation. Neurosis has a purpose, which is to compensate for or adapt to a conflict between two unresolved tendencies, one which is expressed consciously, and the other which is a complex split off from consciousness. Sharing brings this out into the open, where these opposing tendencies can be integrated, thus resolving the conflict and obviating the need for neurosis. He believed there is often a secret that underlies neurosis; revealing the secret will cure.

Jung utilized two types of therapy, *reductive analysis* and a *synthetic hermeneutic approach.* The former was for younger patients and commonplace problems; for this, he used analytical methods like Freud and Adler. The synthetic-hermeneutic approach was a uniquely Jungian analysis reserved for more mature patients, who collaborated with dream reporting, journal writing and self-analysis. Jung's holistic view is evident throughout this process:

> In therapy the problem is always the whole person, never the symptom alone. We must ask questions which challenge the whole personality.[23]

Jung moved beyond therapy into a learning and educational model. We had a similar odyssey. We did not like to diagnose people or merely treat symptoms. We believe that so-called neurosis is generally a form of adaptation; when the meaning of the symptoms becomes clear, the person can engage in the more central work, that of becoming responsible and individuated. As Jung writes,

> The psychic processes of neurotics differ hardly at all from those of so-called normal persons – for what man today is quite sure that he is not neurotic?[24]

Rather than assuming a postured therapeutic distance, Jung engaged with his clients as equals, as fellow travelers. Our own work with clients is in the same vein. Anthony Stevens credits Jung as an early pioneer in this process of engaging:

> Jung offered the radical proposal that analysis is a dialectical procedure, a two-way exchange between two people, who are equally involved. Although this was a revolutionary idea when he first suggested it, it is a model which has influenced psychotherapists of most schools, though many seem not to realize that it originated with Jung.[25]

For Jung, this was a deeply spiritual engagement. The communication is between the personalities of the practitioner and the client, but the issue for both is to connect with their deeper nature. Jung believed in the availability of ancient wisdom:

> Together the patient and I address ourselves to the two million-year-old man that is in all of us. In the last analysis, most of our difficulties come from losing contact with our instincts, with the age-old unforgotten wisdom stored up in us.[26]

Individuating persons come more and more into harmony with the deeper structures of the universe, and manifest the archetypal nature of their own being, which is isomorphic with the deep pattern of the universe itself. The events of one's life, rather than mere whimsical accidents, are manifestations of synchronous occurrences that are part of the universal theme. We are mortal beings in a context of infinity and eternity. Individuation reveals the self, the deep nature of the individual being which is a time-space representation of timelessness and eternity of the Self.

We see this process occur in engaged relationships where each person participates in the individuation process. So although we are not "Jungians," we definitely agree with this central tenet of Jung's work.

Causality, Teleology and Synchronicity

Ira Progoff describes an important aspect of Jung's thinking:

> The soul ... contains a purpose in its nature, and its life consists in the working out of this purpose. The soul is therefore teleological in its operation, while the body follows causality.[27]

To understand this requires considering the notions of causality and teleology. Jung agreed with the scientific notion of *causality* as it applies to the physical world. By this idea, specific events are effects of particular causes. When you turn on your shower in the morning, the turning of the tap is the cause and the water flow is the effect. As the water strikes your head, your hair becomes wet. The water flow is the cause and the wetness is the resulting effect. So, the same phenomenon (the rushing water) can be both cause and effect, depending upon what you are considering. Western science has been grounded in the notion of causality, and the research to find the background causes for things has been the underpinning of scientific advances.

The philosophical idea of *teleology*, on the other hand, explains phenomena by the purposes they serve, rather than hypothetical causes. The word derives from the Greek *telos* meaning "end." Jung proposed that a human life has a purpose that is revealed through life experience. Individuals can resist their destiny, but the situations of our lives are preconfigured, much in the same way as the structure of an oak tree is preconfigured in the acorn. The teleological operation is the unfolding of the acorn into the oak (and the folding back up again of the oak in the seeding of a new acorn).

For Jung, as Progoff explained, the physical body operates in a causal way, while the soul operates teleologically.

Jung also developed the concept of *synchronicity* to explain the deeper operations of the psyche, beyond the day-to-day effects of causality. Synchronicity (Greek *syn* = together and *chronos* = time) means "meaningful coincidence in time." Synchronicity does not compete with the notion of causality; rather, it maintains that events can be grouped by meaning rather than by cause. An oversimplified version of this view is "there are no accidents." Events that occur together have a shared meaning even if the causes cannot be determined. Jung later cautioned that the notion of synchronicity was too limited, since it addressed only intersections in time; he said the archetypes also expressed themselves in meaningful coincidences in space.

Jung and Albert Einstein met periodically for lunch conversations and shared many ideas; according to Ira Progoff, Einstein's theory of relativity was Jung's "base and starting point for his own thinking about synchronicity."[28] Jung perhaps saw in relativity theory a solution to his puzzling about the relationship between substance and invisibility. Ira Progoff studied with Jung later in the last decade of Jung's life; he discusses Jung's ideas about synchronicity, including the Einstein connection, in his book *Jung, Synchronicity, and Human Destiny*. Progoff describes the invisible structuring of the archetypes which manifest in the life of the individual:

> The specific archetypes that are active at the depth of an individual's experience are the means by which the general orderedness of the larger patterns of the macrocosm can come to specific expression at any moment of time.[29]

On the human level, events occur which are meaningful, since they are the manifestations of the hidden operations of the archetypes. Progoff writes,

> The archetypes are the vehicles by which the encompassing patterns of life are individualized in experience, and Synchronicity is the explanatory principle by which chance and meaning of the intersection of these experiences in time may be recognized and comprehended.[30]

Jung, Synchronicity and the Ancient Chinese

In 1928, Richard Wilhelm sent Jung the manuscript of his translation of an ancient Chinese text. Jung was deeply stirred when he read this material. He wrote, "*The Secret of the Golden Flower* is not only a Taoist text concerned with Chinese yoga, but is also an alchemical treatise."[31] When he studied these ideas from antiquity, he no longer felt so alone. He realized that ancient Daoist practitioners had reported similar experiences to those he encountered in his journey to the underworld. He later wrote an extensive commentary for the English translation of the *Golden Flower*, relating the text to his own studies of gnosticism and alchemy. Jung said that Westerners should not copy Eastern practices, but rather find their own way compatible with their own heritage. Nevertheless, he noted the lessons that could come from more familiarity with Eastern approaches for all avid seekers. He wrote, "By understanding the unconscious, we free ourselves from its domination."[32]

Jung studied and used the ancient Chinese classic the *Book of Changes* (*Yi Jing*), which is based on the fundamental notion of two worlds, one bound by time and space, and the other one nontemporal and nonspatial. He found an affinity with this book and its principles; he wrote an extensive introduction to Princeton University's English translation, in which he proposes that the oracle text shows the operations of synchronicity. We have studied the *Book of Changes* for over 40 years, and find much wisdom in this classic that has relevance to our work in the current era.

Religion and God

In contrast to Freud, who viewed religion as an illusion that provides security for neurotic people, Jung believed that humankind is essentially religious, with an inborn urge to connect and celebrate life. He suggests that humans long for wholeness:

> The religious need longs for wholeness, and therefore lays hold of the images of wholeness offered by the unconscious, which independently of the conscious mind, rise up from the depths of our psychic nature.[33]

Jung said that the psyche spontaneously produces images with religious content; indeed, he said the psyche is "by nature religious."[34] Jung's ascribed a "numinous" quality to the archetypes. In simple terms, one could say the archetypes are the expression of God or universal spiritual intelligence.

As we have noted, Jung saw each person as having two personality dimensions – a superficial personality structure that lives in the daily world, and a timeless entity that is connected to the universe beyond time and space. In one of his last interviews, he is reported to have said that God is at the same time the voice of the conscience speaking within us, and also the hidden force behind inexplicable fateful events.[35] About the existence of God, he said, "I do not take His existence on belief – I *know* that He exists."[36] Jung carved a Latin inscription above the door of his home that translates as "Called or not called, God is present."[37] Jung used this same inscription on the labels that identified his personal books, and it appears on his gravestone.

Individuation and the Purpose of Human Existence

Jung felt a deep responsibility to become fully human and to fulfil his destiny as a purveyor of psychological secrets to humankind. This process of individuation was for him the purpose of human existence; his psychotherapy was aimed to help others engage in the process of individuation too. Near the end of his life, Jung collaborated with Aniela Jaffe to share his thoughts and perspectives in *Memories, Dreams and Reflections*. Jaffe interviewed Jung at length. Jung writes:

> But man's task is ... to become conscious of the contents that press upward from the unconscious ... As far as we can discern, the sole purpose of human existence is to kindle a light in the darkness of mere being. It may even be assumed that just as the unconscious affects us, so the increase in our consciousness affects the unconscious.[38]

Jung saw individual development as a kind of cosmic adventure, an untold story to be discovered by courageous individuals:

> We do not know how far the process of coming to consciousness can extend, or where it will lead. It is a new element in the story of creation, and there are no parallels we can look to. We therefore cannot know what potentialities are inherent in it. Neither can we know the prospects for the species Homo sapiens.[39]

This individuation involves a radical responsibility: to come to know oneself deeply and to differentiate oneself from others.

> It is really the individual's task to differentiate himself from all the others and stand on his own two feet. All collective identities, such as membership in organizations, support of "isms," and so on, interfere with the fulfillment of this task.[40]

In his advanced years, he identified with the archetype of the old man who has seen enough and rests assured:

> This is old age, and a limitation. Yet there is so much that fills me: plants, animals, clouds, day and night, and the eternal in man. The more uncertain I have felt about myself, the more there has grown up in me a feeling of kinship with all things.[41]

Looking back over his life, he identifies what has really mattered:

> In the end, the only events of my life worth telling are those when the imperishable world erupted into this transitory one... All other memories of travels, people and my surroundings have paled beside these interior happenings ... But my encounters with the 'other' reality, my bouts with the unconscious, are indelibly engraved on my memory. In that realm there has always been wealth in abundance, and everything else has lost importance by comparison.[42]

Jung was satisfied that his endeavour was not to further science, but to cast a new vision for human beings:

As a young man my goal had been to accomplish something in my science. But then, I hit upon this stream of lava, and the heat of its fires reshaped my life. That was the primal stuff which compelled me to work upon it, and my works are a more or less successful endeavor to incorporate this incandescent matter into the contemporary picture of the world.[43]

The doorway to the universe, he wrote in *The Red Book*, is not through the mind and scholarship, but through the human heart. He asserts

The knowledge of the heart is in no book and is not to be found in the mouth of any teacher, but grows out of you like the green seed from the dark earth.[44]

In the introduction to *Memories, Dreams and Reflections*, Jaffe quoted Coleridge to summarize Jung's contribution to psychology and to humankind:

He looked at his own Soul with a Telescope. What seemed all irregular, he saw and shewed to be beautiful Constellations; and he added to the Consciousness hidden worlds within worlds.[45]

II.11

Accepting the Unknown: Ben's Perspective

All neurosis is, at root, an issue of loss of faith.[1]

I wrote the words above years ago, along with much of the material in this short chapter. Now, in my ninth decade, I still abide by these views. As I look back on my life, I recognize common themes that apply to me and most of the people I have encountered. These are contained in the following metaphors, which sum up the way I see things.[2]

The Landscape of Our Lives
I have found that people tend to be goal-directed. They frequently wish to fix problems in their lives, to let go of unfortunate situations, to forget unhappy relationships, to finally deal with their feelings about the past, to be able to face the future changed and unimpeded. After spending much time and money with counsellors and other people helpers, they are often astonished to discover their demons are still with them. I now have arrived at the belief that nothing will ever be finished, that we will never be rid of the past, and that ultimately, the essentials about ourselves will never change!

I have shifted from a belief that human experience is linear – from past to present to future – to seeing that each of our lives is an immutable landscape of experience. We all have our mountains of exhilaration, surrounded by our cliffs of danger and hardships. Each of us has places of contentment and placidity, like soothing lakes and gentle forests; similarly, each has deep, exciting and sometimes threatening waters as well as scary, unknown jungles. In everyone are parched deserts and lush, productive wetlands. Our landscapes are endless in their variety of appearances and the multitude of experiences they offer.

Although our choices are numerous, most people tend to limit themselves to living in only a few parts of the total possibilities. Some are mountain folk, while others tend to live in their valleys. Yet, no matter where in their landscape they may find themselves, if they look carefully in all directions, they can see that the entire landscape is always there. At any given time, one part of the landscape is *foreground*, while the remainder is in the *background*. Nothing has been exterminated or altered. All that has changed is the location of the present experience.

So a person who is feeling happiness should be aware that somewhere in the background still lurks an area of sadness. While experiencing joy in the foreground, despair has only been relegated to the background at that time. Some people become fixated in one location; even when they are in safe and happy circumstances in their present lives, they are unable to shift the dangerous, harmful childhood memories from their foreground into the background. Thus, they remain anxious and depressed, even when the current context could provide ideal circumstances for security and pleasure. By remaining stuck in one area of the landscape, they have diminished the scope of experience: it is like looking through a small window that has no view of the larger picture. Such narrowing and fixation is what accounts for neurosis.

To ensure good mental health, people should be encouraged to visit all parts of their landscape, to become familiar with the differing terrains and climates, thus remaining aware of the wide range of possibilities. Those who are able to remain flexible, to shift readily, can stay attuned to present circumstances. That is a sign of good mental health. Those who remain rigidly in one place (as occurs in a fixed moral position) limit their viewpoints and possibilities; their lives have less energy and fulfilment. The task for rigidly limited people is to develop their ability to live in other parts of their landscape; by so doing, they increase the size of the container of their experience.

Now consider another set of dynamics. What about people who are unable to settle in a particular portion of the landscape for any length of time? For those who are given to sudden shifts and wide ranges of movement, foreground and background do not remain stable. These people can become severely dislocated, and have difficulty maintaining a stable sense of identification. Others would describe them as being "all over the map." The ability to sustain a chosen foreground is another sign of good mental health.

Now that I have this picture of mental health, I no longer waste energy trying to fix anything or anyone. I now focus on helping myself and other people to move more easily through our personal landscapes.

Climbing the Mountain

Life is a struggle. You're climbing a mountain, and the ascent is very, very difficult. The slope is steep and the terrain is treacherous. Often the ground is slippery, and hand holds are hard to find. Yet you keep struggling on, trying to climb higher. Your hands are bleeding, you sweat and struggle, all the time trying to ascend. You have been told that at the top of the mountain is the view of what will make it all worthwhile. You will see the promised land, the land of milk and honey, where there are treasures and pleasures and perfect weather, and everything you could ever desire. It will all be yours, once you have made the climb and endured the trials. So you struggle on, with your goal in mind. Occasionally you think, "This is all too hard." But you press on.

As you near the summit, you hear voices coming from the other side of the mountain. Their message brings a chill of disappointment.

"There's nothing over here!" "We've been tricked!"

Despondent, you stop climbing, and for the first time in your life, you look backwards from where you have come. The view is dizzying. In discouragement, you begin to slip back. Suddenly, your footing slips and you find yourself sliding downward rapidly. A sudden grab, and you arrest your downward momentum. Heart pounding, you look around and realize you are on a narrow ledge. As you hesitantly peek over, you see a sheer drop into nothingness. You are facing the Pit of Despair.

The Pit of Despair

When I am working with people, they commonly report to me their loathing and fear of moving into a part of the personal landscape that they sometimes refer to as "the pit." This is called by other names too, such as a "well of despair," the "void," "blackness," "chaos," "emptiness" and "meaninglessness." Apparently, we all have a pit, although most would prefer to deny it; as we travel through our landscapes, most of us give our pits a wide berth.

No matter how much we attempt to avoid the pit, it seems that we always tend to slide towards it and into it. Many of us have found that if we move fast enough, rapidly running around the brink through busyness, obsessions and compulsions, we can generate a centrifugal force to avoid the inevitable slippage. Of course, by becoming so occupied, we fail to explore all the many other aspects of our landscapes, and our worlds become narrow and rigid. Furthermore, deep and meaningful relationships are impossible to establish and maintain.

Such a picture of life is very unappealing. In the past, all of this movement was justified by a belief in a god (capital "G" God in Western cultures). We were admonished to run quickly, work hard and suffer long, because the more we did so, the greater the reward we would enjoy sometime later. In Judaism and Christianity, the pit was dealt with by positing a God who lived in Heaven on the other side of the cliffs of Life. Instead of sliding into the pit, we were encouraged to scale the mountainside, painful and difficult as that might be, because on the other side, after death, we were promised an eternal resting place with God in

Heaven. There, after suffering life's trials and tribulations, so long as we remained faithful to God's commandments, we would be rewarded with pleasures for eternity. The promise of such future rewards made suffering acceptable.

Picture us hanging on with desperate fingernails, always looking upward to the top of the mountain, on the other side of which we could spend eternity in Heaven with our God. We began to hear voices from over the mountain top calling out to us, "Hey, there's nothing over here! No Heaven, no God!" Hearing those "No God " theories was not good news to all who were suffering. Suddenly, struggling painfully to climb to the top made no sense at all.

So many stopped climbing. As they did, they began to slip downward; looking below, they got glimpses of the pit into which they were being drawn. At this time, some gave up and sank into meaninglessness and oblivion; others decided to live it up and party all the time on their way down. The more fortunate decided to expand their horizons, becoming more aware of the backgrounds of their landscape. They decided to explore their inner territories, to experience the lengths and breadths of their dominions. The more flexible they were and the more curiosity they possessed, the more interesting and broadening were their journeys. They discovered whole new worlds emerging into the foreground of their consciousness. Their pits receded into the background, even though they did not disappear.

The promise of future rewards is no longer necessary. A happy, fulfilled life is available if I learn to accept.

In the present, life is full!

II.12 Existentialism: Finding Meaning in a Modern World

There was a man walking across an open field, when suddenly a tiger appeared and began to give chase. The man began to run, but the tiger was closing in. As he approached a cliff at the edge of the field, the man grabbed a vine and jumped over the cliff. Holding on as tight as he could, he looked up and saw the angry tiger prowling out of range ten feet above him. He looked down. In the gully below, there were two tigers also angry and prowling. He had to wait it out. He looked up again and saw that two mice, one white, the other black, had come out of the bushes and had begun gnawing on the vine, his lifeline. As they chewed the vine thinner and thinner, he knew that it could break at any time. Then, he saw a single strawberry growing just an arm's length away. Holding the vine with one hand, he reached out, picked the strawberry, and put it in his mouth. It was delicious. – Zen story [1]

Introduction
This old tale of the tigers and the strawberry highlights some of the main concerns of existentialism. A human being is at the centre of the action, and is assailed by nature and the threat of death. He takes action to avoid the inevitable, succeeding at least in prolonging his own life. As he does so, his world view becomes very restricted, and the perilous condition of his existence, as he hangs with straining muscles over the abyss, can be felt by the reader. Annihilation is above and below him. Yet, in this impossible situation, he is free, free to move past his fear into an appreciation of the moment, to use his consciousness to look beyond his immediate concerns and relate to the world of his immediacy, which offers him a tasty strawberry.

Existentialism is not really a philosophy – rather it is a *style of philosophizing*. There is no common body of doctrine. There are many points of view and many modes of presentation. Indeed, there are existential approaches in novels, short stories, painting, drama, poetry and dance, as well as in philosophy, psychology and psychiatry. In regards to religion, there are both theistic and atheistic existentialists. In fact, most philosophers generally identified as existentialists would reject being categorized in this way. Existentialism is individual-focused, and defies the objectification of such a grouping. Sartre complained that the word existentialism had been virtually emptied of meaning. Heidegger, Jaspers and Marcel, key contributors to existentialist perspectives, would have rejected the label. None of them wished to participate in a "school of thought."[2]

Unlike most philosophy, existentialism is an approach that begins with the subjective, not the objective world 'out there'. The experience of the human subject is the starting point; the process works from the inside out.

Furthermore, most philosophical approaches focus on human thought and devalue human feelings. In existentialism, feelings are valued along with thinking, as a way to be involved in the world. More than mere theory-making or abstract intellectualizing, existentialism values the actual *experience* of the individual human as the central point of concern.

Existentialist thought has been a long time in gestation. Its roots go far back into the history of philosophical questioning. For example, the ancient Hebrew prophets raised the issue of humanity's place in the universe. The pre-Socratic Greeks gave value to human beings as thinking subjects. The ancient Daoist practitioners in China pointed out the absurdity of life. The Buddha turned people's attention to issues of emptiness and nonbeing. Jesus Christ preached a gospel of personal responsibility based on individual conscience. Galileo, with his telescope, alerted us to our insignificance in a vast universe. The topics that they raised are all within the purview of existentialism. Existentialism deals with human beings in the context of society and the world, rather than in abstraction. As Thomas Flynn puts it:

> It should be clear that existentialists are scarcely ivory-tower intellectuals. Long before Sartre spoke of 'commitment', Kierkegaard and Nietzsche were addressing the social ills of their time and, in Kierkegaard's case at least, could be found right in the thick of local polemics.[3]

There was a brief period in the middle of the 20th century when existentialism enjoyed wide popular appeal, especially in Europe and North America. The style of philosophizing seemed well suited to dealing with the events surrounding World War II and the social change of the 1950s and 60s. Although it has been overshadowed by other approaches in recent decades, it never fades away completely, just settles into the background.

Existentialism has a tradition of radical questioning. All theories and explanations are seen to be simply narratives about being. Being itself is not confined to theory or doctrine or dogma or belief. Existentialism recognizes that explanations or systems of thought often function as deflections from central issues – its admonition would be "Question your answers!" As one writer puts it:

> Radical questioning and readiness to doubt are built into the existentialist position, and where faith does finally emerge, it will be the stronger for having looked into the abyss.[4]

For existentialist thinkers, life is without inherent meaning, or at least without such meaning that can be known; the situation is sometimes described as absurd. Individuals can find a way to address this, but it requires courage and fortitude. The existentialist tradition offers "a way of life and not a mere parlour game."[5] The road is not easy, and relatively few choose to walk it.

For Sartre, the core of existentialism is humanism:

> There is no other universe except the human universe, the universe of human subjectivity. This relation of transcendence as constitutive of man ... with subjectivity ... it is this we call existential humanism.[6]

We are alone, free to choose without recourse to external authority – lost and abandoned, but possessing vast possibilities:

> This is humanism, because we remind man that there is no legislator but himself; that he himself, thus abandoned, must decide for himself; also because we show that it is not by turning back upon himself, but always by seeking, beyond himself, an aim which is one of liberation or of some particular realisation, that man can realise himself as truly human.[7]

The Authors' Perspective

Some find existentialism dry, dark or depressing. We ourselves have found existentialist approaches to be invigorating, and very confirming of human beings. With its emphasis on personal responsibility and responsive action, existentialism provides a perspective that is expansive and illuminating. We recoil from false romanticisms that gloss over deep human concerns; existentialism addresses people as they are and investigates practical approaches to the challenges of life. We find the concepts of individual freedom and responsibility to be very close to our own views of human issues. Living fully in the moment, in face of the demands of a numbing culture – we have attempted to do this in our own lives, even at the risk of not "fitting in." We have tried to help our clients do the same.

Reading the existentialist writers has challenged and fascinated us for decades. We especially appreciate the writings of Camus, Kafka, Kierkegaard, Sartre and Buber, in addition to a host of other philosophers of this style. The novels and stories of Franz Kafka often shock us into sudden awakening, in the same way the Zen teaching stories and haiku poetry bring sudden transformation.

We also appreciate the existential influence in the arts, and have enjoyed many presentations of this genre. The paintings of Miró and Kandinsky and Canadian Tom Thomson depict bleakness and angst in remarkable ways. As theatre buffs, we especially enjoy the Theatre of the Absurd; we thrill at the starkness, yet the deep familiarity, of the bleak characterizations of life in plays by Samuel Beckett or Eugène Ionesco. For us, the angst-infused music composed in the last century by such composers as Mahler and Shostakovich is very compelling.

In psychology, we have embraced the "here-and-now" approach to working with people. Existential thought offers depth of understanding to those who wish to live fully and responsibly, rather than explain away their symptoms and issues with theory.

Existentialism provides a rich blend of radical questioning that satisfies our minds, and a respect for feelings that appeals to our hearts. We value a philosophy of involvement that is human centred. Furthermore, the stark insistence on personal accountability suits us well. This is a style of philosophizing that is, for us, relevant, practical, and generative.

> Dive headlong
> into cold water
>
> You are suddenly
> chilled to your core
> immediately present.
>
> You don't really like it
> But you definitely know
> You are alive.[8]

Existence, Being, and Nonbeing

In existentialist thought, existence means "to stand out." When people affirm their being, they stand out from nonbeing, from the impersonal background of life. In the language of existentialism, therefore, only human beings "exist." Martin Heidegger wrote, "The being whose manner of being is existence is man." He elaborates,

> Man alone exists. A rock is, but does not exist. A tree is, but it does not exist. A horse is, but it does not exist. An angel is, but he does not exist. God is, but he does not exist.[9]

To exist, to stand forth in being, is always done in face of nonbeing. The more being I embrace, the more nonbeing I necessarily encounter, and must absorb to continue. Theologian Paul Tillich shows in *The Courage to Be* how being is dependent upon nonbeing (and vice versa)[10] Or, as Sartre puts it:

> Here then is nothingness surrounding being on every side and at the same time expelled from being. Here nothingness is given as that by which the world receives its outlines as the world.[11]

Ontology is the study of being. The ontological perspective is that we exist only when we stand forth; this involves confronting nonbeing. When we do not stand forth, we fade into the oblivion of nonbeing. We are still alive in a biological sense, but not present, not distinctly standing forth, not *existing*; this has been called "the death in life" and describes a zombie-like simulacrum of a vital being.[12] When we do not stand forth, we join the herd, do not distinguish ourselves, and fail in the possibility of being what we could be.

Humans are shrouded in mystery. We are deeply uncertain, yet capable of remarkable imaginings and deeds. We are also capable of self-deception, and adept at avoiding the central issues of our existence. Our fertile imagination can be used to stand forth, to exist, or to deny the profoundly perilous situation of human life. André Malraux wrote:

> The greatest mystery is not that we have been flung at random among the profusion of the earth and the galaxy of the stars, but that in this prison we can fashion images of ourselves sufficiently powerful to deny our nothingness.[13]

This summarizes the human condition. We are here, alive, on earth, thrust here by unknown forces; we have no say in the matter. There is no escape, we are imprisoned here – this is our existential state and dilemma. We can use our imagination to become more of what we are by embracing nonbeing; or we can abuse our imagination in trying to opt out of the game, and succumb to nonbeing.

Existence and Essence

The central concern for existential thought is existence itself. In contrast, most philosophies are essentialist, proceeding from a root assumption that there is a basic nature of human beings, an "essence." The existentialists turn this on its head by insisting that existence comes first, that the essence of humans follows the existential decisions that define the individual being. Sartre brings this into focus in *Existentialism and Humanism*: "Existence comes before essence," he says. "We must begin from the subjective."[14] He maintains (and we agree) that existence is human, and depends upon self-encounter.

> What do we mean by saying that existence precedes essence? We mean that man first of all exists, encounters himself, surges up in the world – and defines himself afterwards.[15]

The usual categories of definition do not hold for human existence.

> If man ... is not definable, it is because to begin with he is nothing. He will not be anything until later, and then he will be what he makes of himself.[16]

The Paradoxical Nature of Humans

Ernest Becker's book *The Denial of Death* has been an important touchstone for us as we have pondered the existential issues in our own lives and in the lives of others. The following statement by Becker addresses a puzzling and disturbing issue:

> We always knew that there was something peculiar about man, something deep down that characterized him and set him apart from the other animals ... For ages, when philosophers talked about the core of man they referred to it as his "essence," something fixed in his nature, deep down, some special quality or substance. But nothing like it was ever found.[17]

Why is this so? Why is no essence accessible to those who seek it? Becker answers,

> The reason it was never found ... was that there was no essence, that the essence of man is really his paradoxical nature, the fact that he is half animal and half symbolic.[18]

The human existent is more-than-animal, and yet still a creature of nature.

> Man has a symbolic identity that brings him sharply out of nature. He is a symbolic self, a creature with a name, a life history. He is a creator with a mind that soars out to speculate about atoms and infinity, who can place himself imaginatively at a point in space and contemplate bemusedly his own planet.[19]

Human capability is vast:

> This immense expansion, this dexterity, this ethereality, this self-consciousness gives to man literally the status of a small god in nature ... [20]

Yet we cannot overcome our mortality. We are going to die, and we know it.

> Yet, at the same time ... man is a worm and food for worms. This is the paradox: he is out of nature and hopelessly in it.[21]

As Alexander Pope said long ago, man is "a being darkly wise and rudely great ... the glory, jest and riddle of the world!"[22] We are in the world and also transcend that world. We exist only in relation to the world to which we are tied. Yet this same world that enables us to exist also threatens to diminish our existence or even take it away. Our symbolic identity takes us out of nature; in this way we are creators of the universe; at the same time, we live in a body which hurts, degenerates, and ultimately dies. Lower animals are spared the fate of self-awareness, since they lack a symbolic identity and the self-consciousness that goes with it. Becker states the paradox starkly:

> Man is literally split in two: he sticks out of nature with a towering majesty, and yet he goes back into the ground a few feet in order blindly and dumbly to rot and disappear forever. It is a terrifying dilemma to be in and to have to live with.[23]

So, to the existentialist, there is no given essence. The essence of what we are is derived from our own decisions and actions, as Paul Tillich asserts:

> There is no essential nature of man, except in the one point that he can make of himself what he wants. Man creates what he is.[24]

The Death of God

Nietzsche repeated his statement "God is dead!" in several of his writings, including his classic work *Thus Spoke Zarathustra*.[25] He meant that the concept of a Christian God is no longer valid for humans as a basis for moral principles. He is taking the existentialist position that there is no absolute cosmic order in which we can take comfort or guidance; we are alone, and our existence is determined by ourselves and our decisions, not by some external principle or deity. Heidegger understood Nietzsche's statement to include the death of metaphysics as a consoling function.[26] We cannot retreat into philosophical explanations that grant us our place in the cosmos. Everything is up to us.

We are thus free to choose whether we exist, and how we live. Without predetermined meaning, we can ask radical questions. Since there is no fixed essence to the human, we can transform ourselves through our imagination, decisions and actions. It is this emphasis that makes it possible for theists as well as atheists to take an existentializing approach. The human being is the central concern, whether there is a God or not. As Alexander Pope advised,

> Know then thyself, presume not God to scan/The proper study of mankind is man.[27]

Theistic approaches are most often essentialist – God conceives and creates humanity. Sartre, an atheist, declares the absence of God in the following statement:

> Thus there is no human nature, because there is no God to have a conception of it. Man simply is.[28]

Perhaps Sartre is too dogmatic, asserting his atheism as a fact rather than a philosophical position. However, to the existentialist, the issue of God is not the central concern anyway; human beings are the originators of their existence. This position applies equally to atheists and theists of the existential style of philosophizing. In this approach, human beings do not simply conceive themselves any more than a God would. Sartre continues:

> Not that [man] is simply what he conceives himself to be, but he is what he wills, and as he conceives himself after already existing – as he wills to be after that leap towards existence.[29]

The choice is a willed one, and the conception, the image, comes afterwards. Will precedes conception – existence precedes essence.

Condemned to Freedom

We are thrust into the world, having had no say in the matter. We did not create our situation, and yet, utterly alone, we must make of it what we will. As A.E. Housman put it, "I, a stranger and afraid/ In a world I never made."[30]

We cannot depend upon anyone else to save us from our fate. Sartre contends,

> We are left alone, without excuse. That is what I mean when I say that man is condemned to be free. Condemned, because he did not create himself, yet is nevertheless at liberty, and from the moment that he is thrown into this world he is responsible for everything he does.[31]

We are beings who can choose to exist by affirming our being in face of nonbeing. We are free to choose existence, and free to refuse. In Hamlet's famous words, "To be or not to be, that is the question." Albert Camus takes up the idea:

There is but one truly serious philosophical problem, and that is suicide. Judging whether life is or is not worth living amounts to answering the fundamental question of philosophy. All the rest – whether or not the world has three dimensions, whether the mind has nine or twelve categories – comes afterwards. These are games; one must first answer.[32]

Camus is not just talking here about physical suicide; any stepping back from life is a choosing of nonbeing, a kind of nonphysical suicide, a choice of "the death in life."

We are free to make a choice to exist or not. Once having chosen existence, one experiences the further challenges of freedom, which can be addressed by the human imagination. The imagination is the expression of our freedom, and how we live is a product of that imagination. Tillich writes:

> Man is what he makes of himself. And the courage to be as oneself is the courage to make of oneself what one wants to be.[33]

We surpass our limits, transcend ourselves, through our imagination. The individual is not impotent; one person can influence others by imagining other possibilities. Rather than fading into the anonymity of the herd and nonexistence, one person can stand forward and be an inspiration to a group movement, bringing transformation of groups and society at large. Sartre develops this theme:

> Man is all the time outside of himself: it is in projecting and losing himself beyond himself that he makes man to exist; and, on the other hand, it is by pursuing transcendent aims that he himself is able to exist. Since man is thus self-surpassing, he is himself the heart and centre of his transcendence.[34]

We understand Sartre's concept of transcendence to mean that through imagination, individuals can create new vistas of possibility that overcome alienation. Our own view is that relationships transcend the isolation and alienation; we imagine a world where people can connect with each other, and we are dedicated to living this vision ourselves.

Living with Dread

Edward Munch's famous painting "The Scream" is a swirl of chaos and harsh colours, with a tormented individual clasping his head, eyes agape, with a look of abject pain. This work depicts the experience of the individual in the modern world, alone, alienated, in despair.

Writing about Nietzsche in his book *Report to Greco*, Nikos Kazantzakis admonishes humans to avoid the traps of hope and fear, which

can be used to step back from being, and thus from our fulfilled lives in
the living present.

> Shame on us if we continue to become intoxicated in the taverns of
> hope or the cellars of fear.[35]

Our task is to live with dread, without recourse to hope or fear. There
is no protection from nonbeing. We exist, and intensify our being by
embracing the dread and nonbeing.

In a previous book, we addressed the issues associated with meaninglessness, and the urgency people feel to put on a false self rather than
individuate.[36] The result of adopting the false self is an illusion of security and belonging; the cost is being objectified and out of touch with
one's deepest nature. This is the neurotic solution to the threat of nonbeing. In terms of the Dynamic Empathy Model we outlined in Part I, this
represents a fixation at the stage of objectification/isolation, and inhibits
participation in the fuller human community.

In Colin Wilson's book *The Philosopher's Stone*, the central character
is scathing about the limitations of most people, who lack the courage to
embrace life in its fullness:

> The trouble with most people is an obsessive desire for security. They
> want domestic security and sexual security and financial security, and
> they waste their lives pursuing these until one day they realize that
> death negates all security, and they might as well have saved them-
> selves the trouble from the beginning … they might as well have saved
> themselves the effort of being born.[37]

They then succumb to the death in life, the eclipse of existence by
nonbeing. Kierkegaard writes about non-involvement:

> Most people live dejectedly in worldly sorrow and joy; they are the
> ones who sit along the wall and do not join the dance.[38]

To the existentialists, the solution is to join the dance. Wilson's character says, "I grasped the reality, the truth of my own death. The horror
almost choked me."[39] But then, he goes on to an insight with which we
have much resonance:

> The strange thing is that the experience was not all horror. Somewhere
> deep inside me there was a spark of happiness. To see the emptiness of
> things brings its own exultancy. Perhaps because to grasp futility is to
> recognize that its opposite is implied.[40]

The Age of Anxiety

Originally German, the word *angst* is often used by existential writers to refer to "existential anxiety," an intense feeling of apprehension or inner turmoil which is a feature of existence. Simply put, humans are anxious in being alive. This is not just that we are afraid of death (although, of course, we generally are); fear of death is a diminished aspect of the all-encompassing phenomenon of angst. Fears have an object (for example, one might be afraid of snakes, or of high places), but existential anxiety has no object. Angst is intrinsic in our being. The more we exist, the more anxiety we feel. The challenge is to embrace and accept this anxiety; this is self-affirmation in face of nonbeing. The more anxiety we can encompass, the more nonbeing we can face, and the stronger and larger we become. The larger we become, the more anxiety of nonbeing we have to face.

Angst – "existential anxiety," "anxiety of being," "root anxiety," "ontological anxiety" – is related to existential guilt: individuals recognize they are not all that they could be, and experience guilt over the nonbeing they fail to embrace. For Kierkegaard, a Christian, angst comes with the awareness that we are not living up to the standards of God; for atheistic existentialists, God is not part of the equation. For both theistic and atheistic existentialists, ontic anxiety accompanies our recognition that we are not all that we could be – we are not living up to the potential we can see and imagine. We are disappointing ourselves, and we are not living up to the possibility of participating fully in the human community.

Paul Tillich (a theistic scholar) maintains that nonbeing threatens being in three different dimensions – the *ontic*, the *spiritual* and the *moral*. This means that humans contend with *impotence* in relation to one's fate on the ontic level, with *emptiness* on the spiritual level, and with *guilt* on the moral level. Tillich summarizes:

> Nonbeing threatens man's ontic self-affirmation, relatively in terms of fate, absolutely in terms of death. It threatens man's spiritual self-affirmation, relatively in terms of emptiness, absolutely in terms of meaninglessness. It threatens man's moral self-affirmation, relatively in terms of guilt, absolutely in terms of condemnation.[41]

These aspects of anxiety have been present throughout history. Tillich maintains that different eras had a predominance of one of the three types of anxiety.

> We find that at the end of ancient civilization ontic anxiety is dominant, at the end of the Middle Ages moral anxiety, and at the end of the modern period spiritual anxiety.[42]

In earlier periods, anxiety of fate and death predominated. But in the Middle Ages, "the impact of the Jewish-Christian message changed this situation, and so radically that toward the end of the Middle Ages the anxiety of guilt and condemnation was decisive."[43] Tillich says this persisted until the modern era, when the spiritual form of anxiety assumed dominance:

> The breakdown of absolutism, the development of liberalism and democracy, the rise of a technical civilization ... these are all the sociological presupposition for the third main period of anxiety. In this the anxiety of emptiness and meaninglessness is dominant.[44]

The 20th century, particularly the era after World War II, has been called "The Age of Anxiety." (W.H. Auden wrote a long poem in 1947 with this title, addressing the human quest to find substance and identity in the uncertain, industrialized post-war world.) We propose that we in the West in the second decade of the 21st century are still in the same dilemma. This continues to be an era of emptiness and meaninglessness, a spiritual void in the midst of development and uneven prosperity. Human beings now can have the freedom of self-determination; but this comes with the cost of increased anxiety. In the past, religion and political ideologies kept the individual insulated from the existential starkness. Tillich maintained that we have lost these protections in this new age of anxiety; however, the rise of fundamentalisms indicates to us that these forces are once again more potent. Many seem to be utilizing ideologies as a refuge in the current era. Still, some people continue to seek meaning without retreating into the protections of religion or politics; for ourselves, this remains the focus of our concern. Those who awaken to individual possibilities seek a form of inquiry that can address the challenges of the age. Becker suggests this is the origin of modern psychological perspectives:

> Modern man became psychological because he became isolated from protective collective ideologies. He had to justify himself from within himself.[45]

Existentialism is no longer popular in the way it once was. Nevertheless, it continues to play a role in philosophical conversation as it "voices the abiding moral concerns of the human condition."[46] Flynn states the reason for existentialism's abiding relevance:

> It continues to defend individual freedom, responsibility, and authenticity in the midst of various forms of determinism, conformism, self-deception, technologism, and the like so prevalent in our day.[47]

Responsibility

As Sartre asserts, we are responsible, each of us, for our own lives:

> If ... it is true that existence is prior to essence, man is responsible for
> what he is. Thus, the first effect of existentialism is that it puts every
> man in possession of himself as he is, and places the entire responsibil-
> ity for his existence squarely upon his own shoulders.[48]

Sartre also says this responsibility is not only to oneself, but to the
community at large:

> And, when we say that man is responsible for himself, we do not mean
> that he is responsible only for his own individuality, but that he is
> responsible for all men.[49]

We are connected with each other in the commonality of our fate
and existential aloneness. We must choose our own existence, and in so
doing, we affect the world around us. This involves moment to moment
decisions, which we must make with insufficient information.

There is no recipe that will answer life's questions. Unlike the essen-
tialists, who would suggest that the appropriate decisions can be discovered, the existentialists are left with the starkness of decision with no
perfect blueprint. As Flynn says,

> Like the prudent person, the existentialist judges 'in-situation'. But
> where the prudent person *discovers* what is the right thing to do, the
> existentialist *decides* what is the right thing to do.[50]

Any decision "for" is also a decision "against." When we choose a
course of action, we select against alternatives. For example, when the
motorist decides to turn right, the possibilities that would unfold from
turning left fade in the rear view mirror. The self is created through
individual decisions that determine the quality of one's existence. Macquarrie writes:

> What is really chosen is *oneself.* It is out of decisions that the self
> emerges. A self is not given ready-made at the beginning. What is
> given is a field of possibility, and as the existent projects himself into
> this possibility rather than that one, he begins to determine who he
> shall be.[51]

No external authority or code of conduct can guide a self-affirming
decision. Sartre tells individuals to choose their actions, from their own
values:

> You are free, therefore choose – that is to say, invent. No rule of general

morality can show you what you ought to do; no signs are vouchsafed in this world.[52]

And thus we define ourselves through decisions and actions. We "invent" ourselves.

Courage

In this self-defining activity, each person is alone, unhampered, and aware of the nonbeing that threatens being at every second. We are free to choose to face the nonbeing and embrace it, or to shrink back from it, and be enveloped by it, and thus not exist. This is the existential dilemma, which persists, moment to moment, throughout our lives. The more one stands forth in face of nonbeing and exists, the more nonbeing there is to address. Being is threatened always by nonbeing. Tillich writes that the choice to exist takes courage: "Courage," he says, "is self-affirmation ... in spite of nonbeing."[53]

This courage is not the commonplace martial notion of bravery in battle. This courage is to engage with heart (French "cœur" = heart), and to stand forth in life with one's own unique attitudes and values and actions. To be courageous is to incorporate anxiety, to "own" it. In this process, the anxiety is not reduced – one exists with it. Tillich writes of this process:

> Courage does not remove anxiety, since anxiety is existential, it cannot be removed. But courage takes the anxiety of nonbeing into itself.[54]

In this way, we can no longer project evil "out there" and dissociate ourselves from it through the moralistic dismissal of "I'm good, they're bad." Whatever evil or darkness there is in the world is an aspect of humanity, in which we are each a participant. We are each capable of supporting life or acting against it. Tillich suggests that, in order to affirm oneself, one must take ownership of dark and light forces within one's being; one must "affirm one's own demonic depth."[55]

The courage to be is not only a project for oneself, but for all of mankind. We are challenged to participate with others, to be in community. Tillich writes of participation:

> Self-affirmation, if it is done in spite of the threat of nonbeing, is the courage to be. But it is not the courage to be as oneself, it is the "courage to be as a part."[56]

So, we cannot simply retire behind our walls and gates and disassociate ourselves from the rest of the world. The violence and torment and chaos in the world that we see daily on the television and internet are not separate from us. We are responsible as members of the human community for what occurs, even far away. We are called to take part, to find solutions to human problems. Tillich calls for us to participate:

> But being as a part points to the fact that self-affirmation necessarily includes the affirmation of oneself as "participant."[57]

The alternative to courage is despair, which Tillich describes as a neurotic solution, stepping back from life into nonbeing.

> Anxiety turns us toward courage, because the other alternative is despair. Courage resists despair by taking anxiety into itself.[58]

The relationships that are closest to us are where we live and learn courage, and where we learn to participate. Tillich agrees with Buber that we become and remain persons through dialogical engagement:

> Only in the continuous encounter with other persons does the person become and remain a person. The place of this encounter is the community.[59]

Even short casual engagements have significance in our community participation. As we affirm existence individually, we contribute to the existence of humanity. The individual life is not futile, irrelevant or unimportant – in existing, we have significance. Tillich points out the contribution one makes to the whole through self-affirmation:

> In self-affirmation is the affirmation of oneself as a participant in the creative development of mankind.[60]

This affirmation of life neutralizes despair and embraces the sorrow of existence. Ignazio Silone writes:

> But there is a sorrow inherent in our human fate which we must learn how to face and make into our friend. We must not fear even despair ... as long as it is serious and sincere and has some fundamental reason. We must not fear to ask ourselves: Who am I?[61]

Dialogue with The Absurd

According to Albert Camus, humans are limited to their own experience; all else is conjecture. He writes,

> I don't know whether this world has a meaning that transcends it. But I know that I cannot know that meaning ... What can a meaning outside my condition mean to me? I can understand only in human terms.[62]

To the existentialists, life has no inherent meaning – or at least not one we can know. The situation is absurd. No logic or explanation or theory will encompass life or answer "why?" We live without any operating manual or dependable authority to guide us. We're each on our own. As Efran and Lukens put it, "Life is a meaningless drift, to which we add our own meaning as we go along."[63]

Camus proposes that there are three solutions to the problem of the absurd – suicide, belief in transcendence, or embracing the absurd. For Camus, physical suicide to eliminate subjective experience is not an acceptable option. He contends that adopting a belief in a transcendent realm constitutes philosophical suicide. His third choice is the one he lived – acceptance of the absurd. Embracing the absurd is accomplished through subjective affirmation of inherent meaninglessness, and despite this, creating meaning. Maurice Friedman writes, "Camus sees his art itself as a Dialogue with the Absurd, a dialogue from which emerge not only values but hope and joy."[64]

Camus' novels, plays and stories depict situations in which humans contend with the absurd. The central character in *The Plague*, Doctor Rieux, continues to work tirelessly as a physician, ministering to the sick even in the face of hopelessness and the inevitability of death. Rieux is what Maurice Friedman calls a "modern Job." He joins the often nameless humans "who, while unable to be saints but refusing to bow down to pestilences, strive their utmost to be healers."[65] Like the biblical Job, he refuses to take solace in religious hope for salvation or in trying to be saintly or through passive submission to external fate. He toils on in spite of the situation, deciding for himself in each moment. Sartre advocates for this approach too:

> Man can will nothing unless he has first understood that he must count on no one but himself; that he is alone, abandoned on earth in the midst of his infinite responsibilities, without help, with no other aim than the one he sets himself, with no other destiny than the one he forges for himself on this earth.[66]

Affirming in Face of the Absurd: Two Examples

Psychiatrist Viktor Frankl was a longtime prisoner in a Nazi concentration camp; he survived to write about his experience, while most of his other family members perished in the death camps. The conditions were bestial and many prisoners succumbed to psychological dehumanization, either by giving up or turning against their fellows. But Frankl refused to succumb, and found an affirmation of life in this hideous environment; upon his release, he developed a psychological approach he called logotherapy ("meaning therapy"), based on his experiences in the camp. In his book *Man's Search for Meaning*, he tells of his analysis of how some prisoners kept their humanness and heart in the midst of obscene dehumanization:

In the concentration camps ... in this living laboratory and on this testing ground we watched and witnessed some of our comrades behave like swine while others behaved like saints. Man has both potentialities within himself; which one is actualized depends on decisions but not on conditions.[67]

Frankl points out the choice that is available to each one of us, even in the most horrific circumstances.

In the final analysis it becomes clear that the sort of person the prisoner became was the result of an inner decision, and not the result of camp influences alone. Fundamentally, therefore, any man can, even under such circumstances, decide what shall become of him – mentally and spiritually.[68]

This is individual freedom, with vast responsibility.

A human being is not one thing among others; things determine each other, but man is ultimately self-determining. What he becomes – within the limits of endowment and environment – he has made of himself.[69]

Czech writer Franz Kafka's novels and stories are full of darkness, emptiness and meaninglessness. They deal with isolation and anonymity and depersonalization in a bureaucratic world. Reading Kafka, one is subjected to shocking images in the bleak stories, where no real human contact is ever made. Kafka depicted some of the gloomiest aspects of existence. But his thrust was always to affirm in face of absurdity, both in his writing, and in his own life.

In such a godless time one must be gay. It is a duty ... sorry has no prospects. And all that matters is prospects, going forward. There is danger only in the narrow, restricted moment. Behind it lies the abyss. If one overcomes it, everything is different. Only the moment counts. It determines life.[70]

Kafka died of tuberculosis at age 40 after a prolonged debilitating illness. His personal positivism, which he maintained through his suffering right to the end, is in sharp contrast to the very dark situations he depicted in his writing. Kafka's mantra was "Say yes to everything!" Whatever he encountered, he would embrace positively, even when he was weak and nearing his death. His friend Gustav Janouch wrote of his last hours:

His voice broke into a dry convulsive cough, which he quickly mastered. We smiled at each other. "Look," I said, "everything will soon be all right." "It is already all right," Franz Kafka said slowly. "I have said yes to everything. In that way suffering becomes an enchantment, and death – it is only an ingredient in the sweetness of life."[71]

Every moment is special, even in face of suffering. Even pain and obstacles can be cause for celebration, since they are aspects of our lives.

We must not substitute blind adherence to rules in place of a responsive life in the present. Our ultimate recourse is always to our own individual decisions and the actions we choose. Macquarrie writes:

> Only when he stops listening to the voice of the 'they' can the existent truly hear the call of conscience. From where does the call come? It comes from the depth of one's own being. It is the call of the authentic self struggling to be born.[72]

Evil, Sin and Grace

From an existential perspective, evil occurs from a failure to live up to one's possibilities, not from breaking some external code of conduct. Maurice Friedman declares that "evil is the product of unlived life."[73] This "unlived life" is graphically depicted in Georges Bernanos' novel *Diary of a Country Priest*:

> Many men never give out the whole of themselves, their deepest humanity. They live on the surface, and yet, so rich is the soil of humanity that even this thin outer layer is able to yield a kind of meagre harvest which gives the illusion of real living … how many men will never have the least idea of what is meant by supernatural heroism, without which there can be no inner life! Yet by that very same inner life shall they be judged … Therefore when death has bereft them of all the artificial props which society provides such people, they will find themselves as they really are, as they were without even knowing it – horrible undeveloped monsters, the stumps of men.[74]

Theologian Paul Tillich defines sin as separation. He says that human beings are estranged in three aspects: from themselves, from each other, and from the Ground of Being (Tillich's vision of God). Sin and grace, he says, are bound together; grace is the unity that is lost in sin. In *The Shaking of the Foundations*, Tillich says that grace comes with responsible existential decisions and actions.

> "Sin" and "grace" are strange words; but they are not strange things. We find them whenever we look into ourselves with searching eyes and longing hearts. They determine our life. They abound within us and in all of life. May grace more abound within us![75]

We like Tillich's outline, and we echo his appeal to emphasize grace through joining. Our central position is that relationships heal, that life can be rejoined in any moment. This takes enormous strength and courage; the challenge is for each of us.

Martin Buber too is concerned with separation. There is a split, he says, between the instinctual aspect of humans and their spiritual possibilities. He disagrees with Freud about the origin of this split, and maintains that modern humanity is ill. Friedman contrasts Buber's view with Freud's:

> Buber's view of man leads him to assert that the chasm between spirit and instincts is not an inherent structure of human nature, as Freud holds, but is a product of the sickness of modern man – the destruction of organic confidence and of organic community and the divorce between man and man.[76]

For Buber the misery of life can be overcome by hallowing the everyday: "The wretchedness of our world," he says, "is grounded in its resistance to the entrance of the holy into lived life."[77]

This "entrance of the holy into lived life" is expressed in the existentialists' urgency to relate in the real world, to real human beings, with a social concern. Each can participate in his or her own way. Friedman offers the example of Thomas Merton as exemplifying continuous participation, even in solitude:

> Thomas Merton was a man who spent a good deal of his life in a Trappist monastery. But his greatness is that he never left the secular world. He never ceased to contend in it, book after book, until his unfortunate death. We cannot leave the world for someplace holy. We are all sharers in the crisis of values. We are sharers of the eclipse of the human.[78]

Existential Psychotherapy

Existential psychotherapists focus on the "here and now" rather than delving too deeply into past or future issues. While they attempt to relate to the client as a whole, which must include past and future considerations, the emphasis is on life in the present. They utilize encounter (a more subjective and personal experience) rather than transference (which is impersonal and objective). In keeping with existential emphases, they focus on issues such as awareness, responsibility, decisions and consequences, anxiety and acceptance of death.

Freud said that the primary repression is of the libido energy. Reich tended to agree, using different language. Ernest Becker contradicts both Freud and Reich: "Consciousness of death," he says, "is the primary repression."[79]

Rollo May argues that existential psychotherapy bases its approach on an understanding of what makes people human, and "stands for defining neurosis in terms of what destroys man's capacity to fulfill his own being." He states, "It is based on the assumption that it is possible to have a science of man which does not fragmentize man and destroy his humanity at the same moment as it studies him." He concludes:

> Existential psychotherapy is the movement which, although standing on one side on the scientific analysis owed chiefly to the genius of Freud, also brings back into the picture the understanding of man on a deeper and broader level – man as the being who is human.[80]

As such, existential psychotherapy is closely related to gestalt, humanist, and dialogical psychotherapy, which we discuss in following chapters. Our own careers have also been deeply rooted in a belief in the humanity, wholeness, responsibility and potential of the people with whom we work.

The Real

Poetry, too, can be a vehicle to discover authenticity in the midst of the numbing death-in-life that substitutes for most people's lives. In *The Duino Elegies*, Rainer Maria Rilke describes the empty world of distractions that tempt people with their denials of death's imminence. In the last elegy, he describes "the real" beyond the civilized organization of denial, beyond the last advertisements of diversions, where the river of life flows; the poet bids us wash ourselves clean again, to embrace existence by relinquishing the distractions. We can come to life at any moment. Now is the time. Here is the place.

> Oh, but just outside, behind
> the last billboards plastered with posters of "Deathless,"
> the bitter beer so sweet to those who drink it
> while chewing on plenty of fresh distractions
> just behind the billboards, right behind them, the REAL.
> Children are playing, to one side lovers are holding each other,
> earnest in the thinning grass, and dogs are doing nature's bidding.[81]

The existential position is that we are responsible for ourselves and the world we create and inhabit. The following statement is a call to life:

> Even if I knew that tomorrow the world would go to pieces, I would still plant my apple tree.[82]

II.13　Participation

KZ = Confucius (Kong Zi), CJ = Carl Jung, BW = Ben Wong, JM = Jock McKeen

JM: The existentialists, with their emphasis on the here and now and their inclusion of feelings in their philosophy and psychology, have had a huge impact on Ben and me and on the world we live in.

CJ: Yes, and I recognize that my scientific – secondary process – training limited my perspective. It did not address many of the deeper issues of human beings. The existentialists understood this. To me, these issues seemed better addressed in myths and dreams. This is why I became fascinated with primitive cultures.

BW: What did you find in primitive cultures that related to these issues?

CJ: Well, primitive human beings already had experiences with the deep strata of the mind, because these layers are inherent in their own nature. They addressed issues of this domain (which I called the collective unconscious) through dreams, myths, ceremonies, magic, and ritual.

JM: Are you saying that the contents of this level of mind are not "primitive?" I gather you mean the contents of the collective unconscious are universal and trans-human.

CJ: Yes, this is what I mean. The primitives were in touch with this. In some ways, the primitives were ahead of modern people. Some who have retained the mind frames of the primitives can still access this realm of mind. I mean, for example, aboriginal people, seers, psychics, and some artists. But with the advent of science has come a pre-emptive dismissal of this domain of the mind.

BW: This happened to Western psychology and philosophy and psychiatry in the Enlightenment's emphasis on the intellect.

CJ: Yes.

BW: The access to the immediate "here and now" – the starkness of experience – is lost by focusing only on the mental-intellectual realms. This is what the existentialists have criticized about many "scientific" philosophies.

JM: So you think they were anti-scientific?

BW: The existentialists by and large were not on a "mission" to prove some point. They were simply using a method of philosophizing that included human feelings and personal experience, rather than discounting them. In this context, they criticized philosophical and scientific approaches that discounted feelings.

JM: This is part of my puzzle. How does this relate to the scientific idea that the presence of the observer influences an experiment – that it is impossible to be completely objective?

BW: Jock, I see that you become confused when you associate the existentialists' inclusion of subjective feelings with the problem of objectivity, which separates the observer from the observed. It is relevant, but not the central theme. The main issue is that human feelings are part of the reality of our experience, and need to be considered in relation to the phenomena of the present.

JM: Please say more.

BW: Although the existentialists saw human feelings as part of the area for study, they did not focus on the other topic – namely that in an objective scientific experiment, the presence of the observer can often influence the results of the experiment. This is something else.

JM: Thanks ... this is a dilemma for me. When we are in touch with our feelings and can distinguish these from our thoughts, we recognize our own particular viewpoint on the world in the present moment. In this way, we are participants, rather than mere observers.

CJ: That's the important word – participating.

BW: This is an important contribution of gestalt therapy ... the understanding that connection is everything. When people make contact, their life energy flows and they can connect with themselves and with others.

JM: Dr. Jung, how does this idea of participating relate to the concept of "participation mystique?"

CJ: I used this concept in my book *Psychological Types,* and I continued to use it in my thinking. I always used the French language to name the concept, because I originally borrowed it from Lévy-Bruhl. He used it in an anthropological sense, suggesting that primitive people participated in the world around them, and did not separate themselves from it. In a fundamental way, primitive man did not clearly distinguish himself from the objects around him. Modern man, by contrast, has learned to *think about* the world; as a result, modern man can objectify the world, and thus separate from it. There is a gain and a loss from this.

JM: How so?

CJ: The gain is logic, which allows for science and the modern technological advances. The loss is the sense of belonging to the universe. Modern man is lost in his intelligence, and is an orphan in the universe through his own actions. This was what I addressed in my book *Modern Man in Search of a Soul*.

JM: Gain and loss. Interesting – and a kind of tragedy of progress.

KZ: I am fascinated. For the Chinese, we never completely let go of our participation. The loss for us is we don't have the full experience of being an individual. The gain is we know we belong. We belong to our family, we belong to our Chinese people, we belong in the universe. But we don't have a clear sense of our individual beings.

BW: In the West, we have been obsessed with individualizing and objectifying each other, and taking advantage of the objects around us in a most inhuman way. Now it seems the Western way has gained a dominance in the world whereby participation and belonging are seen as weak or primitive.

CJ: Yes, and our romance with science has clouded the issues further.

JM: Please say more.

CJ: Science has accomplished some astounding advances. Since the time of my death in 1961, the world has been linked electronically in ways that I would never have envisioned. It's magical, and perhaps demonic.

BW: We are prisoners of our own progress. We have come so far, and we have lost ourselves in the process.

JM: So we need a return to human values, and our connection with the universe.

BW (chuckling): There you go mounting a political campaign again. I can see you raising the trumpet to your lips to summon the troops!

KZ: The modern world is what it is. We can gain nothing by trying to go back to a golden age of the past. Humans must consider and deal with where we are now. I must admit that I would find the task daunting. The world was a much simpler place when I was living.

CJ: Indeed. I explored the territories of the mind and the dark underworld of the psyche, and I almost got lost so many times. But you gentleman *(nodding to Jock and Ben)* have siren calls that are very different. Technology is so appealing. You can easily become lost. I fear for the young people of today.

KZ: I also am very concerned.

JM: I frequently do become lost. Checking my email, responding to the electronic offers and information that inundate me. This applies to anyone who is connected to cyberspace.

BW: I'm glad I'm now retired, and can relax and leave this be. It is interesting, but to me not compelling.

JM: What is compelling to you?

BW: My connection with my loved ones, and friends and associates. I also have a keen interest in the world community. The technology helps me to stay in touch with the world, and for that I am grateful. But I mostly enjoy my quiet inner life and the affection of my friends and family. This is an old man's privilege, and I am very appreciative.

JM: So it's appropriate that the next chapter is about the gestaltists, with their emphasis on here-and-now connection and contact! Ben and I have learned a lot from them.

II.14 Gestalt Therapy: Contact, Awareness, Movement

We stop.

In this
stop

we come to life.

We stop concepting.

– Reps[1]

Anyone who has attended a Come Alive program at The Haven will likely have experienced or witnessed the gestalt process known as "two-chair" or "two-pillow" work. This form is based on a method created by gestalt therapy pioneer Fritz Perls, and we discuss it in this chapter. However, the influence of gestalt on our work runs deeper than this. A wealth of theory and understanding underlies this seemingly simple approach to contact, awareness, revitalization and becoming present and free. In this chapter, we address these theoretical underpinnings, which we find very compatible both with Reichian and Chinese energy theories.

Before looking at the ideas of Perls and other gestalt therapists, we want to say a few words about gestalt *psychology*, a theory of mind and brain which the gestalt therapists drew on.

Gestalt Psychology

Gestalt psychology is concerned primarily with perceptual processes. When you look at the image on the right by Roger Shepard,[2] you may see a woman's face … or a saxophone player. When you see the face, however, the saxophonist is not "gone." Rather, he is in the background. Likewise, when the saxophone player comes foreground, the face goes into the background. Foreground and background are all part of a whole.

A gestalt is a configuration or pattern or organized field that constitutes a whole. The properties of a gestalt cannot be derived from the summation of its component parts; rather, it is an instance or example of such a unified whole. A gestalt includes the whole thing or person being considered, its context, and the relationship between the two.[3] In gestalt psychology, gestalt formation is the creation of a figure in a field; the field itself is always present, though it may recede as the pattern of gestalt becomes foreground in our awareness. In the image of the saxophone player/woman's face, the *field* is the entire rectangular area outside this text that contains white spaces and black spaces. When the black section becomes foreground you see the saxophone player as the gestalt (the *figure* in the field), and the white part recedes into the background. When the white section is brought foreground in perception to create the gestalt of the woman, the black portion becomes background. Latner writes,

> The figure/ground relationship is a differentiation of part of the field into a place of centrality and importance, without losing touch with the rest of the field. This is holistic differentiation – the gestalt is a manifestation of the field, sharp and clear and distinct, and yet imbedded in its background.[4]

There is a tendency not only to see whole gestalts, but also to complete them when only part of the information is provided. The human being 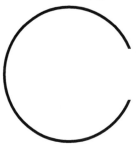 sees wholes, even when only part is visible. In the image to the left, the curved line is not joined; nevertheless, one sees a circle. The gestalt completion is created by the process of "closure," which is one of the many laws of gestalt perception. When an incomplete experiential gestalt is completed, it tends to disappear into the field. This is not only the case with visual images. For example, gestalt psychologist Kurt Lewin noticed that a waiter could easily remember the details of a customer's unpaid bill, but as soon as the bill was paid the waiter tended to forget the details. Lewin suggests that this is an instance of gestalt closure in the area of memory and motivation.[5] As we shall see, the idea of closure or resolution of "unfinished business" is a central concern of gestalt therapy, to which we now turn.

Fritz Perls: Pioneer of Gestalt Therapy

Fritz Perls (1893-1970) was a German psychiatrist who founded gestalt therapy, along with his wife, Laura Perls, and Paul Goodman. He had a time of association with the psychoanalytic movement, including an analysis with bodywork innovator Wilhelm Reich. Perls was a complex and controversial person – innovative, gifted, insightful, and at the same time, dismissive and authoritarian. Virginia Satir encapsulates the conundrum about Perls: "The man had many sides to him. I've often said that when Fritz was gestalting he was magnificent; when he was Fritzing, he could be a bastard."[6] Another writer puts it this way:

> Fritz Perls co-created and disseminated one of the most creative approaches to psychotherapy developed this century. He was an extraordinarily perceptive and intuitive trainer and therapist. Yet many aspects of the man engender personal distaste. Fortunately, as is often the case, the ideas are greater than the man.[7]

In this chapter, we outline some of the many innovations in perspective that this distinctive and highly unusual individual brought forth. We ourselves did not work with Perls, but many of our colleagues did, including Virginia Satir, John Enright and Erving and Miriam Polster. The Polsters' foundational book *Gestalt Therapy Integrated*, to which we refer in this chapter, provides clear details about the intricacies of gestalt therapy.[8]

Foundations of Gestalt Therapy

Gestalt therapy draws upon concepts from gestalt psychology, but is distinct from it. Gestalt therapy is an existential/experiential form of psychotherapy, focusing on personal responsibility, the individual's experience in the present moment, the therapist-client relationship, the environmental and social contexts of a person's life, and self-regulating adjustments. It moves toward action, away from mere talk therapy.

The Polsters name the foundations of gestalt therapy as:

1) power is in the present;
2) experience counts most;
3) the therapist is his own instrument and
4) therapy is too good to be limited to the sick.[9]

Countering Freud's orientation on the past, they propose a "here-and-now" ethic that is characteristic of gestalt therapy ("power is in the present'):

> Instead of looking for symbols from the past to illuminate present experience, present experience *itself* produces symbols which are valid statements and which extend beyond the limits of the therapeutic interaction. The symbolic quality of an event projects it forward because of its power to take on newly created meaning for the individual.[10]

Furthermore, the experience is significant in itself, without external interpretation being necessary. This point of view ("experience counts most"), shared with existentialist philosophers, is a central feature of the gestalt ethos:

> The emphasis on experience itself rather than on the interpretation of experience reflects the spirit of protest against the authoritarianism that entitles one person, who presumably knows more, to put something over on another person, who presumably knows less.[11]

This egalitarian attitude is vital in gestalt – the client knows for herself, and the therapist knows for herself. They can share their experiences and learn from each other in dialogue, but one is not more knowledgeable than the other. Either person can become more aware of what he or she already knows.

This issue is central to our own attitude to education and therapy. Gestaltists have generally referred to their work as therapy, while we ourselves have relinquished the therapy model entirely, replacing it with an educational approach. Our objection to therapy is focused on its inbuilt assumption that the therapist knows more than the the patient. Instead, we have wholeheartedly embraced an educational model that emphasizes sharing in dialogue. But what we call it is not the point. We acknowledge that gestalt therapy has contributed enormously. At the heart of the matter is whether there is a human-to-human cooperation between professional and client (as occurs in here-and-now psychologies such as gestalt therapy), or a one-up, one-down power dynamic as often occurs in traditional therapy.

Erving and Miriam Polster stress the client-centred approach of gestalt therapy, which we think has much in common with Adler's desire to help clients clarify what they want, so that they can make responsible choices to pursue an individually chosen goal:

> Instead of playing intellectual guessing games, we prefer that a patient get inside his own experience, trusting that when he gets a clear sense of what is happening inside him, his own directionalism will propel him into whatever experience is next for him. His internal dynamic needs recognition and reawakening.[12]

Furthermore, unlike traditional psychoanalytic therapy, where the professional must remain hidden and uninvolved, gestalt therapy permits and encourages therapists to use their own experience in the dialogue ("the therapist is his own instrument"). The Polsters note that this occurs in other humanistic approaches too:

> Recognition of the centrality of the therapist's own experience exists

not only within gestalt therapy, but also within Rogerian work, experiential therapy, sensitivity training, and among the psychological workers who are existentially oriented and who see therapy as a two-way human engagement.[13]

The Polster's fourth foundation point – "therapy is too good to be limited to the sick" – is also basic to our own attitude. Indeed, a central motivation in our own move away from therapy towards education is the belief that people are not broken and needing to be fixed, and in that sense are not sick. We can all benefit from greater awareness of our own patterns.

More Gestalt Therapy Concepts

The individual is at every moment a part of some field. It is at the *contact boundary* that psychological events take place, experienced as thoughts, actions, behaviour, and emotions. The contact boundary is where interaction and relationship occurs with other people and the environment. The human being has psychological "contact needs" in addition to physiological needs in order to survive and grow. When several needs occur simultaneously, the dominant need becomes the foreground figure and the others recede into the background. The need organizes the field. For example, a mother might wish to spend time with her husband in the evening. However, when her child becomes ill, her desire to provide care for the child becomes primary and she postpones her interaction with her husband. The child has become foreground and the husband goes into the background. Objects in the field that meet our needs become "figure." The rest is "background." People have the capacity to discriminate, to choose *contact* or *withdrawal*. In a person's life this may be a rhythmic interactive process, as one exercises freedom of choice in regard to contact or withdrawal. However, a person may also become stuck or fixated in this process.

Becoming fixated leaves people with "unfinished business" – they may, for example, block or interrupt their emotional response; this constitutes an "incomplete gestalt" and the individual's energy is reduced by the fixation that maintains the incompleteness. In gestalt terms, emotions are the forces that energize the person to action. Excitement at the contact boundary brings an emotional response, which is a stimulus to action. Emotions are thus feelings in motion. When the person "works through" a fixation and releases the energy, the gestalt is closed. This is important for personal development and individual freedom and has some resonance with the Buddhist notion of "letting go" of attachment. In gestalt terms, one finds wholeness when fixations are released.

In gestalt therapy, the "experiment" is a means of releasing fixations. Human beings operate on two different levels: thinking and acting. In gestalt therapy, the client tells his story (the thinking) and the therapist encourages the client to express the story in action. Gestalt uses the "experiment" to find a satisfactory expression of the story in action. The goal is to gain awareness of the deeper significance of the story, and to find resolution for incomplete aspects of it.

The Gestalt Experience Cycle

Gestalt is a theory with a dynamic quality. In the image of the saxophone player/woman with which we began this chapter, as foreground and background shift in the field, the picture changes and different responses are invited. Perls outlined, and other writers developed, a series of stages that illustrate the dynamic balancing of a live organism. Gordon Wheeler[14] summarizes these ideas into a model of six stages, which has variously been called the contact cycle, the cycle of experience, the cycle of self-regulation, or the gestalt cycle.

The stages are: Sensation → Awareness → Mobilization → Action → Contact → Withdrawal/Resolution. Here's an example of the process. You notice that your throat is dry (this is sensation) and think to yourself "I'm thirsty" (awareness). You stop what you are doing, and your attention shifts to finding a drink (the mobilization of energy). You get up and go to the fridge to get a soda (action). You drink the soda (contact). With your thirst satisfied, you leave the kitchen and return to where you were (withdrawal/resolution). If you fully experience this cycle, you will now be open to whatever comes next. You will be able to move on.

These stages are summarized in our own diagram on the facing page, which condenses the original six stages into five (melding mobilization and action into one). We note the similarity in this diagram with the Chinese Five Stages model (see Chapter IV.2) and with our Dynamic Empathy Model (see Chapter I.7).[15]

This is a generic map of any contact episode. James Kepner writes in his useful book *Body Process*:

> Roughly the same process occurs in any experience cycle, whether one is concerned with contacting food, contacting disowned aspects of oneself, contacting other people, or contacting and working through a major developmental life theme.[16]

The five circles overlap, indicating that they are not separate, but are interrelated aspects of a whole. When focusing on one circle, the other four circles are all available. In order to fully appreciate this process, one should imagine the cycle going around and around – each new sensation

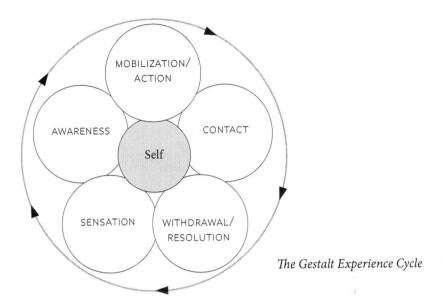

The Gestalt Experience Cycle

opening into a new contact and resolving into a new withdrawal, which allows for a new engagement. This is not merely a repetitious circle, but an expanding and contracting spiral, ever mutating. Thus, it is quite different from the analytic model of Superego/Ego//Id, which tends to be limited and more static. In the analytic model, the individual is more a passive victim of psychic forces in counterbalancing battles; here the individual is an active player in interaction with the environment. It is this concept of the person as a dynamic energy being that links the cycle with other energy theories such as Reich's and the Chinese Five Stages. The process involves episodes of tension, release, and resolution.

Difficulty arises when the cycle is habitually interrupted by the *contact boundary resistances* such as introjection and projection, which we discuss in some detail later in this chapter. The Polsters say that a person either makes good contact with the environment, or resists it. When contact is successful, one confronts the environment "with appetite, confidence, even daring." But, if people are frustrated from getting what they want, they are "stuck with a whole laundry list of troublesome feelings: anger, confusion, futility, resentment, impotence, disappointment and so on." Then they must divert their energy to deal with these feelings, "all of which reduce possibilities for contactful interaction."[17] The energy gets tied up in these interruptions, and the cycle slows down or even becomes arrested. An incomplete gestalt leaves an emptiness; people generally fill this emptiness with a neurosis. The challenge is how to release the tension, to get the cycle moving again. In gestalt therapy, the release of tension comes in completing a gestalt.

In the individual, courage drives the circle clockwise, allowing expansion; fear reverses the cycle, bringing restriction. This can be likened to the notion of growth and defence we have described in Chapter II.2 and elsewhere.[18] Courage brings growth; fear encourages defence. Fixations and their resolution occur in the present and the development is ongoing throughout one's life, as Kepner writes:

> From the viewpoint of Gestalt therapy, the process of separation and individuation outlined in child development literature is not one that is accomplished (or not) only at a given point in one's childhood. Rather it is characteristic of the *ongoing* contact and withdrawal process.[19]

The gestalt therapy process involves enhanced awareness of sensation, perception, bodily feelings, emotion and behaviour. The client is encouraged to work through the "experience cycle." All disturbances (interruptions) in the cycle may be traced back to a problem of awareness. By focusing on fixations and blocks to the gestalt cycle, the client can develop increasing awareness of self-blocking behaviour.

Goals of Gestalt Therapy

Well-being in gestalt theory is the capacity to be self-supporting and self-regulating. Growth is the movement from environmental support and regulation to self-support. The human infant acquires self-reliance, both physically and psychologically, in the process of learning and development. This saga is life-long, with more self-reliance possible as awareness grows.

To gestaltists, neurosis is a defensive maneuver to protect the self from being overwhelmed by the environment. It arises from people's inability to find and maintain the proper balance between themselves and the rest of their world (that is, their inability to make *contact*). Neurotics meet unbalancing situations by *interrupting* themselves in the gestalt experience cycle; criminals, say the gestaltists, interrupt the environment. Both neurotics and criminals are making misguided efforts to achieve a balance. Criminals overshoot the contact boundary, impinging on society; neurotics permit society to impinge on them, pushing and molding them. The use of the term "neurosis" arises out of the gestaltists' therapeutic model. Although we ourselves were trained in therapeutic approaches, we choose to think in terms of growth and learning rather than therapy and healing. The therapeutic model is prone to be moralistic (neurosis is bad, overcoming neurosis is good). In our educational model, on the other hand, everyone has issues of incomplete gestalts and fixations; in this model the terms "neurotic" and "criminal" are less meaningful. To put it another way, everyone has some sort of difficulty in making contact!

As we have seen, gestalt therapy is an existential therapy that focuses on the present. Psychoanalysis, focused more on the past, asks "Why?" In contrast, gestalt therapy asks "What?" Some questions a therapist might ask are "What are you doing with your hands now?", "What do you feel?", "What do you want?" The aim of such questions is to help a person develop self-awareness, autonomy, and self-responsibility. The ultimate goal is free expression of the authentic self.

Awareness in gestalt therapy is an awareness of process, rather than the traditional therapist's focus on the *content* of a client's history. The gestalt therapist assists the person to become oriented and located, finding the proper balance between the self and the rest of the world; the goal is to shift from environmental to self-support. The more aware people become, they more they can make sound existential choices. Clients can find meaning and pattern to their lives by increasing awareness of and responsibility for the total field. In order to help clients become aware of how they interrupt themselves, the therapist focuses on fixations, blocks, and the client's structure of experience. The therapist attempts to disequilibrate or destructure habitual patterns that maintain the fixations.

Gestalt therapy aims to introduce energy and action, to revitalize the individual's experience away from abstract intellectualizing ("aboutisms"). Breathing and body awareness techniques are used to help to bring the client into the present, embodied and aware. The Polsters elaborate:

> By integrating action into the person's decision-making process, he is pried loose from the stultifying influence of his aboutist ruminations. Decisions are best made when one's action begins to indicate a recognizable direction to which he can say yes.[20]

If the goals of gestalt therapy are to be achieved, the personal presence of the therapist is vitally important. This is not a mechanical process; it is a human-to-human engagement. This requires that the therapist be present, empathetic, accepting, authentic, confirming, and inclusive.

Contact

The ability to make contact – between the self and the rest of the world, between self and other – is essential for growth. When defences are utilized to evade the contact boundary, the self does not remain open and capable of development; instead, there is a fixated stasis that restricts the life of the individual. Erving and Miriam Polster write clearly about the importance of contact and the risk involved:

> Contact is not just togetherness or joining. It can only happen between

separate beings, always requiring independence and always risking capture in the union.[21]

But we can both fully develop only through contact:

In contacting you, I wager my independent existence, but only through the contact function can the realization of our identities fully develop.[22]

Change and growth occur naturally through contact:

Contact is the lifeblood of growth, the means for changing oneself and one's experience of the world. Change is an inescapable product of contact because appropriating the assimilable or rejecting the unassimilable novelty will inevitably lead to change.[23]

The Polsters describe the difference between contact and joining:

What distinguishes contact from togetherness or joining is that contact occurs at a boundary where a sense of separateness is maintained so that union does not threaten or overwhelm the person.[24]

In our own Dynamic Empathy Model, contact opens up the possibility of resonance and inclusion. In these stages, the sense of separateness is maintained and togetherness is possible. However, the possibility of union or joining – in our terms 'fusion" – still remains.

Gestalt Therapy and Resistance
Perls and his co-authors wrote:

In the usual character-analysis, the resistances are 'attacked,' the 'defenses' are dissolved and so forth. But on the contrary, if the awareness is creative, then these very resistances and defenses – they are really counterattacks and aggressions against the self – are taken as active expressions of vitality, however neurotic they may be in the total picture.[25]

Psychoanalysis, Reichian therapy and gestalt therapy all see resistance as more than mere defence; in all these approaches, resistance has meaning to be uncovered. The gestalt approach diverges from psychoanalysis and Reich in that "resistance is not considered a mechanism or tool of the self; it is seen as the self *itself* in action ... both the defense and the defended are self."[26]

Take a situation in which a client becomes angry at the pain experienced in a deep tissue massage. An analyst might interpret the anger as a transference projection, believing that the client is (for example) exhibiting unresolved issues with his invasive father. A Rolfer might try to convince the client to inhibit or bypass an emotional response so that the work can continue to a "new place" for the client's physical structure. A Reichian approach could use breathing and touch to facilitate release of the anger, to undo the body armouring and allow streaming of energy. A gestalt therapist, however, would see both the tension in the body and the client's response of anger toward the therapist as valid expressions of the client herself. Seeing both defence and the defended as aspects of the self, gestalt therapists do not attack the resistance, but work with the client to appreciate it, to become more aware of it. The goal is to allow the client's full expression and ownership of the tension and the pain and the anger. The therapist is intent upon helping the client make the messages from the body intelligible.

> To the Gestalt therapist, to break down or eliminate resistance would be the same as breaking down and eliminating a capacity of the self. Resistance in this view is an expression of self.[27]

The exploration of resistance can be accomplished through the gestalt experiment. For example, the practitioner might encourage the client to exaggerate tension in a holding area and explore the feelings that accompany this. An angry outburst at the practitioner might lead to encouraging the client to physically push back at the therapist, or convert the feelings of lashing out into pounding on a foam block. The range of possibilities is extensive once a practitioner has familiarity with experimentation with resistances.

Contact Boundary Resistances
The standard contact boundary resistances in early gestalt theory were confluence, introjection, projection and retroflection. To this list, the Polsters added "deflection." Instances of these boundary phenomena can have pathological or non-pathological aspects.

CONFLUENCE
Confluence involves the loss of boundary between the self and the environment. This may occur in ecstasy, extreme concentration, and ritualistic trance states. When it is pathological, it can result in loss of identity. The pathologically confluent person doesn't know who is doing what to whom. The defensive use of confluence involves "going along" with trends, rather than asserting an opinion or a desire; little energy is invested. In confluence, people might not get to do what they want, but also they don't have to take responsibility for what occurs. Confluence is an inadequate basis for relationship; when there are not clear boundary distinctions, little genuine contact can occur. This is the issue in the co-dependent relations that addicted people frequently have, evidencing their lack of boundary clarity. To reiterate the possibility of both

pathological and non-pathological instances of confluence: it might be appropriate for an infant and mother to merge, or become "confluent," but inappropriate for a client and therapist. If client and therapist become confluent, the client's learning is inhibited because the therapist is experienced as an extension of the client, rather than as a separate being.

INTROJECTION

Gestaltists distinguish between introjection and assimilation in relating to the environment. Normal growth involves the capacity to discriminate, which is a function of the ego-boundary. With discrimination, a person can *assimilate* his or her experience by de-structuring and digesting it. If swallowed whole, without discrimination, however, the experience is said to be *introjected* and the person is less able to develop his own personality. The introjector passively incorporates what the environment provides, expending little effort to identify personal requirements or preferences. If two or more incompatible concepts are introjected, attempts to reconcile them may result in personality disintegration. In relationships, the introjector does as others would like him to do. This is a common situation when a child is being "good" and does as the parents wish without questioning, which can be especially problematic as the child grows older. For example, a young person who becomes a doctor because his parents want him to, ignoring his own desires, will likely experience the consequences of introjection.

PROJECTION

Projection involves disowning aspects of the self, ascribing them instead to the environment. The environment is made responsible for what originates in the self. The problem with this is that the individual abdicates responsibility and becomes passive and powerless to effect changes. Much of gestalt therapy is dedicated to overcoming the irresponsible, energy-restricting effects of projection. For example, if a client complains that his father does not want to talk with him, the therapist might turn this around, and ask the client to experiment with the idea "I don't want to talk with my father." In this experiment, the son might discover that he has some participation in the alienation from his father. In a situation where a client is disowning a body experience through projection, the use of "I-statements" is useful. For example, "It hurts" can be restated as "I hurt."

RETROFLECTION

By reinvesting energy into the self instead of directing it outwards, a person limits interchange between the self and the environment. The retroflector gives up trying to have an effect on the environment, becoming a separated, self-sufficient isolate. In this process, self-destructive behaviour often is a substitution for aggressive impulses that one is afraid to direct out at others. The Polsters describe retroflection:

> Retroflection is a hermaphroditic function wherein the individual turns back against himself what he would like to *do to someone else*, or does to himself what he would like *someone else to do to him*. He can be his own target, his own Santa Claus, his own amour, his own whatever-he-wishes. He condenses his psychological universe, substituting manipulation of himself for what he conceives of as futile longings for attentions from others.[28]

Talking to oneself is a retroflection, a division of oneself into the one talked to and the one talking. As with all these resistances, retroflection can be useful as well as pathological. Sometimes, it is helpful for a person to grant themselves what they have not experienced from others; for example, people can gain some comfort from holding themselves instead of asking to be held, or complimenting themselves instead of asking for approval from others. The self is substituted for the environment. This does not go all the way to resolution, which necessitates contacting others. But it can be a useful step:

> Movement that breaks the immobilization and restores live energy to the system is movement toward eventual restoration of contact with the outside world even though it may, in the intermediate period, be directed towards one's self.[29]

DEFLECTION

Deflection is a means of avoiding sustained or significant contact. The deflector engages with the environment on a haphazard basis, with only a few actual connections, which are mostly accidental. Examples of deflection include circumlocution, excessive verbiage, laughing off what one says, avoiding eye contact, being vague rather than specific, not getting to the point, excessive politeness in place of directness, talking about the past instead of the present, talking *about* rather than talking *to*, and shrugging off the importance of a topic under consideration. The deflector either does not invest enough energy in engagement for it to be sustained, or invests it without focus so that the energy scatters and disappears. The Polsters describe the defensive and life-inhibiting function of deflection:

> Deflection is a maneuver for turning aside from direct contact with another person. It's a way of taking the heat off the actual contact.[30]

We include exercises in programs at The Haven where we ask people not to respond when hearing another person's feeling towards them, whether positive or negative. Many people find this quite difficult – the urge to laugh off or otherwise deflect even a "compliment" can be very strong. As they become aware of this tendency, people may choose to more fully experience the "heat" of the actual contact.

Gestalt Therapy and the Body

"I am my body" is the catch-phrase that sums up the mindbody awareness process used in gestalt and other forms of humanistic psychology. James Kepner introduces his book *Body Process* with the following statement:

> What happens to us as persons happens to us in physical ways as much as in psychological ways. We live not only through our thinking and imagining, but also through moving, posturing, sensing, expressing. How, then, can we ignore the fundamental physical nature of the person in a profession where the aim is to heal the self, the whole person?[31]

In the gestalt approach, the self is embodied as well as thoughtful. People experience themselves in their body movements and sensations, just as they experience themselves in their thinking, imagery and ideas. Human growth and self-development occur through physical as well as mental interaction or contact with the environment. Gradually people learn to adapt and relate to their environment, developing patterns of life and interaction. Kepner writes:

> Just as the patterns of family interaction, behaviour, or sense of self become persistent, so too does the way in which we shape our bodily nature until it is so habitual that it seems a part of our bones and fiber.[32]

He describes how this becomes a physical pattern in the body:

> What was a momentary and flexible *process* of adjustment becomes a constant and fixed *structure* of your body posture.[33]

Frequently, the bodily aspects of self are disowned through the process of objectification, making the body a "thing." When the body is an "it" rather than an "I," people curtail their experience of themselves and their relationship to their world. Body patterns and habits and movements are disowned, and not immediately available as self-referents for growth and learning. Disowning of bodily feeling and sensation is done through tension; this tension blocks the body experience from sensation, awareness and expression. Kepner says:

The self has been split into parts and is in conflict with the self. The emotional conflicts that are most important to the individual, and thus are persistent, inevitably become structurally manifest in the body.[34]

Gestalt therapy practice is experiential and phenomenological. The practitioner concentrates on how the client experiences the body, rather than merely analyzing the client's body structure. This orientation underlies the gestalt "experiment" – a creative investigation into activities that can help the client heighten awareness. Kepner summarizes:

> The Gestalt body therapist is interested in finding ways for the client to experience the body more fully and to define the meaning of these experiences for himself or herself, rather than in interpreting the client's body and experience.[35]

Perls differed from Reich in his view of body processes in two major ways. First, Perls did not see physical expression, and withholding of expression, as merely the product of internal conflicts and events; rather, he saw this in the context of contact with the environment. Second, as Kepner suggests, Perls was not so much interested in body movement and expression in themselves, as in *how the client experienced them.* Kepner says, "His concern was with the client's sense of self, the "I" of experience as an embodied self."[36] He continues:

> To Reich the muscular resistance was a defense that impeded the course of therapy and proper functioning, and therefore must be broken down and eliminated. To Perls and the Gestalt therapist, the muscular tension is an ego-function, part of the self, albeit disowned and unaware.[37]

Perls would first focus on body sensation to enhance awareness, and then work with the client to undo the muscular repressions as the meaning was revealed. Reich had the idea that the body can be used as an analytical tool; Perls took this idea further. The physical body and its expression is a process in itself, and can be dealt with phenomenologically as a pathway to awareness, beyond mere analysis.

Kepner maintains that gestalt therapy has not been developed as a full range of somatically focused techniques to the degree that has occurred in Reichian approaches and Rolfing. He thinks that the use of breathing is better understood in Reichian work than in gestalt therapy. (In our own work at The Haven we have made breathing a central part of gestalt-type experiences.) Perls was critical of methods that attempted to train the body mechanically to relax or change posture. He did not hold an idealized vision for the client, and rejected change for the sake of change. He maintained that malpositions and stances are expressions of the self; his approach was to bring awareness through gestalt experiments, which often involve movement.[38]

> The value that Gestalt therapists place on action and movement is one of the things that distinguishes Gestalt therapy from some other insight-oriented therapies. Awareness remains lifeless unless the blocks to the transition of that awareness into action are freed. This is what makes Gestalt therapy an *expressive* therapy as well as an insight and existential therapy.[39]

In the gestalt approach, movement or action brings the client into contact with the environment. Kepner describes the importance of action in the process of a fully lived life:

> It is through action that we move what is inside of us – our energy, liveliness, vitality, needs, feelings – across the organism/environment boundary.[40]

> We express our commitment and courage to be fully in the world when we carry our feelings and needs into the environment: when we express our caring or sadness, protect our integrity, move with grace and exuberance, voice what is unsaid, reach out for comfort or contact.[41]

Gestalt therapy practice uses many expressive physical exercises, movements and vocalizations that can help the client to reintegrate disowned actions. Some examples are hitting or kicking a foam block, twisting or biting a towel, vocalizing emotionally laden sounds or phrases, stamping, reaching out, hugging and comforting oneself. Expressive movement in gestalt therapy is more often in the form of experiment, rather than as set exercises (as for example in Lowen's bioenergetic work). Movement may start as a deliberate exercise, but the nature of the gestalt experiment means that movements can be modified as required to reflect the expressions that a client is missing.

Catharsis can occur dramatically in this type of work, but it is not an end in itself. The main goal is enhanced awareness of one's patterns of resistance, and enhancing connections with one's world.

Gestalt Therapy Work with Transference and Other Projections

Transference is a term used to describe a projection that occurs between a client and a therapist. In daily life, people commonly project onto others; what makes a projection a transference is that it occurs in the context of the therapeutic situation. The gestalt therapist will work with transference issues, which are seen as the client organizing the present encounter in terms of the *felt realities of the past*. In other words, the client experiences feelings in the present, directed at the therapist, which are habitual feeling responses based on projections from the past.

For example, the client might feel irritation if he thinks the therapist is not paying full attention. In order to work through this transference, the therapist would encourage the client to mobilize and express the energy of the felt reality, acting out his emotions towards the therapist. This is done through breathing and experimentation, in order to find a way of physicalizing the feelings (for example, by loud vocalizing, or twisting a towel). Once this is done, the client can be assisted to take ownership of his feelings as a projection. The therapist and client can investigate the meaning of the experience with such questions as "When else in your life have you experienced this?" With a skilled facilitation, the client can become more aware of the projections from the past that have been interfering with contact with the therapist in the present. When the client takes ownership of the feelings and expresses them, more genuine contact is possible with the therapist as a person, rather than an object of projection of past feelings. The client shifts from blaming the therapist for the feelings to the awareness that the feelings are a consequence of the client's expectations.

Perls devised an ingenious technique to deal with different elements of a gestalt, called the "two chair approach." For example, if the client has two inner voices, one dictatorial and harsh, the other gentle and passive, Perls would assign the voices to two chairs. The client would be instructed to sit on one chair, then the other, to inhabit the feelings and body sensations of each voice fully. The client would be encouraged to use the two chair positions to have an interaction between the two voices. This was often referred to as "underdog/topdog" work. This two-chair technique can be modified to suit various situations. For example, Perls would commonly work with transference projections directed to him by telling the client to "put Fritz on the empty chair." Then he would encourage the client to give full vent to the feelings towards the Fritz on the chair. He was very skilled in helping clients to take ownership of the projection, thus helping them to be more responsible, more autonomous, and less transferred to him.

The Authors' Work with Projections

In a related fashion, we have often worked with clients' unresolved feelings towards their parents. In our groups, a common situation involves a "mother projection" wherein a younger person (we'll call him Jim) becomes aware of having negative feelings to an older person in the group (we'll call her Ida). We encourage Jim to express the negative feelings to Ida (after obtaining Ida's permission and participation).

We maintain safety by insisting that physical acting out be only done to inanimate objects (such as a pounding block or a towel). In working with the feelings, we encourage the client to breathe deeply, become embodied and give full vent to the feelings, often with loud vocalizing. This usually results in some form of physical release (a feeling of relaxation, or spontaneous crying). As Jim settles into his newly revealed feelings, we might say, "Now look at Ida and tell her what you are experiencing." This often evokes personal feelings in both Jim and Ida. We also ask Ida to share her experience, and she can respond with her own personal feelings and awarenesses from her own life. Jim has the opportunity to see Ida as a genuine person in the present, separate from the mother projection; as he finds tender feelings to Ida, he is encouraged to explore the possibility that he might also have these for his mother. At the same time Ida can gain awareness of her own projections onto younger people, and understand how this can interfere with her interactions. Both the original projector (Jim), and the object of projection (Ida) can gain awareness and become more present in the moment.

Projections interfere with contact. As people take ownership of their projections, they gradually recognize that what they have been projecting are aspects of themselves. We have had the experience of a young woman complaining bitterly in a group about "my mother, the bitch," with numerous examples of how unfeeling and controlling her mother was. Some months later, we met the mother as a participant in another program, and found her to be warm, compassionate and relaxed. We had a different experience of the mother than the daughter did. We told the mother about this, and she laughed warmly, saying, "Yes, my daughter has a lot of difficulty with me. I hope she can someday get over it!" Sometime later, we worked with the daughter again, told her how we experienced her mother, and helped her to see that her representation of her mother was where she had trouble, not the actual person who is her mother. Mother and daughter ultimately worked together to resolve these projection issues (they each had projections onto each other), which were limiting their genuine contact in the present. In working with such projections, you never deal with your real mother, but with *your version of your mother* – which is you, not her, and which can be integrated by taking it back to yourself.

Dream Work

Perls disagreed with Freud's view of dreams as representing unconsciously disguised intrapsychic conflicts. Gestalt therapists, more in line with Jung, view the dream "as creative expression rather than camouflage."[42]

Perls himself liked to work with dreams, and many of the transcripts of his work contain dream work sessions. He would ask his client to report the dream in the present tense, in order to convert memory into a current action. To Perls, the structure of the person was in the dream content. He didn't want people to talk *about* the dream; rather he encouraged them to express the feelings that accompany the stating of the dream sequence. In this way, he would encourage a person to live the dream through and integrate it with awareness. To Perls, all parts of the dream are aspects of the self. He often would get different aspects of the dream to interact with each other, guiding the client to take ownership of each of the parts, which he saw as unconscious projections of the self. He wrote:

> I believe that every part of the dream is a part of yourself – not just the person, but every item, every mood, anything that comes across.[43]

We ourselves, in our occasional work with dreams, find the gestalt approach to be efficient and practical. We use Perls' method of relating the dream in the present tense, to convert the memory into present feelings and actions. Then we might use gestalt or psychodrama techniques along with breathing to mobilize the fixated energy.

Gestalt and Intuition: Reading Energy

The concepts of gestalt psychology with which we started this chapter, and which were taken up by the gestalt therapists, offer some useful insight into questions about intuition and "energy reading." Consider the following description of a pencil drawing depicting three people meeting:

> It requires a certain training to see lines on a sheet of paper as three people having a conversation. For a dog, it would be a sheet of paper with lines on it; not a picture.[44]

Human beings learn to interpret the lines and put them together in a "gestalt," a wholeness, to see the "picture" rather than just lines on a paper. The person who looks at the paper fills in the missing elements to make a whole picture. Just as it is possible to do this with an ordinary drawing, one might also do this in reading the pattern of "energy." To the trained eye of a person practised in reading energy, more connections of significance appear. In Colin Wilson's novel *The Philosopher's Stone*, a character with enhanced psychic abilities describes them as well-honed intuition: "I was simply able to see deeper than an ordinary person," he says.[45]

With this understanding, 'reading energy', as for example in classical

Chinese medicine, is not as strange as it might seem. In gestalt terms, one is seeing the whole, including the invisible associations between elements and their activities. The classical Chinese doctor was able to "read" a person's energy by feeling pulses, and thus delve deeply into the *patterns* of that person's being, physically, mentally, emotionally and spiritually. This notion of the "pattern" is central to Chinese ideas in health, medicine, and indeed in society. One could easily substitute the word "gestalt" for the word "pattern." A Western doctor learns to "read" the significance of seemingly disparate symptoms, including the psychological/emotional factors that the patient is not speaking. In the West, psychotherapists learn to "read" the family dynamics, the energy of a system. Some, in the tradition of Reich and others, utilize the idea of energy reading in the body – detecting hidden relationships between things and events, a *pattern* that can be described as "energy." And as we have seen, the gestalt therapists themselves developed creative, practical and powerful methods for investigating and working in the present with these often hidden patterns.

The Art of Living

Gestalt therapy is an art, which can only be learned in direct human contact, perhaps guided by a skilled teacher. In this way, becoming a here-and-now people worker can be likened to becoming a fine actor, painter, sculptor, or dancer. You might have a lot of raw talent and desire. And you can get some of the rudiments and perspectives from books (including this one). But the art – you must develop this in your own being, in your own body, through your own effort and dedication and breath and practice. Having a teacher is helpful, especially at the beginning stages. Furthermore, you need a willingness to experiment (experiment is of paramount importance in gestalt), to discover for yourself. Finally, you learn not only from a teacher, but from the patterns of life itself. And we are all students, until our last breath.

> *Do you want to live, to BE?*
> *If your answer is yes,*
> *comfortably, oh so comfortably*
> *slightly, slowly begin*
> *an invisible nod "yes."*
>
> *You are the way.*
> *Don't stop here.*
>
> – Reps[46]

II.15 Unusual Realities

KZ = Confucius (Kong Zi), CJ = Carl Jung, BW = Ben Wong, JM = Jock McKeen

JM: In the last chapter we touched on some of the gestaltists' ideas about "neurosis" and "criminality." Basically they thought that people had problems making contact, trouble finding a balance between themselves and the rest of the world. We've talked about this a bit before, but I'd like to continue our conversation. Dr. Jung, you worked with so-called psychotic people in your training ...

CJ: Yes.

JM: What did you learn?

CJ: They were often more honest than I was. They were in touch with other realities. I was taught they were crazy ... but I sensed that, in some cases, they were more open, more sensitive, to other hidden dimensions.

JM: So you became interested in them, rather than dismiss them as mere cases?

CJ: Yes. In particular, I was interested in people who had psychic experiences. My cousin was a medium, and in my family, séances and the idea of communicating with departed souls were not unusual.

KZ: Interesting. In our Chinese culture, we also have a connection to the ancestors. Many homes have a shrine with the photographs of deceased relatives, who remain in the family through the honouring of them. To the Chinese people, the idea of the closeness of the dead brings much unease, since we tend to believe this is possible.

BW: I saw people in psychiatry wards who had special talents, including, I think, paranormal abilities. Some of my patients experienced voices and visions that challenged me to open up my viewpoint to the possibility of other realities.

CJ: As I mentioned, this was a factor in my separation from Freud. He adamantly refused to accept that for some people, issues of God or psychic realities are important. He dismissed them all as mere illusions.

JM: Whereas, to you, they were just unusual realities?

CJ: Yes, that's right.

BW: When I was training, and in practice, some of my most talented and insightful patients were those who had been dismissed as psychotic. But as I saw it, the problem was one of connecting and communicating. I'm with the gestaltists on that. People entered what I could call "craziness" or "psychosis" when they disconnected from other people, and their environment. They became lost in their own inner world of imagination.

CJ: When I was in my retreat period and investigating my inner worlds, I feared I would go crazy. So I made sure that I kept a regular schedule, which included time with my family and associates, and I had a regular practice where I was responsible to be present with my patients. I think I could have become psychotic if I had not disciplined myself to keep a regular connection with usual reality.

JM: What has been called "craziness" is just being unrelated, out of touch with usual reality, not in contact.

CJ: Exactly! I believe that people can bring themselves back if they want to do it. Often, they have to learn the skill and practice being present. But if they are willing to learn and make the effort to stay in contact, they can keep touch with usual reality.

BW: This was a cornerstone of my work. I believe that people need to take responsibility for all their situations, including whether or not they go crazy. I vividly recall a group I was leading with Jock that had two participants who both flirted with psychosis. They were women of a similar age, but they dealt with their situations very differently. One decided to learn how to get hold of her so-called craziness, became more grounded, and poured her unusual sensibilities into developing her art creations. The other woman did not want to be responsible for her situation, and refused to acknowledge her part in the going crazy process. She ultimately ended up in a locked psychiatric ward because she insisted on not taking care of her reality contact.

KZ: How did this come to be?

BW: Instead of eating and sleeping, she would stay up night after night, fascinated with the visions she was having. As her physical condition declined with sleep and food deprivation, she had more and more difficulty staying in touch with others. We were urging her to eat and sleep, and come back to contact, but she seemed to be in a romantic affair with her visions. Remarkably, when she woke up in the locked ward, she was shocked and asked herself, "What have I done?" She immediately set to work to learn to keep herself grounded through diet, sleep and regular contact (which she had to learn in counselling). She made very fast gains, and never returned to the psychiatric ward again; instead she worked to help others learn what she had discovered about taking responsibility for psychological illness.

JM: I recall those two people very well. We devoted a lot of attention to teaching our counselling students the skills to help others become grounded and make contact.

KZ: A remarkable and fascinating story! So far from my experience – but it makes sense.

JM: Yes, this has been most interesting ... and our discussion leads very nicely into the next chapter, which explores further some of these ideas about contact and connection.

II.16
A Psychology of Dialogue

Therapy consists in experiencing the self in a wide range of ways in an emotionally meaningful relationship with the therapist. – Carl Rogers[1]

From Objectification to Dialogue
We have already seen that psychology was profoundly influenced at the beginning of the 20th century by Freud, who aspired to cast the net of the medical model over psychological understanding. Maurice Friedman, from whom we'll hear more below, acknowledges Freud's importance:

> Sigmund Freud is one of the great Promethean explorers of our age who has pushed back the limits of human knowledge. No one in our age can have an image of man which has not been in some decisive way influenced by Freud.[2]

Friedman also contends that the Freudian style of therapy objectifies people and misses what is specifically human. In the situation of the analyst "treating" the patient, there is a dichotomy of roles wherein both parties are depersonalized. There has been an evolving trend over the last century to a more existentialist-humanistic view. Existential psychotherapy, says Rollo May, "is based on the assumption that it is possible to have a science of man which does not fragmentize man and destroy his humanity at the same moment as it studies him."[3] He notes that "Eastern thought never suffered the radical split between subject and object that has characterized Western thought, and this dichotomy is exactly what existentialism seeks to overcome."[4]

The shift in focus from diagnosis and treatment to relationship has developed gradually. The traditional objectifying approach is still prominent, but more human elements have emerged in the work of different practitioners and theorists. Wilhelm Reich added insights about body and energy, expanding psychotherapy past the limitations of purely mental interactions, but his work remained set in the analytic framework in many ways. Alfred Adler was a bridge from Freud's objectifying view to a perspective more focused on equality and interpersonal communication. Fritz Perls and gestalt therapists such as Erving and Miriam Polster introduced notions of contact, boundaries, and being in the here and now. Martin Buber, Carl Rogers and others spoke further for a humanistic viewpoint and Maurice Friedman, Richard Hycner and Lynne Jacobs have focused on the integration of existentialism, gestalt and dialogue. In this chapter, we discuss the work of the innovators whose perspectives have helped us in our own investigation of dialogue and relationship.

Dialogue

Martin Buber's book *I and Thou* is foundational for understanding dialogue, though Buber's writing is not easy to digest. In addition, different translations suggest different nuances of meaning. Even the 'word pair' of the title is variously rendered: the more familiar term "I-Thou" is sometimes "I-You." We will use I-Thou and I-You interchangeably here, depending upon the sources we are quoting. Buber writes,

> The attitude of man is twofold in accordance with the two basic words he can speak. The basic words are not single words but word pairs. One basic word is the word pair I-You. The other basic word is the word pair I-It.[5]

He asserts that the "I" of human beings is twofold:

> … the I of the basic word I-You is different from that in the basic word I-It.[6]

Furthermore, there is no "I" distinct from the contexts that these two words depict:

> There is no I as such but only the I of the basic word I-You and the I of the basic I-It.[7]

These two "basic words" depict two different human worlds:

> The world as experience belongs to the basic word I-It. The basic word I-You establishes the world of relation.[8]

Buber, as an existentialist, proposes that full being arises only in I-Thou relationship:

> The basic word I-You can only be spoken with one's whole being. The basic word I-It can never be spoken with one's whole being.[9]

Dialogue occurs in an I-Thou relationship when two people witness each other humanly, beyond projections and objectifications, and share their individual experiences with each other. According to Buber, certain "elements of the interhuman" must be present in order that dialogue can occur in an "I-Thou" process. These elements include *presence, genuine and unreserved communication,* and *inclusion.*[10] Lynne Jacobs defines presence as "bringing the fullness of oneself to the interaction." "Genuine and unreserved communication" involves the willingness to share one's thoughts and feelings, even when one is fearful of how they might be received. Inclusion involves imagining the reality of the other while still retaining one's own self-identity. We discussed this in Part I in our Dynamic Empathy Model.[11]

Richard Hycner says, "A genuine dialogical approach requires a radical paradigm shift from an individualistic model of the self."[12] He refers to the "between" as a ground of relationship:

> Any contact and awareness work needs to be grounded in the "between." Out of this "between" arises an awareness and differentiation of self from not-self.[13]

Erving and Miriam Polster emphasize the contact boundary in their Gestalt therapy work:

> The contact boundary is the point at which one experiences the "me" in relation to that which is not "me" and through this contact, both are more clearly experienced.[14]

In our Dynamic Empathy Model, we see contact as the initial phase of establishing an interpersonal relationship, which requires further development to become fully dialogical. In our sequence, contact emerges from the isolated position of objectification and develops as the interpersonal feeling is established. Richard Hycner distinguishes between dialogue and contact:

> All dialogue is contact, but not all contact is dialogue.[15]

I and Thou
Buber described the "I-Thou" relationship as being an elemental tendency to combination, and the "I-It" relationship as a natural separation. These are not morally tinged concepts; they simply refer to contact and separation, similar to contact and withdrawal/resolution in the Gestalt Experience cycle. Hycner explains:

> The I-Thou experience is one of being as fully present as one can to another with little self-centred purpose or goal in mind. It is an experience of appreciating the "otherness," the uniqueness, and the wholeness of another, while at the same time this is reciprocated by the other person. It is a *mutual* experience. It is an experience of profoundly valuing being in a relationship with this person. It is an experience of "meeting."[16]

In contrast, Hycner describes the I-It stance:

> In contrast to an I-Thou moment, the I-It stance is thoroughly *purpose-full*. There is a goal in mind. There is a subservience of the personhood of the person to this goal. It is an objectifying of the other. Everyone must, at times, have to do this in order to accomplish a goal. It often is a by-product of so focusing on a goal that the other persons become secondary. It is an inevitability of human doing.[17]

He notes that when one is task-oriented, the I-It stance becomes more foreground:

> At times the task takes precedence over focusing on the relational: the task becomes figure, the "other" becomes ground.[18]

While asserting that the I-It is natural, and not a moral issue, Hycner does suggests that there is a serious imbalance in human life:

> The I-It attitude is not wrong, or evil: Rather, it is its overwhelming predominance in the modern world that is problematic, even tragic.[19]

We agree that people need to live in both I-It and I-Thou. But dialogue occurs only with I-Thou. The most human experience is through dialogue in relationship with another. The I-Thou relationship is always temporary, and both parties will inevitably return to the I-It world. But without intimate relationship, people are severely stunted, as Buber emphasizes:

> And in all the seriousness of truth, listen: without It a human being cannot live. But whoever lives only with that is not human.[20]

In our own relationship, and in work with clients, the I-Thou moment emerges when the impediments to direct communication are relinquished. Sometimes this happens in a conversational interaction, where we share our feelings, interpretations and perspectives with each other. At other times, it occurs after a moment of revelation by a member of a group, which provides an invitation to the other group members to drop their defences and share openly. The I-Thou does not persist, but gradually recedes to be replaced by I-It once again. A creative, healthy life involves finding a dynamic balance between the two states.

Gestalt Therapy and the Dialogical

Fritz Perls' catch phrase "I and Thou, Here and Now" has long been seen as a ready encapsulation of gestalt therapy. But Perls has a different interpretation of "I and Thou" from Buber. Although Perls does write of "We," he values individualism more. His main goal is personal growth and awareness, more than relationship. For Perls, an interpersonal encounter is a vehicle for awareness, rather than a goal in itself. This is evident in the following passage from Perls:

> The *We* doesn't exist, but consists of I *and* You, is an ever-changing boundary where two people meet. And when we meet there, then I change and you change, through the process of encountering each other.[21]

Perls valued being present, aware, and independent. His "Gestalt Prayer" with its famous line "I do my thing and you do your thing" was purportedly written by Perls in reaction to the symbiotic merging of individuals without regard for each other's boundaries that he frequently observed in his day. For Perls, autonomy is of ultimate importance and he is cautious of the pitfalls of dependency in relationship. Maurice Friedman says,

> For the therapist as well as the patient, Perls recognized that the alternation between contact and withdrawal is a healthy one and that the extreme of either is pathological. But in the end, I-Thou was for him a means to the end of autonomy, rather than a value in itself because autonomy was, to him, the final goal.[22]

In our view, Perls' style was at times similar to the Synanon "shot-calling" approach that was common in the 1960s, where one person in a group would be on the "hot seat" and others would barrage that individual with criticism and admonishments to change. We found this approach to be moralistic, dismissive, and contemptible. Perls was prone to tell a client what was so for the client, rather than acknowledge that he was merely expressing his own perspective.

John Enright, a student of Perls, explicitly rejected this approach. Rather than tell someone, for example, "You are boring me," he would use a personalized I-statement such as "I am finding it difficult to listen to you." Enright's style was decidedly dialogical:

> The goal we set for the patients as they sit down together in a group or family is an I-thou relationship in which each person is aware, responsible, and direct in his own communications and listens as fully as possible to the other person as an equal.[23]

Also in contrast to Fritz, his wife Laura Perls valued both autonomy and interdependence. "What was important for her," writes Friedman. "was not how she 'did therapy,' but rather how she was with people. In this she proved herself to be as dialogical as her husband Fritz ... was not."[24]

Our colleagues Erving and Miriam Polster were well aware of the human dilemma regarding contact and separateness:

> All our lives we juggle the balance between freedom or separateness, on the one hand, and entry or union, on the other.[25]

> We each need individual space and, at the same time, there is a potential loss if we insist on our "territorial rights."[26]

> We see all around us how the reduction of contactfulness can choke man into a condition of personal malaise which festers amid a deadening accumulation of habits, admonitions, and customs.[27]

The Polsters' personal and professional relationship is a testimony to their belief in dialogue. They succinctly describe the wonder of meeting:

> At the moment of union, one's fullest sense of his person is swept along into a new creation. I am no longer only me, but me and thee make we.[28]

Turning Toward, and Inclusion

The preliminary and necessary step in establishing a genuine dialogical connectedness involves what Buber termed "turning toward the other." This requires a momentary turning away from self-preoccupation.[29] Hycner elaborates:

> This "turning toward" is far more encompassing than what is ordinarily meant by "attending." It is viewing the other in her/his unique "otherness" – which is different from me, and any of my needs.[30]

A genuine dialogue proceeds beyond contact into inclusion, which Hycner defines as

> an existential turning of one's existence to the other and the attempt to experience that person's side as well as yours. In the true moment of inclusion, neither side of the dialogue is ignored.[31]

This is a rare experience, one that requires strength, courage, and caring. One must remain centred yet flexible if one is to accomplish the "back-and-forth movement of being able to go over to the 'other side' and yet remain centred in [one's] own existence."[32] In our work this ability is developed through practice of the Communication Model.

Dialogue in Therapy

The process of dialogical psychotherapy involves a steady attempt by the therapist to establish a genuine relationship with the client. Often, the client is unprepared for such an encounter, and is incapable of moving past the projections that objectify the therapist, maintaining an I-It stance. As the client gradually works through projections and other impediments to the flow of the gestalt experience cycle, genuine meeting become more possible.

Change occurs organically in this atmosphere. The therapist does not try to change the client or force awareness. Rather, awareness emerges in the relationship. Lynne Jacobs writes:

> The acceptance of the I-Thou relation permits a deepening of awareness, and is itself an embodiment of the prerequisite for change, which is acceptance of what is.[33]

The I-Thou relationship is, however, not equal in therapy: the client is the focus and there are restrictions to the extent of friendship between therapist and client outside of the therapeutic situation. Even so, writes Friedman,

> The one-sided inclusion of therapy is still an I-Thou relationship, founded on mutuality, trust, and partnership in a common situation, and it is only in this relationship that a real healing can take place.[34]

Carl Rogers was a pioneer in humanistic psychology. He espoused a similar sort of relationship in his Client-Centered Therapy; he later called this a Person-Centered Approach, reflecting his view that personal engagement should not be limited to therapy, but is relevant in other contexts too. Although Rogers' style is characteristically nondirective, it is not mere laissez-faire, but rather involves an active acceptance of the client as a worthy person for whom the counsellor has genuine respect. Rogers says that a person comes to accept others through self-acceptance; as this is fostered through the acceptance of a child by a parent, so it can be nurtured by the acceptance of a client by a counsellor.

For Rogers, the nuclear concern of therapy is not past memories, exploring problems, or developing awareness. The central issue is direct experiencing in the therapy relationship. In *On Becoming a Person*, published in 1961, Rogers describes his transformation as a therapist from being a dispenser of treatments, to recognizing that changes occur through experiences in a relationship.[35] He came to believe that the more genuine he was, the more aware of his own feelings, the more willing he was to share his feelings and attitudes, the more the therapeutic relationship became growth-enhancing for the client. He also notes the importance of acceptance and respect for the other; the more one can find this, the more one is helping to create a relationship that the client can use. This involves curiosity and caring, free from moral or diagnostic evaluation.

When I hold in myself the kind of attitudes I have described, and when the other person can to some degree experience these attitudes, then I believe that change and constructive personal development will *invariably* occur.[36]

He describes his fundamental attitude, which moves beyond objectification into dialogical relationship:

I enter the relationship not as a scientist, not as a physician who can accurately diagnose and cure but as a person entering into a personal relationship. Insofar as I see him only as an object, the client will tend to become only an object.[37]

Rogers believed that the most effective traits for therapy are *congruence, unconditional positive regard,* and *empathetic understanding.* When counsellors expresses their feelings, which might even include boredom or irritation, they overcome a barrier to communication and their clients are more inclined to respond in kind with genuine revelation. Rogers summarizes:

Personal growth is facilitated when the counselor is what he is, when in the relationship with his client he is genuine and without "front" or facade, openly being the feelings and attitudes which at that moment are flowing in him ... It means that he comes into a direct personal encounter with his client, meeting him on a person-to-person basis. It means that he is being himself, not denying himself.[38]

While this humanistic evolution was occurring in North America with Rogers and others, the dialogical approach was also developing across the Atlantic Ocean. Harry Guntrip, an important contributor to the British object relations school who worked extensively with detached, withdrawn, schizoid patients, wrote in 1969:

The psychotherapist must be primarily a human being who has faced and sufficiently understood himself to be worthy to be admitted into the patient's private pain and sorrow. He will understand the patient's inner life ... because he can feel with and for the patient; and he knows, not just theoretically but in his own experience, what the patient is passing through ... Only that enables the patient no longer to feel alone.[39]

Guntrip echoes Buber in his assertion that the experience of relationship brings the possibility of breakthrough for the client:

What is therapeutic, when it is achieved, is the 'moment of real meeting' of two persons as a new transforming experience for one of them.[40]

The Authors' Perspective: Group Work and Relationship

Our goal is always to discover connection. Our work focuses on breathing, undoing fixations, mobilizing energy, releasing, becoming more aware – all of this as preparation for enhanced contact and awareness. This can occur in a private one-on-one hour with a therapist, and it can readily occur in a group. The approach should be tailored to the specific situation of the client.

To us, the attitude of engagement is more important than what methods are used. Regardless of the technique used in working with a client – body work or gestalt or psychodrama or acupuncture or dream work – we always aim to bring the individual into contact with the others in the room, and to share humanly. When we worked in private practice, we saw the client's relationship with us as an important feature of the work. When we work in groups (which we have done almost exclusively for the past 40 years) we always focus on helping the person doing the work connect with the rest of the group. Once the individual work is done, we ask the other attendees to share their feelings; we are not so interested at this point in observations, and definitely not in analysis. We are interested in the possibility for more *contact* between the person who did the work and the others who witnessed it.

In the group process, everyone can learn by participating with caring attention. Everyone can benefit, not just the person who is the focus in the centre. If people pay attention during the individual's process, remaining aware of their own thoughts and feelings, they can identify any meaning the experience might have for their own lives. Often new group members are surprised, and sometimes unsettled, by how deeply they feel for the sufferings and anguish of others. As they learn about resonance and open sharing, they discover how they can develop their own awareness of themselves and their connection with others. What they learn in the group can help them with their daily lives. We always say that the real work of the group begins when it is over – the challenge for participants is to take what they have learned and translate it into their regular lives with co-workers, family and friends. For us, relationship is at the centre, always.

The Communication Model and the Dynamic Empathy Model are keys to all this. As people learn to access their thoughts and feelings beyond their conscious or unconscious preconceptions, they come to see others with soft, fresh eyes and open hearts. They discover how to connect with themselves and others. We encourage them to take home what they have learned and begin the long practice of the art of living in dialogue with others.

Beyond Therapy

We have long maintained that therapy is a temporary engagement; the ongoing work for people is in their own lives. Contact between counsellors and clients is limited by professional boundaries. Our wish is that people extend what they learn in our groups into their personal relationships. Thus we have consistently urged our clients to establish an intimate friendship with a peer and work on their deepening communication together.

We have embraced a learning, educational model, letting go of much of the medical-therapeutic model. In our groups and seminars, we encourage participants to think for themselves and come to their own conclusions about what kind of life they want. On the way, we teach them communication processes, methods to breathe more effectively, and ways to release the body and the mind from habitual constraints. Ultimately, it is up to each individual how he or she chooses to live. People first need to clarify what they want in their lives, and then settle into the process of living with clear goals and intentions.

People can learn much on their own. But our lives are severely inhibited in isolation. Humans are relationship beings; we believe that people can realize their fullness only in dynamic relationship with at least one other person. For this reason, we encourage people to develop the skills to communicate clearly, honestly, and openly with themselves, and with others. Furthermore, we recommend that people practice these skills as a life style. In our longer programs, we frequently advise people to establish an "intimacy experiment" with one other person for the duration of the program, wherein they agree to devote time each day to being clear and sharing with each other. In the program, this is a practice engagement; however, the eventual objective is to establish an ongoing dialogical relationship with at least one other person. This intimate other need not be a sexual partner; indeed, many times intimacy is easier with someone who is not a sexual partner. We wrote about this process and many of the tools and methods in our book *The Relationship Garden*.[41]

For us, this is a spiritual practice in Tillich's sense of finding meaning. As people get to know each other more clearly, they can increasingly find the acceptance and curiosity that takes them deeper. They are able to experience the liberation of unshackling from previous constraints and addictions. As the process deepens, being in dialogue becomes more foreground and people can find freedom from fixations, objectifications, and self-limiting behaviours.

Therapy and counselling are fine along the way. But eventually, we each must live the life we choose, and live without dependency upon a therapist, counsellor or teacher. We all have to forge our own way. In dialogue, self-reliance can be achieved in concert with another. We are still existentially alone and responsible, but we can share.

> Love consists in this, that two solitudes protect and touch and greet each other. – Rilke[42]

PART III

Chinese Philosophy

Fire

Fire is associated with the summer season and the sun at midday. Fire expresses the heat and expansion of the life force. It is said that "creatures recognize each other" in the sign of fire; thus Fire is associated with the awakening of psychic consciousness and interhuman communication. With Fire comes the contact that begins the transformation from isolation into empathy. The potential of Wood is manifested in the stage of Fire. Fire is expansion, realization, execution, warmth, heart, love and connection.

III.1
The Place of the Yellow River

On our second trip to China, we made a journey to Xi'an, the area of the Yellow River, to see the ancient sights. This is reputed to be where calligraphy and writing began, and is near the birthplace of Confucius. There we met Feng Zheng (Sean Feng) and began a decades-long friendship. He was at that time our tour guide, and was exemplary in teaching us about the dynasties of ancient China and showing us the museums and historical collections. Jock had studied Chinese philosophy intensively for years; now he wanted to fill in the gaps in his knowledge of Chinese history and so studiously took notes as Feng spoke. As we wandered around, Jock noticed, again and again, evidence of Daoist and Confucian symbols and design that were not mentioned by Feng, nor by the museum's guidebooks. Also, having visited many Christian cathedrals in Europe and North and South America, we were struck by the presence of the cross in the architectural design of the space. We had been aware of the arcane meaning of the cross, to represent the four directions; North American aboriginal people, for example, had incorporated the cross and directions into their medicine wheels.

Jock would say things like, "See that symbol? That's an old Daoist icon. Look at this – the museum is actually an old temple laid out as a cross to mark the four directions. The ancient roots of China and the ancient roots of the Christian world have similar iconic structures." Linda Nicholls, who was accompanying us, took Jock aside and whispered, "Have you noticed that every time you speak about what you see, our guide is taking notes?"

So Jock was learning from Feng, and Feng was learning from Jock as we discussed ancient China. Feng knew the official history but not the expunged philosophy; Jock knew the philosophy, but lacked knowledge of how it fit into the modern Chinese context and the official Chinese version of history. We began to talk more openly about this with our studious guide. Thus began a dialogue that has continued for nearly twenty-five years. Feng eventually came to Canada and studied at The Haven for many years. We have returned to China over and over to assemble these missing pieces. Often when we have taught in China, Feng has been our interpreter.

Jock was intensely interested in the Confucian library we visited in

Xi'an. The ancient writings were mostly on carved stone tablets called "steles," large erect creations that contain the words of the Master for posterity. The following poem marked our experience, which has been pivotal in our learning and growth in studying East and West.

Forest of Steles

(Xi'an, November 1988)

At the top of the garden
of the ancient Confucian temple grounds
we are surprised to recognize
the buildings are laid out to form
a cross
marking the four directions

Inside
cold winter sunlight,
remote in dirty high windows
casts pale shadows across uneven floors

Imperturbable
lines of stone tablets
stand in the silence
as they have for centuries
row on row
facing forward, without speech
ancient reminders of enduring attitude
patiently waiting for the sensitive
to be initiated

Moving closer
in the dim light
I see
sharp characters,
cut deep
into the smooth erect stones
dancing across time

Silence hangs dense
in these timeless chambers
a church of ancient mysteries

Another room
crammed with stone treasures
        filled with an insistent, rhythmic sound
Whap! Whap! Whap!

        the pads of the stone rubbers slap
ancient figures reappear as spectres
        from other times
on the thin paper mounted on the stones

        How strange –
paper derived from a living plant
        now serves to bring life to images
forever cut into lifeless stone
        death   and   rebirth   amidst   the   stone
garrisons
which hold the forms for future generations

        Life again
and again
        where there appeared to be
only cold smooth
        waiting

        Emotion swells
as I find what I have been searching for
        the place of the Yellow River
bringing new images
        from an archaic time
        Our guide tells me that
the finest calligraphy
        sings –

music
        in the flow of the characters
prompts
        a response
deep within the chest
        of the human who listens

This was the centre of the world
Now the survivors of this time stand mute

except to one who has prepared
for the initiation

You must peer through the gloom
to make out the shapes
and in the dance of the characters
hear the rhythm
inviting the mind and heart to sing

How marvellous!
the outside appears so lifeless
yet the interior is teeming with vitality
a once-Confucian temple
now a museum for a government who
wants to forget
relics from another time
that I have grown to love

Inside my breast
is awakened
music, movement, colour
light, joy,
present with past time
Possibilities loom
seeking me to awake
urging my pen to finally move

– Jock McKeen[1]

III.2
Emptiness and Fullness

The four men are assembled again. Jock is eager to start the meeting and opens up the conversation with apparent restlessness and force.

JM: I have been trying to write about the Chinese classics and the evolution of Chinese thought and Chinese civilization. For me, the ideas and the subjects are very meaningful. But I am having difficulty getting started at this. Do you have any suggestions?

BW (chuckling): Well, I expect you're trying to condense the entirety of Chinese culture and civilization into a few chapters that say absolutely everything and resolve all the dilemmas of translation that have kept East and West apart! Perhaps you're biting off too much.

JM (sheepishly): Well, yes, I certainly do want to dig in and make a new mark on this.

KZ (benignly and kindly): Sir, do you know about emptiness and fullness?

JM: Perhaps ... I certainly have a shiver when you say this, much like I used to get when Reps would say something pithy. Please tell me more.

KZ: You are so full at this moment that you don't know what items to display. Just become empty and feel the deep resonance in your heart for all of life.

JM: I often feel this resonance when I listen to music. It seems to bring forth my feelings for nature, and our place in it.

KZ: Exactly. You have been trying to describe the Chinese way in ideas. But the Chinese way is first and foremost a feeling way. To do it justice, you must settle, relax and let the ideas flow from within, rather than reaching for them.

CJ: I am feeling aligned with you Jock. For years, I was eager to explain everything, even translating my ideas into different languages, and probing into alchemical language to try to get at the "meaning" of everything. But as I grew older, I realized that I must first relax before I can get anywhere with these ancient ways.

BW (still chuckling): My heart is warm with your fervent enthusiasm Jock.

You are so earnest. I hope you can listen to these men, and settle for a few minutes. Master Kong, please tell us more about emptiness and fullness.

KZ: There is nothing more to say once you are feeling it. The emptiness is always, and when we settle and accept, the depth of the earth and the bounty of the skies are ready to wait on us. Nature is our friend and servant, and the sky is our friend and servant.

JM: Now I am feeling moved. Can you tell me why?

KZ: I see that your mood and feeling have changed, and your eyes are now open. Your thinking brain is quieter, and you seem more at rest. Whenever you find this position of rest and stillness, everything else can be experienced in relation to it. From here, you will never lose your way. You are always at home, resting in the stillness.

JM (eyes tearing): This is so simple, yet so meaningful. And I am filled with gratitude that you can so gently help me find my way back to myself. I had been getting very wound up.

KZ (bowing slightly): This is my pleasure. I am enjoying the harmonious relationship with you men, and for me it is a privilege to listen and share.

CJ (also moved): Gentlemen, I have just been "brought down a peg" myself. Jock is a lot like me – intellectual, active, seeking – and I am prone to get lost as he does. (Nodding to Jock) Welcome back, my friend.

JM (now crying): Thank you.

BW: I feel so close to you as you humbly show your openness to us.

KZ: So, that is emptiness and fullness. This is at the centre of the Chinese way. The ancients knew this and tried to teach their people about it. But people have become lost in the fullness, and forget the emptiness.

JM: Thank you for your guidance, gentlemen. The ideas seem so vast, and to me they are so beautiful. Yet their elegance rests in their simplicity. I will try to show this.

III.3 The Book of Changes

The *Book of Changes* (*Yi Jing, Book of Transformations*) is one of the treasures of Chinese culture. Among the oldest of the Chinese classic texts, the written version of this book of wisdom is at least 2200 years old, compiled from an oral tradition that extends back into antiquity. Its influence on Confucian, Daoist and other thought has been profound. Legends tell of the shaman of old who would investigate the markings on the back of a tortoise or the spiderweb-like cracks on oracle bones, in order to discover the deeper meaning of circumstances and find a pathway to the most positive future. Over time, such methods of divination developed into an intricate system of thought, which was codified and ultimately written into the structure of the *Book of Changes*. Based on the concepts of *yin* and *yang*, the *Book of Changes* can be used to investigate the hidden meaning of situations. A core assumption in the book is that there is a pattern that underlies events, ever shifting and transforming. By seeing the movements of this pattern, one can come to understand the flow and unfolding of events in time. The more one understands the hidden patterns that underlie our daily life, the more one can become a responsible operator in life instead of a mute victim of fate.[1]

In consulting the *Book of Changes*, one asks a question and casts coins or yarrow stalks to determine which hexagram (made up of two trigrams, as explained below) applies. By reading the text associated with the hexagram(s), one can penetrate the meaning of the situation; thus one can learn in each of life's circumstances. Through dedicated contemplation and study, one can develop increasing freedom in this process of studying the hidden meaning of events; one can move from being a helpless victim of life, to becoming an ever-learning active agent.

This system is intricate, elaborate and very elegant. One of the authors (Jock) has studied the *Book of Changes* for over 40 years, and this has instigated much discussion between the two of us. The *Book of Changes* is a rich resource for study and reference for contemplating human beings' place in an ever-changing world. Ira Progoff described in detail a session he had in consulting the book with Carl Jung, saying that Jung "was convinced there was a deep and subtle wisdom" that "constituted an important area to be explored by the modern mind."[2]

Between Heaven and Earth: *Yang* and *Yin*
Human beings are born, live and die in the context of two poles, Heaven and Earth. The principal of heaven is *yang*, a moving force; the principle

of Earth is *yin*, the receptive quality that responds to heavenly *yang* by manifesting forms and structures. Heaven initiates life by its energetic activity and Earth responds by transforming the invisible energies of Heaven into the forms of life on earth:

> Whenever Heaven initiates life, breath (energy) is sent to Earth. Earth obediently receives and transforms, developing unceasingly the forms that correspond to the endless creative movement of Heaven.[3]

Time and space and the material universe all arise in the polarity between Heaven and Earth. In this context is human life, nature, and the life of all beings.

Yang and *yin* are not things; they are descriptive terms to express changing relationships. They are more like adjectives and adverbs than nouns. *Yang* is known as the creative force, and *yin* is receptive to *yang*. Traditionally, *yang* is associated with the father of creation, and *yin* is the mother that gives birth to all things. Any situation can be described (and thus clarified) in terms of *yang* and *yin*. *Yin* is dark, cold, still, feminine, receptive, nutritive, form, physical, deep; *yang* is bright, warm, moving, masculine, generative, stern, formless, nonmaterial, high.

Yin/yang is a very convenient and flexible construct to show the binary aspects of wholeness. They can be used to describe all situations and events. When considering anything (an idea, a phenomenon, a thing) *yin/yang* allows one to consider *all that this is not* at the same time. For example, up implies down, in implies out, and *yin* implies *yang*. The notion was probably derived from watching the day-night cycle (*yin* is associated with night, darkness, coldness and stillness; *yang* is associated with day, light, warmth and activity. This dual aspect occurs in many cycles, exemplified in the cycle of the seasons. The first aspects of the cycle (from spring through summer) are expanding, and therefore *yang*; the later aspects of the cycle (from late summer though autumn into winter) involve a closing, a compression, a quieting, which is *yin*. This *yin/yang* expanding and contracting goes on throughout all cycles (a daily cycle, a yearly cycle, a life cycle, an epoch).

The complementary opposites of *yin* and *yang* are often represented by the symbol of a circle with dark and light parts. The circle itself represents the unity of the cosmos. The dark portion represents *yin* and the light portion represents *yang*. The curved line demarcating the border between the dark and light parts shows the interrelatedness of *yin* and *yang*; the line is curved to indicate the organic nature of the flow between the related opposites. The small light circle within the dark portion indicates that there is always some *yin* within *yin*; conversely, the small dark circle within the light portion indicates that there is always some *yin* within *yang*.

Yin and Yang in The *Book of Changes*: The Structure of the Trigrams

By convention in the *Book of Changes*, *yang* is represented by an unbroken line (—) and *yin* is represented by a broken line (– –). By arranging *yin* and *yang* lines in groups of three, the ancients derived eight primary images (*ba gua*). These elemental arrangements are called trigrams in English. These trigrams (*gua*) represent the eight elementary "images" (literally symbols) that underlie the phenomenal universe. The following are the eight primary images and the trigrams that depict them.

乾 (*Qian*) Heaven ☰

兌 (*Dui*) Lake/Marsh ☱

離 (*Li*) Fire ☲

震 (*Zhen*) Thunder ☳

巽 (*Xun*) Wind ☴

坎 (*Kan*) Water ☵

艮 (*Gen*) Mountain ☶

坤 (*Kun*) Earth ☷

Arranging the Trigrams

The trigrams are arranged traditionally in two patterns, one for the *invisible world*, and another for the *phenomenal world*. These two arrangements facilitate understanding of forces and effects in the two different realms. The invisible world is depicted by the Sequence of Earlier Heaven (also called the Primal Arrangement), and the phenomenal world is shown in the Sequence of Later Heaven.

The Sequence of Earlier Heaven is the "world of idea" and underlies cyclic change and nonchange; the Sequence of Later Heaven is the world of phenomena, and operates as sequent change, within the laws of cause and effect. The Sequence of Earlier Heaven is chaotic; the Sequence of Later Heaven is linear, showing itself in time and space. Let's take a closer look at these ideas.

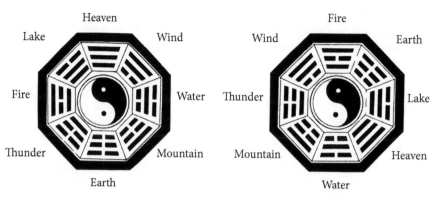

The Sequence of Earlier Heaven   The Sequence of Later Heaven

The Two Worlds: the Invisible and the Phenomenal

> The wind blows over the lake and stirs the surface of the water. Thus
> visible effects of the invisible manifest themselves. – *Yi Jing*[4]

The ancient Chinese notion of two worlds, the invisible and the phenomenal, is key to the understanding of the *Book of Changes*. Beyond
the world of familiarity, filled with things and events, is a hidden world,
largely invisible. The nonmaterial forces of the invisible world direct the
unfolding of activity in the material world.

The invisible world is beyond words, infinite and eternal. No constraints of space or time limit this world. There are no "things," no phenomena, no change, no separations, no distinctness. One could say that
the inner world, the invisible world, is the unity of the universe (in the
West we might say "God"). This world is a timeless unchanging flow of
forces that do not contradict each other.

The phenomenal world is the realm of time and space. Things come
into existence and ultimately transform and pass out of existence again;
all life beings are born, live and die in the passage of time in three
dimensions of material space. A characteristic of this material world
is the dualistic nature of phenomena; everything is in relationship to
its opposite (up/down, in/out, hot/cold, high/low, better/worse, male/
female). In this world is life and death and material existence.

This conception of two worlds is embedded in the eight primordial
images, which are formations in relation to a basic axis of heaven and
earth. The *Yi Jing* scholar John Blofeld describes the two worlds this way:

> The heavenly trigram, Chien, doesn't really mean heaven. It stands
> for the invisible world in which yin and yang archetypes act together

to produce the forms that are primarily represented by the so-called earth trigram which stands for the realm of form. So 'heaven' is the formless realm and 'earth' is the realm of form in which we find ourselves now.[5]

Much of classical Chinese philosophy rests on this notion of the two worlds, the interrelated concepts of change and nonchange and the flow of forces that underlies material existence.

Change: Living in harmony with the eternal flow

On a background of *nonchange* (the invisible and eternal world), are two different kinds of change – *cyclic change*, and *sequent change*. Cyclic change shows in the annual cycle of nature, where one season transforms into the next, and eventually the earlier season recurs for another repetition of the cycle. Many possibilities for change occur within this, but the cycle itself is stable; what is constant is change. At this level, cause and effect are not relevant. At the same time, the phenomenal world manifests "things" which go through transformations that obey the laws of cause and effect; these are sequent changes (changes in a sequence).

The ancient sages who studied the *Book of Changes* codified the ways the universe functions in these two worlds (the invisible and the phenomenal), and interpreted them over centuries, accumulating deepening understandings of the cosmic operations underlying nature and the human world. They saw the phenomenal world as a manifestation of eternal principles that are not constrained by time and space. The universe is in a pattern, a flow, which they called *dao*. When humans can distinguish the patterns of these forces and flows, they can choose to live in harmony with these forces.

The more individuals learn to be in balance and harmony with the universal flow, the more life-giving and regenerative will be their life process. Indeed, even set-backs and obstacles are only temporary situations for learning; when people learn to "go with the flow" rather than oppose it, their lives become enriched, nourished and regenerated by the cosmic forces. This is a key element in understanding the notions of Confucius (Kong Zi) about learning as well as the teachings of other Chinese sages such as Lao Zi and Zhuang Zi.

The Sequence of Earlier Heaven (the Invisible World)

The Sequence of Earlier Heaven (or the Primal Arrangement of the trigrams) was attributed to a legendary person of ancient times named *Fu Xi*. In this representation, Heaven and Earth are on a vertical axis opposite each other, representing the dualism that underlies the nonmaterial and the material worlds. On the horizontal axis, Fire and Water are primordial elements that interact and balance each other. In the same fashion, the other four *gua* are paired in complementary opposites.

Note that the trigrams are read from the inside to the outside (in other words, the bottom of any given trigram is closest to the centre of the circle). Recognizing this, close scrutiny shows you that each trigram has its exact opposite structure facing it on the other side of the eight-sided figure (if the lowest line is a *yin* broken line on one side, it will be a *yang* unbroken line in the trigram directly opposite).

This ingenious arrangement of broken and unbroken lines provides a basis to describe a double process of folding and unfolding; this double movement is the core of the pattern of ideas that underlies events. The *Book of Changes* states, "When the trigrams intermingle, that is, when they are in motion, a double movement is observable: first, the usual *clockwise movement*, cumulative and expanding as time goes on, and determining the events that are passing; second, an opposite *backward movement*, folding up and contracting as time goes on, through which the seeds of the future take form."[6] This interaction of complementary opposites underlies the process of cyclic change. The clockwise movement unfolds into time and space, while the backwards movement folds up as a seed principle into timelessness.

The Sequence of Later Heaven (the Phenomenal World)

The Sequence of Later Heaven (the Inner World Arrangement of the trigrams) shows the engineering of the world of phenomena, the unfolding of events in time. King Wen (*Zhou Wen Wang*) is generally credited with devising this arrangement over 3000 years ago. This sequence is read in a clockwise circular fashion, beginning at the left side of the horizontal axis, which corresponds in Chinese thinking to the east, the place of beginning, and the spring, the season of beginning. The sequence describes the cycle of the seasons, unfolding of vegetative life in nature, awakening in the spring after an apparent death in winter, and then going through another iteration of the process of sprouting, budding, fruit, seed and withering, decline and back to winter again. This is the process of sequent change, which obeys the laws of cause and effect, wherein "the forces of the preceding year take effect."[7]

The Two Arrangements and the Will of Heaven

By placing one below another, the trigrams can be paired to make 64 possible combinations, each one comprised of six lines. These are called hexagrams. It is these hexagrams and the texts associated with them that people refer to when using the *Book of Changes*, in order to better understand both the circumstances they find themselves in, the invisible world behind them, and, ultimately, the unity of the two worlds.

The Will of Heaven expresses itself in both worlds. Indeed, it is the unity that integrates the entire process of the two worlds. The notion of the Will of Heaven is an ancient concept referring to suprahuman forces that influence not only the lives of humans, but the entire universal order. Although this is often understood primarily as a *moral* order, it can also be understood without this right-wrong emphasis as an inclination towards harmony and balance. When someone disregards the Will of Heaven, misfortune is likely to follow, since harmony and balance are disrupted; conversely, an individual who follows the Will of Heaven can live in the most fortunate circumstances possible for each situation.

The invisible world often goes unnoticed, unless one is alert to find it in dreams and unexpected happenings. In literature, especially poetry, the hidden realm appears in imagery. As Jock once wrote:

> Beneath the impersonal hustle of daily life runs a quiet subterranean stream – a wellspring that trickles into the occasional moment.[8]

Wang Bi: Images, Text and Meaning

Wang Bi, a scholar said to have lived between AD 226 and 249, wrote a treatise that elucidates the relationship between the primordial images (ba gua), the words that describe them, and the meaning that can be inferred. Wang Bi exemplifies a classical Yi Jing scholar who studied the images of the oracle to penetrate more deeply into the meaning of life situations. Hellmut Wilhelm writes, "To Wang Pi, the I Ching is no longer a compendium of superstition or a playground for speculation, but a book of wisdom from which precepts for action and endurance are derived."[9] Wang Bi says that the eight images carry inherent meaning that can be described in words in order to clarify the images:

> It is the images that give the meaning, it is the words that make the images clear.[10]

He goes on with similes that elucidate his understanding:

> It is like following a trail to catch a hare. Once one has the hare, one forgets the trail. Or it is like putting out wicker traps to catch fish. Once one has the fish, one forgets the traps. Now, the words are the trails of the images and the images are the traps of the meaning … the images arise from the meaning … the words arise from the images.[11]

The images hold the meaning, and the meaning ultimately is the oneness of the universe. In our life situations, we are always related to the whole; difficulties arise when we lose sight of our place in the whole scheme and separate from this wholeness. The images show the relatedness of different aspects of a situation in order to "close the gestalt" and arrive at a complete picture, which places the situation in the context of the whole. In a Zen-like fashion, Wang Bi describes how one has to move past attachment to these vehicles:

> Thus, only by forgetting the images can one grasp the meaning, and only by forgetting the words can one grasp the images.[12]

This is the idea in Zen's "finger pointing at the moon." The finger is an indicator of where to direct consciousness; once the moon is seen, the finger is no longer needed. So too for the images in the *Book of Changes*; they are forms that can organize the mind towards deeper understanding, that can be released once the comprehension occurs. This is especially challenging for a Western mind, which tends to reify and hold onto separate elements. For example, neophyte dance students are tempted to analyze each distinct element; skilled teachers encourage students to "let go" and "feel the rhythm of the dance." The same applies in studying the images of the *Book of Changes*. The images and the words that describe them are tools of study that can help to clarify understanding. But they are not the object in themselves, and ultimately must be surrendered for us to enter the dance and participate in life fully.

The *Book of Changes* and Personal Responsibility

According to *Yi Jing* philosophy, hidden forces influence our lives. Hellmut Wilhelm writes:

> Not only is human action guided in those surface realms in which cause and effect can be surveyed with relative accuracy, but in addition this action is based on psychic strata not immediately accessible to consciousness but nevertheless, as individual and social agents, at least equally as significant as purely external influences – if indeed they do not surpass them.[13]

This could seem like a denial of personal responsibility, a passive acceptance of fate. But this was not so for the ancients. Wilhelm continues:

> The individual must adjust to the fated order of heaven and earth, and only then does the framework of reference emerge within which action is possible and is demanded. To be guided by the contents of such a system did not appear to the Chinese as a loss of freedom; they never felt it was incompatible with their self-respect to seek an example and a standard outside the limits of the ego.[14]

Father Thomas Kwan, former Dean of the School of Theology in Hong Kong and a personal friend, put it this way:

The Book of Changes regards the unconscious self as the basic stratum of conscious self ... the former sets up a clear guideline for the concrete decision of the latter.[15]

For Father Kwan, a Roman Catholic priest and theologian, there is no problem with divination, and he finds it quite compatible with living a Christian life:

Divination is a means to activate our unconsciousness, which provides us a frame of reference ... divination does not provide a final decision for moral responsibilities. It simply provides the trend or the movement of the ethical situation by which we make our actual decisions.[16]

Father Kwan goes on:

In a framework of the permanent principles of the Tao of Heaven and Earth, divination puts the user into a sphere of reference which includes the wisdom of the past (the oracles), the co-relation of events (the unconscious) and the concrete situation; then it leaves man to make a conscious and responsible decision, adaptable to the here and now.[17]

We ourselves find this approach to the *Yi Jing* compelling. Furthermore, we see parallels in the two worlds of the *Yi Jing* and themes in Western psychology, especially in the ideas of Jung. The Sequence of Earlier Heaven describes eternal principles beyond time and space that are operative in the depth of the psyche, generating primordial images that constellate into universal themes that inform the individual; this echoes Jung's collective unconscious or perhaps the *Self* archetype, or "God within." The Sequence of Later Heaven shows the movement of energy in the external world unfolding in the life of the individual, through a process that Jung referred to as individuation.

This is the human possibility, the opportunity to follow the Will of Heaven in an individual life on earth, working patiently to become ever more sensitized to cosmic forces that underlie events. In our own experience, although we live very much in the day to day, there are times when we glimpse larger contexts for our lives. The ancient Chinese believed that harmonious interaction between humans and the Will of Heaven was the key to life regeneration. This is living with the *dao*, the natural flow of the universe.

Man follows the earth.
Earth follows heaven.
Heaven follows the Dao.
Dao follows what is natural.[18]

III.4
Teachings of the Ancients

KZ = Confucius (Kong Zi), CJ = Carl Jung, BW = Ben Wong, JM = Jock McKeen

JM: Master Kong, you say that many of the ideas you taught were not from you, but passed on from the ancients.

KZ: Yes, this is so.

JM: Who were these ancients?

KZ: It's not "Who were they?" but "What are they?" As human beings, we think of a past history and the ancient beings as human figures in that history, but from a universal perspective, the ancients always were, always are, and always shall be. So it is not a question of "Who?" That's a human question. I would rephrase the question to "What is the nature of the ancients?"

CJ: This is what I gradually came to see in my journey into the unconscious. As a human, I anthropomorphized what I was experiencing and put a human face on many of the archetypal forces I was encountering. Now, after much study and experience with these forces and patterns, I think they are "more than human." They fit into the human context in some ways, but they are much, much more. They are the archetype of the self, timeless and spaceless, the image of wholeness.

JM: So they are not entities? Rather, "they" are a pattern beyond space and time?

CJ: Yes. When I had discussions with Einstein, I saw that his theories regarding relativity related to my notions of archetypes. Whereas human beings exist in a time/space world, the archetypes are timeless and spaceless.

JM: Ben, your mother was told by a Chinese fortune teller that you would be the reincarnation of a Chinese sage.

BW: Yes, this is a story in my family. But I have never made much of it.

JM (earnestly): Maybe you are Master Kong reincarnated!

BW and KZ and CJ all laugh at this outrageous but relevant suggestion.

KZ: I would be honoured if it were so, sir.

BW: Likewise.

CJ: I suggest something different. There are indeed deep and abiding truths available to the heart that opens and listens. Ben, I know that you are open to the ancient wisdom. The idea of reincarnation is a human conception; it represents in human language something that is trans-human, universal. So you are not Master Kong's reincarnated being, but you both share the same life, and you speak the same truths, albeit in different languages, in different times, in different places.

JM: I see this thread throughout the history of Chinese culture. For example, the ideas from the ancients, expressed so well by Master Kong, were later expressed by Sun Yat Sen in the early part of the 20th century. The ideas are the same – they're isomorphic, transformed into the context of the time period in which they are revealed.

BW: Sun Yat Sen's vision for China was a unified country where the central government listened to the peripheral states and local communities.

KZ: This notion follows the pattern of ancient politics. We Chinese have understood that the natural harmony is revealed when the rulers listen to the will of the people.

BW: This is like the North American aboriginal idea of the chief serving the people by listening deeply to them. The ruler governs by serving.

CJ: I think this was also the principle of ancient governance in the teachings of Lao Zi.

KZ: Yes. It is also the principle of leadership that is found in the *Yi Jing*, the *Book of Changes*.

JM: You studied the *Book of Changes* throughout your life, and you were responsible for many of the commentaries.

KZ: Yes, to me this is a treasure of the wisdom of the ancients, and I devoted much of my time to studying this important book. If I had another lifetime to live, I would concentrate on studying the *Book of Changes* more intensely than ever. This is a limitless storehouse.

CJ: I, too, was fascinated with this ancient book. I was very happy when the English translation brought this to the attention of people in the West.

JM: Dr. Jung, I read your introduction to this edition when I was in my twenties, and you helped to put me on a path of study into Chinese ways. I have returned to this book repeatedly since then, and I continue to find much wisdom in it.

CJ: It seems we are linked, we four, through the wisdom contained in the *Book of Changes*. It is a way that the universe speaks across time and eras.

BW: I think this can be discussed in terms of structuralism. In structuralist thinking, there are three levels – superficial, middle and deep. The superficial level of human endeavour is the individual unique pattern; this can be called the "idiosyncratic structure." In the middle is a social pattern that shows the behaviour of the community in which that person lives; this has been called "contingency structure." The deep level is the universal dimension, which has been called "universal deep structure."

KZ: That's interesting that they consider three levels, like we Chinese would do.

JM: I also see similar themes in your notions of archetypes, Dr. Jung. The archetypes are the deeper patterns that are revealed and expressed in each human personality in a unique fashion. In structuralist terms, these are the idiosyncratic structures of the individual personality. The individual interacts with contingency structures of the culture through the family and social connections. Underlying it all is the ancient wisdom of the universal deep structure, the archetypes. Do you agree?

CJ: Yes, this is an apt comparison. I chose the word "archetype," which literally means "ancient pattern," to indicate that timeless forces inform and direct life, not only today, but along through the ages.

JM: And this can be spoken of in Chinese terms as *dao*?

KZ: Definitely. The *dao* is the flow of the ancient patterns.

JM: The *dao* is thus expressed in the time and space incarnation of each person?

KZ: Yes. We Chinese understood that the task of the leader was to help educate the people into the ways of the deeper forces. Since most people are not leaders, they need compassionate and intelligent instruction to help them live the best life possible. It is the task of the leader to teach the common people to not make a mess, and to keep the world in order, by living in harmony.

CJ: There is a universal consciousness beneath culture. The task of the leader is to teach his people about this ancient wisdom and help them to express it into their own lives.

KZ: I agree with this view.

BW: The same applies to a caring psychologist or counsellor. The task of the leader (in this case the professional counsellor) is to help to educate his clients into a life style that is in harmony with their deeper nature.

CJ: When I was corresponding with Bill W., the originator of Alcoholics Anonymous, I suggested to him that the roots of addiction were a loss of spiritual connection. AA addressed this issue in groups of people with open sharing.

BW: We dedicated our professional careers to group process because of this same idea. We wanted to help people get in touch with themselves, and share with others. Our goal was healing, both psychological and emotional, to help them to open to a new world.

CJ: Goethe said, "What you have inherited from your forefathers, you must work to make your own."

KZ: His view was entirely compatible with the Chinese perspective. He said in his words what I believe. For myself, I saw the human being as the centre of growth and change. The more a person grew and developed, the more responsibility would come on his shoulders. If we are students of life, we have the task of working hard to learn the secrets, and then we have the responsibility to teach others what we have learned.

JM: Master Kong, we have devoted the next chapter to your teachings. I hope we have done justice to your profound contributions.

KZ: Thank you for bringing me into this presentation.

III.5   Confucius: An Early Humanist

> Confucius exerted great influence on Chinese philosophical development in that, first of all, he determined its outstanding characteristic, namely humanism. – Wing-Tsit Chan[1]

Along with Daoism and Buddhism (which we discuss in the next two chapters), Confucianism is one of the "Three Doctrines" or "Three Teachings" of the Chinese. Confucianism is a practical, human-centred philosophical approach with political and social overtones. It is not a religion and does not focus on superstition. That said, Wing-Tsit Chan clarifies, it is "not the humanism that denies or slights a Supreme Power, but one that professes the unity of man and Heaven. In this sense, humanism has dominated Chinese thought from the dawn of its history."[2]

While it is more common to trace humanism's roots to Greece of the 5th century BC – when the Sophists and Socrates "called philosophy down from heaven to earth," as Cicero put it – Confucianism too contains within it the germs of much later humanist, and also existentialist, thought.

Karl Jaspers, considered one of the founders of existentialism, called this period (very broadly around the 5th century BC) the axial age, "the point most overwhelmingly fruitful in fashioning humanity." While the West has focused largely on the achievements of Greece and Israel in this period, Jaspers is at pains to include the influence of the East – this was the time of Confucius and Lao Zi in China, of Zarathustra in Iran, and the Upanishads and later the Buddha in India.[3] In this axial age, wrote Jaspers,

> Man becomes conscious of being as a whole, of himself and his limitations. He experiences the terror of the world, and his own powerlessness. He asks radical questions. Face to face with the void, he strives for liberation and redemption. By consciously recognizing his limits, he sets himself the highest goals. He experiences absoluteness in the depths of selfhood and in the lucidity of transcendence.[4]

Confucius and Ancient Wisdom

Confucius (Kong Zi or Kong Fu Zi; traditionally 551–479 BC) was a thinker, social philosopher and government employee whose ideas have deeply influenced Chinese, Korean, Japanese, Taiwanese and

Vietnamese thought and life. He systematized much of the Chinese classical *Ru* thought, including concepts we touched on in our discussion of the *Book of Changes* (many of the commentaries on which are said to have been written by Confucius). Confucianism is thus an organized expression of the *Ru* philosophy that has been dominant in Chinese social and political life for more than two millennia. The Chinese characters making up the word *Ru* represent "human" and "necessity"; the word implies a virtuous scholar who cares about the harmonious functioning of society. A *Ru* must be first a scholar and teacher, focusing on the morals and order of their society.

"Confucius did not consider himself the author of what he taught," says Thomas Cleary, "but rather an heir and transmitter of ancient learning developed over the course of many centuries."[5] He believed he was revitalizing an ancient culture for posterity. That culture was "epitomized in the enlightened reigns of several illustrious leaders of ancient times, dating as far back as the twenty-fourth century BC, nearly two thousand years before his own time."[6] The ancient Chinese believed that there were beings of antiquity who were sources of much later wisdom:

> Huang Di declared: I know through tradition that at the time of high antiquity, there were authentic men who had grasped Heaven Earth, held yin yang in their hands, and breathed with the essences and qi. Established in themselves by keeping the spirits, in their flesh they realized the unity. And this is why they attained the longevity of Heaven Earth itself, which knows no end. Those men lived in the Way.[7]

Confucius lived at a turning point in Chinese history when the old feudal system of "saints on the throne" had broken down. Wilhelm says that Confucius, a man of the people rather than a ruler, "marks the point in Chinese history where the guidance of society passed from the theocratic ruler to the human philosopher."[8] Confucius maintained that leadership should come from learned scholars who have studied life deeply and have developed themselves in an authentic process of self-investigation and self-reflection. Such leaders are inspirational from the deep roots of their genuineness, and express without guile the forces of the universe.[9]

Whereas Lao Zi, the traditional originator of Daoism and an older contemporary of Confucius, was suspicious of attachment in the world and preferred a kind of detached philosophical mysticism, Confucius affirms the development of culture. Wilhelm writes, "His striving is only to preserve this development from becoming mechanically superficial and chaotically confused in its ideas of right and wrong and thereby to keep it supple and adaptable to the demands of the age and the locality."

The main texts of Confucian thought are found in three works: the

Analects (*Lun Yu*), the *Great Learning* (*Da Xue*), and the *Doctrine of the Mean* (*Zhong Yong*). In this chapter, we will take a look at some prominent Confucian themes as they occur in these texts.

Learning: Perspectives on A Famous Text from the *Analects*

The Analects of Confucius (*Lun Yu*), more literally "a discussion over Confucius' words," are usually interpreted in a political or a social way, but there can be a personal dimension to them too. Although many translators approach this text from a more *essentialist* viewpoint, seeing humans as relatively passive and helpless, having little influence, but rather conforming to the dictates of the universe, we believe that Confucius advocated individual development. Thus we translate his famous statement about learning in *Lun Yu* II.4 with a more individual perspective:

> At 15 I set my heart on learning. At 30 I was well established. At 40 I had no more doubts. At 50 I began to glimpse the will of heaven. At 60 I was ready to listen. At 70 I could follow my heart's desire without interrupting the melody of the universe.[10]

This "I statement" (where other translations might use "we") reflects a more *existentialist* understanding of the text and a more humanist view of man's place in the cosmos. Here there is an individuating autonomous being, making decisions from a self-chosen ethical standard, "without interrupting the melody of the universe." This individuating person is responsible for all his or her own thoughts, feelings, choices and actions, and their consequences. We find this view very fruitful. In this modern world, ancient writings and rituals become relevant when they are experienced within a current context. The West can embrace the treasures of the East and bring an existentialist viewpoint to bear upon them. Furthermore, we think that this existentializing, humanist viewpoint is closer to Confucius' own ideas than the more essentialist interpretations that have frequently attached to his tradition.

Li, Yi, Ren: A Frame for Self-Cultivation

In Confucian thinking there are three levels of concern, named *Li*, *Yi* and *Ren*. The most superficial level is *Li* (proper conduct, a gentleman, the rites and rituals, "ritually proper"). At a deeper level is *Yi* (righteousness, appropriateness), and the deepest is *Ren* (humanity, benevolence, goodness, humaneness).

We see these three levels as isomorphic with ideas we have set out earlier, reflecting human development from fusion to objectification, through contact and resonance to inclusion, which we have described in our Dynamic Empathy Model. The superficial level involves observing rules of social conduct; in the middle is a relatedness and contact beyond objectification; and at the deepest level (*Ren*) there is the connection to humanity. Confucius believed that people are all connected in their depths, and furthermore, an individual can learn to be in touch with this connection at all times. We ourselves subscribe to this viewpoint.

SUPERFICIAL: *LI* (THE RULES, ETIQUETTE, PROPER CONDUCT)
Parents and caregivers teach their children rules of conduct and, in their desire to please and be "good," the children learn these behaviours. These involve socially appropriate activities and rituals such as shaking hands, bowing, polite discourse, respectful body language and so forth, all of which are situation and context specific. These differ from culture to culture; in communicating with someone who was raised in another country, it is important to learn the "rules of conduct" that show human respect. The rules can be simple, such as a handshake between two people when greeting, or very intricate, such as the specific duties required of a best man at a wedding.

The proper conduct for Confucius is never arbitrary; it should always express the deeper human nature of caring and connection. *Ren* (humanity) is expressed in social contexts through *Li*. Confucius has often been misunderstood as being doctrinaire and rule-bound. But for him, the rules are not the important part; the relevance of rituals is that they provide a social shorthand for demonstrating connection and caring in human relationships. These formal rules of behaviour are ways to express deeper human values, not a substitute for human connection. *Ren* is expressed through *Li*.

This training of children in *Li* is useful to establish the patterns of conduct. In light of modern brain research and developmental theories, one could say that this helps to establish links in the nervous system that permit further and more expansive connections with higher brain areas at a later stage. The scaffolding of human development comes first with patterns and rules and the objectification involved in understanding roles and the behaviour attached to them. In learning to communicate, for example, a child needs to learn some basic "rules," such as when to speak (not just interrupting) or the need to stay more or less "on topic." The rules in themselves are not the goal, however. Learning them is intended to help communication and understanding between people. The other dimensions or layers are necessary for the person to become a full and freer being.

DEEPER: *YI* (RIGHTEOUSNESS, APPROPRIATENESS)
Whereas the rules (*Li*) can be executed in an empty fashion, they are most appropriately done with a sensitive appreciation of the context and everyone in it. The next level, appropriateness (*Yi*), allows for listening

to others and taking consideration for the world of the other. This facilitates the movement from objectification to empathy and curiosity and human consideration. This has been often translated as "righteousness" but it is much more than a moral right/wrong approach. The notion involves a sensitive awareness of what a situation requires, doing what fits so that no one is disrespected or disregarded or forced to stray from his or her inner nature. *Yi* involves a deep sensitivity to oneself, to others, and to life. *Yi* is a refined awareness of "what fits" the demands of a situation. In order to develop *Yi*, people must move beyond prejudices and utilize their genuine human concern (*Ren*). To express *Yi*, one lets go of a particular outcome:

> A proper man is not absolutely bent on, or absolutely averse from anything in particular, he will be just.[11]

The virtue of knowing and acting according to "what is right" is thus more than just living by the rules. A person sensitive to *Yi* is a team player with an autonomous conscience; one does not need the rules when one has the inner sensitivity of ethical conduct, a well-developed conscience. A person who lives *Yi* is motivated to cooperate and participate with others, not to seek personal selfish gain: "The proper man understands equity, the small man, profits."[12]

DEEPEST: *REN* (HUMANITY, CONNECTION)

The Chinese term *Ren* can be translated as human-heartedness, humanity, virtue, benevolence, morality, or goodness. In essence, *Ren* is what makes humans truly human and distinguishes us from animals. Individuals can develop themselves to express their *Ren* in everything they do. When people are expressing *Ren*, there is harmony. *Ren* means having a felt sense of one's heart connection with oneself, deep nature, and all other beings. Alan Watts notes that Confucius valued *Ren* above righteousness (*Yi*):

> For at the head of all virtues Confucius put, not righteousness (*i*), but human-heartedness (*jen*), which is not so much benevolence, as often translated, but being fully and honestly human.[13]

Watts quotes Lin Yutang's translation of the Confucian classic *Li Chi* (Record of Rites), where once again the connections with later humanism and existentialism are clear:

> True manhood requires a great capacity and the road thereto is difficult to reach.[14]

> The superior man goes through his life without any one preconceived course of action or taboo. He merely decides for the moment what is the right thing to do ... The goody-goodies are the thieves of virtue.[15]

The term 'superior man' used by Watts and others is a translation of *jun zi*. People become a *jun zi* by self-development, becoming more and more in touch with *Ren*. In the words of Confucius:

> He who in this world can practice five things may indeed be considered man-at-his-best. What are they? Humility, magnanimity, sincerity, diligence, and graciousness. If you are humble, you will not be laughed at. If you are magnanimous, you will attract many to your side. If you are sincere, people will trust you. If you are gracious, you will get along well with your subordinates.[16]

The notion of "superior" meaning "better" is somewhat of a Western interpretation expressed in the main translations. We think this was not necessarily Confucius' meaning. He more likely intended to distinguish between those who are sensitive and in harmony with the flow of the universe, in contrast to those who are out of touch with *Ren*. A *jun zi* is a person who is closer to the heart of life. These are the characteristics of such a person, from the *Analects*:

> Of Zichan, the Master said that in him were to be found four of the virtues that belong to the Way of the true gentleman. In his private conduct, he was humble and courteous, in serving his superior, he was respectful and punctilious, in providing for the needs of the people, he was kind, and gave them even more than their due; in ordering the people, he was just.[17]

Watts notes Confucius' humanistic notion of the 'righteous' person as one who is fully human:

> A true human is not a model of righteousness, a prig or a prude, but recognizes that some failings are as necessary to genuine human nature as salt to stew. Merely righteous people are impossible to live with because they have no humor, do not allow the true human nature to be, and are dangerously unconscious of their own shadows.[18]

We humans don't have to be perfect; indeed, this is an impossible ideal. The pursuit of the "ideal self" and the associated striving for perfection take us off the track of following the flow moment by moment. We believe that the process of self-development facilitates people being in touch with their *Ren*, their deepest nature.

The *Great Learning*: Translating *Ren* into actual living

The Great Learning (*Da Xue*), which includes Confucius' text and commentaries by Zengzi, is a small classic with great importance for Confucian thought and is a main text for the doctrine of *Ren*. Known in English as the *Great Learning*, it discusses the "eight steps": the investigation of things, extensions of knowledge, sincerity of the will, rectification of the heart, cultivation of personal life, regulation of the family, national order, and world peace. Wing-Tsit Chan describes the eight steps as, the "blueprints for translating humanity [*Ren*] into actual living."[19]

A basic notion is that all levels of society, from the individual to the family, to the nation, to the cosmos, are isomorphic with each other. The *Great Learning* describes the keys to development towards being in harmony with the universal rhythms. The goal is not for mere accomplishment; the development of the individual is rooted in the state of the heart and is the natural outgrowth of internal authenticity.

The practice of self cultivation aims towards a state of being and awareness that exemplifies an ethical approach to life. This cultivation is a process of self-development that has rippling effects through one's family, and further into society, and ultimately to humankind and the universe.[20]

> The great learning ... takes root in clarifying the way wherein intelligence increases through the process of looking straight into one's heart and acting on the results; it is rooted in watching with affection the way people grow; it is rooted in coming to rest, being at ease in perfect equity.[21]

There is an orderly procedure to this learning which emanates naturally from coming to rest in awareness:

> Know the point of rest and then have an orderly mode of procedure; having this orderly procedure one can "grasp the azure," that is, take hold of a clear concept; holding a clear concept one can be at peace [internally], being thus calm one can keep one's head in moments of danger; he who can keep his head in the presence of a tiger is qualified to come to his deed in due hour.[22]

Confucius saw learning in terms of the growth and development of a living plant. Knowledge can acquire a deep root, and a strong trunk from which supple branches of learning can extend.

> The virtue, i.e., this self-knowledge [looking straight into the heart and acting thence] is the root; the wealth is the by-product.[23]

He was insistent that leaders should keep self-knowledge as the root of life and let whatever wealth came from it occur naturally. He counselled against acquisitiveness and making accumulation of wealth a goal. Since all levels are isomorphic with one another, such inappropriate focus would invite a loss of humanity in the people and consequent violence against each other:

If he make the root his secondary object, and the result his primary, he will only wrangle with his people, and teach them to rob and despoil.[24]

The inner conduct of the ruler is the key to the healthy and harmonious life in the family and throughout the country. Most Chinese people are familiar with the following statement, showing harmony between individual, family, state and humankind:

The ancients who wished to illustrate illustrious virtue throughout the kingdom, first ordered well their own states. Wishing to order well their states, they first regulated their families. Wishing to regulate their families, they first cultivated their personal lives. Wishing to cultivate their persons, they first rectified their hearts. Wishing to rectify their hearts, they first sought to be sincere in their thoughts. Wishing to be sincere in their thoughts, they first extended to the utmost their knowledge. Such extension of knowledge lay in the investigation of things.[25]

Central to this process is the notion of filial piety, *xiao*. When children are raised with reverence for their parents and other family members, they develop a respect for others and learn their place in the family and in society. Children learn to respect their parents as the source of their life, and learn through this to cherish and respect their other family members. This becomes a framework for their discovery about their place in a larger world. The key is development of a sense of one's place, one's location, and a familiarity with the heart connection with self and others. When one goes astray, one can participate in a process of "rectification of the heart" to come into resonance with self, others, and the larger context. (This is sometimes translated as "rectification of the mind" but this neglects the Chinese notion of the heart-located synergy of thinking and feeling. For the Chinese, thought and feeling are intricately woven; both are the domain of the heart.) Rectification of the heart is similar to what we describe in our Dynamic Empathy Model as the process of moving through isolating fixations into the stages of contact, resonance and inclusion, which constitute human empathy. The individual who aligns with the deepest purposes of the heart finds enriching relationships with others, which can have ripple effects into the rest of society. This is at the core of the teachings at The Haven.

In line with the practice of "rectification of the heart," Confucius counselled against self-deception and advised constant self-scrutiny. Memorably translated by Ezra Pound, Confucius says (*Lun Yu* II.2)[26] that the ancient Odes, an anthology of 300 poems, can be gathered into the one sentence: "Have no twisty thoughts."

The Doctrine of the Mean

The *Doctrine of the Mean* (*Zhong Yong*) is another classic Confucian text. Whereas the *Great Learning* is concerned with social and political affairs, The *Doctrine of the Mean* is concerned more with psychology and metaphysics. Wing Tsit-Chan wrote, "The *Great Learning* discusses the mind but not human nature, whereas with the *Doctrine of the Mean* the opposite is true." He further notes, "The *Great Learning* is generally rational in tone, but the *Doctrine of the Mean* is religious and mystical."[27] The following is a summation of the whole work:

> What heaven has disposed and sealed is called the inborn nature. The realization of this nature is called the process. The clarification of this process [the understanding or making intelligible of this process] is called education.[28]

The task of education is to bring the animalistic nature into the service of the integrative heavenly nature that is inborn as a potential. This notion is not foreign to Christianity or other faiths from both East and West; it is the concept of taming the passions so that they can serve a more inclusive nature. The process of self-education involves constant self-examination and reflection:

> Only the most absolute sincerity under heaven can bring the inborn talent to the full and empty the chalice of the nature.[29]

The process of self-realization does not require striving, but only attentiveness, since there is in people a natural inclination to growth and awareness. One has only to focus on revealing the natural process:

> The inborn nature begets this activity naturally, this looking straight into oneself and thence acting.[30]

The individual who becomes adept at this process becomes an inspiration to others, to facilitate their learning and self-development. They, in turn, become teachers of others in a ripple effect:

> He who can totally sweep clean the chalice of himself can carry the inborn nature of others to its fulfillment.[31]

A person can first find the balance and harmony in themselves. Then they can help others to do the same. They can also become more insightful about the operations of life on earth, the ways of nature, and even of cosmic patterns.

> Getting to the bottom of the natures of men, one can thence understand the nature of material things, and this understanding of the nature of things can aid the transforming and nutritive powers of

earth and heaven [ameliorate the quality of the grain for example] and raise man up to be a sort of third partner with heaven and earth.[32]

Even if the process is not carried on to its ultimate cosmic conclusion, people can have full and meaningful lives by practising to the best of their abilities:

> He who does not attain to this can at least cultivate the good shoots within him, and in cultivating them arrive at precision in his own terminology, that is, at sincerity and clear definitions.[33]

Each contributes in his or her own way, at his or her own level. Such a life of clear practice encourages the manifestation of bounty, and an illumination that begins to bring changes. So the humble life of an earnest person has life-giving, regenerative possibility. Each person contributes to life and renewal in his or her own way.

> Proceeding in this manner, even a fellow who is a bit stupid will find the light, even a weak man will find energy.[34]

Remarkably, people who study diligently both the external life patterns and the structure of their own personality inclinations begin to see previously invisible threads that allow them to peer into the future. This is the essential teaching of the *Yi Jing*, which Confucius was said to have studied extensively. Such people develop what seem like supernatural spiritual strength and abilities.

> When calamity or happiness is about to come, the good shall certainly be foreknown by him, and the evil also. Therefore the individual possessed of the most complete sincerity is like a spirit.[35]

To Confucius, such people have undergone the process of enrichment through self-examination and honest discipline. They are manifesting life in its fullness. This is available to anyone who dedicates the time and effort with a pure heart. A realized person is not a soothsayer or wizard forecaster, just an alert human.

Self-examination, *Ren*, and the Feeling of Shame

We have already seen how the process of self-examination facilitates people getting in touch with *Ren*, their deepest nature. This is necessary for a true leader. Confucius believed that a ruler should function by serving the people, teaching by example, and "governing by the light of one's conscience."[36] The essence of leadership is found through learning, self-examination and continual practice towards the cultivation of character. "Government," says Confucius, "is rooted in men, it is based on man. And one reaches men through oneself."[37]

This idea leads to an understanding of *shame* that we think is most important:

> Confucius said, "To be fond of learning is to be near to knowledge. To practice with vigor is to be near to humanity. To possess the feeling of shame is to be near to energy [or near to courage]. He who knows these three things knows how to cultivate his own character. Knowing how to cultivate his own character, he knows how to govern other men. Knowing how to govern other men, he knows how to govern the kingdom with all its states and families.[38]

Many people think of shame as a negative thing. Writers confuse shame with guilt, or use the terms interchangeably. We have written at length about this topic in another book to distinguish these two from each other.[39] We propose that guilt is a condition of non-being when the self and others are objectified and separated from life. In contrast, shame is a condition of being, where the individual is revealed as truly human in an expansive, receptive open state of being. Confucius recognized, as did Buddhist scholars, that shame is a condition that arises when a human being is revealed, present and open. In ancient Buddhist texts, shame is one of the nutritive states of consciousness, in the same potency as love and compassion. Shame is linked with the courage of the heart, the warmth of connection with all of life, with *Ren*.

The "Inner Elasticity" of Confucianism

Confucianism has been in and out of favour at different eras of Chinese history. Yet the philosophy of the sage has arisen transformed over and over, with relevance to the time in which it recurs. In the 1930s, Wilhelm wrote:

> The most difficult test of Confucianism must be met in the present. For the European-Occidental civilization which has so irresistibly penetrated China is, of course, the most powerful enemy that Confucianism has ever encountered.[40]

How prophetic this was! These thoughts remain so pertinent in the tumultuous days of the early 21st century as China undergoes fantastic growth, and with it the challenges of asserting classical Chinese values in the global community. Wilhelm was certain that Confucianism "possesses sufficient inner elasticity to accommodate itself also to modern conditions … it will be a question of finding people who grasp these doctrines in their essential depth, and of finding new forms with which to make the old content alive."[41] Wilhelm summarized his vision:

If a reawakening of Confucianism ensues today, this reawakening will once more signify a new stage of development for Confucianism. But just here lies the secret of Confucius. As he naïvely took over Chinese antiquity and did nothing more than inspire it with new motivation, just so his influence has again and again been that of offering a new dynamic. And this spiritual impulse which he represented may, in all probability, have still further effect at the present time. It is only a question of the right people.[42]

To deeply penetrate to Confucius' meaning requires years of study. For ourselves whose native language is not Chinese, this has involved much pondering and comparison of different translations, and numerous conversations with our Chinese speaking colleagues and friends. We have found that for modern Chinese people the study is not easy either; although they have the basic language skills, they often do not have ready access to the rich cultural overtones and associations that are intricately woven into the apparently simple words of the Master. For us, the effort is well worth it – and at the same time we recognize that such study is not for everyone! We hope our summaries of our discoveries to this date are helpful for you. We continue to discover new riches in returning repeatedly to the teachings of Confucius.

III.6
Three Levels and the Heart

KZ = Confucius (Kong Zi), CJ = Carl Jung, BW = Ben Wong, JM = Jock McKeen

JM: Master Kong, it seems that the heart is at the centre of your teaching.

KZ: Yes. If people would learn to look straight into their own hearts and act according to what they see, they would be in harmony with the universe. This is not my idea – this was an idea from the ancient masters.

JM: If you ask a Westerner where he thinks, he will tap his head. If you ask him where he feels, he will touch his chest, over the heart. For them, the heart is the place of feeling and connection; the head is for thinking. So were you asking people to look into their heart and feel and connect, but not think?

KZ: Not exactly. To the Chinese, the heart can think and feel.

BW: As a Chinese person, I understand this. The Chinese people are different in their ways. Non-Asians think with their brains and feel with their hearts and guts. But Chinese people think and feel with their heart, and only calculate with their brains.

KZ: This has been our way from antiquity.

CJ: There is a basic split between mind and emotions in the West – between thinking and feeling. Some called the thinking way Apollonian, referring to the sun god Apollo. Thinking was associated with light and revelation. The other side is the feeling way, related to Dionysus, god of the dark places, and of wine and inspiration. So human nature is split into Apollonian and Dionysian. Apollonian is structured, logical, thinking. Dionysian is chaotic, earthly and feeling.

BW: So, the Chinese person does not have this Apollonian/Dionysian split that we take for granted in the West?

CJ: Not so much. For the Chinese person, thinking and feeling are done together, and cannot be fully distinguished. This does make a problem for Chinese people when they attempt to address abstract intellectual issues. On the other hand, it makes them much more ready to feel a human emotional connection to any subject.

JM: Thank you, Master Kong. I also want to ask you more about the traditional Chinese way of seeing things on three levels.

KZ: Well, since ancient times, we have seen everything in terms of three levels – heaven above, earth below, and human in the middle. The number three is very significant to us. It is the number of movement and transformation.

JM: Please tell me more. How does this relate to human life?

KZ: When we Chinese think about the universe, we think of three levels. Since a human being is part of the universe, these three levels also apply when considering an individual person. In an individual, the lowest level is associated with nature, and with the animal characteristics of our being. The middle level is the human level, the qualities associated with human society. The high level is associated with heaven, and addresses the spiritual qualities that are often hidden to a casual look.

JM: Is one level "better" than the others?

KZ: Of course not. They are all part of the structure of the universe. To make something better or worse involves a human overlay of morality. The universe is amoral.

JM: So there is heaven, there is human, and there is nature. How are they connected?

KZ: These three are separate, and one. They are not connected as such. They are different aspects of the same.

BW: They come together in the human heart.

KZ: Yes, this is the core of my teaching. The human being contains both spiritual (heavenly) forces and earthly (natural) forces. They are often in opposition, but they can be united in the heart.

CJ: Goethe said something similar – that there are forces of dark and forces of light, and they are in a battle. He noted that the outcome of the battle was determined by the individual in the decisions made through earnest self-examination.

JM: I want to continue with this idea of three levels. Chinese medicine considers three types of doctor – superior, mediocre and inferior. What is intended in the statement from the medical classics concerning superior, mediocre and inferior medical practice?

KZ: This is somewhat different than the notion of heaven, earth and human. The three statements from the medical classics are the following.

"An inferior doctor deals with symptoms only. A mediocre doctor deals with the people. A superior doctor deals with the country." Many Chinese people know this saying.

BW: This makes sense to me. In my medical training, I was constantly aware of the temptation to provide something for a patient to alleviate suffering, without considering the broader context. That would be the "inferior doctor" approach.

KZ: Yes, exactly.

JM: The mediocre way would be to go a little deeper, and see that patient beyond the symptoms, and address the contextual influences in the illness, including family dynamics and social concerns.

CJ: And the high level would be to see the illness as part of a much bigger picture, larger than the life of that individual. This is the spiritual level.

KZ: Yes. I know you gentlemen all understand this. In regard to the three ways, one is not better than the other. Each has its use. But the superior way is much more comprehensive and far-reaching.

BW: Some have said that a master doctor is somewhat like a priest, addressing the spiritual level of any illness.

KZ: Dr. Jung, this is what you were trying to do in your advanced psychology, going much deeper than conventional approaches to get to the level of spirit.

CJ: This certainly was my goal. I wanted to help people find their way in the big picture, which included their religious feelings and their more universal concerns.

JM: This modern Chinese idea of upper, middle and lower is actually a misrepresentation of the ancient *Ru* philosophy as I have come to understand it. Master Kong, please comment on this.

KZ: Yes, people are obsessed with upper, middle and lower, and miss the key point, that all levels are equally important and one is not better than the other. To be specific, there are two notions of levels - *shang/zhong/xia* (superior, mediocre, inferior) and *Li/Yi/Ren* (rules, awareness and humanity). People confuse these two "level" ideas.

JM: Please continue.

KZ: The former (superior, mediocre, inferior) refers to doctoring: a superior doctor deals with the country, the mediocre doctor deals with the people, and the inferior doctor deals with symptoms only. We discussed this already.

JM: Please say more about the latter – rules, awareness and humanity.

KZ: The latter *(Li/Yi/Ren)* is the basis of the ancient *Ru* philosophy. When people are in touch with their deepest humanity, they will naturally be in harmony with the flow of the universe and they will be aware of what is required in every situation, which means they do not have to slavishly follow automatic rules, since they will always do what is appropriate. This comes from a life-long study of self-cultivation. But people get caught up on whether they themselves are middle, superior or inferior, and miss the central point that it requires a life-long pursuit, not something that gets a grade or a report card.

BW: I like to think that each person is all three, and at any moment can choose to express middle, superior or inferior. In that way, we are not static beings; these three move back and forth from foreground to background.

CJ: Very insightful, Ben.

JM: What about the concept of the "superior man?"

KZ: Many people have interpreted the idea of *jun zi* to mean "superior man." But this is not what I intended with this concept. Indeed, women too can be exemplary people, and it is not an issue of superior or inferior. So neither the word "superior" nor the word "man" is appropriate.

JM: What did you intend with the idea of *jun zi?*

KZ: I only wanted to single out the individuals who are diligent in self-examination, who become more deeply in touch with life and themselves. I think I would translate *jun zi* as "one who knows the deepest humanity." These people are humble and do not promote themselves. They are not "superior" in any sense of worth. All beings have their worth. Superior does not mean more worthwhile; it just designates someone in touch with universal patterns.

BW: The other interpretation of "superior" comes from the Western idea of achievement, and the guru system has promoted this idea. If the students obey the master, they are said to be superior.

KZ: Yes, we talked about this in a previous discussion. To understand guru and master is an important key to becoming free of limitations.

JM: Master Kong, are you aware of the modern movie in China made about your life? It depicts you as someone who resisted nature and tried to dominate society. They say you wanted to be like a king, or at least to brainwash people into respecting the king of the day.

KZ (sighing): I know people see me this way. Too stiff, too rule-bound. But I only wanted to show people how the structure of the universe could be learned and practiced. I showed them "the rules" so that they could see the structure of life. I was very persistent, and did not sit back and "let nature take its course."

JM: So, you were "pushing the river."

KZ: In this way, I suppose I could be seen as pushing. I was different than Zhuang Zi in this way, who was more ready to accept without trying. But if I was pushing people to consider, it was so that they would think for themselves.

JM: I understand that Zhuang Zi believed one has to relax to the will of nature and give up trying to have an influence.

KZ: Yes, we were different in this way. I saw the value in making an effort.

JM: In modern China, there has been a resurgence of interest in the teachings of Zhuang Zi, and we talk about both him and Lao Zi in our next chapter, on Daoism. Master Kong, some scholars suggest that you and Zhuang Zi are not compatible in your philosophy. What do you say about this?

KZ: Master Zhuang and I had a difference in emphasis. But both of us had our focus on the *dao*, the source. So if we could talk, I think we would have much more overlap in our philosophy, and the differences would be interesting, not disruptive.

JM: What would you say were the main differences?

KZ: I wanted to emphasize education of every human, to develop his or her full potential. Some people are not experienced, or not privileged, and these people benefit from dependable principles by which to conduct their lives. People who have more curiosity and more opportunity to study can question the principles and develop unique approaches. Zhuang Zi wanted people to let nature have its way. He had his eyes on the sky; I had my eyes on the individual human being and the relation to the developing social order.

CJ: So the difference is one of focus and emphasis, rather than a fundamental disagreement. You were not merely interested in rules and regulations.

KZ: Definitely not. I tried to show people the rules of the universe as tendencies of how things flow, consistent with the ancient *dao*. But I never wanted them to blindly follow the rules without thinking them through for themselves. It would be no use if they accepted everything without consideration. They would not be humans; they would merely be monkeys.

JM: The Buddha taught, "Do not believe anything because I say it to you. Make it true for yourselves."

KZ: Yes, you understand. This was the spirit in which I tried to show people the rules of the universe.

CJ: The modern Chinese do not really understand you, Master Kong. Part of the problem is that some of your sayings are so familiar to them that they think they know the deeper levels of your teachings.

BW: Yes, they disregard the universal themes, thinking the ideas are superstitious or old-fashioned.

JM: Your character in the movie was middle level, not understanding the ways of nature, and needing your universalist teacher Lao Zi to set you right.

KZ: Yes, many think I am a middle man. But it is their lower and middle persons that see things this way. Since they are not in touch with the high level in themselves, they project their imagination of what they think high level should be, from their lower level.

JM: Since Ben has been my teacher, many people have seen me in this way too – as lower or middle level, needing instruction from a wiser person. (Then laughing) And for so many years, it was true!

BW: Yes, but Master Kong, in this way, they reduce what you have to say.

KZ: I don't care for me. I don't need to be important. To me it does not matter what level I am. These are just words.

BW: I feel bad for those who think they understand you, and dismiss you without knowing the breadth of your teaching. They miss out on harmonizing with nature when they disregard your teachings.

CJ: You do not speak for yourself. You speak for all the ages.

Confucius and Ben are both softly sad, and look meaningfully at each other.

BW (with moist eyes): Yes, it's sad how people prefer to project onto leaders rather than thinking for themselves.

KZ: This has been my longstanding dilemma: how to show people the deeper structure of the universe without their turning me into some kind of social director who teaches only rules.

BW: People see you in two inaccurate ways, either underestimating you or inflating you. They either see you as a low-level dictator who insists on the rules or some kind of guru who can teach them everything.

KZ: They miss that I am just another human being, learning through a life of practice. I am learning now, still, even in death. There is no end to the ancient teachings.

BW: I understand. You wanted people to be aware, awake, and responsible – to learn about life, and to be of service.

JM: Thank you all. This has been most illuminating. The next chapter is about Daoism, and especially the ideas of Lao Zi and Zhuang Zi.

III.7 Daoism

Daoism is a philosophical and sometimes religious approach that has been influential in China for over two millennia. Like Confucianism, it has its roots in classical Chinese thought, especially the *Yi Jing* or *Book of Changes*. Chinese people are steeped in both Confucianism and Daoism, in the way we in the West are steeped (whether we know it or not) in the ancient tales from the Old Testament. Northrop Frye wrote that for Westerners, "The Bible is clearly a major element in our own imaginative tradition."[1] The same is true of Daoism, Confucianism, and Buddhism in China.

The word *dao* literally means a "path" or a "way" and has associated with it a host of other meanings. Older methods of romanizing Chinese have used the words "Tao" and "Taoism." We use the more modern pinyin versions, *dao* and Daoism, except when we are quoting authors who have used the former spelling. *Dao* is the undefinable, unnameable, eternal, underlying, unifying principle upon which reality rests. R.L. Wing offers this explanation:

> Awareness of the Tao cannot be reached through the senses: it cannot be seen, heard, or felt. It resides in the realm of the intuitive mind and can only be perceived through its effect in the environment: its effect on ideas, events and social transformations. Worldly events occur in ever-repeating cycles, and those who follow the Tao learn to employ these cycles ... with an intuitive understanding of the patterns of life, the outcome of events can be apprehended and reality can be altered.[2]

Dao stands for what cannot be expressed in language. It is a signpost to a deeper reality beyond words and thought. Alan Watts called it "the ultimate reality and energy of the universe, the Ground of being and nonbeing."[3]

Daoism shares with Confucianism an emphasis on humanism, valuing compassion, moderation and humility. Central concerns in Daoism revolve around humans living in close harmony with nature and the cosmos; when one follows the "way," one can achieve health, longevity and success. Other concerns are *wu wei* (action through inaction), spontaneity, and freedom. One aligns with *dao* through the practice of *wu wei*. *De* (strength, virtue, integrity) is associated with living in harmony with *dao*. *De* is the cultivating of a life style that is in harmony with "the way."

Our own understanding of *dao* is of an ever-changing pattern, an invisible flow that manifests in the events of the material world. Gestalt therapist Barry Stevens' 1970 book *Don't Push the River (It Flows By Itself)* explicated her attitude to self-development and helping: stay out of the way and help people get into harmony with this flow. One could say that the movement of the gestalt cycle (which is interrupted with defences) is the flow of *dao*. When people are interrupting the gestalt cycle (or the Dynamic Empathy cycle for that matter), they are out of the flow of the *dao*. When people become aware of their interruptions and complete a gestalt process, they reenter the flow of the universe, of which they are a part. Becoming aware of the flow and letting go to join in the flow is the attitude of *wu wei*.

The emphasis in Daoism is not on a deity, but rather on learning about life in order to become harmonious with nature and all of existence. Daoism focuses on consciousness and learning, rather than moralistic rules of conduct. The emphasis is on the human experience in relationship to other people, nature and the cosmos.

In Chinese thinking, all is pattern, expressed in the Chinese character *li*. The pattern of heaven is the same pattern as that of the earth; heaven is non-material, while earth is physical. The human being exists at the interface of heaven and earth, and participates in both as another isomorphic pattern. The holistic Chinese approach sees that there is just one universal pattern expressed in different contexts: in this case, heaven, earth and human are three dimensions of expression of the universal whole.

The invisible *dao* can be seen displayed in the patterns of flowing water. Organic structures have this flow, which is seen in the grain of wood, wrinkles in a face, and the windswept curves of sandstone. Alan Watts writes:

> Tao is the flowing course of nature and the universe; li is its principle of order which ... we can best translate as "organic pattern"; and water is its eloquent metaphor.[4]

Watts notes that the concept of *li* embraces the organic order that is seen in nature.

> Li may therefore be understood as organic order, as distinct from mechanical or legal order, both of which go by the book. Li is asymmetrical, nonrepetitive, and unregimented order which we find in the patterns of moving water, the forms of trees and clouds, of frost crystals on the window, or the scattering of pebbles on beach sand.[5]

In the West, we would say a photograph is more true to the subject than a painting, which is more fanciful and subject to the artist's interpretation. But ask any Chinese person this question: "If you compare a photograph of a landscape and a painting by a Chinese master of the same scene, which will have a truer representation of the landscape?" Most will say the painting. The Chinese perspective allows that the deeper integrity of the landscape is not contained in the physical phenomenon; rather, its distinctness is in the pattern, the unique flow of *qi*, the energy of life, which is more deeply shown in an artistic rendering. This unique dynamic pattern is expressed as *li*. Alan Watts writes:

> The beauty of Chinese calligraphy is thus the same beauty which we recognize in moving water, in foam, spray, eddies, and waves, as well as in clouds, flames, and weavings of smoke in sunlight. The Chinese call this kind of beauty the following of li.[6]

The texts we discuss in this chapter are those associated with the names of Lao Zi (the *Dao De Jing*) and Zhuang Zi. Lao Zi is traditionally regarded as the founder of Daoism; Zhuang Zi developed the concept of *dao* with a different emphasis, especially in his understanding of *wu wei*, or action through inaction.

Lao Zi and the *Dao De Jing*

Lao Zi, the traditional originator of Daoism, was said to be an older contemporary of Confucius. There is some controversy as to whether he actually existed or was a mythical figure, perhaps a synthesis of more than one historical person. Most sources say he lived in the 6th century BC. Lao Zi was said to be the author of the *Dao De Jing*, a classic made up of poetic chapters that set out the principles of *dao* and its power or virtue (*de*).

Much like existentialism, Daoism as a philosophy decries the limitations of intellectual constructions. Words are not the point; experience is the central concern. The *Dao De Jing* is a small book of wisdom containing elemental ideas of Daoist philosophy and practice. According to legend, Lao Zi refused to write down his ideas during his lifetime, and only relented shortly before his passing, pressured by his followers, who wanted something to study when they lost their master. The story reflects a belief that *dao* cannot be contained within a book or indeed within an idea. Readers of the *Dao De Jing* are warned in Chapter One that words cannot substitute for direct experience:

> The Tao that can be told is not the eternal Tao.
> The name that can be named is not the eternal name.
> The nameless is the beginning of heaven and Earth.
> The named is the mother of the ten thousand things.
> Ever desireless, one can see the mystery.
> Ever desiring, one sees the manifestations.

These two spring from the same source but differ in name;
    this appears as darkness.
Darkness within darkness.
The gate to all mystery.[7]

The impossibility of containing or grasping *dao* is further explored in Chapter Fourteen, which also hints at the two dimensions of being, the eternal world and the world of phenomena (as we have already seen in the *Book of Changes*):

Look, it cannot be seen – it is beyond form.
Listen, it cannot be heard – it is beyond sound.
Grasp, it cannot be held – it is intangible.

The text continues:

Stand before it and there is no beginning.
Follow it and there is no end.
Stay with the ancient Tao,
Move with the present.
Knowing the ancient beginning is the essence of Tao.[8]

In their accessible English translation, Gia-Fu Feng and Jane English say, "Whereas Confucianism is concerned with day-to-day rules of conduct, Taoism is concerned with a more spiritual level of being." Chapter Sixteen suggests that the spiritual can be merged into daily lived life (the "ten thousand things"):

Empty yourself of everything.
Let the mind become still.

The ten thousand things rise and fall while the Self watches their return.

They grow and flourish and then return to the source.
Returning to the source is stillness, which is the way of nature.

The text continues with a methodical approach towards a harmonious blending of the individual with the cosmos:

The way of nature is unchanging.
Knowing constancy is insight.
Not knowing constancy leads to disaster.
Knowing constancy, the mind is open.
With an open mind, you will be openhearted.
Being openhearted, you will act royally.
Being royal, you will attain the divine.

Being divine, you will be at one with the Tao.

Being at one with the Tao is eternal.

And though the body dies, the Tao will never pass away.[9]

Zhuang Zi

Zhuang Zi was said to have been born around 370 BC, after both Confucius and Lao Zi. He developed the notion of *dao*, advocating non-action in face of nature (*wu wei*) while maintaining personal freedom of body and mind.

Zhuang Zi was an original thinker, and developed the perspectives of Daoism into a philosophy that still has relevance in modern times. He and Lao Zi were concerned about the same things, but each had a different focus for how to deal with them. Zhuang Zi was less interested in the social aspect and the dynamics of "living in the world." Both were mystical in their outlook, but Lao Zi was more concerned with life in the world. Noting that Lao Zi encouraged people to live in the world in harmony with *dao*, de Bary emphasizes Zhuang Zi's transcendentalist approach:

> Chuang Tzu, on the other hand, is almost indifferent to human society. He seeks neither to reform things nor to keep them as they are, but only to rise above them.[10]

This does not necessarily mean an abandonment of society or people. It does call for a shift in perspective, a change in awareness that is liberating. Zhuang Zi's conception involves rising above the concerns of the world and living freely in the universal. This concept of liberation, says de Bary, distinguishes Zhuang Zi's approach from the more humanistic perspective of Confucius:

> What [man] must be freed from are his own prejudices, his own partial view of things, his tendency to judge all else in terms of himself. Man is not the measure of all things, as the humanistic philosophy of Confucius had seemed to imply. What is of man, says Chuang Tzu, is artificial and unnatural; what is of nature or the Tao alone is enduringly, and universally true. Thus Chuang Tzu is a skeptic where human or worldly values are concerned.[11]

A central issue in Zhuang Zi is the recognition that each of us has a unique perspective. This calls for understanding and a broader vision, as expressed in this passage attributed to Zhuang Zi:

> Our experience of the world is relative to our perspective. The world of our experience is always changing. Therefore we must be wary of our tendency to adopt fixed or dogmatic judgments, evaluations, and standards based upon a narrow viewpoint, since this leads to conflict and frustration.[12]

Zhuang Zi advocated a life of integrity and the maintenance of an inner calm and mindfulness. Only when one is quiet inside can one have a lasting effect on the external world. This inner quiet seems to be at the heart of *wu wei*:

> Water, when it is still, reflects back even your eyebrows and beard. It is perfectly level and from this the carpenter takes his level. If water stilled offers such clarity, imagine what pure spirit offers! The sage's heart is stilled! Heaven and Earth are reflected in it, the mirror of all life. Empty, still, calm, plain, quiet, silent, non-active, this is the centredness of Heaven and Earth and of the Tao and of Virtue.[13]

The two stories that follow, I Dreamed I was a Butterfly and Pao Ting Separates the Ox, are characteristic of Zhuang Zi's thought. There are similarities in their style to the teaching stories of Zen, the subject of the next chapter. The Pao Ting story illustrates a sensitive awareness of the ways of the universe and nature. The Butterfly story shows the relativity of things, and the duality of visibility and invisibility.

Zhuang Zi: I Dreamed I Was a Butterfly
Zhuang Zi's story of dreaming of being a butterfly invites perplexity and discussion. On the surface, it is a simple tale, but it points to the possible relationship between the waking state and the dream state, or between the "real" world and the world of illusion. Furthermore, it suggests a subtle seamless relationship between the world of appearances and the invisible process of transformation that underlies it. Others have interpreted Zhuang Zi's dream as describing a process of self-transformation or spiritual awakening; just as one can wake from a dream, one can enter another dimension of awareness.

> Once upon a time, I, Zhuang Zhou, dreamt I was a butterfly, fluttering hither and thither, to all intents and purposes a butterfly. I was conscious only of my happiness as a butterfly, unaware that I was Zhou. Soon I awaked, and there I was, veritably myself again. Now I do not know whether I was then a man dreaming I was a butterfly, or whether I am now a butterfly, dreaming I am a man. Between a man and a butterfly there is necessarily a distinction. The transition is called the transformation of material things.[14]

Caring for Life ("Pao Ting Separates the Ox")
This famous passage is widely known by Chinese people, and characterizes Zhuang Zi's philosophy of caring about life in every moment. There are similarities in tone to the Zen teaching stories of "every minute Zen," which requires minute attention to precise details. The cook Pao Ting describes his method to Lord Wen Hui:

A good cook changes his knife once a year because he cuts. A mediocre cook changes his knife once a month because he hacks. I've had this knife of mine for nineteen years and I've cut up thousands of oxen with it, and yet the blade is as good as though it had just come from the grindstone. There are spaces between the joints, and the blade of the knife has really no thickness. If you insert what has no thickness into such spaces, then there's plenty of room, more than enough for the blade to play about it. That's why after nineteen years the blade of my knife is still as good as when it first came from the grindstone.[15]

Zhuang Zi continues by focusing on the special awareness required when life presents challenges:

However, whenever I come to a complicated place, I size up the difficulties, tell myself to watch out and be careful, keep my eyes on what I'm doing, work very slowly, and move the knife with the greatest subtlety, until flop! the whole thing comes apart like a clod of earth crumbling to the ground. I stand there holding the knife and look all around me, completely satisfied and reluctant to move on, and then I wipe off the knife and put it away." "Excellent!" said Lord Wen Hui. "I have heard the words of Cook Ting and learned how to care for life!"[16]

The story should be understood as an allegory. Pao Ting (the cook) represents the self, the knife is life itself, and the ox is the social organization, which requires separation into distinctions. Zhuang Zi tells us that Pao Ting understood the ox, the knife, and himself. He worked carefully and slowly. He could make the knife swim in the smallest ligament or tendon. Here, Pao Ting, knife and ox combine in oneness. This is an art work by the soul, not by the hands or by the eyes.

In Zhuang Zi's philosophy, caring for life involves understanding life and its relation to the world, because caring for life should be present as part of our living environment. So caring for life is managing the relation between self, others and society. It means caring for the heart or spirit; this is how to survive freely and easily in a "difficult world."

Confucius, Zhuang Zi and *Wu Wei*
Zhuang Zi is currently experiencing something of a renaissance amongst scholars in China.[17] There seems to be a growing valuation of Zhuang Zi as offering a kind of spiritual liberation philosophy. Conversely, we have observed in our interactions with Chinese people a tendency to disregard Confucianism as outmoded, feudalistic, and inherently limited. It seems possible to us that the existential, humanistic approach of Confucius could be eclipsed by emphasizing the transcendental aspects of Zhuang Zi's writings. We note the human tendency to seek solutions

to current dilemmas in otherworldly pursuits. A superficial reading of Zhuang Zi might interpret him as devaluing humanity and suggesting that people lie passively in the cradle of nature.

We see this as a critical issue. We do not think that Zhuang Zi devalued humanity. Rather, he urged people to study, learn and increase their awareness of the ways of the universe, the *dao*. The modern Chinese person, however, drawn to Zhuang Zi's emphasis on freedom, seems likely at the same time to adopt a philosophy of passivity in face of the universe, and thus miss opportunities for the deeper possibilities in humanistic development. Neo-Confucianists, in turn, have for centuries criticized followers of Zhuang Zi for their transcendent passivity, resulting in an ongoing "us and them" dispute. We think Zhuang Zi would not have approved of such a moralistic, right and wrong approach in either camp, evidenced in this writing of his:

> Now I have something to say, namely that there is no such thing as right and wrong.[18]

We think that Zhuang Zi and Confucius themselves would probably find much to agree about; their differences would be of emphasis, rather than fundamental disagreements. Their followers, however, accentuated the differences.

According to Gia-Fu Feng, Zhuang Zi spread the teachings of Lao Zi in the same way that Plato explicated Socrates' teaching or St. Paul spread the gospel of Jesus. In each case the students furthered the teachings of the Master they followed. Unlike the followers of Confucius, who concerned themselves with practical matters of government and social conduct, Zhuang Zi focused more on the illusory nature of the world, and thus anticipated the perspectives of Zen Buddhism and ego transcendence.[19]

Zhuang Zi certainly advocated *wu wei*, non-action, but he was not a completely passive person. He wanted people to be involved in life, but not trapped by the usual limitations.

> The Confucianists teach full development of one's nature, fulfillment of one's destiny and participation in the creative work of Nature. Chuang Tzu, on the other hand, believes in nourishing nature, returning to destiny, and enjoying Nature. The Confucianists want people transformed through education, but Chuang Tzu leaves transformation to things themselves.[20]

Zhuang Zi's approach is indeed different from that of Confucius, but his understanding of nature does not at all deny the individual human's capacity to make ethical decisions about how to live life. Thomas

Merton writes, "The secret of the way proposed by Chuang Tzu is therefore not the accumulation of virtue and merit taught by *Ju (Ru)*, but *wu wei*, the non-doing or non-action, which is not intent upon results and is not concerned with consciously laid plans or deliberately organized endeavors."[21]

To Westerners, this non-action might seem like inattentiveness to planning or laziness, or inscrutable noninvolvement. But *wu wei* is something quite different, which artisans and masters of many disciplines understand in both the East and the West. Alan Watts explores the idea of not forcing things, noting that a pine branch, being rigid, will crack under a load of winter ice, whereas a willow tree, being sinewy and yielding, can tolerate much greater loads without breaking. He continues:

> Wu-wei is thus the life-style of one who follows the Tao, and must be understood primarily as a form of intelligence – that is, of knowing the principles, structures and trends of human and natural affairs so well that one uses the least amount of energy in dealing with them … Wu-wei is a combination of this wisdom with taking the line of least resistance in all one's actions.[22]

A simple every day example would be when a parent watches two children playing happily together. An over-eager parent might join in and change the mood of the already-successful interaction. A *wu wei* approach would be to "leave well enough alone" since the children are getting along; intervention from the parent would be unnecessary and possibly disruptive. We could think of *wu wei* as "don't tamper unnecessarily."

> Thus wu-wei as "not forcing" is what we mean by going with the grain, rolling with the punch, swimming with the current, trimming sails to the wind, taking the tide at its flood, and stooping to conquer.[23]

These expressions are commonly known among educated people in China:

Knowing it could not be done, I tried to do it. – Confucius

Knowing it could not be done, I did not do it. – Zhuang Zi

Herein lies the central difference between Zhuang Zi and Confucius, who is remarkably closer to the Western ideal of action and decision, and whose emphasis on personal, individual responsibility marks him as a kind of existentialist. On the other hand, Zhuang Zi seems more accepting and in this way is an *essentialist*, relaxing and letting nature go its way, accepting passively what nature provides. Zhuang Zi's mark is deeply noted on the Eastern psyche, where non-action and patience are seen as consistent with the *dao*. We ourselves see value in both perspectives. We are clearly advocates of the existentialist position of individual responsibility and socially contributory actions. At the same time, we believe that the *wu wei* approach of moving in harmony with the *dao* is wonderfully efficient and life-enhancing. Thus, we propose a mixture of watchful awareness to recognize the flow in any situation, with a responsible attitude of contribution through individual efforts that go with this flow. *Dao, wu wei*, and existential choice can be harmoniously blended.

III.8

The Search for Cold Mountain

On a trip to China in 1989 we went to Suzhou, the "Venice of the East," in search of the Cold Mountain temple. For years we had been steeped in the Zen writings of Han Shan, the fabled poet of Cold Mountain, which you can read about in the next chapter. The journey to Cold Mountain depicted in Han Shan's writings was for us a metaphor for our own personal development and that of our relationship. On this trip to China, we took a train from Shanghai to Suzhou, where the fabled temple was reputed to be, to see for ourselves.

Suzhou was beautiful, filled with canals and ancient gardens. Our guide was a young modern Chinese man, who was puzzled by how two scholars from the West could be interested in the superstitions of archaic times in China. He knew we were interested in *qi* (which he called "air"). He had heard of this ancient notion, and was ready to dismiss it as quaint nonsense or humorous superstition – certainly nothing befitting the time or attention of two professors from the West! We told him we were looking for the Cold Mountain temple.

The temple itself was a big disappointment. It was well maintained, but the atmosphere was cold and uninviting, and it lacked the special quality of spiritual intensity that we had seen in other cathedrals and holy sites in Latin America and Europe. We told the young guide that we were disappointed, that the temple seemed to "lack *qi*." (A piece of the gold-coloured plaster had fallen from the wall surrounding the temple, and Jock collected it, bringing it home to Canada in his suitcase. We thought this might be all that we would find. A piece of the temple now rests in the display case in the Phoenix auditorium at The Haven and another piece is under the totem pole in front of the lodge.)

By this time, the young man was curious about us, and was doing his best to satisfy our curiosities about old China. But he did not have any formal training in Daoism or Confucianism and did not relate to many of the terms that we were using (such as meridians, harmony, heaven and earth, flow). He said, "I think I know where we can find a place that has the *qi* that you are seeking."

He took us to Sky Flat Mountain, which is an hour's drive outside of Suzhou. When we arrived, we immediately could see that something was different about this landscape. The mountain was flat-topped across the skyline, very different from the peaked crags of Guilin or the rolling cones we saw in North America. Furthermore, the sides of the mountain featured gigantic boulders, which were standing upright as if inserted into the slopes by giant hands. At the base of the mountain was a stone quarry, with many people working away at carving stones, many of them for tombstones. There was a small temple at the base of the mountain, and the setting was lush, quiet, and filled with *qi*. We could immediately see that immense care had been taken to fit this temple into the geography of the landscape. Everywhere we looked, there were gentle depictions of a warm nature that welcomed humans. A soft path led through scented forest to a small burbling river. A gigantic boulder in the river was carved with Chinese characters, painted red. The guide told me that he had some difficulty in translating the characters, which were in an ancient style. He said it was something like "stones that transform."

In ancient China, people would show their reverence for the Emperor by bowing low and holding up a stone tablet with words of praise or specialness. Remarkably, the Emperor himself had a similar relationship to the sky and heaven, and would bow low at the Temple of Heaven holding a stone tablet aloft over his head in homage. We learned that this temple site was in honour of a local governor, who had been given the land as his place of burial. The governor, being a humble man, said "I am not worthy of such a place; give me a lesser land, and I will dedicate this area to nature and to the people." Local legend says that the spirits of the mountain were so moved that they knelt in homage before this humble offering by the governor, raising the massive stones on the mountain side to stand erect in honour of this harmonious human action, and they continue to do so to this day.

We set out to find a temple, and instead we found a natural surrounding that marked the harmony between earth and sky, with human beings welcome participants. We had found Cold Mountain, but not in the temple of the external. It was in our hearts and minds and our relationship to nature. Jock wrote a poem about this experience, which you can read in Chapter III.10. Read it now if you like, or carry on to find out more about Chinese Buddhism and Zen, and about our relationship with the Cold Mountain Poems.

III.9
Buddhism and Zen

Buddhism in China

Buddhism originated in India around the 5th century BC, and had spread into China by the middle of the first century AD. In time it became the third of China's 'three religions', though it never quite managed to shake off its foreign associations. Buddhism brought a systematic philosophical framework that Daoism lacked – this was very appealing to the Chinese gentry, who valued scholasticism and learning.

Buddhism was in some ways strange to the practical Chinese. At a time when Confucianism, which regarded the family as the centre of society, was the dominant philosophical force in China, the Buddhist invitation for young people to leave their families and renounce the world provoked considerable suspicion. Furthermore, the Buddhist communities were seen by some as a challenge to the emperor's power and a disruptive influence to the social structure outlined in Confucianism. For example, in India, monks were revered by the populace; in China, they refused to bow in obeisance to the emperor.

Nevertheless, Buddhism also had considerable appeal to the Chinese people. Whereas Confucianism is a philosophy of the practical everyday life, Buddhist thought included unseen, spiritual worlds. When Confucius was asked about how to relate to spirits and divinities, he was reputed to have said, "You cannot treat the spirits and divinities properly before you learn to treat your fellow men properly." He gave a similar answer when asked about death: "You cannot know about death before you know about life." (*Analects* XI.12).[1] Damien Keown writes:

> In relegating the supernatural to second place, Confucianism left unanswered questions about which many Chinese were curious. Buddhism seemed to have answers to these questions, especially those concerning death and the afterlife, a subject which was of particular interest to the Chinese in view of the deep respect in which the ancestors were held.[2]

> Buddhism proved to be a welcome addition to the Confucian approach.

> Thus while many Chinese accepted Confucianism as the authoritative guide to this world, they turned to Buddhism for guidance about the next.[3]

Buddhism had some overlap with the well-established philosophy of Daoism, especially in the realm of meditation. Both approaches valued the goal of inner stillness. Some scholars, including Keown, argue that the Chan Buddhism of China (which is the ancestor of Japanese Zen) arose from the interaction between Buddhism and Daoism. The Chinese word *chan* can be translated as "meditation" or "meditative state."

Our own interest is primarily in the Zen or Chan form of Buddhism. In part this has come about through personal circumstances, and especially our friendships with both Alan Watts and Paul Reps. Alan Watts' writings helped to make Asian ideas accessible to occidental readers; *The Way of Zen* (1957) was one of the first widely selling books on Buddhism in the West. We have rich memories of provocative discussions with him. We have already quoted his work in this book and we refer to him further in this chapter. Watts trained as a theologian and became an Episcopalian priest, but found much more personal fit with Asian practices and approaches. We wish he were still alive, so that we could discuss this text with him.

Alan Watts wrote that there are built-in obstructions to easy communication between the great cultures of East and West. He believed that West could learn much from East, and vice versa; but because of the extreme differences in their perspectives, this was fraught with problems. For those who have been steeped in ways of seeing life with a deity in the foreground, coming to either Daoism or Buddhism can be a strange and difficult shift in perspective. The issue in Christianity is salvation; the issue in Islam is living by the will of Allah; the issue in Buddhism is awakening to life itself:

> If Christianity is wine and Islam coffee, Buddhism is most certainly tea. Its quietening, clarifying, and slightly bitter taste gives it almost the same taste as awakening itself.[4]

Our friend Paul Reps was an artist, poet and author, whose life and work were profoundly influenced by Zen Buddhism. In the last two years of his life he lived with us at The Haven. He published a number of books, perhaps the best known of which is *Zen Flesh, Zen Bones*. We refer to him throughout this book, and devote a whole chapter to him later. Our discussion of Zen below relies heavily on what we learned from Watts and Reps.

Zen

According to tradition, Zen originated at the moment of the Buddha's enlightenment in the 5th century BC, and was passed down through a line of Patriarchs until it came to Bodhidharma, who brought Zen to

China in the 6th century AD. Scholars differ on the early history of Zen, although its emergence is first documented in China in the 7th century. Alan Watts saw Zen as the fulfillment of long traditions of both Indian and Chinese culture, but thought it "much more Chinese than Indian" and its origins "as much Taoist as Buddhist."[5]

Watts relates that "according to legend, spiritual insight was passed from one to another without any intermediary of scriptures or doctrinal teaching; it was a 'direct transmission', a communication which passed immediately from mind to mind, understandable only by that person who was far enough developed to grasp his master's Enlightenment."[6] While this secret direct transmission of knowledge was passed on, the Buddha's teachings were codified by different sects. Watts notes that "none of the Buddha's teachings was committed to writing until at least 150 years after his death."[7] So, similar problems exist concerning this material as with the teachings of Jesus, whose words were not written down until many decades after his death.

According to Watts, Chinese Buddhism, coloured by familiarity with Daoism and Confucianism, became a more practical, everyday approach, "a possible way of life for *human* beings, for people with families, with everyday work to do, and with normal instincts and passions."[8]

A common theme in Chinese Buddhism is liberation from *maya*. Commonly understood as "illusion," *maya* has a subtler meaning. Watts notes that the roots of the word in Sanskrit are related to measurement and division. Our world of experience is coloured by notions of boundaries and measurements that are byproducts of mental theories, which project the world out there for us to experience. We do not so much experience the world directly as we witness the projected interpretations of our measuring of reality.[9] Thus, says Watts, "the maya doctrine points out, firstly, the impossibility of grasping the actual world in the mind's net of words and concepts, and secondly, the fluid character of those very forms which thought attempts to define ... It is precisely this realization of the total elusiveness of the world which lies at the roots of Buddhism."[10]

Zen shares with Daoism an absence of pompous gravity and seriousness. This is also a feature in sayings of Lao Zi and Zhuang Zi, and was certainly characteristic of our friend Paul Reps. For example, many Buddhists believe in a round of birth and death and reincarnation, associated with the notion of *karma* that shapes the individual destiny, life after life until the ultimate insight and awakening closes the process. In Zen, the process of rebirth is from "moment to moment" so that one is reborn "so long as one identifies himself with a continuing ego which reincarnates itself afresh at each moment of time."[11] Reps, the Zen master, put it more succinctly. When someone asked, "Reps, do you believe in reincarnation?", he grinned and replied, "Ask me again."[12]

Zen Challenges to Western Thinking

> Human experience is determined as much by the nature of the mind and the structure of the senses as by the external objects whose presence the mind reveals. – Alan Watts[13]

In Western thinking, we conceive of a subject acting on an object and responding to the resulting change in the object; this occurs within the constraints of cause and effect. To the Chinese way of thinking, subject and object are inseparably linked in the circumstances of their interaction, and cause and effect are not foreground. Alan Watts wrote, "We do not sweat *because* it is hot; the sweating is the heat."[14] He asserts,

> Our problem is that the power of thought enables us to construct symbols of things apart from the things themselves.[15]

"The life of Zen," says Watts, "begins … in a disillusion with the pursuit of goals which do not really exist – the good without the bad, the gratification of a self which is no more than an idea, and the morrow which never comes." Zen begins at the point where there is nothing more to be sought or gained. Watts says, "Zen is most emphatically not to be regarded as a system of self-improvement, or a way of becoming a Buddha."[16] He notes the challenge in Zen:

> The difficulty of Zen is, of course, to shift one's attention from the abstract to the concrete, from the symbolic self to one's true nature.[17]

Some have interpreted this to mean that one should give up thinking. But this is an impossible trap: to conceive of giving up thinking is itself a thought process. There seems indeed to be a paradox in achievement generally: it is impossible to accomplish anything, since one can only try to achieve one's idea of what that accomplishment would be. The paradox, however, dissolves if we realize that "the mistake arises in the attempt to split the mind against itself."[18] If we accept that we are capable of mental activity and see it for what it is, we will gradually learn to give up the impossible and come to rest more in the present moment, able to think about it without trying to change it or achieve something else with it. Watts writes:

> From the Buddhist point of view, reality itself has no meaning since it is not a sign, pointing to something beyond itself … To Zen and Taoism alike … the very life of the universe … is complete at every moment and does not need to justify itself by aiming at something beyond.[19]

While thinking itself is not the central problem, says Watts, philosophers would do well to recognize that "there is a point where thinking – like boiling an egg – must come to a stop."[20]

Watts echoes here the classical Asian view that the mind is a tool that can also become a trap. In Buddhism, Daoism and Zen, holding onto mental images limits consciousness; by not holding on, not fixating, people can achieve "soft eyed vision" and release from mental constraints. This is the non-grasping mind:

> When we have learned to put excessive reliance upon central vision, upon the sharp spotlight of the eyes and mind, we cannot regain the powers of peripheral vision unless the sharp and staring kind of sight is first relaxed. The mental or psychological equivalent of this is the special kind of stupidity to which Lao-tzu and Chuang-tzu so often refer. It is not simply calmness of mind, but 'non-graspingness' of mind.[21]

When the mind does not grasp, it is a very useful source of information and perspective for awareness. Zhuang Zi says:

> The perfect man employs his mind as a mirror. It grasps nothing: it refuses nothing. It receives, but does not keep.[22]

This is the context in which meditation can be developed as a tool for dealing with the limitations of mental (as well as physical and emotional) activity. There are many types of meditation; the common thread between them is a goal of transformation, clarity and freedom. In his groundbreaking book *Zen and the Art of Motorcycle Maintenance*, Robert Pirsig expresses the classical Asian view of the limits of the logical mind and the use of Zen meditation to move past these limits:

> Logic presumes a separation of subject from object; therefore logic is not final wisdom. The illusion of separation of subject from object is best removed by the elimination of physical activity, mental activity and emotional activity. There are many disciplines for this.[23]

Zen Perspectives on Individual Transformation

Both the West and China have literature about personal transformation, wherein individuals disengage from the expectations of their culture and set out on a solitary journey of discovery. Indeed, this theme of leaving the known world and embarking on a mythic quest occurs in literature and legends throughout the world. Joseph Campbell described the hero's journey in many cultures, depicted in stories of quests and trials. Jung's period of self-investigation (his *nekyia* or journey to the underworld) during the period 1914 to 1919 has the same theme.[24] The

Zen Ox Pictures and the Cold Mountain Poems which we discuss next are explorations of this theme from China.

ZEN OX PICTURES

Paul Reps included the Zen Ox Pictures in his early collections of Zen stories, to illustrate an ancient Asian view of individual spiritual development. We associate these pictures with Reps and his own unique life of seeking. Sometimes called the "Ten Bulls," the "Ten Ox Herding Pictures" (*shi niu*) are a sequence of pictures accompanied by short poems that describe them. They illustrate the stages of a Buddhist practitioner's progression towards enlightenment. The date of this work is uncertain, but likely around the 12th century AD.

The pictures and accompanying words tell how a student ventures into the wilderness (the unknown) in search of the ox (a common metaphor for enlightenment, or the true self). At first his efforts are unproductive. However, he perseveres and eventually finds footprints that encourage his further quest. After a long search, he is amazed when he first glimpses the ox, finding it marvellous – it represents either Buddha nature or his deep self. But he has to work hard to accomplish the taming of the wild ox; this is an allegory of subduing the passions through awareness and self-discovery. A later picture shows him riding the ox home, demonstrating his mastery of the lower nature. In the next frame, the ox is gone; this is the stillness that comes when the passions are put to rest. The next frame is empty; the boy, the ox and the entire environment have disappeared, showing that all the effort of the search and the taming of the passions are now forgotten, left behind in the oneness of all. The last pictures show a river and a tree with neither ox nor boy in evidence; this represents the source of all life. The last frame shows the return to society of the now wise person, who spreads his enlightenment by mingling with other people.

The Zen Ox Pictures, then, are an allegory of the search for one's true nature. When the boy ultimately finds the ox and tames it (that is, he tames his passions), he is released from attachment to his desires and can forget them. He finds his place in the universe, embracing the source of everything. Then he rejoins the familiar world with an enlightened perspective to help others in their search for self and meaning.[25] In his commmentary, M.H. Trevor adds this perspective:

> Why the search? The ox has never been missing from the beginning. However, it so happened that the herdsman turned away from himself; thus his own ox became a stranger to him and eventually lost himself in the far, dusty regions.[26]

THE COLD MOUNTAIN POEMS

The legends and the poems associated with the poet Han Shan (The Cold Mountain Poems) are another example of the lineage of personal development in ancient China. The poems are dated to the 7th or 8th century.[27] For years, the legend of Cold Mountain was compelling to both of us. At one time, the poems were a companion to our own search for connection to each other, and to ourselves. We will say more about this below, but first here is a flavour of the poems.

Han Shan, literally Cold Mountain, and his friend Shi De were Chinese Zen recluses who lived at a place called Cold Mountain in the Tiantai range near the city of Suzhou. Han Shan appeared to be crazy, his words nonsensical; he has been regarded as a high spiritual being of the Zen tradition. Paintings of Han Shan and Shi De often depict them as laughing, robust, and enjoying life.

> When men see Han-shan
> They all say he's crazy
> And not much to look at –
> Dressed in rags and hides.
> They don't get what I say
> And I don't talk their language.
> All I can say to those I meet:
> "Try and make it to Cold Mountain."[28]

"Cold Mountain is often the name of a state of mind rather than a locality," said Arthur Waley in an introduction to his translations of some of the poems.[29] Climbing Cold Mountain involves leaving the world of civilized, conventional life and striking out on one's own. People who follow the mountain path experience isolation, loneliness and fear. They proceed without maps and find their own way in the universe.

> Cold Mountain has many hidden wonders,
> People who climb here are always getting scared.
> When the moon shines, water sparkles clear
> When the wind blows, grass swishes and rattles.
> On the bare plum, flowers of snow
> On the dead stump, leaves of mist.
> At the touch of rain it all turns fresh and live
> At the wrong season you can't ford the creeks.[30]

The journey is experienced as a very difficult solitary climb up a steep mountain:

> Clambering up the Cold Mountain path,

The Cold Mountain trail goes on and on:
The long gorge choked with scree and boulders,
The wide creek, the mist-blurred grass.
The moss is slippery, though there's been no rain
The pine sings, but there's no wind.
Who can leap the world's ties
And sit with me among the white clouds?[31]

The Cold Mountain poems describe a process of leaving the known world and its conventions. In relinquishing society's usual perspectives, one can discover oneself. Not really a place, Cold Mountain is a domain of consciousness. To arrive there involves a challenging spiritual journey that can leave the individual derelict, lonely, lost and apparently crazy. As in other legends of seeking (such as the Grail knights or the Navajo youth), to find oneself, one has to give up the security of belonging.

The Zen Ox pictures describe a process of self-discovery that we might describe as essentialist, since they assume that there is a deep nature to find. The journey to Cold Mountain is different; it is an abandonment of previous constraints, a risk of everything, a leap of faith into the unknown, and is more existentialist in its perspective.

People ask the way to Cold Mountain.
Cold Mountain? There is no road that goes through.
Even in summer the ice doesn't melt;
Though the sun comes out, the fog is blinding.
How can you hope to get there by aping me?
Your heart and mine are not alike.
If your heart were the same as mine,
Then you could journey to the very center![32]

Our Own Path to Cold Mountain

As we have said, these poems have been important to us in our own lives, in our search for connection with one another and with ourselves. We find our deep natures in our relationship, wherever we are. We propose that this journey that is Cold Mountain can be made by anyone, anywhere. For us, the pathway has been through deepening relationships.

This journey is allegorical; there is no need to physically leave to discover your true nature. You can do this wherever you are. You don't have to abandon your regular life to have a spiritual life. You can read some poems quietly, share them with a friend, contemplate inner nature in yourself and in your dialogues with others. You can go for a walk in nature, or just look out the window and reflect.

So many people, in their earnest desire to connect with deeper life, believe they have to change the external structure of their lives. For example, people who have been experiencing limitation in a marriage sometimes think that leaving the marriage will automatically bring them into a more life-fulfilling situation. Sometimes people think they are with the "wrong" person, then separate in order to find the "right" person ... only to enter a new relationship and find that they are no freer than before.

Freedom does not come from leaving anything in the external world. Freedom comes from deep insight into one's attachments and cravings, and a methodical inner work to see fully the extent of the fixations that underlie the traps of one's life. The issue is fixation. For instance, if someone is a workaholic, driven for success and monetary gain, the problem is not the work or money. The problem is in the *attachment* to the meaning of what is seen as success or enough cash.

Others think that by leaving the pressures of modern existence behind and entering a monastic or bucolic life style, they will find spiritual growth and freedom. But when you leave the city for the mountain top, you bring your fixations and desires with you. Without a clear, insightful investigation into attachments, people will remain in the prison of their own desires. To be clear, it is not desire that is the problem, but the fixation. We will gain nothing by leaving behind the trappings of the external world if we stay stuck in our rigid attitudes, prejudices and aims.

There is another trap in the belief that you must find a guru to tell you how to live, so that you can advance spiritually. Dependency upon a teacher can be a fixation that limits growth; by letting go of this, the individual is forced back onto personal resources, to work out life in a unique and creative fashion.

Sharing one's insights about oneself, especially the "ouchy" ones that are embarrassing, can be a path to openness and freedom from fixations. This has been the method of our spiritual life, to share with each other our day-to-day limitations, quirks, and neuroses. We have grown closer and closer to each other and less attached to these inner fixations as we continue to share and grow and know each other more.

So, in summary, you don't have to leave, even though the Cold Mountain Poems and the Zen Ox Pictures suggest you have a journey to make. The journey is inward, and can be done in the context of one's regular life. We recommend that people dedicate a portion of each day to what has deep meaning to them (art, literature, friends, family, nature), to maintain and intensify the lifeline to their deepest concerns.

Enlightenment comes gradually to most, through a process of self-cultivation. Whether this is through a practice such as yoga, meditation, prayer, journal writing, or an ongoing intimate relationship, the path is not important. The process of opening, self-investigation, and self-cultivation is what matters. When one achieves some degree of illumination, life is both exactly the same, and utterly different:

Before enlightenment; chop wood, carry water. After enlightenment; chop wood, carry water. – Zen saying

III.10   Sky Flat Mountain

Suzhou, December 1989

I. THE SEARCH

In life's strange
        winding paths,
many times we seek
        one thing, and find
another

We came believing
        we were to see
the Han Shan temple
        and the Cold Mountain with it.
and we did - but this proved not to be
        the reason for our journey
That temple was cold
        form perfect
                but without spirit
There was a mountain
        but not at the Buddhist temple of Han Shan.

Instead
We found the Sky Flat Mountain
        with its singing hills
and erect choirs of stones
Legend says that the stones
        rose to worship,
honouring the generous heart
        of a man;
the landscape was touched
        moved, by an act of
kindness and selflessness.

Now, ages later, huge stones still stand
        in proud worship

II. PURIFICATION

I had felt like this before
     at Assisi
the landscape sings
     and hints
at a deeper presence

At the base,
     we were prepared
and underwent a
     gentle purification:

The steady clatter of
     stone carvers
provided a rock chant;
     they were
     working earnestly
to make gravestones

Evidence of previous times and peoples:
     the care of the human architects
was revealed in the precise
     statements of
graceful buildings,
     gently placed
          to protect the placid lake
and vibrant gardens laid out
     in harmony with the surrounding

In the lush, peaceful woods we found
     large carved stone animal figures,
and a band of chattering women
     dressed in blue
worshipping in the fragrant forest
     they spoke of Buddha
          and gods that are alive
joining heaven and earth

We saw a huge rock
     marked with arcane calligraphy
even our guide

had difficulty translating:
something like "changing rock" –
    evidence of the stone that transforms

III. THE ASCENT

God is with us here
or rather, I have returned to my God
as I open my heart,
    the stones of my soul
        stand erect
I am moved to tears
    emotional, flooded
with relief
    at the return

Thanks be to God

On the hill, the rocks are carved
    sculpted, and inscribed by patient chisel
        with timeless Chinese words
indicating the deeper meanings of this place
    calligraphy singing
pulling us up
    effortlessly in a climb
        to the sky

We ascend into
    the huge erect stones,
discovering grottoes, stairs
    alive places of present remembering

The rough rock feels warm
    beneath my fingers
as I grasp for a hold
    pushing to the top
We become intimate with the hill
    seeing, feeling
up close

As we peer up at the massive boulders
    corridors of light

break through narrow cracks
        making windows of the sky

behind, over our shoulders
        the retreating earth
rests in a pastoral vista
        we can see for miles

in the bushes near us
        we hear the rattle
of birds and unseen little creatures

The dry morning sunshine
        warms our deep beings

We are surprised, near the top
        to be met by a gigantic
carved stone Buddha,
        fat-bellied, smiling
                welcoming us
such heart-felt religion!

Invigorated by the climb
        my interior jewels glisten
and the externals fall into retreat
        my inner life dances
        my heart swells
and God takes root
        fills my veins and soul
with gardens and pictures

IV. SKY VIEW

We rest in heaven but a few moments
        sitting together in gentle fraternity
                three generations of men
sharing ancient secrets and feelings
The earth below is imminent
        from this Chinese Olympus
        Outside reflects
inside

both are alive, full
        vibrant

Descending, we feel the sun
        and our cleansed blood flows freely
through our invigorated frames
        wondrously, a peace descends with us
as we move down the rocky slope

V. CONSECRATION

We have been carved now
        with the calligraphy
                of ancient feeling
Initiated,
        marked
                for eternity
the inscriptions tell
        our secret names

Now, the stones of our inner mountain
        etched with the winds and hands of time
speak the ancient poems
        written upon them

White clouds circle about our heads
        and dry leaves
crackle in the winter wind
                – Jock McKeen[1]

PART IV

Chinese Medicine

Earth

Earth is associated with the late summer season, the time of the bounty of the harvest. It is a time of joy and fulfilment on earth, with images of baskets full of apples and gathered vegetables. The intensity of the summer's sun has mellowed, and yet the cold winds of autumn have not yet arrived. It is a time of balance. In the life of humans, it represents nourishment, physically and spiritually. The birth of a child is an earth manifestation. Earth is at the centre, the focus of a life that integrates the forces of heaven and the forces of nature in harmony. Earth represents stability, calm, generativity, fecundity, seeding, the interface between past and future, the now.

IV.1 Science and Intuition

KZ = Confucius (Kong Zi), CJ = Carl Jung, BW = Ben Wong, JM = Jock McKeen

JM: Gentlemen, as a preliminary to writing about Chinese medicine, I want to address the topic of science and intuition. When I was studying Western medicine, I had the impression that I should hone my scientific, logical side and suppress my artistic nature, at least in my professional life.

CJ: For me too. At first, I saw the artistic side of things as recreation, not as something fundamental.

JM: When I studied classical Chinese medicine, I was excited to discover that an artistic approach was highly valued. Finally, I could apply all of myself to my professional life, not just my brain! Ben, how do you see the approach of science?

BW: Well, it is objective, logical, analytical. It uses experiments to prove hypotheses, which once proven can substantiate theories. Science is very useful in sorting out the trends of behaviour for large groups of people or phenomena. But a statistic is not a prediction. Statistics can never tell the story for the individual situation. Statistics are useful only to recognize patterns. These patterns are only tendencies, not cut and dried fates in the particular.

JM: Dr. Jung, please talk about your view of intuition.

CJ: Intuition involves an inner subjective experience. So it is different from science, which strives for objectivity. One gets an "inner feeling" about something, a hunch, or sometimes even a vision or a voice. Intuition is not objective, and does not bear up to the scrutiny of analysis, insofar as nothing intuition brings can be proven as "true." But intuition is very useful in the specific situation in the here and now, with individuals and small groups. One cannot count on an intuitive event to be reliably predictive, but these feelings are often a more clear indicator of the deeper meanings of an individual situation. This is the realm of the artist and the mystic.

KZ: The Chinese *Book of Changes* has a formalized structuring of the intuitive approach, to reveal the hidden significance and trends in a situation. We Chinese pay attention to our intuitions about people in social and business settings too. We don't just analyze them mentally; we also feel with them.

BW: Science has valued objectivity and statistics so highly in its urge to prove things. Thus science has been very suspicious, or overtly dismissive, of intuition.

CJ: An artistic approach to life is not objective, but expresses a deeply felt subjectivity. And the structure of science must avoid subjectivity.

KZ: I myself valued logic and wanted to see the patterns. If I had been born into the modern world, I could easily have been a scientist. But I also wanted to be practical, to use the patterns that I discerned to teach people about life. Lao Zi and Zhuang Zi were more intuitive than I was.

BW: When science dismisses art and intuition, a large source of information is often lost. A broad-based healer would use both science and art.

KZ: I agree. Modern China has become enamoured of science, and now tends to dismiss classical Chinese medicine and Daoism as mere superstition. In this they are in danger of ignoring the richness of their spiritual heritage and the ability to deal with invisible forces. They become limited with the insistence on reality being "proven."

CJ: Western science has done the same thing, dismissing art as "soft" and irrelevant to the furthering of knowledge.

BW: Psychiatry, as a branch of medicine, has remained wedded to logic and science, and the art of the endeavour has been threatened.

CJ: Freud struggled hard to make psychoanalysis a scientific, provable system. In the process, he denied his artistic nature. He was quite an artist when he was plying his craft, especially when he wasn't stuck in being righteous. We separated over our disagreement in this area.

JM: Would you agree, Dr. Jung, that you were more intuitive than scientific?

CJ: I certainly valued my intuition, and I struggled to wrestle logically with what I found. But I would say that I was a scientist with strong intuitive leanings. Indeed, I was very interested in science. But it is impossible to be "cut and dried" about intuition and intrapsychic events. Intuition is awash with feelings and hunches and artistic impressions and nuances and whiffs and vapours and tendencies.

JM: The "pattern" of the *dao*?

KZ: Yes, this is the "forever flowing constancy" of the *dao*.

CJ: My research approach was to use my own experience as my laboratory.

BW: This is the same approach that Jock and I have taken. We have not been "anti-scientific." Like you, Carl, we studied ourselves and our clients and included our subjective experience as data.

JM: I have gradually learned that science is neither "right" nor "wrong" but is constrained within its own method. In my rebellious youth, I railed against scientific dogmatism; as I have ripened, I have come to value what science has to offer. At the same time, I recognize its limits.

CJ: Art and intuition often cannot be contained within the definitions of science. This has been an issue in the development of psychology and psychiatry.

JM: There has been a long history of separation between doctors and priests. In modern times, this involves a difference between issues of faith and religion on the one side, and issues of science and logic on the other.

BW: Yes, priests follow the paralogical, and their roots go back to the primitive, to childhood (where emotions and feelings hold sway), to darkness, to the subterranean, mystical, nonlogical forces. Doctors are wedded to the logical, to the world of analysis and objective reality and daylight; doctors are seen to be the civilized healers.

KZ: So much of classical Chinese medicine relates to priesthood, to paralogic, to the primitive. Western medicine prides itself in being associated with logic and analysis. But the finest doctors of both traditions, Chinese and Western, use both logic and intuition.

JM: Psychology has the same dilemma in regard to logic and intuition.

CJ: Yes, it feels like this often. Psychology has its origins in the faith healer priests of antiquity, who could connect with their patients and facilitate genuine healing. But as science developed, there emerged a growing suspicion of contact, believing that objectivity was necessary to find truth. We have gained much objective knowledge, but this has limited the healing that comes from contact and connection.

JM: In a way, psychology has a foot on the dock and a foot in the canoe!

CJ: Yes.

JM: You, Dr. Jung, were more of a priest. Would you agree?

CJ: Not "more," but I was interested in priestly things. I did my research on myself, as well as my patients. I always wrestled logically with what I found.

KZ: But you used your own experience as a laboratory. You didn't study external things; you studied yourself and your clients.

CJ: Yes. This is phenomenonological research, which includes the observer as part of the experiment.

BW: We identify with this approach too. It is a different kind of research. It does not use techniques like "double blind" and control groups. So it is impossible to make predictions about the behaviour of groups. We try to be objective, but the focus of study is the individual and small group relationships. We use a heuristic research of discovery, learning through experience.

KZ: Your research techniques are akin to journalists. You try to look with honest eyes at what you see and experience, report on it, and develop your theories from your experience. This is quite existential.

CJ: It doesn't prove anything in the abstract; nor does it extract universal truths. It is the stuff of Kierkegaard's "Knight of Faith," who abandons the certitude of the universal in order to walk the narrow lonely path of the personal. And every step that is taken leads on into the darkness, into the fearful unknown, and no certainty or security accrues. The anxiety and the uncertainty are part of the life style of personal inquiry.

KZ: Your description applies to my life experience too. For years, I felt alone and misunderstood.

CJ: Usually, there is a great chasm between art and science. But they are not incompatible, just different domains. This can be overcome by a dedicated life of study and reflection. With a wider consciousness, they are quite harmonious. I called this the "individuation project."

KZ: Your words echo my own desire for human growth and development. This is what I wanted people to accomplish by looking straight into their hearts.

BW (addressing the others): We have common goals for learning. We are all on the same team.

JM: Thank you, gentlemen. This seems like a good context for our chapters on Chinese medicine.

IV.2
Classical Chinese Medicine

Health is the natural state of the universe.[1]

Chinese Medicine and Western Medicine: Vast Contrasts

A medical system expresses the biases, prejudices and assumptions of the culture in which it develops. Chinese medicine grew in the context of the history and philosophical evolution of this enduring civilization, which we have discussed in the preceding chapters. Today it is very different from Western medicine, even though many of its basic goals (health, wellbeing, longevity) are the same.

The differences between Chinese medicine and Western medicine are based on the divergent world views of the two cultures. One fundamental difference concerns the relationship between the physical world and energy. To the Westerner, physical reality is primary and energy is a derived phenomenon, an expression of this physical reality – physical is first, energy second. For the Chinese, energy is primary and manifests in various dimensions, including the physical dimension – energy is first, physical second. So, everything is topsy-turvy when one system is seen from the vantage point of the other. Furthermore, just as Western medicine has evolved over the centuries, Chinese medicine has also undergone radical shifts and transformations in the tides of political and cultural changes. In their noblest application, both systems have the focus of the health and wellbeing of human beings. But they are very, very different in many ways.

YELLOW RIVER AND BLUE SEA PHILOSOPHIES

Confucian teachings have deeply influenced the learning style of Chinese people (the Yellow River way); the investigation methods attributed to Socrates show in the mental operations of Westerners (the Blue Sea way).[2] This distinction, which we detail in Chapter I.5 and Appendix 1, is helpful in understanding Chinese medicine and its relationship to the medicine of the West. The Blue Sea way permeates the logical-analytical, objectifying approach of Western science. The Yellow River way underlies the approaches in Chinese medicine and in other medical forms of Asia. In the Western approach, illness results from malfunction of the parts of the organism. In the Chinese view, illness is an expression of an impedance to the free flow of *qi* energy in the meridian channels of the bodymind.

ANTICIPATORY VERSUS REPAIR MEDICINE

There is an inherent danger in generalizations; nevertheless, they can be useful to begin to appreciate a new way of thinking. So we risk the following overview. Chinese medicine has classically placed more emphasis on a preventive life-style approach, anticipating the disease process by reading energy. Western medicine has become a repair medicine to correct problems that occur in the physical being. Certainly, Western medicine has respect for prevention, and Chinese medicine also attends to existing problems with the goal of correcting them. But these generalizations point to habitual trends in the evolution of these two medical forms. Asian energy perspectives anticipate the disease process with the goal of correcting problems before they manifest physically. Western medicine focuses on the diagnosis of problems after they have occurred, and concentrates on sophisticated and subtle ways to bring the physical system back into health. Chinese medicine is prospective, looking forward; Western medicine is inclined to be retrospective, coping with what has arisen from previous situations.

PHYSICAL AND NONPHYSICAL

For Western science, the physical realm is foreground and objective investigation is the mode of research. Western medical training is grounded in anatomy, coupled with basic sciences and physiology; these approaches help the practitioner learn deeply about the physical being, which is seen to be the primary reality. The cornerstone of Western medical practice is the objectivity of scientific observation and analysis.

For the Chinese practitioner, the primary reality is invisible to the casual eye. The physical being is a manifestation of an underlying (and often hidden) energy organization, the flow of universal *qi*. The *qi* flows in the meridian pathways (*jing luo*). Its emanation is manifested on the other dimensions of being, and illnesses are expressions of the interruption of the flow of *qi*. Practitioners hone their sensitivity to the subtle behaviour of *qi* by enhancing intuition and closely observing phenomena in the patient, in themselves, and even in the environment. The life force energy, *qi*, is not regarded as a physical phenomenon; rather, this is a descriptive term for a phenomenological experience. The same applies to the notion of Chinese meridians, *jing luo*. In a way, the flow of *qi* in the meridians is not really "there"; rather, the meridians are more an experiential phenomenon, not anatomical realities. The meridians and their activity can be discerned in the way that an artistic performance can be experienced, but one cannot dissect out fully what makes the experience itself. Indeed, one might say that the movement of *qi* in the human being is one of nature's most elegant symphonies, beyond words and descriptions.

SEPARATION OR PARTICIPATION

In the West, practitioners strive to be objective and separate, to get themselves "out of the way" and disregard their own subjective state. In Chinese medicine, practitioners hone a focused subjectivity that includes observation of self and other and invites a closeness between the practitioner and client. This makes for very different approaches to health and medicine.

The Western system tends to appreciate separate parts in a way that facilitates fixing problems. The Chinese approach is more inclined to see the entire human system and does not focus on separated parts.

Classical Chinese Medicine and Traditional Chinese Medicine

Traditional Chinese Medicine (TCM) and Classical Chinese Medicine (CCM) are two different systems of thought and treatment. Classical Chinese Medicine evolved from the ancient cosmic viewpoint outlined in the *Book of Changes* and other Chinese classics. Thus, there is a spiritual dimension to CCM, associated with the idea systems of Daoism, Confucianism and Buddhism. CCM receded in China over the past two hundred years, during which period it was transplanted to Europe, where it grew and flowered (see Chapter I.4). In recent years, there has been a renewal of interest in and approval of Classical Chinese Medicine in China, and it is gradually being reintroduced into its country of origin.

Traditional Chinese Medicine (TCM) is a relatively recent arrival, coming into being in Communist China after 1949. Thus TCM uses old ideas in the sociocultural context of China today. Begun under Mao Zedong to bring needed medical care to the masses, TCM tends to be pragmatic, often using formulas and mechanistic approaches to medical care. In TCM, there is little association to the philosophical and spiritual perspectives (from Buddhism, Daoism, and Confucianism) that are included in the CCM approach. In the mind of the average Chinese person, TCM is synonymous with the Chinese medical practice, and there is little recognition of the often subtle differences that denote the CCM approach.

Both TCM and CCM utilize diet, exercise, and physical therapies such as massage, acupuncture, herbs, and moxibustion. What largely distinguishes them is the spiritual and philosophical emphasis of CCM that is generally disregarded in TCM. Indeed, amongst the general populace, these aspects of CCM were, for years, often seen as quaint superstition.

In Chinese medicine as a whole, there are three basic forms – the local ("barefoot") doctor approach, symptomatic treatment, and integrative-therapeutic, which is most characteristic of CCM. Their conceptions of *qi* and meridians are similar; but the attitude and the approaches are very different in the three forms.

The local doctor approach was devised in the early days of the post-1949 China, to bring health care to the multitudes of the Chinese populace. Barefoot doctors are trained in courses lasting only a matter of weeks, to deal in straightforward and practical ways with common health conditions. Their treatments come from formulas; they do not approach the *qi* from the philosophical viewpoint of the master CCM (or TCM) practitioner.

Symptomatic treatment is somewhat more comprehensive than local doctor, and its practitioners will have received more training. However, just as in Western medicine, Chinese medical practice is open to the dangers inherent in a purely symptomatic approach. Those who are trained in either system can use complex formulas (whether Western drugs or Chinese herbs) to treat symptoms without getting at the underlying cause of the illness process itself. If the underlying disease process is not properly understood, it can persist even when the immediate symptoms disappear.

In CCM, with its ideal of an integrative-therapeutic approach, these various levels are addressed like this:

> A superior doctor deals with the country. A mediocre doctor deals with the people. An inferior doctor deals with symptoms only.

The meaning of this is profound. Symptom relief without addressing the underlying cause of illness is seen by CCM to be an inferior form of medicine. The hallmark of an inferior medical approach is regarding the patient in isolation, without seeing the disease process in the context of the person's psychology, past experiences, and social relationships. A superior medical approach is to relate to the individual in all aspects, and anticipate the flow of *qi* as it becomes unbalanced, resulting in disease. By delving into the disease process, the practitioner can have a subtle and far-reaching appreciation of the balances and imbalances of the individual's *qi*, both past and present, and thus can anticipate the movement of the *qi* in the future. A superior practitioner is said to be able to know the disease processes from the past, to appreciate the current energy condition, and to predict the probable outcomes of the ensuing imbalances if they are not rectified.

More Detail: The Fundamentals of the CCM Approach

In the remainder of this chapter, we explore some details of the Classical Chinese Medicine approach. Some, but not all, of this material is also referenced in the training of TCM practitioners.

LIFE-FORCE ENERGY (QI)

Qi (often written in older romanization as *ch'i*) is the universal life-force energy. This is named in other disciplines variously as ki, prana, vital essence or, in pop culture, the force. Western scientists have described bioelectric behaviour in the human body; Reich talked of orgone energy; Mesmer described magnetic force fields; those who lived in the 1960s are familiar with "vibes." All of these various names may be seen as attempts to describe an invisible energy of life.

In the classical Chinese view, at the moment of conception *qi* begins to circulate in a uniquely human pattern (the meridian system). Indeed, what makes us human is the particular human organization – the human meridian matrix – of the *jing luo*. So, the difference between you and your family dog is one of patterning: Fido expresses a canine *qi* matrix, whereas you manifest a human variety. A tree has a different *qi* pattern, a starfish another one again, and so on, every life form having its own distinct configuration.

Within the pattern that denotes a particular life form, the uniqueness of each person (or dog, or tree) arises from subtle variations in the patterning of this *qi* flow in the meridian matrix.

A modern image might help to make this clear. *Qi* is eternal; a person is an expression of the universal whole, manifesting in time and space. Consider an ordinary light bulb in your room: when the circuit is turned on with the switch, that shining bulb is an expression of the energy circuit. When the light bulb burns out, it "dies"; the circuit remains, although there is no illumination until a new light bulb is connected into the circuit. In this way, an individual human being is like a light bulb in the universal circuitry of *qi*, blinking on at conception, shining throughout the lifetime, and going out at the time of death. The different human beings are different "events" in the universal energy stream. We can extend the metaphor to consider different life forms. Just as a heater that radiates warmth is another form of expression of the household's energy circuit, other live beings are also events in the cosmic *qi* circuitry, and their different forms are expressions of a unique patterning of the universal *qi*, temporal beings in an eternal context.

THE MERIDIAN PATTERN (JING LUO)

The ancient view of the *qi* circulation involves the notion of the meridian system, the doctrine of *jing luo*. In this view, the jing are 12 longitudinal pathways that flow one into the other in an ongoing sequence. The luo are transverse linking channels that connect the jing. What are described in English as "meridians" are noted in Chinese as *jing luo*. The acupuncture points occur on these meridians.

These meridians are not substantial entities; they are dynamisms of flow of the universal *qi*. The meridians are like pathways in which the *qi* can travel (although this is a physical metaphor for a nonphysical phenomenon). *Qi*, which is the unity force of the universe, has *yin* and *yang* aspects. In the human being, there is a central channel up the front of the person called the Conception Vessel (*ren mai*), and a central channel down the back called the Governor Vessel (*du mai*). Although the terms seem to refer to separate channels, they are descriptors for a dynamic flow between Heaven and Earth; in the Conception Vessel is a flow of *qi* from earth to sky (*yin qi*) and in the Governor Vessel is a flow from sky to earth (*yang qi*). So, the notion of Conception Vessel and Governor Vessel describe a constant movement between Heaven and Earth; thus, the two vessels are aspects of one process. When the flow is from ground to sky, this is the *yin* movement, and is called the flow of the Conception Vessel. When the flow is from sky to ground, this is the *yang* movement, and is named the Governor Vessel. If they are not reified as physical entities, the Governor Vessel and the Conception Vessel are one dynamism. The *yin* aspect is the Conception Vessel; the *yang* aspect is the Governor Vessel. But, they are the same; each is the other in a different aspect, like two sides of the same coin.

Seeing this two-in-one, we can now conceptualize these two meridians giving rise to 12 pairs of secondary channels, which also are not separate from each other. There is a continuous circulation of *qi* in this meridian system, passing through 12 different phases in a 24-hour period. The meridians are often named for the organs they pass through; but they are much more extensive than the specific organ, which is merely an event upon the pathway of the meridian itself. This is the key to understanding the meridians. They are not things; they are descriptions of a process. It is all one circulation in the individual, and the circulation in the individual is included in the larger circulations that include friends, family, community, state and cosmos. This understanding links Chinese medicine to the Confucian notion of interrelationship of individual and culture and universe.

As we mentioned, the meridians are named by the major organ systems through which they pass. Thus, there is a Heart Meridian, a Small Intestine Meridian, and meridians for Bladder, Kidney, Gall Bladder, Liver, Lung, Colon, Stomach, and Spleen/Pancreas. In addition, there are two "function meridians" that do not have a major physical organ associated (Heart Protector and Triple Heater). To indicate the notion that each of these meridians has a two-hour period of the day when the energy dynamics are most emphasized, they are numbered in the order of this emphasis (starting around mid-day), and often the meridians are referred to by their roman numeral equivalent. This convention provides a useful shorthand to indicate a specific pathway and its activity.

I Heart	II Small Intestine	III Bladder	IV Kidney
V Heart Protector	VI Triple Heater	VII Gall Bladder	VIII Liver
IX Lung	X Colon	XI Stomach	XII Spleen/ Pancreas

In considering the meridians, we must keep in mind that it is only a mental convenience to think of separate pathways. They are all one pathway. What appear as distinct meridians are actually one meridian in different phases and aspects. The *qi* of the universe is manifested in the individual human as a circulation of personal *qi* (which is not separate from the *qi* of the whole, but rather is an expression of it). The life-force energy pulsates, expanding and contracting; in contraction we say it is in a *yin* phase, and in expansion it is in a *yang* phase. A practitioner's goal is to interact with the flow of *qi* in the meridians and influence it through the acupuncture points that occur on the meridian channels. The aim is to facilitate balance between the different meridians.

Bodymind Unity

The *qi* is manifest on various dimensions – body, mind, emotions, spirit and environment. In Western thought these are generally considered separate. In Chinese thought, however, these dimensions are actually all one, in different aspects. This is commonly expressed as "bodymind unity." The basic pattern is the same for each dimension, and exhibits itself in different ways on the different levels. This is a holistic notion of oneness: the parts are all aspects of the whole.

The human being is a whole – body, mind and spirit are a unity – and the individual human is not separate from humanity as a whole. Furthermore, humanity is intricately related to the entire planet, which is a wholeness that includes the seemingly separate parts of human and nature. And so on, right up to the stars. The universal patterning of *qi* is unified in the realm of nature, the human world, and the cosmos. The 4th-century poet Tao Yuan-Ming explores this idea:

> I pick chrysanthemums underneath the east hedge
> The mountains to the south are clear.
> The mountain air at sunset is so wonderful,

and the birds coming home, one after the other.
In all these details there are secret truths;
but when I try to shift to language, it all slips away.[3]

Health and Illness

If the flow of *qi* in a person is unrestricted and balanced, there will be a harmony in the manner in which the *qi* behaves and manifests. The graceful flow on the energy level will manifest as ease and health on all the other dimensions (body, mind, emotions, spirit, environment). If there is some disturbance in the flow of the *qi*, its manifestation will show evidence of disturbance, and eventually, disease. The imbalance in flow of *qi* is what underlies illness on any of the dimensions of being. Furthermore, an imbalance on any of the levels of being will, in time, influence the other levels. For example, excessive worry on the mental-emotional level will eventually express in some physical manifestation (maybe headaches or bodily weakness). Similarly, a physical injury will generally have a psychological component. This is the meaning of body-mind unity – each so-called "level" is an expression of the movement of *qi*, and in this way, each level is the other levels. They are not merely similar; they are expressions of the same *qi* in differing dimensions. Thus, the body is the mind, and the spirit is the environment. This is isomorphism (see Chapter I.5). For this reason, healing efforts directed at any level can be effective at all levels. The *qi* is the integrating factor. The goal of the classical Chinese practitioner is to diagnose the energy imbalances that underlie disease and prescribe treatments to rebalance the energy system, thus encouraging health and rejuvenation.

Five Stages of Change *(Wu Xing)*

The Five Stages of Change model outlines the phases and interrelationships in the complex, ever-changing process of life. This ancient theory describes a recurring process of beginning, development, fruition, decline, and stillness. This cycle of life, death and rebirth is based on observations of the cycles in nature. The Five Stages are Wood (*mu*), Fire (*huo*), Earth (*tu*), Metal (*jin*) and Water (*shui*).

The model of the Five Stages of Change (*wu xing*) elaborates the relationship of the hidden eternal world and the revealed world of phenomena. Sometimes incorrectly translated as "five elements" (which would imply individual parts), the *wu xing* model is not made up of distinct "things," but rather is a cyclical process of energy in a complete system. This misnaming as the "five elements" is an example of the Western proclivity to reify nonmaterial phenomena. Nonetheless, holistic modeling is familiar to Western physiology, which is similarly integrative:

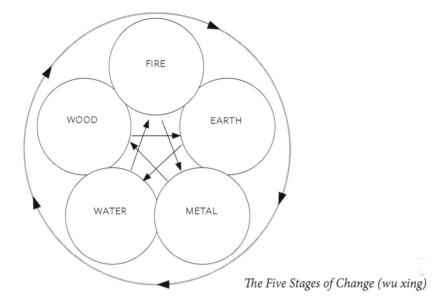

The Five Stages of Change (wu xing)

although Western physiologists talk of the pulmonary, cardiac, and digestive systems, these are in fact all aspects of a whole body system. The "parts" cannot really be isolated from the whole.

For the Chinese person, the notion of oneness is intricately woven throughout philosophy, language and life. While the idea of a cosmos that is undivided, whole, universal, may seem so vast to a Westerner as to be almost incomprehensible, from the classical Chinese perspective, it is quite easily accepted. The concept of the Five Stages of Change elaborates this principle of wholeness.

The Five Stages of Change – Wood, Fire, Earth, Metal and Water – are stages in a cycle that folds back on itself. The ancients watched the seasons in nature and noted a repeating cyclic process. One stage follows another in a sequence. And one stage inevitably gives way and becomes the one that follows it. The next stage incorporates what came before, develops and synthesizes it, and offers it to the next stage for another transformation.

Wood is associated with spring, Fire with summer, Earth with late summer, Metal with autumn, and Water with winter. Understanding these associations, the ancient Chinese made vast inferences about the behaviour of nature and the cosmos. The movement from Wood to Fire to Earth is an unfolding expansion (*yang*); the Earth process involves an involution (*yin*), a turning inward and a progressive contraction, through the Metal stage into an extreme contraction and stillness in Water. The Water stage of winter reawakens in the spring, and the cycle repeats, but in a current fashion. The structure of the process is the same but each year is different, determined by events of preceding years and anticipating transforming possibilities for the future.

The *yin-yang* expanding and contracting go on throughout all cycles (a daily cycle, a yearly cycle, a life cycle, an epoch). So, too, for every cycle there is a five-stage evolution and involution, expansion and contraction. When you think of it as five stages, this is *wu xing*. When you consider this as one or the other, this is *yin/yang*. They do not contradict each other. They are different forms of notation for natural cycles and events.

In considering the Five Stages, begin at Water, a resting stage associated with winter, stillness, and apparent death. From the Water stage of winter, the new rebirth of Wood in the spring reawakens the cycle after a dormancy. The budding and shoots of spring show the reemergence of visible life after the stillness of winter. Wood expands and spreads, transforming into the next phase, which is Fire. In Fire, associated with the dramatic expansion of summer, the life force is abundant and operative in many domains. The Fire season gradually softens and transforms into the Earth phase, associated with late summer. As the expansion continues, there also occurs a diminution, a shrinking; thus the Earth stage checks the expansion of Fire by the counterbalancing shrinking. The Earth stage is the time of fruiting and abundance. The Earth phase gradually transforms, through condensing, into the Metal stage, the time of autumn, where the life process begins to become quieter, and a reflective mood upon the year begins to hold sway. This phase leads back into the next Water phase, opening into another round of an iterating process.

Every cycle has a beginning, a middle and an end. There is a birth, an evolution, then decline and death. From the death is a rebirth and a new cycle ... and so on. By convention there are five stages; but there could be any number of divisions in a continuous process. The stages depict the transformations that occur in the context of a whole system. The central theme is oneness. Beneath the Five Stages theme is a vastness, one without second, universal wholeness.

The movement between Water → Wood → Fire → Earth → Metal is the *sheng* cycle (the creative or generative cycle). Water generates Wood, which generates Fire, which generates Earth, which generates Metal, which generates Water, and then around the cycle again. The arrows that are in the centre linking the Five Stages are the *ke* cycle (the "balance cycle," often misrepresented as the "destructive cycle"). There is a common phrase known to many Chinese people, "*sheng* and *ke* mutually support each other." The meaning is that a dynamic balance is always occurring between the *yang* function of generation in the *sheng* cycle and the *yin* function of restraint that is in the *ke* cycle.

Relation of the Five Stages with the Meridians and Organs

Each stage of change is associated with two meridian pathways, except for Fire, which is associated with four. For example, the Wood stage of change is associated with the Gall Bladder and Liver meridians. For each of the stages of change, there is one *yin* organ (*zang*) and one *yang* organ (*fu*). For Fire, there is an additional *zang* and an additional *fu*, indicating the complexity and the dynamic importance of the Fire state of change.

The Chinese Organs (*Zang Fu*)

The meridians make up an energetic matrix, a system of interconnected *qi* dynamics that can be described in terms of flow and balance and association. Within this conceptualization, the Chinese conceive of "organs" – but they are not merely the physical organs understood by Western anatomy. In the Chinese medical view, the term "organs" includes the physical structures to which Western medicine refers, but also appreciates their energetic dynamics and context within an overall active system. We could say that the meridians are known by the major phenomenon that occurs physically on their specific pathway, but they are not limited to this. As an analogy, a highway stretching from a smaller centre to Chicago and beyond could be called the Chicago Highway, but the highway is much more than the largest city on the route. Larre and his associates put it like this: "The heart, for example, by controlling the circulation, commands the entire vascular system and thus the total vitality of the body."[4] Nevertheless, the meridians tend to be named for the major organ that occurs on their passage; thus we have a Heart Meridian and a Lung Meridian and so on.

We have already seen that each state of change has one *yin* meridian and one *yang* meridian (two of each in the case of Fire). Another way to look at this is to say that half of the meridians are *yin* (these are the *zang*) and half are *yang* (these are the *fu*). The *yin zang* are associated with the "solid" organs (Heart, Liver, Lungs, Spleen, Kidney and Heart Protector), which hold on to precious aspects of life; the *yang fu* are associated with the "hollow" organs (Small Intestine, Stomach, Colon, Bladder, Triple Heater and Gall Bladder), which direct the activity of the processes of growth and transformation. Claude Larre and his collaborators offer the following imagery:

> Zang means to dissimulate, to hold and conserve in a safe place, to gather, to amass actively, hoard, and hide in safety, as one would a treasure ... fu means a depot or storehouse for precious objects, a

marketplace for the transit of valuable merchandise, a public center of distribution through which goods come and go.[5]

At first sight, this is perhaps puzzling to a Westerner, but it reflects a level of sophistication in considering the dynamic relationships between energy and physicality that the ancient Chinese system addresses. Thus, images taken from the very physical world of commerce are used to express the qualities of *yin* and *yang* energy.

Energy Imbalance: Root of Disease

To the Chinese practitioner, the Five Stages are five different energy states that can be distinguished from each other; the practitioner is able to detect alterations in Fire, Wood, Earth, Metal and Water. As well, the practitioner is attuned to the variations in the energy of the 12 meridians, and can detect subtle shifts that indicate imbalances in the flow in these pathways.

In theory, the amount of energy in each meridian should be approximately the same as in the other eleven. There is some ebb and flow, but overall they should be relatively balanced and harmonious with each other. In this situation, the other levels of the bodymind will also be in balance, with no sickness or dysfunction. Illness can occur on one or more levels of the bodymind when the meridians are imbalanced with each other. When one or more meridians have too much or too little energy, this constitutes an imbalance with a shift in the configuration of the energy matrix. Imbalances tend to lead to more imbalances. Illness is an expression of persistent imbalances between the meridian channels.

Once again, a modern analogy may be useful. Consider a freeway system in a large city. Twelve major roadways could be seen as 12 meridians of automobile traffic. In this system, let's assume that the traffic flow is roughly the same on each of the 12 roadways. If one were to observe this traffic system from a helicopter at dusk, the lights of the cars would show a free flow of the traffic, and there would be a gentle glow emanating from the traffic system, which is "in balance." This is analogous to the state of harmony that occurs in the human bodymind when the meridians are conducting *qi* in a balanced way.

In the traffic system, a rear end collision represents a temporary blockage in the energy flow. Suddenly, the traffic behind the accident becomes plugged up, stagnated; ahead of the accident, the freeway gradually empties of cars. There is too much energy behind the blockage and too little ahead of it. If this situation can be rectified quickly by towing the damaged cars away, the traffic flow will gradually reconstitute and rebalance. However, if the situation persists, the drivers behind the accident will become impatient and one by one will decide to take another route, travelling down subsidiary streets to enter another freeway. However, this freeway already has as much traffic as it can handle, so when the new cars arrive it will be overloaded; this is the situation of excess energy on a meridian. Meanwhile, ahead of the blockage on the first highway, the retail outlets that depend upon drivers stopping into their stores to buy goods begin to see their business diminish ("a slow night"); this is deficiency on a meridian. As this imbalance continues, with more and more traffic coming onto the other freeways, the likelihood of another accident is increased; when this occurs, the situation becomes more complex – there are more blockages, more impatience, more diversions and increasing imbalance, which in turn leads to more accidents – and the situation deteriorates further.

In the human being, every blockage on the system contributes to holding, tension, and the shifting or diversion of energy to compensate. When this is temporary, no lasting harm is done. But if the situation becomes repetitious and chronic, the imbalances no longer return to balance, and the insidious process of increasing energy imbalance continues. This energy imbalance begins to show as disturbance on one or more of the levels of the bodymind. At first, this is possibly only a feeling of physical malaise or headache, or an emotional experience of feeling "down" or lacking energy. As this process develops, a full-blown disease state can ensue. The illness is a manifestation of the underlying energy imbalance.

The Chinese practitioner learns to sense these different energies and to build up a picture of the relative state of balance/imbalance in the energy body matrix. This training takes years to ripen, requiring diligent practice and observation. The methods of energy diagnosis are varied.

No human being is in perfect balance or harmony; blockages and disruption are part of human life. A resilient system will be able to compensate for momentary imbalances; just as it is necessary to "go off balance" to be able to walk (you have to thrust yourself off balance in order to move forward), temporary imbalances are part of the design of the system. The problem, then, is not restriction or blockage; this is normal and expected. Troubles begin with fixation; if fixations persist, this can lead to chronic disruptions in energy flow, which will eventually manifest as illness states.

We note the similarity in this dynamic energy model with the gestalt cycle we have discussed, where fixations at a particular part of the cycle inhibit movement and growth. We also see a fit with our Dynamic Empathy Model; in this case, fixations lead to inhibition of the energies of interaction.

Chinese pulses

Western medicine recognizes only one physical pulse, which represents the effects of the systole and diastole of the heart on the blood vessels. For Chinese medicine, there are twelve pulses, detected at different positions on the radial artery pulse. The pulses are felt by the practitioner with index, middle and ring fingers placed next to each other on the radial artery pulse. Each of these three fingers feels a superficial (*yang*) and a deep (*yin*) pulse. The left hand superficial pulses show the activity in three *yang* organs (Small Intestine, Gall Bladder and Bladder) and the deep pulses show the state of the three *yin* organs (Heart, Liver and Kidney). The right hand superficial pulses show the activity in the other three *yang* organs (Colon, Stomach, and Triple Heater) and the deep pulses reflect the behaviour of the three associated *yin* organs (Lung, Spleen and Heart Protector). Thus, by feeling these three positions on the radial artery, superficial and deep, on both sides, the practitioner gets a pulse reading of the quality and quantity of energy on all 12 meridians. Although everyone has some degree of fluctuation and temporary imbalances, disease states arise from chronically fixated imbalances, which the pulse taker can detect.

Since each meridian is associated with with either a *yin* or *yang* aspect of a particular stage of change, each pulse position also refers to an aspect of one of the stages of change, either Water, Wood, Fire, Earth or Metal. Thus one might speak, for example, of an imbalance in the *yin* aspect of Wood, detected through the Liver pulse.

Five Stages of Change: Correspondences and Associations

Each of the five stages of change is associated with a different season, time of day, colour, smell, odour, taste, and other parameters. These associations are sometimes called "The Laws of the Five Elements." But, as we have pointed out, these are not "elements" but rather "stages." Furthermore, these "laws" might be more helpfully thought of as "systems of correspondence."[6] By assessing these various parameters, the practitioner can build up a picture of the imbalances and balances in the different meridian channels. These associations are assessed along with the pulses, tongue diagnosis and other features, to arrive at a "Five Stages diagnosis." For example, often a seasonal variation will give a clue as to which stage is disturbed. Patients will sometimes say, "My aches and pains are always worse in the summer"; instead of assuming that the heat is the problem, the practitioner, knowing that summer is the "Fire" season, will think of Fire disturbances that might not be directly associated to heat. Perhaps this person's Fire is generally excessive and the extra energy in the summer season tips the balance to a point where the person experiences exacerbation of symptoms.

Each stage of change also has an associated colour. In the healthy state, all five colours should be produced. In an imbalanced meridian matrix, there will be too much or too little of a particular colour showing on that person's skin. A skilled practitioner can detect changes in the colour balance and can infer the energy imbalances on the meridians that correspond. The five energies can also be heard as sound vibrational qualities in the voice; again a skilled practitioner can detect changes in the sound balance. Since the five energies can also be detected as odours, an experienced Chinese practitioner can literally smell imbalances. In a similar fashion, the five energy states give rise to predilections for five basic tastes. Furthermore, a healthy individual will show an ebb and flow of expression of five emotions; when an emotion is expressed too frequently or less often, this indicates an imbalance on the meridian or meridians associated with that emotion.

The following table summarizes this system of correspondences.

	WOOD	FIRE	EARTH	METAL	WATER
DIRECTION	East	South	Centre	West	North
SEASON	Spring	Summer	Late Summer	Autumn	Winter
COLOUR	Green	Red	Yellow	White	Blue/Black
SOUND	Shout	Laugh	Sing	Weep	Groan
ODOUR	Rancid	Scorched	Fragrant	Rotten	Putrid
TASTE	Sour	Bitter	Sweet	Spicy	Salt
EMOTION	Anger	Joy	Empathy	Grief	Fear
ORIFICE	Eyes	Ears	Nose	Mouth	Lower Orifices
ORGAN	Liver/Gall Bladder	Heart/Small Intestine	Stomach/Spleen	Lung/Colon	Bladder/Kidney
BODY PART	Ligaments/Nails	Arteries	Muscles	Skin/Hair	Bones/Teeth
CLIMATE	Wind	Heat	Humid	Dry	Cold

The Eight Principles or Guiding Criteria (*Ba Gang*)

Acupuncture schools in the English-speaking world have tended to focus on Five Stages diagnosis. Another system in Chinese medicine is known as the Eight Principles or Guiding Criteria (*ba gang*). The use of the Eight Principles is an elaborate study, and we will say only a few words about it here. The four pairs of considerations that make up the Eight Principles are *yin/yang*, superficial/deep, cold/heat and excess/deficiency. These paired considerations are utilized to discern alterations in the patterns of the human energy body matrix, with the intention to find the state of balance and imbalance. Just as the Five Stages are not "things," so the Eight Principles are descriptors for the behaviour of *qi*. In terms of *yin* and *yang*, a person who has a *yang* excess or *yin* deficiency will show hyperactivity and heightened wastage of energy; a person who has *yang* deficiency (or *yin* excess) will manifest torpor and blockages and stagnation. In a similar way, some diseases result from imbalances in heat or cold, or from excess or deficiency of a particular kind of energy; the considerations of superficial or deep add more subtlety.

Chinese and Western Diagnosis

In the West, diagnosis focuses on answering the question "what is wrong?" In Classical Chinese Medicine, whether working with the Five Stages of Change or the Eight Principles, the purpose of diagnosis is to sense the state of energy in the meridian system. Where is the energy too high? Where is the energy too low? What is the relative state of harmony/disharmony? As we have seen, the Chinese practitioner builds up a picture of the pattern through pulse reading and observing colours, sounds, and smells, and integrating this information with questions about season, time of day and so on. Legend has it that a master practitioner is able to feel the pulses of an unknown patient through a slit in a screen and, without speaking or observing the person, tell all the illnesses that person has experienced and know their current state of health. Furthermore, through pulse diagnosis alone, the master practitioner is reputed to be able to predict future trends and possibilities for illness and health, based on the current state of pulses and the patterned history they carry. Rather than impute magical properties to fabled practitioners of old, we can see the message of "pattern recognition" that underlies these tales. We practice and teach this approach in our own work. There are many ways to accomplish this without using any of the specific approaches from CCM.

This is not pertinent only to an old medical system rooted in a distant past. The relevance of subtle pattern recognition is timely in the world today, beyond the confines of a strictly medical approach. For example, this understanding of seeing a pattern and being able to predict its effects into the future is now finding its way into modern psychology and business approaches. Daniel Goleman, for example, identifies pattern recognition as the one cognitive ability that distinguishes star performers in large companies: he describes this as "big picture" thinking that allows leaders to pick out meaningful trends from a welter of information around them and to think strategically far into the future.[7]

This way of thinking is quite different from the traditional Western medical diagnosis, which includes history taking, physical examination, and diagnostic tests (laboratory and special radiology). These elements lead the practitioner to a differential diagnosis. Based on this, the doctor will prescribe a course of treatment. Throughout this process the doctor carefully remains objective, and sees the patient as a separate entity; the doctor is discouraged from subjective feelings relating to the patient, in order to maintain an objective distance.

In classical Chinese diagnosis, on the other hand, the doctor depends upon sensory information and intuition to build up a picture of the energy body of the patient. So the practitioner is encouraged to be emotionally and psychologically close with the patient, in order to have a subjective experience of the patient's complaints. Classical Chinese diagnosis is summarized as "See" (observe the patient), "Hear" (notice the sound of the patient, and hear the unspoken elements of the patient's presentation), "Ask" (question to get a clear impression and a sense of the history of the illness process) and "Feel" (check the pulses, feel the quality of the patient's physical being). The diagnosis and subsequent treatment emerge from the contact and connection between client and practitioner.

Each system has inherent strengths and weaknesses. In the objective view of the West, the dispassionate attitude of science can be brought to bear on a situation without over-sentimentalizing; however, a practitioner may also be so "cool" and "remote" that the patient is left out of the dialogue. In the subjective Chinese medical approach, a natural healing can occur from the warmth and compassion of the healer; on the other hand, over-identification may cause the practitioner to lose clarity about what is best in a given situation. So, as in many other East-West issues, we propose an integrative approach where each system can learn from the other.

Treatment Methods
All too often, both patients and doctors are prone to look for a "quick fix" – a pill or a treatment to relieve the symptom, without investigating the underlying factors that brought the illness to manifest in the first

place. But this "fixing" the symptoms is only a temporary measure, and does not address deeper concerns. For healing to occur, the root of the illness must be located and deeply understood.

In their evolved forms, both Chinese and Western medicine see a change in the patient's life style as the key to healing. Both systems consider diet and exercise as important. Both often prescribe medicines; in the West, the focus is on drugs, while in Chinese medicine, more emphasis is on herbal remedies. In the West, surgery is often used; in CCM, acupuncture and moxibustion (burning of an herb on or near acupuncture points) are common features of treatment. We focus here on the use of acupuncture.

Acupuncture

Needles are not the same for China and the West. In the West, a hollow needle is introduced into a blood vessel in order to administer a fluid (e.g. an intravenous drug, or blood replacement) or to remove blood for testing. With acupuncture, the approach is very different and does not involve the blood vessels. The acupuncture needle is solid, not hollow; it is introduced into an acupuncture point (acupoint) which is bloodless, and there is nothing applied to the needle. The needle is used to connect to the energy of the patient on one side and the acupuncturist's fingers on the other. The acupuncture needle can be seen as a means of energetic communication between the patient and the practitioner.

Conceptually, the acupuncture points are places on the meridians where action can be taken to adjust the flow of qi in that meridian. Different writings report the number of acupuncture points to be between 365 and 1,000. Each point has its own characteristics and can be utilized in a variety of ways to invite further balancing in the system. Some of the points are used to enhance the energy on a meridian (tonification points); some can calm the energy on a meridian (sedation points); some are used in association with the concept of a 24-hour energy cycle (horary points); some connect the paired meridians within an element (junction points); and some can do a multiplicity of actions (source points).

These are but a few of the remarkable variety of points that can be utilized by a knowledgeable practitioner to take action on the energy matrix to facilitate balance and healing. Needles of different lengths and diameters can be used with a variety of techniques to help adjust energy flow. As well, non-needle stimulation can be quite effective (massage, electrical stimulators, sound). The purpose of treatment of the acupoints is to facilitate the freeing of energy in order to encourage reharmonizing of the energy matrix, thus reducing symptoms on the various dimensions of the being. CCM embraces an attitude of "least action" – use the lightest, simplest treatment with the smallest possible number of needles.

Energy Transfer or Resonance?

As we have said, acupuncture needles can be seen as a means of communication between client and practitioner. This view is in contrast to more mechanistic theories that reify energy as something that can be raised, lowered, gained or lost. In such a physical understanding of medicine, the healer helps by transmitting extra energy, with net gain to patient and net loss to practitioner. This is an aspect of what we describe as power-based medicine, where the healer is responsible for the healing. This concept is utilized often, not only in medical practice (both Eastern and Western), but also in other helping disciplines such as massage, body work, chiropractic and other healing forms. It is an attitude that can lead to dependency on the part of the patient, and often to burnout in the practitioner. Some people take this idea so far as to say that a person who is ill can transmit "toxic" energy, which is dangerous to others. We do not subscribe to this energy transfer notion. Instead, we believe in a concept of resonance, where each individual is responsible for his or her own state of balance and vibratory harmony; nothing physical is exchanged in the healing dialogue.[8]

Interrelatedness is a non-physical concept; each person can vibrate in resonance with the universal *qi* energy, within the boundaries of an individual energy body matrix. Illness occurs from an imbalance in the energy relationships within the organism itself, and in its relationship with other energy entities. Communication between individual beings is not by "energy exchange" but rather by resonance. Hence, no energy is transmitted or transferred. Using the concept of resonance instead of exchange, a healer can influence by proximity without giving any thing to the patient; what is "given" is the focused attention of the healer. In this way of thinking, there is no toxicity from the disharmony of a patient; if the practitioner responds with diminished energy, this is from the practitioner resonating with his or her own energy body matrix. Since no energy is exchanged, the practitioner is not harmed by the patient (and the patient is not "helped" by the practitioner). Therefore, there is no loss or gain of energy. This is the context in which we ourselves use acupuncture or acupressure with people.

Power-Based Medicine and Strength-Based Medicine

Although Chinese medicine and Western medicine are very different in their assumptions and practice, both of them can be practised either in a limiting way or in a manner that enhances health and responsibility on the part of the patient. The key question, as we've already implied, is

"Who is responsible for the patient's illness and health?" We wrote about this at length in an earlier book.[9]

In both the West and the East, there has been a strong tendency to look upon the doctor as the expert, who has superior knowledge and power to fight disease; the patient is the victim of illness and depends upon the practitioner's skill and power to be relieved. The doctor is cast in the role of a priest-healer-shaman. The power dynamic of assigning the healing role and authority to the practitioner results in a power-based medicine that keeps the patient weak and uninvolved with health and healing.

A strength-based medicine, on the other hand, sees patients as responsible for all aspects of their lives, including illness and healing.

This distinction between power-based and strength-based medicine cuts across the categories of Western and Chinese medicine. Either form can be practised with a strength-based or a power-based approach.

In the scientific, objective approach of Western medicine, the goal of treatments is to "fix" something "wrong"; this can be a practical and effective approach and at times will be entirely appropriate, but, as we have seen, it can also degenerate into a mechanistic and moralistic dehumanization. When it is practised inelegantly, disease is seen as an entity separated from the patient, a "thing" to be combated; the doctor "fixes" the patient. The doctor in this approach is responsible for the healing, and resorts to all sorts of external aids to correct the illness, including drugs and specific therapies. The diagnosis and treatment come after disease is manifested. These are all components of the power-based approach in Western medicine.

This objective scientific approach can be practised as a strength-based art, keeping the patient as the centre of the activity, with the practitioner as a counsellor and advisor. The task is to assist the patient to make the appropriate choices to find health and wellness; in this elegant approach, patients are responsible for their healing, health and wellbeing. Drugs and treatments are prescribed in consultation with the patient, and the patient is at the centre of the ongoing process. In this form of medicine, life style counselling and prevention are cornerstones, utilizing the objective evidence from scientific research as a support.

In the classical Chinese approach, diagnosis and treatment involve appreciating energy blocks that underlie the person's symptoms. In its evolved form, this type of medicine is holistic, pragmatic and non-blaming. Illness results from being out of touch with self and life. The patient is responsible for balancing the energy blocks, and the practitioner is the facilitator, catalyst, and focusing agent. Essentially a preventative medicine, the aim is to harmonize the energy body before illness has a chance to manifest in time and space. The practitioner is a life style counsellor and an educator; the patient is the healer. However, while the classical Chinese approach emphasizes the patient's relationship to self and life, Chinese medicine can equally be practised with a power orientation and can easily degenerate into a mechanistic process. Just as a power-based Western practitioner may simply prescribe drugs and therapies, power-based Chinese practitioners can use acupuncture, moxibustion, herbs, and other treatments merely as tools to control patients' symptoms, without regard to their wholeness and responsibility or their life style and relationships.

Western medicine and Chinese medicine can be very compatible as long as there is no need to choose which is superior. They each have their own limitations and appropriate uses. We encourage the movement towards understanding in all aspects of East and West, including the medical field. Perhaps at some future time, we can grow in our understanding of each other to achieve a truly global, transcultural understanding of health and healing.

IV.3
Spirit Guides, Reincarnation, Ancestors

KZ = Confucius (Kong Zi), CJ = Carl Jung, BW = Ben Wong, JM = Jock McKeen

JM: Dr. Jung, I share with you a strong interest in China. I have been intrigued with the ancient Chinese culture since I was introduced to the *Book of Changes* in my early 20s. What about you?

CJ: My deep introduction came in the late 1920s when Richard Wilhelm sent me the manuscript for *The Secret of the Golden Flower*. When I read it, I knew I was not alone. Unseen people from another time in China had been practising what I was just discovering. We were connected across time, across space. I felt very confirmed by this.

JM: I'm glad to hear this. We talk about the Golden Flower in our next chapter! I understand what you say you about connection. I always feel remarkably comfortable with Chinese people. No matter where I am in the world, when I am in a Chinese restaurant, whether it is fancy or simple, I am always completely at home, amongst "my people." Often, I am the only Caucasian, yet I never feel out of place.

BW: As for me, I am racially Chinese (with some aboriginal blood too). Yet I am more Western in many ways than Jock. I tend to be suspicious of anything that is not strictly logical, and I have adopted Western culture so thoroughly. People often call me a "banana" because I am yellow on the outside and white on the inside!

JM: Yet, in his bones, Ben is Chinese and understands traditional ideas without studying them formally. I, on the other hand, have studied Chinese diligently. Whenever I made a discovery in my studies, I would be very excited to bring things to Ben that his forefathers had said, and he would say, "So? That's obvious!" I think he is both Chinese and a banana! I am a Western boy, yet I am internally more Chinese than Ben ... I am an egg.

KZ (smiling at the levity): Jock, your Chinese nature is very apparent to me. It's not on the outside, it's on the inside.

JM: I have taught Chinese philosophy and medicine for four decades. Even when I have not studied something, I seem to be able to figure it out, or guess at the meaning of Chinese characters that I don't know.

BW: Sometimes, students in China would argue with Jock when he was teaching about ancient ideas. They thought that Jock's scholarship was superficial and that he didn't know what he was talking about. They were so sure of themselves. But Jock would never back down. He was often so assured about what he was saying.

JM: I have a brash personality, but I was especially audacious to challenge Chinese scholars in class in China and argue them down about ancient Chinese issues. At first, they would dismiss me as a crass foreigner; but then, slowly, surely, something would happen, someone else in the class would say, "I have heard of such a thing from my grandfather" and the debate would be on. How was it I could have such confidence in things I should not know? Was I just foolhardy and lucky?

BW: This has happened over and over. Often our Chinese students would ask us a question about the East, expecting me to know the answer. I often would say, "I don't know – that's Jock's area, ask him."

JM: I have never known how I could be so certain about Chinese issues, even before I studied the Chinese language. How could I be so sure about facts from ancient China that even my Chinese-speaking friends rejected as being untrue?

BW: It has happened so often that Jock now has a reputation as a true egg!

JM: I gradually have developed an ever-increasing confidence that I am being aided, assisted, and if I am clean in my intentions to learn, the revelation will come.

CJ (Looking mysterious): Our lives and learning are often under strange circumstances. We are directed by invisible agencies.

JM: Do you mean spirit guides?

CJ: I think there are deep forces within the psyche that express themselves to guide us. Call them spirit guides if you like. My inner forces also seem to be very harmonious with Chinese ways.

JM: Do you think I might have a Chinese spirit guide? Or maybe I was Chinese in another life? I don't really know what to think of such things as spirit guides and reincarnation.

CJ: We all have Chinese spirit guides, and Jewish spirit guides, and aboriginal spirit guides, and all manner of other guides. They are aspects of the universal psyche. These are available to anyone who tunes in to them.

KZ: These are not actual physical entities "out there" that help us. They are within.

CJ: I agree. These are not separate from us ... they are part of our deep nature. For you, Jock, the Chinese aspect of your spirit guide is foreground in your psyche; for someone else, they would tune into different cultural variations.

BW: I agree that they are not separate from us. Call them spirit guides or guardian angels, or God, or deep nature, or individual conscience. Whatever you like. We must not get trapped in the words.

JM: I like to think of this as my intuition, or my inner voices, or my conscience.

KZ: Certainly. Except that they are not "yours." They cannot be owned ... they are of the universe. Vast wisdom is available to us at all times in the present moment.

BW: They are the universe, of which we are a part; they are in us because we all participate in the collective unconscious.

CJ (making an unaccustomed joke): You are becoming a Jungian!

BW: In this way I guess I always was!

JM (earnestly): Since we are addressing such topics, let's talk about reincarnation. I wonder if I might have been Chinese in another lifetime.

KZ: This idea of reincarnation is so prone to misunderstanding. You, Jock, as a particular personality, were never in existence before. Each life form that manifests is new, and has never appeared exactly the same way previously. We are not "reincarnated" from the past ... we are *incarnated* in the present. Incarnation, yes. Reincarnation, no.

BW: This has puzzled me too. As Jock mentioned in an earlier discussion, my mother was told that the baby she was carrying (me) would be an incarnation of an ancient Chinese sage. (Turning to Confucius) Maybe I am you!

KZ (eyes twinkling with mirth): Of course you are! We are all each other. We are a whole, with individual parts. Just as the flower is a part of the plant, each flower that opens is new and individual. When the blossom dies, another blossom takes its place. Each human flower that comes into life is new in the same way. This is not a reincarnation ... it is an incarnation. One humanity, different human flowers.

JM: The notion of ancestors has been significant to both you, Master Kong, and you, Dr. Jung.

KZ: We Chinese are always aware of our ancestors. This is not only our personal blood relatives, although it includes them.

CJ: My ideas about the collective unconscious and archetypes include the idea of ancestors. This is our heritage as a people, as a race, which is embedded in the depths of our psyche, collectively and individually.

JM: Dr. Jung, I know you believe that the primary archetype of the individual self, which is at the centre of the deep unconscious, is an expression of the universal archetype of the Self. Is this God?

CJ (with a deep gaze): Yes, I could say that the centre of the human being is God. We are small manifestations of God in our little lives.

JM: Some say that we are all God. We are the ancient wisdom struggling to incarnate, impeded by the obstinate pedantry of current assumptions and beliefs. How can God break through?

KZ: We Chinese don't talk about God so much – we talk more about deepest nature. But I am comfortable with inviting God into the discussion. I think it all depends upon an individual person opening the heart.

BW (smiling at Confucius): Exactly. God, or deep nature, or human meaning – it doesn't matter what name you use – they all occur in the heart.

KZ: The centre of human beings, and their connection to the universe, is in the heart. I once said that if people would look honestly, straight into their hearts, and then act in accordance with what they found, they would never need rules or regulations. They would be in harmony with the universe. For those in earnest, they don't need rules – if they listen to the rhythm of the universe that beats in their heart of hearts, they will remain in the centre.

JM: But Master Kong, you wrote so much about rules, and structures and ways of being. They seem to be very important to you.

KZ: This was for people who were not ready to do the intense self-investigation needed to operate from conscience. Structures and politics, and rites and rituals are superficialities for people who are not ready to plumb deeper.

BW (laughing appreciatively): Yes! Being a human being can be hard work!

IV.4

The Spiritual Dimensions of Classical Chinese Medicine

There are more things in heaven and earth ... than are dreamt of in your philosophy.[1]

When we first went to China in 1987, our intention was to learn more about Classical Chinese medicine. We have already told the story of how we were surprised, even shocked, to discover that much of what we had found illuminating and exemplary in Chinese medicine was being utterly disregarded in China in those days. Classical Chinese Medicine's ancient grounding in spirituality, we realised, was in danger of being lost in the place of its origin. However, the European schools, where Jock had studied, had maintained what China was forgetting. We found ourselves in the strange position of becoming teachers when we had intended to be students. Throughout our careers, we have sought to bring the hidden elements of the Chinese classics to light, in ourselves, in our students, in our school; ultimately we hope this remarkable material is returned to the Chinese people.

In our first chapter on Chinese medicine we discussed how Classical Chinese Medicine (CCM) has a much more comprehensive view than its modern version, Traditional Chinese Medicine (TCM). Yet it is TCM that receives most attention. Classical Chinese Medicine included the deeper philosophical perspectives of Daoism and Confucianism, and other ancient wisdom. We have already introduced many of these ideas. But there is more – much, much more. The ancient wisdom that brings the spiritual dimension to Chinese medicine and philosophy has been receiving more attention of late; however, some of it has already been lost. The deepest significance of Chinese medicine lies in the appreciation of the philosophy of the spirits that informs the ancient vision of the human place in the world. J.R. Worsley – Jock's teacher and one of the most influential Five Stages theorists and practitioners of the 20th century – insisted in his lectures that the deepest healing is at the level of the spirit. In this chapter, we will outline some of the poetic and imaginative approaches to spirituality found in the ancient Chinese classics.

Dao and Shu

The Chinese make a contrast between *dao* – a word we have already met in several contexts – and *shu*. This is the distinction between something universal and encompassing and deep (*dao*) and something simplified, practical, but often superficial (*shu*). In both Western and Chinese medicine, the *shu* approach would be to treat the symptom without appreciating the underlying cause. The *dao* approach would be to get to the root of the matter and treat the deep cause of the disorder.

Much Chinese medicine outside China has been practiced from a *shu* point of view. This has occurred not only in the West – where one might more expect superficiality due to a lack of familiarity – but also in the modern practice of Chinese medicine inside China. However, in contrast to the modern views, classical Chinese ideas are subtle, supple and complex.

A practitioner of the *shu* approach often disregards the patient, looks at the part that is malfunctioning, assigns a diagnostic label, and then treats the label. In Western medicine, this has been a growing issue: objectifying, depersonalizing approaches have been supplanting the art of medicine. The same is occurring in China with TCM. As we discussed in Chapter IV.3, we associate these trends with a power-based approach to medicine. The *dao* approach would treat the whole person, in his or her life context; the treatment is dynamic and holistic. CCM was, and is, a *dao* approach based on a universalist, humanistic, strength-based philosophy of life.

The Yellow Emperor's Classic: The Heart at the Centre

The most famous of the ancient classics of CCM is the *Huang Di Nei Jing* or *The Yellow Emperor's Classic of Internal Medicine*. Much of this cornerstone text was written in the Han Dynasty (206 BC – AD 220). The book takes the form of a dialogue between the mythical Yellow Emperor and his minister Qi Bo.

The *Nei Jing*, as it is commonly called, comprises two parts: the *Su Wen (Simple Questions)* and the *Ling Shu (Spiritual Axis)*.[2] Some parts of the *Nei Jing* provide a straightforward outline of the "nuts and bolts" of the thought system; these practical chapters of the *Nei Jing* are the source of much of what we wrote in Chapter IV.3. Other chapters of the *Nei Jing* are mysterious, esoteric, poetic, mystical; some of the information we discuss in this chapter comes from these texts. These writings suggest there are influences from invisible realities that have effects on our everyday world.

For the ancient Chinese there are two poles, heaven and earth. The *qi* of heaven flows down to the earth, and the *qi* of the earth flows up to the sky. In the ancient Chinese system, the human being is in the middle of this dualism and lives in the flow of these two forces. In this sense, the human being participates in the forces of heaven and earth, and integrates them in human being-ness. The downward flowing force from heaven is *yang qi,* and the upward flowing force from earth is *yin qi.* Heaven denotes the world of invisible forces, the abstract world of no time, no space; the earth represents the manifest world of nature and mortal beings in time and space.

The human being is in relationship to both of these worlds, one infinite and eternal, the other temporal-spatial. Indeed, as Richard Wilhelm put it, "Man is a microcosm and is not separated from the macrocosm by any fixed barriers … [he] participates in all cosmic events, and is inwardly and outwardly interwoven with them."

The interface between the human world and the cosmic world is the heart. For an individual to be completely healthy, the heart must be empty; if the heart becomes full of wordly concerns, the deep connections with the universe are obscured and the vitality of the individual is lessened. Claude Larre and Elizabeth Rochat de La Vallée write:

> As the Chinese saw it, the master-word of psychology is "heart." The heart is the vital center. It occupies the place of ruler. It is sacred vessel, holy land of each being; it welcomes the Spirits sent from Heaven. It contains and controls the Heaven/Earth exchange that makes us human and keeps us alive. By nature man's heart is vast and free like Heaven; always tempted to fill itself, it must seek to become empty.[3]

Meditating on the concerns of the heart, one can attain a deepening awareness of one's connection to the greater order. This involves a periodic de-emphasizing of the daily concerns of the world and a turning inward.

> Man's heart, involved naturally in knowledge coming from the senses and from the motion of the body, will from time to time close its shutters and withdraw. The art of the heart is the mastery of life.[4]

If the individual becomes addicted to the passions of the external world, a progressive spiritual illness can ensue, which will eventually show its effects on the other dimensions of the being.

> The person held prey by passions unravels day after day, along the routes of deterioration implied by the particular passion that he has allowed to inhabit his heart.[5]

One's humility and reverence for the depth of life keep the heart open and ready to receive. We can find our place in the infinity of beings, but only by letting go of our attachments to the toys of the outer world. Implied in this is a belief in free will, and the human individual's ultimate choice to engage in the vital life of the universe, and thus live fully, or to become fixated upon externals and lose touch with the inner resources. In the classical Chinese view, the human being has the ability to open to life and to experience flow and harmony with nature and heaven; or the human being can close up, become defensive and withdraw from life.

We return to the centrality of the heart at the end of this chapter.

Essences and Spirits

A common pairing that often occurs in Chinese texts, including the *Nei Jing*, is that of *jing* and *shen*. *Jing* is the essence energy and *shen* are the spirits that direct the activity of life in the being. As life unfolds in individual humans, their genetic inheritance from their ancestors is involved in the *essences* of their life. These essences interact with *spirits* that assist and guide and shape an individual's being and life. Larre and Rochat de La Vallée write:

> The essences coming from the mother and the father meet in an embrace that gives structure to the individual of the species; then the Spirits appear that guide the individual life.[6]

Jing, essence, is the material substrate for life inherited from one's parents. The Chinese character has radicals for "rice" and "green," implying a meaning of "the best, the purest food of spirit and flesh." *Jing* is maintained by the function of the kidney. The interplay of essences and spirits is the interplay of earth and heaven in the human realm:

> Essences form us, spirits animate us. The spirits that dwell in us emanate from our essences. In me, Heaven manifests through the spirits, Earth manifests through the essences.[7]

Five Spirits

The five spirits or spiritual aspects (*wu shen*) in ancient Chinese thinking are an arrangement of the psychic authorities of each individual. They do not *inhabit* a being; rather, they represent the Chinese understanding of the psychic structures that influence and guide the organ systems. The *wu shen* are *shen, hun, po, yi,* and *zhi,* and each is associated with a specific organ. Let us consider these in more detail.

SHEN (LIFE SPIRITS)

The *shen* are the life spirits that reside in the heart. The heart itself is empty and is the special place where the subtle spirits can come and go freely. But the heart must be open or the *shen* will not stay. It is said,

"The heart preserves the mental energy." The character for *shen* implies a light spirit; one could say that the light of heaven shines through the agency of the *shen*. The Chinese character has the radical for "revelation," which could be interpreted (depending upon your persuasion) as "God" or "to tell," meaning human speech and expression.

HUN (SPIRIT SOUL)

The *hun* is the "spirit soul" that is preserved by the liver. The character for *hun* shows an upward movement from earth to sky. The sense of the *hun* is that material potential (the physical being) moves towards a non-material state. The *hun* directs the imagination and the emotions (the vehicles through which humans strive upwards to the sky). The Chinese characters contain elements for "cloud" and "spirit"; literally, the *hun* is a "spirit you cannot catch." The liver is a solid organ; the solidity is necessary to hold the vaporous upward rising *hun*.

PO (ANIMAL SOUL)

The *po* is the animal soul that resides in the lung. This represents the downward movement of spirit from sky to earth. This is the transformation from insubstantiality into materiality, a process of increasing densification. The *po* directs the instincts through their activity. It is said, "The lungs preserve the sap of life." The flow of *qi* is guided by the *po*, whose roots are in the sky and whose life is in the body in the lung. The Chinese character means "white spirit" or "transparent spirit." The lung is a full of air, and this characteristic permits the dense *po* to have a balanced place to be (that which is already dense would be excessively constrained by more density).

YI (PURPOSE, THOUGHT)

The Chinese character *yi* has numerous associations. *Yi* is usually translated as "thought," but the meaning of it is more complex. It includes aspects that imply "to stand out," "light" and "heart"; the character implies "preserving" (as thought can preserve a principle). By extension, it can be associated with consciousness, contemplation, and principles. *Yi* is associated with the spleen; it is written that "The spleen preserves thought." The characteristic of the Chinese spleen is movement and transport throughout the being; in this way *yi* suggests "spreading an idea throughout the being." *Yi* can be translated as "purpose" or "something which resonates with the heart" with a "musical resonance in harmony with the way of the universe." This implies a purpose and a thought process that is sensitive, responsive to the ways of heaven and nature. So, this is thought that is harmonious with the ways of the universe, which can be intensified into "reflection" and "meditation," which have far-reaching effects.

ZHI (WILL)

Zhi is will, and is preserved in the kidneys. In this way, it is associated with *jing*, the essences, the strength of life, which are also associated with the kidney. Will develops from maintenance of *yi*, the purposeful thought that is in harmony with the will of heaven. In this way, the individual will can be integrated with the will of heaven. This human will is developed through a life of reflection and contemplation to maintain the inner balance of the being in harmony with the *dao*, the way of the universe.[8] Thus, in our terms, will is a strength- rather than power-oriented capacity.

The Yellow River Map and the Five Spirits

The Yellow River map is an ancient organization of the Five Stages of Change that has Earth at the centre, rather than the more familiar arrangement with Earth in sequence with the other stages. This organization implies that the other four Stages are all in a special relation to the Earth Stage, which is profoundly involved in the material world and the manifestation of the living being. All the energies find integration in the physical manifestation of the being, through Earth.

It is useful to consider the five "spirits" in relation to the Yellow River Map. The *shen* are associated with Fire, *hun* with Wood, *po* with Metal, and *zhi* (and the essences, *jing*) with Water. *Yi*, purpose, is associated with Earth, denoting its centrality in the process of manifestation and materialization.

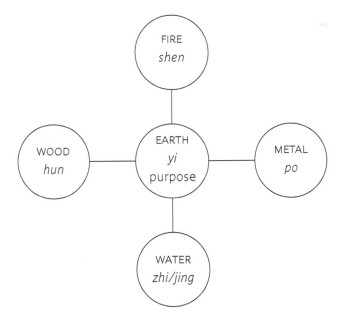

The Secret Treatise of the Spiritual Orchid: The 12 Officials

Chapter Eight of the *Su Wen*, known as *The Secret Treatise of the Spiritual Orchid*, is a short text that describes the 12 meridians as 12 "officials" of a city-state. Each official has specific duties and functions, and has particular relationships in the organization and politics of the body-mind. This arcane and obscure text has been very ably translated into English by Claude Larre and Elizabeth Rochat de la Vallée.[9] The translated text follows in the precise order of the original; we have added the numbering to the statements to show the sequential relationship between the different officials:

1   The heart holds the office of the lord and sovereign; the radiance of the spirits stems from it.
2   The lungs hold the office of minister and chancellor; the regulation of the life-giving network stems from it.
3   The liver holds the office of general of the armed forces; assessment of circumstances and conception of plans stem from it.
4   The gallbladder is responsible for what is just and exact; determination and decision stem from it.
5   The heart protector has the charge of resident as well as envoy; elation and joy stem from it.
6   The spleen and stomach are responsible for the storehouses and granaries; the five tastes stem from them.
7   The large intestine is responsible for transit; the residue from transformation stems from it.
8   The small intestine is responsible for receiving and making things thrive; transformed substances stem from it.
9   The kidneys are responsible for the creation of power; skill and ability stem from them.
10 The triple heater is responsible for the opening up of passages and irrigation; the regulation of fluids stems from it.
11 The bladder is responsible for regions and cities; it stores the body fluids; the transformations of the *qi* then give out their power.

"These twelve charges," the text continues, "form an interdependent group that allows of no failing." These officials thus function together; their interconnection and relationships bring a strength that keeps the integrity and security of the being. This metaphoric description of the human individual as a city-state provides a code of life that is rich with associations, with secrets about the development and maintenance of an evolved and healthy human being. The effective functioning of this body politic requires balance, harmony and integration amongst the twelve officials who conduct the business of the whole. Another way of conceiving this is that within each human is contained a multitude of natures that all have an important role in being whole. From a spiritual perspective, the full expression and integration of all the natures brings forth the emanation of a whole being, a soul in full bloom. Conversely, blocking any of these takes away from wholeness of spirit. The Chinese metaphor of twelve beings helps one to understand the internal dialogues that are necessary for the individual to lead a full and creative existence. This links to Chinese diagnosis and treatment; determining where the blocks exist among the officials and finding ways to release them results in increased flow, harmony and expression within the being. There are vast implications in this for an integrative psychology and spirituality.

If one official is ill, then all the others will lack the clarity of that official's input, and this will result in imbalance and disharmony in the bodymind. For example, the liver as general of the armed forces has a vital task – effective planning is critical for overall health and maintenance of the being. In modern psychological terminology, excessive planning is seen in obsessions and compulsions; inadequate planning leads to impossible situations where opportunities cannot be seized.

Everything that applies in the individual's body politic also pertains to groups of people. For example, an assessment of the functioning of the 12 officials could be used to evaluate the health and productivity of a business enterprise. In an effective business, the activities of the 12 officials would be integrated. An effective classroom would be the same; so would a self-sustaining health care system. The interrelationship between different functions that brings health within an individual human being is equally important in the creation and maintenance of a group.

Return to The Heart
We have already noted the centrality of the heart in Chinese medicine. "Heaven and Earth," wrote Larre and Rochat de la Vallée, "meet in the heart."[10] This is a recurring theme in Chinese spiritual writings. Each of us is connected to our deepest nature (which is the nature of the universe) through the function of the heart. Confucius was clear about this too, and the theme repeats again and again in the texts of ancient Chinese medical practice.

Claude Larre and Elizabeth Rochat de La Vallée translated and discussed Chapter Eight of the *Ling Shu* in a very accessible book *Rooted in Spirit: The Heart of Chinese Medicine*. The text involves conversations between the Yellow Emperor and his Minister, Qi Bo, concerning health, life and treatment of disease. A central theme recurs throughout: treatment is never satisfactory if it is done only on a superficial or symptomatic level.

In response to the Emperor's questions, the Minister Qi Bo notes that all treatment is rooted in the spirits. The key is understanding the relation of the invisible, heavenly world and the visible, earthly world and learning to live in harmony with the forces of the universe, humbly and creatively. The text contains some key concepts of Chinese medicine and health. Peter Firebrace, editor of another book by Larre and Rochat, says in his foreword,

> The … terms roll on like a waterfall and are taken slowly, line by line, character by character, to present the weave and pattern of the cloth as much as the individual threads themselves. These terms are key to a deeper understanding of Chinese medicine with their strong connection to our mental, emotional and spiritual nature.[11]

The character for the heart (*xin*) is the central figure in this "waterfall" of words, and many of the other characters contain the representation of the heart within them. The ideograms for the following terms in the text all contain the character for heart: Virtue (*de*), Purpose (*yi*), Will (*zhi*), Thought (*si*), and Reflection (*lu*). The heart is the centre of the human being, the link between self and nature and heaven. The human being, by living in harmony with the forces of heaven and earth, can grow increasingly aware and responsible in the occupation of tending the garden of life. Human beings, by being in touch with themselves, can harmonize with the movements within and then act on the world in the present, expressing timeless and infinite possibilities. This text summarizes the forces and the development process of a responsible human being. Understanding this process of transformations, one can gain deeper understanding of health and wellness. For us, Larre and Rochat's books are excellent sources for the earnest reader who wants to appreciate the original Chinese text. They carefully show the origins of the thought, the nuances of meanings in the flow of the characters, and gracefully express the poetic layering of this comprehensive treatise on health and life. Our own understanding has deepened through repeated readings of their translations and comments.

A summary might go like this. In the human being is a heavenly aspect (Virtue, *de*) and an earthly aspect (the Breaths, *qi*). The heart is the central location for the human awareness and development of these aspects. Life occurs as the Breaths expand, and is developed in a human fashion by following the directives of the Virtue of heaven within (conscience). The life of the human being is seen in the Essences; when the Essences are in harmony with heaven, this shows the operation of the Spirits. So, the Spirits are from heaven, and the Essences are from earth; their interaction is the life of the human being. In the human, there are

de, Virtue   xin, Heart   yi, Purpose   zhi, Will

si, Thought   lu, Reflection   zhi, Know-how, Wisdom

A "waterfall" of terms from the Ling Shu. *Note that the character for heart appears in all but the last ideogram.*

two processes, one that follows the Spirits as they come and go from the heart (this is the *hun*), and one that follows the Essences as they exit and enter (this is the *po*). So, just as Virtue is on the side of heaven, and Breaths are on the side of earth, so too are Spirits and *hun* associated with heaven, and Essences and *po* associated with earth. All of this is mediated in the human heart, which is the centre of the being. The text reads, "When something takes charge of the beings, we speak of the heart."

The development of the heart's mastery of these forces involves a sequence of learnings and intensifications on a path towards a fully responsible, aware human life. This echoes the Confucian notion of "looking straight into the heart and acting from what you see." The heart is the central intelligence of the human being, and is aware of our place in life and the universe. When one focuses on what the heart speaks and dedicates oneself to expressing the heart's desires, this is Purpose (Intent, *yi*). When one practises living with intention, this is the development of Will (*zhi*). As the Will is developed, the person becomes more flexible and adept in applying the Will; this is the development of Thought (*si*). When one maintains this thought, which is a deepening awareness of life and consequences and other beings, a meditative process becomes stronger and is known as Reflection (*lu*). As one extends this reflection to include awareness of all beings, this is Know-how or Wisdom (*zhi*), in which the individual is aware and caring for all of life, in both its time-space contemporary physical aspect and also for all eternity. The person who exhibits Know-how is a master of life, and a realized human being, caring for all life and all beings.

As we noted, the character for heart appears in many of the complex

Chinese characters that describe this process. The final character, Know-how or Wisdom, *zhi*, does not contain the character for heart, since it is above and beyond human considerations and is the central stream of the universal process, which can be engaged and expressed by a human being who "gets out of the way" of the flow of the universe. This is "letting go," *wu wei* (non-action with awareness). This is the element of "flow" that occasionally comes to trained athletes or the suppleness of thought that can occur when someone has pondered a topic long and deeply. These are stages in a process, not a static sequence with an end goal. This is a way of life.

The Golden Flower

The Secret of the Golden Flower: A Chinese Book of Life is an ancient Daoist alchemical text, translated in 1931 by Richard Wilhelm; a more recent translation has been done by Thomas Cleary. The Daoists were interested in the preservation and regeneration of life. The book contains ideas about an "immortal spirit body" (the Golden Flower of the title). Wilhelm's edition contains an introduction and commentary by C.G. Jung.[12] Jung had a major epiphany after he first read the text he received from Wilhelm; he notes that what he found in the book confirmed so many elements he had discovered in his own personal investigations. He had previously thought that his answers were perhaps only personal to him; when he saw the *Golden Flower*, he realized that others had been working in the same area many centuries before, and he found this very confirming. Nevertheless, wrote Jung, "It cannot be sufficiently strongly emphasized that we [Westerners] are not Orientals, and therefore have an entirely different point of departure in these things."[13]

According to this book, each individual contains a central core that involves both earthly (*yin*) and heavenly (*yang*) aspects. This core "monad" is comprised of universal, impersonal principles, which are represented by two spiritual principles, *hun* and *po*, which strive for mastery over each other during the life of the individual. As we have discussed earlier, the *po* is the earthly soul, the *yin* downward movement of spirit into matter. *Po* directs the instincts and resides in the lungs; a translation of the Chinese character for *po* would be "transparent (white) spirit." The *hun* is the spirit soul, the *yang* upward moving process of transformation of matter into spirit; the Chinese word contains radicals for "cloud" and "spirit" (clouds come and go, cannot be captured). There is a struggle between the forces of *po* that pull us down into the earth, to materialization, and the forces of *hun* that urge our life force upwards. At death, *hun* and *po* separate and go different ways: *po* sinks to earth as *gui* (ghost beings) and *hun* rises to become *shen* (free spirits).

This struggle occurs in every human being, usually below awareness. The general tendency is for exteriorization, for people to become
attached to the physical world and lose contact with the root of the
spirit; they gradually weaken as the life force becomes more and more
invested in the illusions of the external world. Their life force is lessened
and at physical death they persist as *gui*, hungry ghosts or earthbound
spirits that hover around life, trying to capture lost opportunities. The
alchemical practices of the *Golden Flower* are designed to counteract the
usual tendency towards dissipation and exteriorization, and loss of the
life force. Although this is commonly understood as a manual for preparation for the afterlife, to us, more fundamentally, it is a book about life
itself. The significance of the text lies in its focus on energy conservation
and regeneration and learning to minimize energy dissipation.

While the general tendency, as we have seen, is towards dissipation, it
is nevertheless possible for the the earthly souls (*po*) to be mastered by
spirit souls (*hun*); when this happens, a backward flowing, rising movement of life energies is set in motion. The result is liberation from externals, a freeing from attachment and field dependence. Externals are
recognized but not desired; external illusions are robbed of their energy.
An inner ascending circulation of energies takes place. The self with-
draws from entanglement in the world and remains alive after death
because of "interiorization," which has prevented wasting of life energies in the outer world; a life centre is created in the inner rotation of the
monad, which is independent of bodily existence. Such a self becomes
a *shen*; it survives as long as inner rotation continues. *Shen* means to
create or extend (the opposite of *gui*). The *shen*, even though invisible,
can still influence others and inspire great thoughts and deeds. Saints
and sages are said to be beings like these. They are still limited beings:
they retain their personal character and are subject to the constraints
of space and time. They still are not immortal; only the Golden Flower,
which grows out of inner detachment from all entanglement, is eternal.
The Golden Flower penetrates the magic circle of the polar duality of all
phenomena, and returns to the undivided one, the *dao*.

We see this account as a structure of life enhancement and personal
development. It is a metaphor for the choices facing each individual to
either fritter away life on externals and illusions and superficial attachments, or to concentrate one's life centre and harmonize with the forces
of the universe that flow within us. Each human is free to lose the light
through dissipation, or concentrate it. We can waste our lives, or be eco-
nomical in energy conservation and recycling, participating meaningfully in the whole of the cosmic pattern.

There is no necessity to follow the Daoist practices recommended in the text; the central meaning of the text is relevant to modern people in the West and East who wish to develop themselves. One can grow and learn to be in harmony with life through a process of awareness and self-investigation.

This self-development is clearly a process of living. But, as the text suggests, death may be only the end of the bodily existence. One's life of disciplined conservation may have influence and effect beyond the death of the physical being. The focus is on awareness of the flow of reality, not the preservation of the individual personality:

> For immortality does not consist in the preservation of our ego or our limited personality, but in the awareness of that great flow of reality in which our present life is only a fleeting moment. In this knowledge lies the liberation from death leading to the experience and realization of immortality.[14]

In this view, the path to freedom is through letting go, not holding on:

> Herein lies the secret of immortality: we are immortal not by holding on, but by letting go. Whatever we master, we need not cling to; we can always create it anew, thanks to the creative power of the sovereign spirit within us.[15]

To us, and to Chinese medicine, the sovereign spirit is the heart. In life and in death, what matters most is the heart. In the words of Ezra Pound,

> What thou lovest well remains,
> the rest is dross.[16]

IV.5
A Remarkable Meeting

Jock's account of this memorable experience first appeared in The Haven's *Shen* magazine in 2000.[1]

I had been searching diligently for information about a secret Chinese diagram of the human body for more than two decades, and I thought I was going to fail again. Ten years ago, I had visited the temple in Beijing where this marble carving of the diagram was supposed to be, and after an intensive search, I did not find any trace of the mystical origins of the drawing I was seeking. When Ben and I returned to Beijing in March 2000, we revisited the White Cloud Temple, an old Daoist religious site, where I had a most extraordinary experience. I first learned of the ancient Daoist carving in an esoteric acupuncture book in the early 1980s. I was immediately fascinated with this rendition of a landscape with mountains at the top, and rivers and valleys leading down into lower landscapes. I learned that this was a Daoist view of the human body. I was fascinated by the clear associations to the acupuncture points and meridians. Significant areas occurred in this diagram as special mountains, or temples in rocks, or as major water ways. As I probed and penetrated this diagram, I began slowly to intuit the Tang Dynasty esoteric view of the bodymindspirit as landscape.

I photocopied the picture from the book and made an overhead slide for teaching my acupuncture students in the New Horizons program at The Haven. As I lived with this picture and taught from it, my understandings of the relationship of the forces of nature to the workings of the human organism deepened. I became more confident to show this picture. One day, in a class in the mid-1980s, Father Thomas Kwan, a Roman Catholic priest and moral theologian steeped in Chinese culture, gave me my next clue. Seeing my evident enthusiasm, he said, "I think that drawing is in the White Cloud Temple in Beijing." I then set my sights on seeing this arcane Tang Dynasty diagram for myself.

When Ben and I visited Beijing in 1990, I insisted that I wanted to see a particular place that was not on the tourist itinerary. With some coaxing, our guide searched out the White Cloud Temple, and Ben and I and friends visited. We were quite taken with this dusty old place, where dark costumed monks with ponytails went about their serious business.

They did not seem much interested in a query from a white-skinned foreigner, even with the intervention of our guide. I tried to describe the diagram I was seeking; most of the monks seemed ignorant of my query. Finally, one monk did seem to understand, and motioned with his arm above his head, telling the guide that the diagram was "back there." With the direction of his gesture, I went straight to the very back of the huge temple grounds and searched valiantly in the little meditation rooms and grottos that were there, but to no avail.

Returning to the monk, we questioned again. He was no more helpful or warm than before: he gave a similar vague motion above his head, and we thought, "Maybe he means it's on a second storey somewhere." So we set out again and found ourselves in upstairs portions of the temple, farther and farther away from the few visitors who were in the temple grounds. We made a thorough (fanatic!) search of the area, and found not one trace of the diagram, or anything like it. Dejected, I accepted that I was not going to find the diagram. I checked the souvenir shop on the way out and leafed through the temple rubbings, hoping to find a rendition of the diagram. None was revealed. I satisfied myself with a T-shirt of the White Cloud Temple and left the spot behind. But I never quite let go of my quest.

I continued to teach from this diagram, and my understandings continued to grow. I pointed out the area over the heart chakra to students, where a young boy held on to the end of the little dipper constellation, standing amidst flames (or leaves … I wasn't sure which). I began to intuit the power of the heart region in the Daoist view. At the level of the belly was a lush forest of soft trees, with a maiden weaving in beatific peacefulness. Lower down, in the region of the *dan tien*, the centre of the being, was a depiction of four interrelated *yin/yang* symbols amidst a glowing emanation. Still lower, in the region of the lower belly was the earthly cowherd, a man standing behind an ox-drawn plough. And still lower, two figures seated on a waterwheel, generating waves as they turned the paddles. Each of these special areas marked a place where acupuncture texts noted great power or significance. This was a diagram to help the intuitive questioner go deeper into the structure of being. I decided that if I ever returned to Beijing, I would try once again to find the original.

I had studied Chinese, been repeatedly to Hong Kong, China and Taiwan, had read more ancient books, and had taught acupuncture to the Chinese people through interpreters. I had passed the test of Chinese people who initially disbelieved my intuition, my scholarship. With this heady acceptance, I was in danger of becoming arrogant about my skills and my intuitions about the ancient ways, but I was humbled again when I returned to college to study written and spoken Chinese and realized I would never master the Chinese language. I will be always hobbled by my limitations. I feel deeply for Chinese, and yet I am not a native Chinese speaker. I have old knowledge, but only the rudiments of contemporary communication. It was as if I had to pass through all these learnings and humblings before I was ready to return to The White Cloud Temple.

We arrived at the temple for our second visit after a ten-year period. It was a quiet, overcast day in late winter. This time, I was not so caught up in the ancient symbols I saw everywhere – now they were familiar, part of me. I searched with my Chinese friend Sean Feng as translator, and found the same obstacles as I had encountered a decade before. Repeated questions only brought vague answers about the Daoist diagram. But with persistence, we found ourselves in a part of the temple where we had never been. We were alone in a back garden … just Ben, myself and Sean. We searched diligently and still found nothing that matched the photocopy I had brought. I was about to give up on my two decade long search for the ancient carving and resign myself to the fact that I was never going to get closer to the source. I was about to indicate reluctantly to Ben and Sean that it was time to leave, and tell them that I could "let this go." Just as this release came, when I was ready to give up, a man in tattered clothes appeared in the quiet garden. He was an unlikely person to be in such a holy place; he was rustic and dressed like a farmer. We didn't see him enter; it was as if he appeared out of nowhere. Without much hope, Sean showed him the photocopy of the diagram and asked the man if he knew where the original was. To our surprise, he immediately began to walk quickly towards a back wall, motioning us to follow him. We wended our way through corridors, hastening to keep up with his quick pace.

Suddenly he turned and motioned to a section on the wall where the white stone was marked with indistinct markings. On closer examination, my heart began to race. This was the original picture! The image was vague, and the calligraphy was not clearly demarcated. But the guide knew the symbols, and so did I! We conversed across our heritages and our disciplines. He looked at me with bright eyes, and we recognized that we had both been studying the same information, but from different perspectives. Our respect for each other deepened as we saw the seeker and diligent student in each other. He had devoted himself to Daoist meditation for the past ten years, living apart from the world in privacy and silence. During this time, I had been working with people, practising acupuncture, and probing translations of ancient Chinese classical texts. He said he was following a Chinese master, who never came out into the public; his master had mysteriously instructed him to come to the temple on this day, and he had obeyed without question.

He looked at me pointedly, and said, "You are a white guy, but you and I have the same heart. We were meant to meet. My master sent me here for this encounter today." I said with a smile, "I was here ten years ago ... where were you?" He smiled back, and then said very seriously, "Ten years ago, neither of us was ready." He outlined the details of the diagram, and said that it taught about giving up desires in order to get to heaven. I said in a humorous way, "Maybe Ben will get to heaven, but I don't have much hope. I have so many desires, it's not likely for me to get to heaven." He looked at me sharply, and said, "Desire is not evil – it's your motivator!" He smiled.

I told him that our work with people is to help them to come fully into their physical incarnations, and that we do not emphasize getting to an afterlife, or into higher states. He looked at me knowingly, and said, "Ah ... I see ... You practice and teach, I only practice." We took photographs and hugged each other. Then we parted respectfully and walked back out into the open garden. We paused to bow to each other with mutual recognition. Then I turned to walk towards the gate, across the open garden.

After a few steps, I looked back to bid a final farewell, and to my amazement, the man had vanished! This seemed a physical impossibility, since the garden was so large and open. But he indeed was gone!

His departure was also sudden for my companions. After our initial shock, we accepted this as another part of this most unusual event. I had heard of the Daoist practitioners who lived in caves in the mountains, some of whom are reputed to be hundreds of years old. My Chinese friends who were on spiritual searches frequently sought them, but to no avail. These ancients apparently are rarely seen; it is said that occasionally they send a student to a public place on a mission, who appears for a short time and then vanishes again. I wondered if our new friend was indeed one of those emissaries from the masters. I had also been told that my spirit guide was an old Chinese man who taught and guided me in the Chinese classics. I felt my spirit guide close to me now.

For me, this was a solid confirmation of my long studies and research and probing into the wisdom of the ancient Chinese. My desire, my "motivator," took me to this place and to this meeting. After all my long preparations, I had been visited by an emissary who confirmed that I was on the right path.

We three men walked out of the temple feeling full, warm and close with each other, talking excitedly.

PART V

Integration

Metal

Metal is associated with the fall season, the period of decline. Thus it is the stage in any cyclic process when contemplation can bring insights for future actions. It is a time of learning, reflection, clarity, judgment and resolve. In the human realm, it is associated with self-investigation and principled thought.

V.1   Self and Community

> For the most part, Psychology has been looking in the wrong place! Psychology is mostly studying the individual, and the individual's psyche, rather than studying the "between," and how the individual and her/his psyche exists *within* the relational context.[1]

If you have read our accounts of Western psychology in Part II and Chinese thought in Parts III and IV, you will now be aware of the main sources we have used in coming to our own understanding of the way people operate, grow and live.

You undoubtedly know that we see relationships as the centre of human activity. We encourage people to live in the present with energy, conviction and responsibility. We don't believe in rummaging around in the past for its own sake. We don't believe in political action that is based on an "us-and-them" morality. At the same time, we do support standing up for what you believe and living your life with integrity. We believe in a caring, inclusive attitude to people from different regions and beliefs and cultures. So, some theories work for us much better than others. Dogmatic fundamentalist religions don't get far with us; we believe that openminded philosophical inquiry and dialogue are essential for a lived life of engagement and contribution.

Energy mobilization is important; without becoming embodied and inhabiting our physical being, we are in danger of just thinking about things rather than contributing to those around us. In this way, we are staunchly existentialist; we also find much use in theories from gestalt therapy and Reich and dialogical psychology. Our responsibility is to ourselves, to the community around us, and ultimately to the world.

We don't think human life is some extraordinary accident. We believe that each person is unique, expressing a pattern that unfolds through life experiences. We are each a unique being that needs nurturing from those close to us (parents, teachers and guides). In turn, we can also nurture ourselves and each other.

We agree with the gestaltists and Zen practitioners that a fulfilling and productive life is led in the here and now, with vitality, contacting others while retaining our own boundaries and self-respect. We agree with Adler that social concern is paramount and selfishness can have potentially disastrous consequences for the individual and for humankind. We agree with Jung that the individual human life has significance. And we maintain the existentialist view that it is up to us to express that significance.

We agree with Reich and Chinese acupuncture theory that the energy body can be obstructed, and release is possible with breathing and other approaches. We agree with the ancient Chinese that our human life force energy is in flow with the universe. We can choose to be in or out of harmony. Health occurs with open energy, shared while maintaining boundaries with loving and concern for all beings. Illness occurs in closure and resistance. We can heal ourselves.

Hillman and Ventura's Criticism of Psychotherapy

In their book *We've Had a Hundred Years of Psychotherapy – And the World's Getting Worse*,[2] psychologist James Hillman and journalist Michael Ventura document a series of dialogues about the state of therapy. This book made quite a stir when it was first published twenty years ago, and remains relevant. We were very taken with this book because the authors were discussing topics that we had identified ourselves. We like their irreverent, iconoclastic attitude. They state their views provocatively.

Certainly, Hillman and Ventura were not the first to question the status quo. Carl Whitaker, who was a friend, and who taught at The Haven, was very critical of conventional psychotherapy. Whitaker tersely dismissed individual therapy, saying publicly: "One on one psychotherapy is emotional incest."[3] His family therapy work involved all the generations in the room at once, including mistresses, lovers, and black sheep. In his later career, he refused to work alone, teaming with his wife Muriel, saying he needed a "real human being" in the room with him to keep him honest, because he was a "professional."

Thomas Szasz, best known for his 1960 book *The Myth of Mental Illness*, also taught at The Haven. He remains critical of a mental health system that coddles patients and does not expect them to develop personal responsibility. We watched him provoke audiences in public lectures with his statement that often people are misdiagnosed as schizophrenics when actually they are merely "parasites" in a system that supports irresponsibility.

We ourselves like to question, to challenge. We think that some of the above-mentioned sometimes go too far in their dismissal of the work of conservative, yet earnest, workers and thinkers. But we should not have sacred cows that prevent us from seeing deeper.

Overemphasizing the Self

People tend to be overly self-concerned. Hillman and Ventura maintain that, for decades, many of the most sensitive people in the West have gone into therapy, focusing on their inner concerns while they ignore pressing issues in the outer world. Those in therapy become sensitized to the inner realm, but are more passive in the outer world.

Often this focus on intrapsychic work involves the notion of the "inner child." We have seen individuals become fixated on "healing the child within" to the detriment of their current life and relationships. We think the task for us all is to become more fully present as we are, not to nurture a "child within" – an approach that keeps people psychologically immature. In fact, we would do well to look instead for the "adult within"! Our work emphasizes relationship contact in the present, with only brief investigations of memories from time to time, to provide perspective. Hillman is very strong in his dismissal of inner child work:

> This is a disaster for our political world, our democracy. Democracy depends on intensely active citizens, not children.[4]

When people work on their inner growth, this does not automatically translate into change in the world. "If personal growth did lead into the world," asks Hillman, "wouldn't our political situation be different today, considering all the intelligent people who have been in therapy?"[5] The truth, says Hillman, is that

> therapy, in its crazy way, by emphasizing the inner soul and ignoring the outer soul, supports the decline of the actual world. Yet therapy goes on blindly believing that it's curing the outer world by making better people.[6]

Hillman says that humans have had a long habit of withdrawal that began two thousand years ago with saints and mystics retreating into themselves, away from the natural world of community. He says, "It's a monkish notion. A saintly notion." It is a deeply embedded idea that one somehow becomes "more oneself" in solitude. Hillman turns this idea on its head by suggesting that in fact people become *out of touch with themselves* when they are alone. They are only "with themselves," he says, when they are with other people and engaged with their environment. He envisages a new paradigm in which

> I would be with myself when I'm with others. I would not be with myself when I'm walking alone or meditating or in my room imagining or working on my dreams. In fact I would be estranged from myself[7]

In this alternative scenario he defines the self as "the interiorization of community."[8] We like Hillman's provocative way with words and we agree that people often retreat into isolation and cut themselves off from contact, limiting themselves and their relationships. However, we quickly add that not all solitariness is defensive isolation, as Hillman himself acknowledges:

This is not to deny that you do need to go inside – but we have to see what we're doing when we do that.[9]

In gestalt terminology, healthy people are able to both contact and withdraw in a natural rhythm; both are organic functions. People can be with others, and also can be alone – these are both aspects of human nature. Even when individuals are in withdrawal, they are, to us, still themselves, just separated from others. In the words of the *Yi Jing*:

> In order to find one's place in the infinity of being, one must learn both to separate and unite.[10]

So, with these qualifications, we agree with what Hillman wishes to accomplish, to compensate for the selfishness that personal development and therapy has too often enabled. We like that Hillman envisions a place for participation with others, in relationship, in the development of community. Such a psychology of relationships is a ready fit with our lifelong work on communicating and connecting.

Such participation requires people to reconsider their definitions of themselves and others. The emphasis on engagement recalls Buber and the existentialists of dialogue:

> To begin with oneself, but not to end with oneself; to start from oneself, but not to aim at oneself; to comprehend oneself, but not to be preoccupied with oneself.[11]

Overemphasizing the Past

We have already seen Hillman's disdain for "inner child" work. In the same vein, Hillman points to the profound influence of developmental thought on American psychology. What happened earlier in a person's life is seen to be the cause of what comes later.

> And so when people are out of their minds or disturbed or fucked up or whatever, in our culture, in our psychotherapeutic world, we go back to our mothers and our fathers and our childhoods.[12]

But, as he expresses it in his 1996 book *The Soul's Code*, people are limited not so much by their childhood, but by their viewpoint:

> Our lives may be determined less by our childhood than by the way we have learned to imagine our childhoods. We are ... less damaged by the traumas of childhood than by the traumatic way we remember childhood as a time of unnecessary and externally caused calamities that wrongly shaped us.[13]

We ourselves are firmly convinced that the past has been overemphasized as a source of answers for present concerns. While there is merit in considering the past to give perspective and clues, it is the present lived moment that constitutes the solid ground from which we can ask questions, and, as Rilke said, "live into the answers."

If people are not victims of their history, they can take a different view of their past and present difficulties. We see these as potentially positive challenges, forces that test individuals, encouraging them to develop strength and resilience as they contend with them. Hillman says psychology's insistence on processing the past often has a goal of "leveling things out" so that people no longer have strong, disturbing emotions around events, but these same emotions and events can be seen instead as elements in character building:

> Wounds and scars are the stuff of character. The word *character* means, at root, "marked or etched with sharp lines," like initiation cuts.[14]

People can respect the facts of their history and the strong emotions that sometimes occur – not try to dilute them or smooth them over. We are solidly in agreement with this viewpoint, of making the most out of our experiences and embracing whatever life brings to us. This is character building.

> The so-called traumatic experience is not an accident, but the opportunity for which the child has been patiently waiting – had it not occurred, it would have found another, equally trivial – in order to find a necessity and direction for its existence, in order that its life may become a serious matter. – W.H. Auden[15]

The Acorn Theory and Soul-making

Hillman's views on the relationship of the individual self to the larger world and his de-emphasis of the role of the past in shaping the present both grow out of an underlying perspective he refers to as the acorn theory.

Carl Jung proposed that there is a distinct and unique pattern to each of us, the archetype of the self, which is an individual variant of the archetype of the universe, the Self. This is similar to the ancient Chinese view that the individual is an aspect of the whole of the universe, and our task as humans is to get ourselves into harmony with the flow of nature and the universe at large.

Hillman outlined his own take on this Jungian view in *The Soul's Code: In Search of Character and Calling (1996).* In his view, each one of us is born with a distinct character, an innate image, a calling. "Each person," he writes, "bears a uniqueness that asks to be lived and that is already present before it can be lived."[16] And again, "I am answerable to an innate image, which I am filling out in my biography."[17]

In this understanding, the acorn and the oak are one, manifesting differently in time. It is the same oak, whether it is the folded up seed or the unfolded manifest oak. Similarly, the child and the adult are different expressions in time of the same essential pattern. This is in contrast to the traditional view of Western psychology that maintains that events in the past determine who we are in the present.

Hillman offers an evocative image from Plato's *Republic*:

> The soul of each of us is given a unique daimon before we are born, and it has selected an image or pattern that we live here on earth. This soul-companion, the daimon, guides us here; in the process of arrival, however, we forget all that took place and believe we come empty into this world. The daimon remembers what is in your image and belongs to your pattern, and therefore your daimon is the carrier of your destiny.[18]

This notion of an elemental pattern, an "acorn," matches our experience with ourselves and with our clients and friends and family over many years. Mothers have so often told us that they knew their child's personality while they were carrying them in utero; some children are fighters and kickers from before birth, while others are placid and calm from their earliest days, even before seeing the outside world. Hillman emphasizes the "call of fate":

> I believe we have been robbed of our true biography – that destiny written into the acorn – and we go to therapy to recover it. That innate image can't be found, however, until we have a psychological theory that grants primary psychological reality to the call of fate.[19]

Similarly, in Chinese medicine, each person's energy body matrix is distinct and individual, a pattern that underlies one's personality and proclivities in life style, disease and health.

We resonate with the idea of a prefigured possibility. For us, however, neither Hillman nor Chinese medicine gives enough emphasis to the existential ability of individuals to choose how they express the prefigured pattern. We agree that we are all fated to work with the cards we are dealt, but we think that people are free to choose how to play each hand. While we agree that there is a call of fate, an acorn, an image that offers us possibilities, we staunchly take the existentialist position in regard to individual choice and freedom. We are not doomed by our fate or destiny and we have not been "robbed" of anything. Fate is an offering, a call, to which we can choose to respond in our own individual and unique way. This is the existential challenge.

Life experiences don't generate one's personality; instead, they reveal the pattern that is unique to that individual and provide stimuli to strengthen the expression of what is already given. Certainly, external factors are significant in the unfolding of the seed pattern, but we do not believe that people are mere victims of their childhood, a view that is so common in therapy now. Again, Hillman offers an intriguing image:

> I am not caused by my history – my parents, my childhood, and development. These are mirrors in which I may catch glimpses of my image.[20]

In this rethinking, the notion of a linear development through time is replaced by a process that is not time-bound. Hillman points out some of the consequences of the developmental model:

> Psychology starts with an upside-down premise, that childhood is primary and determining, that development is cumulative, a kind of organic evolution, reaching a peak and declining ... not only is childhood thus overvalued, but aging is trapped in an organic, and melancholy, model.[21]

By contrast, an assumption that people do not *develop* but are *revealed* gives meaning to all stages of life. The oak tree is no more or less fully itself after 400 years than it was as a sapling. This is compatible with the Buddhist view of life as a process in the midst of eternity; in Buddhist teaching, people's problems arise when they fixate on certain aspects of their lives (their troubled childhoods, for example, or their desires, attachments, anxieties about illness and infirmity, and fears of aging and death).

The revelation of the individual who responds to the call of fate is for Hillman a process of "soul-making." But soul-making, he suggests, goes beyond our individual soul to include the world soul, which involves the world out there as well as the world inside. This would then have people being engaged with the world, with the environment, with "deep ecology" – as well as with their individual soul. Comprehensive soul work would include involvement with others, with nature, and with the civilized world. Hillman says that excessive individualism is an imbalance, and "the neglect of the environment, the body of the world, is part and parcel of our personal 'insanity.'" He calls for involvement in the world:

> The world's body must be restored to health, for in that body is also the world's soul.[22]

For decades, we have been counselling people against withdrawal into spiritual practices. We maintain that a reverential practice should enhance one's life and being in the world, not take one away from contact. Hillman's viewpoint is similar; he makes a case against the transcendence of spiritual withdrawal, inviting therapy to reimagine its role, to bring people to earthly concerns:

> I don't think spiritual disciplines take the world enough into account; they're always set on transcending, that is, denying it with spiritual practices. That's why therapy is so important – once it makes the effort of rethinking its base – because therapy stays here on earth, in the mess of life, truly concerned with soul.[23]

We agree that therapy and counselling are well positioned to help people deal with the "mess of life." We ourselves see value in both developmental psychology and the "revelatory" or essential approach espoused by Hillman, though within each perspective we give extra weight to a person's existential freedom to choose. Furthermore, we are invigorated by the conception of psychology becoming extended beyond the therapy hour to address the full life of people, in themselves, in their family life, and in the world. This has been an educational focus of our work with groups of people at The Haven and around the world.

From Imagination to Action

Conventional psychology is rooted in moral value systems. Certain behaviours are appropriate; others are outside the limits. We ourselves are certainly not anarchistic, nor amoral – far from it. The social structure requires laws and conventions in order to function smoothly and harmoniously. But when people achieve a degree of maturity, they feel urgings for freedom, to try their wings, to imagine new ways to live and love and learn. This sometimes leads them to question conventional notions of appropriateness, to find their own style.

The moral outlook is reflected in the opposition between superego and id in the conventional interpretation of Freud, says Hillman. But this is a battle created by therapeutic theory, he says, not by the psyche. He evidently agrees with Reich's view that the passions of the id are potentially constructive: they are the eruption of life energy.

> No need for that war if we imagine the superego to be an aesthetic rather than a moral principle. Then the id would not be condemned for its desires or dissuaded from its pleasures, but would be encouraged from above to find for them more fertile fantasies and superior forms.[24]

We find this viewpoint very appealing. The soul, says Hillman, is "inherently imaginative."[25] But our philosophical view goes beyond just imagining – people have choices to make in order to make their art come to life. In our work at The Haven, we included opportunities for artistic development and self-expression. Working with people over the years using psychodrama and energetic gestalts, we more and more believed that people ultimately need to connect, relate, and express themselves creatively. Overcoming past traumas is sometimes a temporary concern; but eventually, creativity, relationship and expression take precedence. We saw this time and time again. This led us to construct a performing arts theatre at The Haven, so that people could explore the areas of personal expression more fully.

An artistic view is a state of mind, a state of being. Aesthetics is in the eye of the beholder; the perception of beauty is determined by the life and intention of the person who is witnessing it. It's not some chance happening if one sees beauty; one trains for the experience, prepares for it, with a life of participation and dedication. Symphony musicians know this; when their conductor is completely energetic and focused, and if they respond with alacrity and intensity, the beauty that is hidden in the printed scores arises in their instruments and resounds in the concert hall. So it is with each human life; if people are dedicated, earnest, intense, they can create and manifest beauty out of the patterns of possibility in them and around them. In this way, the potential in the pattern is revealed and released through purposeful human action. This is the coupling of essentialism (the underlying pattern) and existentialism (the actions that manifest the pattern). For us, aesthetics (the appreciation of the pattern) in this way couples with existential choice. We choose to show up; we choose to be in earnest; we choose to dedicate our lives to the pursuit of quality.

There is a parallel to this existentialist/essentialist coupling in classical Chinese medicine. The Liver meridian has the psychological function of planning and imagining, and the Gall Bladder is the decision maker. Liver and Gall Bladder are the *yin* and *yang* aspects of Wood energy. The gentle life spirit *hun* is the invisible spiritual agency that creates imaginative possibilities that bring the individual being into closeness with all life; these imaginings of *hun* are expressed by the activities of the Liver. The function of the Gall Bladder as the decision maker is intimately associated with that of the Liver planning. Imagination and decision go hand in glove; one is meaningless without the other. They are opposite sides of the same coin. The Chinese medical books have a saying, "The Gall Bladder and Liver are always together, cooperating to bring mutual enlightenment." We say the interrelation of the Gall Bladder/Liver axis brings the *transformation of imagination into action*. Both aspects are necessary. Imagination without action easily degenerates into pointless daydreaming; action without imagination is impulsive reaction. Human creativity requires an exquisite interplay between the two.

For us, such creativity – this transformation of imagination into action – includes relationships at the core, with self-awareness, personal responsibility and community feeling as vital elements. It is a challenge to the process of conforming that is, Hillman says, "the disease of our times." This conformity invites numbness and limits imagination; in extreme, it is the "sickness unto death" that the existential writers describe. We agree with Hillman that the work of psychology should be "a deanesthetizing … reanimation, reenchantment."[26]

We are excited at what this "little revolution"[27] could bring. We ourselves continuously seek new ways to see, and find our place ever more firmly on the ground, under the wide sky. One can fall in love with life and the inherent beauty that underlies it. People are drawn to artistic expression that illustrates the highest and deepest aspects of humans. This should come into our psychology. Rather than returning people to normalcy, we need a psychological perspective that gives us the possibility of bigger vision. If we achieve such a vision, we can take our place in the larger world harmoniously, contributing as full participants in the flow of the universal symphony.

We are encouraged by Hillman and Ventura's proposals. A psychology of the imagination can fit with a personal philosophy of ethical living. As you will have discovered in reading this book, China's heritage has been more philosophical than psychological, and profoundly aesthetic and imagistic. Hillman and Ventura's perspective can be useful in helping China and the West to find common ground. With this inclusive viewpoint that links the individual with the global world and opens psychology's view of itself to include philosophy and art, we can find a way to teach each other, and to learn from each other, East and West.

We recommend that people consider their basic values and desires deeply, over a long time. Read, attend artistic and community events, and continuously question yourself as to your relationship to whatever you are doing, witnessing and thinking. Talk about life and values and personal inclinations with friends and teachers, especially with people from other backgrounds and cultures. Most importantly, this involves an attitude of curiosity, of investigating and learning. The goal is to discover one's personal philosophy of life, which, if you remain open, will be in evolution during all your days. In working on yourself, the final judge of the validity of a theory or approach is you. This is an all-engaging enterprise, "requiring not less than everything." Nor is it a matter of whim; it requires a critical look at what others have thought, said and done. It requires discrimination and a willingness to make your own choices. And as you do this, the hard work begins, the transformation of imagination into action. Don't just think it … live it too!

V.2   Reps: Joined

Zen master Reps lived with us for years at The Haven. But he would not come to sit at our table at lunch. Jock asked him why.

Reps said, "You guys have important business to talk about, and I don't want to get in the way."

Jock replied, "Reps, you are always welcome to join us."

Reps shot back a sharp look and quipped, "Already joined! Don't you know that?"

V.3   Patterns and Processes

In Buddhist thought, human existence is an illusion, a kind of a dream. Shakespeare's Prospero suggests something similar. We are born, live for a time, and pass back into the sleep of eternity:

> The cloud-capp'd towers, the gorgeous palaces,
> The solemn temples, the great globe itself,
> Yea, all which it inherit, shall dissolve,
> And, like this insubstantial pageant faded,
> Leave not a rack behind: We are such stuff
> As dreams are made on, and our little life
> Is rounded with a sleep.[1]

The idea that there is a pattern to eternity and infinity that expresses itself in time and space appears in many traditions, both Asian and Western. Ancient Chinese sages elaborated this as the inner and outer worlds of the *Book of Changes*. The ancient hermetic words "As above, so below;" the Christian "on Earth as it is in Heaven"; the Jewish Kabbalah's two dimensions that interpenetrate, the invisible world of Keter and the manifest world of Malkut – all these express comparable notions, as do Jung's archetypes that manifest in individual lives.

In China, the *Dao De Jing* indicates the interrelationship between heaven and earth and humans:

> The model ... of man is the earth; the model of the earth is heaven; the model of heaven is the Tao; the model of the Tao is spontaneity.[2]

This is the pattern of wholeness. The pattern is not static, but rather involves continuous movement and transformation. The pattern is all.

Our human life is an aspect of this pattern. Alan Watts notes that Western science can describe this pattern as an aid in our following it:

> Scientific description follows the pattern of nature; it does not lay down, like rails, the rules which nature must follow, for the pattern itself is developing freely. The feedback, the description, simply helps the human pattern to develop in a more orderly fashion.[3]

Structuralism

We have discussed the subject of pattern and process repeatedly in previous chapters. In particular, these notions feature in gestalt therapy, existentialism, classical Chinese medicine and Jungian psychology. We find the structuralism of the mid-20th century useful in integrating these various ideas. Structuralism is more a style of inquiry than it is a core dictum. Its tenets appear in diverse fields of inquiry into language, culture and society; there are structuralist writers in linguistics, anthropology, psychology, psychiatry, biology, and other disciplines. Their common aim is to elucidate the patterns that underlie and unify events in the world of experience.

A central theme of structuralism is holism; every event and element of this world is related to all others. The pattern of interaction of these events and elements is the focus of structuralism. According to Edgar Levenson, a leader in the interpersonal field and an important contributor to psychoanalytic literature, there are at least three dimensions to this patterning. Each "level" has its own structure; yet, each "level" is the other levels when viewed as a whole. This is the phenomenon of self-similarity or isomorphism – each level of structure is the other levels. Structurally, they are the same. Levenson, discussing Piaget, writes:

> Views of structuring occur on a continuum ranging from "deep structure," a rigidly codified set ... through culturally determined configurations to a highly idiosyncratic personal structuring of experience. The range is from deep structure to idiosyncratic structure ...[4]

Levenson names the three levels as deep structure, middle structures and superficial structures. The deep pattern is universal, timeless and spaceless, and manifests in the other two levels – in the middle structures as different social groups, and in the superficial structures as individual personalities. The deep structure is a unified wholeness – a similar notion to *dao* for the Chinese. The middle (social) structures are the organization of people into different cultural groups (races, nations, religious groups); these seem different from each other (e.g. Christian and Muslim), but they are the same in their elemental patterning, as expressions of the universal deep structure of wholeness. The superficial (idiosyncratic) structures are the individual particular variations; each person is unique, with a distinct history, perspective, tastes and prejudices.

The superficial and middle structures are themselves expressions of the universal deep structure; in this way, there is only one pattern, which manifests in different "levels." The superficial and middle levels can transform, whereas the deep level is constant. Each "level" is isomorphic (has the same basic pattern) with the other levels. In this sense, each level is the other levels (they are not just similar). Structurally, they are the same; only their forms of expression are different.

The poetry of the 15th-century Indian mystic Kabir is woven with this theme of isomorphism of level within level, each one folding into the others:

> You know that the seed is inside the horse-chestnut tree;

and inside the seed there are the blossoms of the tree, and the chestnuts, and the shade.

So, inside the human body there is the seed, and inside the seed there is the human body again.[5]

Change and Transformation

We wrote a chapter entitled "Is Change Possible?" in our first book, *The New Manual for Life*. We still hold to the views we expressed there, so we will just touch a few of the main points here and refer you to the other book for more details.[6] Virginia Satir developed her concepts of family therapy around a notion of change; we challenged her with our view that change is not possible. We had many discussions (sometimes heated) with Virginia; she remained adamant in her belief that change does occur. In preparing this book, Jock asked Ben, "Do you now think change is possible?" He replied, somewhat whimsically, "No ... and yes ... and no ... and yes." So, this requires further clarification.

We say that "change" – meaning alteration of the universal deep structure – is impossible. However, "transformation" – meaning a different expression, on the middle and superficial levels, of the universal deep structure – is possible. The ancient Chinese address this in the *Book of Changes* by distinguishing between nonchange, sequent change and cyclic change; the universe is always transforming, but the process itself is unchanging.

Some of the basic facts of one's biography cannot change – you were born in a particular time and place to the parents you had; your family constellation and life experiences are what they are. What you can do is adjust your relationship to these basic facts. This is a freedom wherein transformation of life style and consciousness is possible. The middle and superficial structures become rigidified when not challenged, and can be transformed with new input. People can overcome even the greatest obstacles through awareness, will, dedication, hard work, repetition, and challenging the limits and rigidities of habits.

With awareness, individuals are able to decide what aspects of their middle and superficial patterns they will emphasize. For example, if a child has a musical talent and does not practice, the ability tends to wither in time and development does not occur. Another child with less innate talent practices diligently and becomes an accomplished musician – this is transformation in individual patterning.

When people transform their patterns, this is often disturbing to the security of others around them, who want their behaviour to remain predictable. Their transformation invites chaos by upsetting the established dynamics of a family or cultural system. Nevertheless, this chaos can also be a source of revitalization and creativity for everyone in the system.

Structuralism in Therapy and Dialogue

A structuralist approach to therapy aims to facilitate awareness of the client's personal structure, which is revealed in the interaction with the therapist. The possibility for transformation occurs in the interplay between the security of predictability and the unexpected revelations of chaos that can occur in the therapeutic relationship. The patterns of both therapist and client are involved, as Edgar Levenson writes:

> This tendency to isomorphism is so powerful that it will engage the therapist in some way, pull him in, make him a part of the system he is observing, either as countertransference, participant-observation, authentic encounter, whatever.[7]

In therapy, clients bring their whole life with them. Levenson describes the "thread of continuity," noting that any aspect of the client's life contains the total pattern of his or her life:

> Any small piece of the clinical material contains the total configuration. Both past and future.[8]

Regardless of the particular style the therapy takes – whether body oriented, or gestalt, or analysis, or any other method – what matters is the engagement, so that the patterning can be revealed. When there are interruptions in flow of the pattern, this becomes a focus for the therapeutic engagement. Levenson says,

> Everything – his past history, present behaviour, fantasies, dreams and behaviour in the treatment room – will reflect the same patterning.[9]

Interruptions that occur between the client and therapist are isomorphs of interruptions that will be occurring in other aspects of the client's life (and the therapist's life too!).

> One could say that the same patterning of experience occurs with the mother ... it will appear in his dreams, with his wife, in any situation which lends itself to structuring. It is his pattern.[10]

In the structuralist framework, then, transference is not the central issue in therapy; instead the dialogue facilitates awareness of the patterns of the existence of each. Levenson describes how this challenges the therapist to move past roles, to be a genuine human in the encounter with the client:

> The interpersonal therapist must grapple with the real matrix of events and personalities in which every therapy is embedded. It is not a question of what the patient has projected "onto" or "into" the therapist, but of really who the therapist is, and what he brings to the therapy encounter.[11]

In our own work with people, we take a position similar to Levenson's that the goal is not change, but rather awareness. For us, this can lead to transformation. The more awareness people have, the more they can address incomplete gestalts and regenerate movement where stasis has occurred. In this movement, transformation can occur.

When the gestalt cycle is stuck in unawareness, the client's life is linear and movement is inhibited. Honest feedback from a therapist or a friend can challenge this stasis, bringing forth turbulence, and with it, new possibility. In this chaos, the client's gestalt cycle can be opened again, the fixation addressed, and the lost movement can begin again. From the feedback comes awareness, challenge to the defences, and the possibility for new action.

Importantly, we maintain one does not require therapy or personal growth programs to accomplish this. Indeed, genuine feedback from friends and family can invite the same transformative possibilities. One can learn about patterns in ongoing dialogue with dedicated partners, friends and associates. We developed our Communication Model as a way of practicing this. The model itself can be seen in structuralist terms. The process begins on the surface level, with simple elements of interaction and verbal sharing. But as the process continues, people find they become more aware of themselves, their location, and their perspectives; furthermore, they become more aware of the patterns and life of their partner too. The simple interactive process can go deeper to address very meaningful aspects of the lives of those involved; they move from superficial patternings to deeper levels. As people practise this process together, they experience a dynamic flow from level to level within themselves as their experience of intimacy grows. They are able to express and transform their middle and superficial structures. At times, they find wordless wonder at the resonance they feel with each other at the deepest levels of their being.

Practicing an Algorithm

An algorithm is a recipe, a pattern with a purpose. For example, there is an algorithm for baking bread that includes flour, water, salt, heat, time, kneading, and the smell of the baking bread, as well as many other elements. At The Haven, we have focused on maintaining a healing algorithm that involves interaction, openness, honesty, dependability, curiosity, reverence for life, and respect for others. For those who come to The Haven, this algorithm can be both comforting and unsettling. People can feel anxious in face of unusual candour and honesty; yet, they also feel the peace of reharmonizing with the flow of life.

The Communication Model is itself an algorithm, intended for communicating and connecting. It is the practice taught at The Haven to help people experience the healing algorithm we have developed at The Haven in their own life contexts, often far away from the physical location of The Haven.

In our own work and lives, we have dedicated ourselves to the Communication Model of relationship; we continue to practice all the time. It is a daily (every minute Zen) exercise that keeps us moving. Meiten McGuire writes:

> Training does its work when we do our little part – when we are willing to ask for help, to acknowledge that we don't know the answers, and to keep moving into unknown territory in good faith that our intention to heal, to return to the place of oneness and peace, will protect us.[12]

Practice is essential. The human brain establishes and maintains patterns of behaviour through a vast web of connections of neurons. New behaviour that contradicts older patterns will bring new neural connections. When these links are reemphasized through practice, they become well established as habits. Research in neuroscience indicates that the brain can actually remap itself; unused pathways tend to fade, and the habitual ones become stronger.

This indicates a link between your brain activity, awareness, decisions, actions and indeed, your physical being. You can transform your physical being, which can transform you. For example, if you decide to eat healthy food, you might have several difficult days as your habitual brain associations encourage you back to your junk food diet; you will likely be called upon to use your will power to keep with your determination of a new style. But, as you persevere, your system will become accustomed to the new diet and your appetites and feelings will transform. The activity trains the physical brain, and the brain supports and stimulates the activity. The changes in your physical body that result become a supportive feedback to the life style change.

We encourage people to find their own healing algorithm. Become aware of something that is beneficial for you, that brings you into harmony with your nature and your surroundings; once you discover it, keep doing it. The repetition of the practice will intensify the transformed pattern, giving it more thrust to further movement.

One's character development progresses through a life of dedication:

> Sow a thought, reap an action; sow an action, reap a habit; sow a habit, reap a character; sow a character, reap a destiny." – Zen Proverb[13]

V.4　Self and Not-Self

KZ = Confucius (Kong Zi), CJ = Carl Jung, BW = Ben Wong, JM = Jock McKeen

JM: A friend who is a Western psychologist asked me recently, "When a Chinese therapist is addressing a client and asking that person to consider the self, is it the same 'self' as we have in the West?" This provoked a lot of heated discussion amongst a group of professionals from various human disciplines. We realized this is a very vague area indeed.

KZ: Well, the idea of "self" is a somewhat strange one to a Chinese person. The smallest unit for the Chinese is the family.

BW: This is also the case for many other ethnicities. My Jewish friends laughingly tell me how their lives are intricately wrapped up with their entire family, and no one can do anything without everyone else being involved! The notions of individual privacy and autonomy seem to be idiosyncratic to the "American dream." Most people who have come from European or Hispanic cultures understand that no one acts alone. Certainly, the Chinese people believe this.

CJ: Fascinating. My work was focused on the unfolding of the unique individual personality; yet I see what you mean. There are social pressures that limit people's capacity to realize themselves.

JM: I have made the extreme statement that the "self" is an artefact, a conception of an individual entity that is distinct from the sociocultural milieu. The "self" does not exist as a separate phenomenon. For over a hundred years, Western psychotherapy has assumed the singularity of an individual self. But lately I have been wondering. Is there really a distinct "self"?

KZ: Historically, we Chinese have not considered a distinct self. Certainly, there is an individual personality that has unique features and attributes. But we see this always in the context of the family and the broader social environment.

CJ: This means that the introduction of Western psychology into modern China brings with it many unquestioned assumptions. I think this is an important discussion to have.

BW: The existential viewpoint – we are born alone, we live basically alone with limited contact with others, and die alone – is severe, and yet it also brings a refreshing capacity for individual responsibility and individual action and decision making. A mixed blessing. This point of view is more common in the West. It does support the notion of an individual self.

KZ: In the East, the family and society at large have always been part of the individual's life and concerns. We are not alone, ever. Thus we don't have the ready experience of making unique and individual decisions. We tend to act as a group, not as singularities.

JM: So, now we Westerners have been going to Asia to teach individual approaches to self-development and individual psychology. We slowly learned that Chinese culture finds the notion of individual self a vague one at best.

BW: There is an irony here. We thought we were bringing Western ideas to Asia to help integrate East and West. Now I wonder what we have actually done.

JM: My Asian friends tell me that many of the concepts of Western psychology are very difficult to grasp. Yet the Chinese group participants are eager to learn. My concern is that they are learning something different than we intend to teach. They seem prone to copy the techniques used by the teachers, rather than penetrate to the process of interpersonal interaction.

CJ: From this discussion, I think Chinese people probably need to develop a different kind of psychology from the one that has developed in the West.

KZ: This is complex, but it is fascinating indeed. I am deeply interested.

BW: I wonder what this means for creativity. In the West, we value individual creativity and hold our idiosyncratic artists up as heroes. In classical China, there wasn't this iconization of creative individuals. Instead, they kept a universal view, seeing human beings within this context. In the West, we have heroes; in the East, there is participation in the whole.

JM: So, back to my provocative proposal that there is no self. Is the self just an artefact of mental objectification? Or is there an entity we can call "the self"? What do you all think?

BW: I would propose that the self is a mental construct, a symbolic representation of our point of view. We tend to treat it as if it has an independent existence. But the self is an idea, not a real thing.

KZ: I concur. I would suggest that there is no thing called a "self." Instead there is a process we could call "self-ing."

JM: I like this ... process, not a thing.

BW: I hasten to add that we recognize that there is a "being" intact in each newborn. Mothers often report that they have felt a connection with their infants from the beginning. We propose that she is not connecting with a "self" but rather with the "being" of the child. The being is present from the beginning; the self is developed over time as a mental construction.

JM: The "being" would be the unique energy patterning of that individual baby – this is what we called the "authentic self" in our Selves Model. There is clearly something distinct and unique about that baby. But the way we are talking now, it's not actually a "self" until the mental apparatus matures some more.

KZ: The mental representation occurs through the connection with the parents and other family members.

BW: Yes, and is developed through language and other forms of communication.

CJ: If what you say is true, it would put my work on individuation into a different light. I like this idea of "self-ing" and I would add the universal "Self-ing." The representation perhaps is not real, but is an expression of the activity of an underlying pattern. This is very interesting.

KZ: I am fascinated too. This "idea" of self pervades Western thinking in a very profound way. To us Chinese, this is very, very strange. Now that Western psychology is coming to China, I imagine this notion of self is invigorating, tempting, and perhaps dangerous to the Eastern mind.

CJ: What do you see as dangerous?

KZ: I am afraid that the new generation will become enamoured of the notion of self and independence, and forget their deep-rooted social and family values. They are in danger of becoming too selfish. I think the idea of individual self-ing is an important step to personal development. But it can be misunderstood.

BW: I see what you mean. To me, individual and the whole are not either/or, but rather issues of foreground/background. When one becomes in touch with individual perspective, one is still connected to others and the whole, but with a unique personal viewpoint. But I am concerned that our work in China is being misinterpreted. We fear that people will try to copy the structure from the West that they see. If they just copy an individual perspective, they can easily break connection to become selfish and objectifying and power driven.

KZ: I agree that this is a foreground/background phenomenon. But to understand this takes experience and a balanced perspective, such as yours, Dr. Wong.

JM: We thought we were teaching individual responsibility and using techniques to elucidate this. But we have learned that the Chinese people are inclined to copy the structure and miss the spirit of what we are teaching. They are in danger of "mistaking the shadow for the substance."

BW: China has had the family and culture in the foreground, more or less, for centuries. The individual has been subordinated, or even just a vague possibility. Now that Westerners are teaching personal perspectives in China, the Chinese people are acquiring a concept of the individual self.

KZ: West is coming to the East.

BW: Yes, and it has a dilemma. I passionately believe that people can individuate *without breaking contact or relinquishing the relationships to the whole*. However, frequently in the West, this does not happen. A common misconception confuses the quest for self-confidence with selfishness. I am afraid in the quick attempt to copy the West, the selfishness will be copied in China too.

CJ: I am in mind of what Adler said, "All neurosis is vanity."

JM: What do you mean?

CJ: The neurotic solution is to reduce the world in an attempt to control it. This selfish attitude, in the service of elevating the self, can be the symptom of a quest for security. One closes off and makes oneself number one, in an attempt to keep control.

BW: So in that way, if people become more self-aware and more self-confident, they can grow past their selfishness. They will be more responsible and less neurotic. They can open up to new possibilities and connect with others.

KZ: This is consistent with my teaching – the issue is to learn deeply about one's place in the universe, and humbly contribute to the whole by living a full and responsible life.

BW: Chinese people are so industrious. Since they have not had much of an idea of individual self, they have concentrated on "doing" rather than "being." They like structure.

KZ: I had a part in this in trying to show them the structure of the universe. They think they should "follow the structure" rather than see that this is only a guideline. They are in danger of being dogmatic and prone to following a recipe rather than engaging in a responsible, reflective process of living.

BW: In both East and West, the people who "do" are rewarded with positions of authority, and those still in touch with "being" end up on the sidelines. The decision makers and leaders tend to be active, assertive "do-ers" who are out of touch with themselves and their deeper being nature.

JM: The problem of rewarding power rather than emphasizing strength.

KZ: It seems this situation is ongoing. This was the problem of my day too. People found the power solutions to be so appealing. I had hoped people would learn to cooperate, to join in harmony.

BW: This is my ever-present concern.

V.5   The Problem of "I"

We have no one law that governs us.
For me there is only one law: I am I.
And that isn't a law, it's just a remark. – D.H. Lawrence[1]

Why are you unhappy?
Because 99.9 per cent
Of everything you think,
And of everything you do,
Is for yourself –
And there isn't one – Wei Wu Wei[2]

D.H. Lawrence and Wei Wu Wei are addressing an important issue. Is there a self, or not? What is "I"? Other questions arise from these: What is an individual, what is a person, and what is personal? What is the relationship between self and others? How can I find my place? East and West have approached these questions in different ways.

The West has emphasized the development of an individual personality, which is known as "the self" (or, in the first person, "I"). In China and other parts of Asia, the individual has traditionally been less important than the group.

In the classical Confucian view, as we have seen, there are four dimensions to human participation: the individual, the family, the state, and humankind. In the West, the emphasis has been on individual and state – the single human being is regarded as a central atom of society. An individual consciousness, a separate "I," relates as a distinct entity in a collection of other separate beings. In contrast, the Chinese have given greater weight to family and mankind; one participates as a team member rather than as a soloist.[3] For Chinese people, the notion of individual is difficult, while social participation is the norm.

As we seek to understand the place of psychology and philosophy in the two cultures, we must keep these differences in mind.

No Foreground Individual for Chinese

We first got a glimmer of the Asian perspective when we were leading a seminar in Hong Kong in the early 1990s. We offered a guided meditation for the group of about 50 Chinese people. As usual, we introduced the meditation by asking people to lie on the floor with eyes closed, to relax and breathe deeply. All was proceeding as usual until Jock said, "As you continue to relax, go down into your self." Immediately, many of the attendees opened one eye with a sharp querulous look, and we knew that something was amiss. The problem, we soon learned, was that they had no idea of a self to go into. When we learned to modify our group meditation instructions to "Go down into your deep nature," people's eyes remained closed. For Chinese people, one's deep nature is a collective – *our* deep nature. This is isomorphic with Jung's Collective Unconscious, in which each individual is a participant.

There is no individual "self" in the Chinese language; or, at least, the notion of "self" is not foreground in a culture that emphasizes participatory values. There is the Chinese world *wo*, which means "I," but it is a notation of a singular subjective position, rather than a "self" in the sense we have in Western culture. This absence of self extends throughout the language, where the smallest unit is conventionally the family. In the West, the notion of "I" refers to an internal mindspace that is replete with individual memories, experiences and attitudes; the reference of Chinese speakers is more to a collective. West identifies as an individual, while the Chinese identify more with the culture.

In our work with people, we have emphasized the importance of sharing oneself by being open, revealed and vulnerable, one to another. Commonly, we talk of this sharing as being "personal." In English, the word "personal" sometimes has a touching delicacy to it that can even imply a spiritual tone. After we had worked with the same Chinese translator in seminars for a decade, we discovered to our amazement that she had difficulty translating our instructions when we told workshop participants to "be personal" in their interactions. We intended for them to be open, revealed and intimate. Our translator, not knowing a direct equivalent, had to use her ingenuity – she faced the language problem by translating "be personal" as "respond as an individual unit." We were shocked and sobered when we realized this vast difference of meaning. The discovery launched an ongoing investigation with our Chinese colleagues to bridge this translation gap. For ourselves, we have learned a great deal – we hope our Asian counterparts have also found benefit from this "personal" dialogue.

Two Theories about Self

There are two distinct groups of theories about "the self": "ego theories" and "bundle theories." One's experience is generally that one is a single continuous self who has experiences that make up a personal history. Ego theorists would say that we have the experience of being continuous selves because that is in fact what we are. Bundle theorists, on the other hand, say this is not true, and look for other ways of explaining the experience of self.

Bundle theories are named from the writings of 18th-century philosopher David Hume. When Hume looked at his own experiences in order to find the experiencing self, he found only the experiences, without finding the experiencer. He concluded that the self is not an entity, but only a "bundle of sensations." People's lives are a series of impressions that seem to belong to a single self, but really are just strung together by memory and associations.[4]

The mainstream of Western psychology and most of the major world religions are based on some form of ego theory, with a notion of an ongoing self entity underlying their ideas about identity, values, and life after death. This is a central assumption for Christians, Jews, Muslims and Hindus. Buddhism is unusual in that it rejects the idea of a self. In the words of the Buddha:

> Actions exist, and also their consequences, but the person that acts does not.[5]

This viewpoint qualifies the Buddha as a bundle theorist. Psychologist Susan Blackmore writes:

> Bundle theory is extraordinarily difficult to understand or to accept. It means completely throwing out any idea that you are an entity who has consciousness and free will, or who lives the life of this particular body. Instead, you have to accept that the word 'self', useful as it is, refers to nothing that is real or persisting; it is just an idea or a word.[6]

Blackmore describes how the illusion of continuity is generated and maintained:

> As for the self who has experiences, this sort of self is just a fleeting impression that arises along with each experience and fades away again. The illusion of continuity occurs because each temporary self comes along with memories that give the impression of continuity.[7]

According to the Buddha, suffering arises in clinging to the false notion of self; the way to relieve suffering and achieve freedom is to alter one's perspective. The task is to let go of desires and attachments that keep recreating the self. Central to Buddha's teaching is the idea of no-self.

So, you are challenged to investigate your own assumptions, and decide whether your personal philosophy is that of an ego theorist, or a bundle theorist. Or maybe you will find – as we do – that both theories can offer something useful.

The Self: Innate or Developed?

As we saw in Part II, object relations theory maintains that the self is only potential at birth, and emerges as the infant matures. But many mothers have told us that this doesn't make sense to them, since they have clear experience of someone looking back at them from their infants' early days. We have struggled to find language that fits for the disparity between mothers' experience and the dicta of theory.

We propose that a *being* is there from the beginning, without a developed "self-concept" (and thus, without a "self"). The being is innate, while the self develops with the maturation of the nervous system. In the words of our colleague Gerry Fewster:

> This is not the cognitively constructed Self that comes from systematic learning but an undeniable sense of being, drawn from internal bio-energetic experiences and external conditions. This then becomes the foundation, the essence from which the newborn will begin to create his or her defined place in the world.[8]

Furthermore, says Fewster, humans are relational from the beginning, even before birth:

> I believe the in-utero relationship is ... the blueprint for all future relationships ... The underlying assumption is that we enter this world as relational beings – we are not 'taught' to be this way (in fact, our socialization works in the opposite direction).[9]

From the viewpoint of attachment theory, the child's relationship with the mother (or other caregiver) is a critical element for social and emotional development.[10]

> What the infant actually experiences is not a passive world of disconnected and impersonal objects but an arena constantly stirred by internal and external personal activity and interpersonal encounters. In other words the 'meeting place' is open for business from the moment mother and child make their first eye-to-eye connection.[11]

Fewster writes that "the authentic Self is a deeply rooted feeling state that reflects our unique essence." He maintains that

> This felt sense is neither biological nor cognitive at the core, although these systems are certainly involved in its expression and elaboration. Its essence is spiritual, its substance is energetic, and its central location is in the body. It is not a creation of the mind but the kernel from which our consciousness continually expands.[12]

We broadly agree that there is an elemental pattern, a proto-image of the self. We suggest that the self emerges from its elemental pattern to be defined in relationships, first with the mothering person and later with others. When we use the word "develop," it is more in the sense of a developing photograph – the image is already there, and is revealed in the developing fluid process. Fewster says, "What I'm referring to is the unfolding of the spiritual essence into the human form."

Children gradually learn to control their body and their environment; as this is accomplished, the project widens for the child to reach out and touch the world, and be touched by it. According to object relations theory, the child must go through a "separation-individuation" project, first objectifying the mother's face and breast, and later learning to move away and keep a stable internal object of the whole mother. The world out there, which is made up of objects, becomes an inner world of stable internal objects.[13] Fewster writes of the separation-individuation project:

> Through the lens of object relations, healthy separation from the mother is seen to occur as the child becomes progressively able to distinguish between inner reality and the external world – between the "me" and the "not-me."[14]

But this is not a strictly sequenced development, rather the unfolding of a pattern. The self does not develop in a mechanical linear fashion, but through the interaction of many experiences.

This early separation involves the use of power, where children learn to control themselves and the external environment. In this stage, children operate in a world of objects, objectifying both others and themselves. Further development as a person will require expanding on this limited viewpoint to see themselves and others as human individuals, not merely objects.

Fewster writes that the goal of the self is to be witnessed, and to witness:

> At the heart of the matter, the Self, the *real* Self, is pursuing its most enduring objective – to see and be seen, by an Other. If I were to insert my own dialogue into the scenario, it would be something like "So, here I am and there you are."[15]

We believe that autonomy and joining are both features of the dialogue. We say a critical transition must be made for a fuller actualization of the self, wherein the heart opens and the individual learns to care about others, and to connect and interact with them in a community way. In that way, we agree with Adler and Confucius. The process of development reaches a mature stage when both parent and child can grow beyond objectifying, past the impersonal expectations of the parent/child roles, to become people to each other:

> Within the developmental continuum, the power that once held everything together is gradually replaced by the 'personal', a more equitable and responsive arrangement in which the 'I' of each participant comes to know and respect the 'I' of the other.[16]

This is a life-long project. In an ongoing adult intimate relationship, people come to know each other more and more clearly. In our book *The Relationship Garden*, we describe this as a state of *recognition*:

> Because partners know each other's experiences so well, separating boundaries seem absent. Union does seem possible. This is a characteristic of the loving state.[17]

This is the ongoing process we describe in our Dynamic Empathy Model.

Beyond Individualism

Bundle theory suggests that the self is illusory. Martin Buber's view is that the self is not a central concern anyway, since relationships are what matter: "The self as such is not ultimately the essential."[18]

Instead, to Buber, all living is a meeting. There is no "I" but only I-It and I-Thou interactions.[19] Buber's perspective is not exactly bundle theory, but he does de-emphasize the habitual concern on the self that is prominent in the West.

As we have seen, James Hillman proposes a comprehensive definition of the self that involves the "interiorization of community." His view is more holistic and less individualistic:

> Once individualism dissolves its notion of self, and self relaxes into a communal feeling beyond bonding (tying, tightening, gluing, adhering, obligating), you can't possibly die alone, because there is no alone ... *existence is multiple* and does not cease with your cessation. The chord, the flow, the herd, the hive dances on.[20]

For ourselves, the issue is to undo the habitual fixation on the self that limits one's participation in a bigger picture. Oxford philosopher Derek Parfit's views are much more in keeping with bundle theory than ego theories. Parfit believes that personal identity is not what matters; instead, he concentrates more on participation with others. When he first learned of the bundle theory of Buddhist thought that disregards the self, Parfit was invigorated. "Is the truth depressing?" he asked. "Some may find it so. But I find it liberating, and consoling."[21]

Realizing that he could not depend upon an imagined future self – a "deep further fact" – he discovered the immediacy of living now, in the moment. He describes this as an escape from a prison:

> When I believed that my existence was such a further fact, I seemed imprisoned in myself. My life seemed like a glass tunnel, through which I was moving faster every year, and at the end of which there was darkness. When I changed my view, the walls of my glass tunnel disappeared. I now live in the open air. There is still a difference between my life and the lives of other people. But the difference is less. Other people are closer. I am less concerned about the rest of my own life, and more concerned about the lives of others.[22]

Transitional Selfishness

When people first do personal development groups, they often feel flushed with the power of being able to express themselves; sometimes they fail to recognize that all individual expression is in the context of a social environment. Having moved from a culturally based false humility, discovering that it is OK to be self-accepting, they sometimes become fixated into a selfish, self-centred attitude. They confuse self-acceptance with self-involvement and narcissism. In this way, they are like children, experiencing the first heady rushes of knowing that they are an individual. This is the issue of the "terrible two's" in child development; youngsters at this age often express their newfound sense of identity with excessive demands and insensitive actions. Some people who attend self-development groups go through a similar phase, being self-centred, lacking sensitivity and concern for others, in the name of affirming their new-found self-determination.

This was very common in the early decades of personal development groups in North America. We witnessed some people selfishly "expressing themselves" with little concern for the consequences, or for others' concerns. They were "doing their thing." We have staunchly opposed this limited viewpoint, and have long advocated for a fuller expression of the individual in sensitive relationship to others. Our work has been to teach the so-called "me generation" to become the "I-and-we generation." We see the same process at work in personal development groups in China, where self-learning is so new. Now that people are discovering the "I" attitude, they are in danger of succumbing to the allure of self-centredness. In our work, we try to help people see this trap and get past it to a more inclusive attitude – one of community concern from a singular point of view.

Other challenges face people in East and West. When Chinese people get into growth environments, they are tempted to follow the lure of catharsis instead of defining themselves. Caucasian people have less difficulty with self-definition; however, they often have felt isolated, and tend not to understand family feeling and group feeling so well. The danger for Chinese people is to remain stuck in repetitious energy release without learning; Western people can easily remain fixated in resentments against family members, blaming them for their sense of isolation. The Western people need to learn more language and action of social concern; the Chinese need to learn to distinguish their own defined individual viewpoints, decisions and actions. Westerners need to learn to connect. Chinese people need more to learn to separate. They have different fixations in the gestalt cycle.

Location

Do we think there is a self? Our answer, as in so many instances, is "yes and no." We believe there is no static thing we could call a self – there is no noun that applies. Instead, we conceive of an ever-changing process of *self-ing*. The pattern that is unique to each individual is preconfigured, but subject to mutation through experience and decision. This evolving self-ing is a learning process that is autodidactic, heuristic, and self-mutational. Individuals can observe their behaviour and experiences and make adjustments to change themselves.

Neuroscience now recognises that the brain can remap itself depending upon experience. We wrote about the consortium of brain activities in another book.[23] We think that more advanced self-learning, wherein people can distil standards, values and sensibilities, occurs through the reflective view of the self-aware prefrontal brain, the 'angel lobes'. We propose that this self-reflective capacity of the prefrontal brain works in concert with the connecting feelings of the heart brain and the integrating functions of the cerebellum to make physical changes in the brain structures as development continues.

Each individual has a unique and particular point of view. No one else looks out through your eyes. No one else has your particular history or frame of reference or educational background. No one else has your exact desires, whims, standards, tastes, dislikes, aversions, and knacks. What is unique is that each individual has a particular *location* in time and space. When I refer to myself, I should refer to my "I-Location."

One of the tasks in life is to develop a "location" in time and place. We wrote about this in a chapter in another book.[24] When people become fixated on the past or focused on possible futures, they are dislocated in time. When people do not have clear boundaries about their relationship to themselves and their environment, they have inadequate sense of their location in place. When one is located, the particular time-space location is often referred to as "the self" or "I." But this is a linguistic shorthand for the phenomenon of individual location experience. Psychology has become confused in trying to identify what is the "self" or the "I" or the "ego." We don't think in these terms; rather, we conceptualize about people in terms of their location in time and space.

In reference to I-Location, Chinese and Western people tend to have different issues to face. As we have seen, Western people are prone to selfishness and isolation, emphasizing their individual I-Location and not so cognizant of the place of others. For a Chinese person, the challenge is the opposite one; their cultural upbringing and language support a view of the "other" and less focus on oneself, which often results in blurred boundaries and mutual dependencies and resentments.

Historically, the traditional Asian perspective and the self-denying Judaeo-Christian ethic of the West have disregarded the I-location. In trying to find an I-location, people sometimes confuse location with being important, but being located has nothing to do with importance. I am singular, and a unique, separate and distinct entity that participates in the whole. If I think I am important, I am in danger of losing my connection by overemphasizing myself. If I think I am unimportant, I will miss the opportunity to bear witness from a unique vantage point. It's a task indeed!

Whether there is a self or not, all you have is your experience. If we shift the emphasis from self or not-self and focus on your particular I-Location, then you can get to work on the project of living a fulfilling and loving life that can bring unexpected bounty:

Pay attention to yourself. There is no great ocean apart from single drops of water. Wake up to the fact that you yourself, your every act is filled with wondrous, marvellous features. – Zen saying[25]

V.6   Paul Reps:
A Modern Zen Master

The problem of our mind, relating conscious to preconscious awareness, takes us deep into everyday living. Dare we open our doors to the source of our being? What are flesh and bones for? – Paul Reps[1]

Paul Reps (1895–1990) was an American artist, poet, and author. Reps (he always referred to himself this way, without his first name) was a phenomenon. Born in Iowa, he went to the Orient as a young man in the early 1900s and studied with the teachers of Asia. Gradually he assimilated the wisdom of the East and began to distribute it to the West in a most unique fashion. He published *Zen Flesh, Zen Bones* in 1939, then went on to develop his ideas about self-expression, believing that there were too many words. He would toss off picture-poems – simple, child-like line drawings and penetrating haiku-like epigrams.

Reps was a wanderer with no fixed roots. He regarded the planet as his home. In his life-long movements over the earth, he would stay in various places, then mysteriously move on. In each of these places, as far separated as Norway, Japan, India, the U.S. and Canada, he had a "family" of friends who looked out for him, loved him, and grew by the grace of his insightful teachings. He lived with us at The Haven during his final years, and a chair was placed near the door of the session room so that Reps could come and go from seminars as he wished.

Reps was one-of-a-kind. He was remarkable for his insights, his quick and sharp philosophical quips, and his respect for all of creation. Reps believed that humans are too aggressive with themselves and with each other. His attitude about body awareness was expressed in this admonition to a group:

Speak to your body softly, lovingly. Say "relax, dear neck" And it will!

But his teaching was full of paradox. Reps maintained that the subconscious is a brute beast. He said to get its attention you must shout at it, loudly. He recounted that he had been a smoker in his youth. He said he quit instantly when he stood in the middle of a room, breathed deeply to centre himself, and screamed at the top of his lungs, "STOP!" He counselled, "But you have to do it loudly, and you have to mean it!" We know others who have done this very thing, and still don't smoke years later!

Jock tells a story of a curious encounter that sums up Reps' teachings:

One day, I was in a hurry and still wanted to get my exercise routine done. I raced into the gymnasium at a break, didn't even take the time to turn on the light, and plunged into my exercise regimen. After a few minutes, a quiet but insistent voice spoke to me. "Slow down!" Out of the shadows, Reps spoke to me; he apparently had been standing in there in the dark, and in my haste, I didn't notice that was there. I stopped in wonder and listened to him. I then went back to my exercises, jumping into the Roman Chair. He said, "Stop! That's all wrong. You shouldn't jump up there. You should float up! Do it again!" I jumped down and tried to float up into the chair; I got up easier, but it was still with effort. "Do it again!" he ordered. As I relaxed, to my amazement, I floated up into the chair. After lifting my legs a couple of times, he said, "That's enough. You've earned your reward." I thought, "That isn't enough time or repetitions to get a good exercise benefit." However, I did as I was told. When I raced to my next exercise, situps, he began to criticize these. "Stop," he said. "Can't you put your mind on what you are doing?" I slowed down inwardly and concentrated on the exercise instead of time. After a couple of repetitions, he said, "That's enough. You've earned it." As I floated out of the gym, with far too little time applied to my exercise to logically get any benefit at all, I felt relaxed, calm, refreshed, and with a quiet mind. Exercise has never been the same.

He enjoyed people expressing themselves in their own unique way. He was the enemy of dogma, and sneered at routine practices which take the life out of humans. In rebellion to the growing trend towards rigid Zen practice involving hours of ritualized sitting, he invented thirty-second Zen sitting meditation! And he resisted the power doctrine of master/pupil, believing in the autonomy and wonder of each individual. Once, when instructing his students in the art of calligraphy, he told them to breathe and express themselves in the ink and brush. After one short session, he promised each of his attendees a diploma in calligraphy, with full and immediate rights to teach! Thus, there is no Reps school, no Reps way – this died with him.

He valued uniqueness, surprise and fun. "If not fun, better left undone" was a kind of mantra for him. One was never quite sure whether he was serious, whimsical, or pulling an existential leg with his surprising comments. One evening in conversation in our living room, he kept glancing out the window. Suddenly, he sprang up and ran to the window to exclaim:

The moon has moved
Something has jiggled loose up there!

He had a sharp mind and ready wit. His chess games showed the workings of a shrewd and alert intelligence, that was belied by his ready laughter and sense of the ridiculous. He enjoyed making himself an object of humour, and referred to himself in the third person always. He was in the spirit of the Zen crazy man, the trickster clown with a huge heart.

He believed in the unity of nature and the human worlds. He was concerned and critical about how humans were ignoring themselves and their own nature in their achievement pursuits. He wanted people to learn to live in the present, to surrender to life and thrive with their own beings, relaxed and flowing, alive like green bamboo.

He believed in a healthy body, fit by exercise and breathing, loose like a young sapling that bends in the wind. Sharp and directive, he once attended a presentation by Buckminster Fuller. After the presentation, Reps appeared at Bucky's hotel door, and without introducing himself said, "You're a disgrace ... the young people listen to you, and you don't breathe properly .... get down on the floor!" Apparently, the astonished Fuller did as he was instructed, and was subjected to a Reps lesson in being in the body with breath and life.

Reps spent much time in his final years at The Haven with us. To the last, he lived as he always had, simply and with enthusiasm. He loved to be with people and always had an insightful bit of wisdom/nonsense to offer. Everywhere on the grounds, people would be reporting each day "what Reps said to me." A perennial child, Reps took delight in his own creations. Once, he arrived at breakfast full of vigour, his eyes shining, to announce, "I just wrote a poem ... do you want to hear it?" The poem turned out to be:

Incredible
as it may seem
it may seem

That one is still reverberating, years later.

We were privileged to have known him. We named a reading room at The Haven "The Reps Room" and Reps took great delight in sitting in this space with its view of the forest, sea and sky. He spent hours poring over the collection of books he had generated over his life. Even in his final months, he was still producing; soon before his passing, he made us the gift of a picture-poem booklet he had just created, with the "best-ever Reps" expressions.

In the last few months of his life, Reps was feeble. Always independent, he found his bodily confinement to be very bothersome. He resisted anyone assisting him, and continued to move with purpose and self-motivated decisions. He did not want to burden anyone, and wished always to contribute to the spirit of place with his presence. He continued to believe in the oneness of the universe, as illustrated by the words he displayed on the wall of his kitchen many years ago:

come from sky
return to sky
no problem

His final days, he was comatose, his body rigid, coiled in the fetal position. In the hours before his death he relaxed, and his body lengthened and loosened into the easy quiet that he had always wished for others. As he lay in relaxed unconsciousness, his hands wondrously formed the mudra of oneness, a yogic posture representing peace, cosmic unity and wholeness. Each index finger touched the tip of the adjacent thumb. One of his attending nurses noticed this and said, "I believe this is an important sign. What does it mean?" We take it to mean that Reps' essential being was and is in touch with the cosmic harmony, and as he surrendered to his next lesson, he adopted the position of worship that demonstrated his joyous embrace of life. As he slipped into death, he surrendered in the same way that he had always encouraged others.

To honour him and his friendship, we use Reps' own words, which he often said so humbly to others: *Thank you for your life.*

Reps ...
your shining eyes
dance

watching
the little bird
hopping on
the tender grass

We know you are here.[2]

Oddly, people still experience Reps on the Haven property, years after his death, especially near the Reps Meditation Room. Without making any judgment about how this could or could not be, the reports are periodic, and indicate that the smiling guy is still in people's awareness. Jock reported an experience when Ben was going into surgery.

WHEN IN DOUBT ...

Ben had been undergoing medical tests for six months because of progressive tiredness and significant weight loss. After many consultations, he was scheduled to have surgery to investigate a probable tumour in the region of the gall bladder. We feared it was malignant.

We were told by the surgeon that she might be able to remove the tumour with a laparoscopy, which involves only an abdominal puncture and a camera. There was a possibility that she would discover more problems, and he might have to have a large incision. If the removal could be done by camera, he would likely go home the same day; if he had the incision, he would likely be in hospital for a week with a much more difficult recuperation. After months of the strain of investigations, we finally were at the hospital and he was in his gown in readiness for his surgery. As they wheeled him into the elevator, we waved goodbye to each other and, as the door closed, I was suddenly very alone.

I walked aimlessly around the hospital, knowing I had to simply endure the next few hours waiting to hear about the surgery. We were hoping it could be done with the camera, but there was still some doubt about this. As I sat in a lonely couch in the back of the hospital, I was suddenly overwhelmed with feelings of sadness and fear and deep concern for Ben. I had not paused to feel such emotions during the preceding weeks as we went from test to test, doctor to doctor. But now I had nothing to do but wait, and I was consumed with desperation and impotence.

Marilyn Rossner, our psychic friend, had told us that she was in touch with the spirit world, and that Ben's deceased mother was watching over him. Dubious, I still held some private hope that such things could be so. I wanted to reach out to the spirit world myself, but all past attempts to get someone from the other side to talk to me had been fruitless. So I sat and stared and fretted.

I tried to read, but the words would not come in. I took out my electronic digital organizer and scrolled through photographs of friends and family, seeking some kind of comfort and reassurance in my desperate loneliness and worry. I saw photos of our kids and faces of so many friends. And suddenly as I flipped through photographs, there was Reps' face smiling and shining.

I felt a wave of love for the old guy, and thought, "If there's anyone from the other side that I could trust, it would be Reps." So I spoke to him. "Reps ... are you there?"

To my shock and relief, I heard a voice inside my head: "Sure."

I said, "Well, I doubt that this is really true. I think you are a projection of my inner fears and hopes. But I still want to know how this is going to turn out."

He was very clear ... "The surgery will be done by camera, with no incision. The surgery will be quite long and involved. Ben will not go home tonight. He will stay in hospital. There is no cancer."

I said, "Reps, I really want to believe you ... but I have been told that with the camera procedure, the patient usually goes home the same day." I continued, "And furthermore, I am too afraid to trust what you say, because I think you are just the projection of my hopes. I doubt everything you say, and I doubt that your voice is really from you."

Reps, as he had often done, responded with a sage and weighty quip: "When in doubt, sprout!"

I burst out laughing, and tears of relief flowed down my cheeks.

Hearing this rhyming, Reps-like reply, I began to trust that maybe it was him after all. But I was still watching carefully to see if his predictions would come true. When I told Ben about this after he had come from under his anesthetic, he laughed quietly and said, "For sure, that's Reps!"

Ben did have the surgery by camera, it was long and involved, and he did stay in hospital overnight to recuperate. So there was one final test of Reps' statements that rested on the outcome of the pathology report that would come ten days later. During those ten days, I was hopeful that the final statement about "no cancer" would also be proven out by the pathology report. But I was afraid to trust, and the doubt persisted.

When the pathology report finally came, Reps was indeed correct. There was no cancer. The growths that were removed with the gall bladder were benign and there was no evidence of any spread. So Ben was cured of what ailed him and we could settle to the task of getting him heftier once again.

As for me, Reps has challenged my doubt, and his record is "four for four" on his predictions. So I am humbled. This is the beginning of a new opening in myself, and the sprouting of a renewed faith after doubt.

"When in doubt, sprout!"

Thank you, Reps.

V.7   Influencing the Future

KZ = Confucius (Kong Zi), CJ = Carl Jung, BW = Ben Wong, JM = Jock McKeen

JM: Science maintains that the future cannot be predicted with certainty. Certainly, one can see trends, which help in anticipating weather conditions and earthquakes. Some occult philosophies propose that it is possible to peer into the future. Dr. Jung, what do you think about, for example, astrology?

CJ: I was for a time deeply interested in astrology. This is an ancient system, like alchemy, that is useful as a tool for learning about cosmic things.

JM: Do you believe in astrology?

CJ: Not really. It is another "story" ... a myth to describe the indescribable.

JM: What about the predictive nature of astrology? Is it possible to use it to predict the future?

CJ: No, that is absurd. We can learn to see the *pattern of events* more clearly, and see our relationship to these. When we understand this, we can avoid future difficulties and make choices that would lead us into more expansive outcomes.

JM: What about you, Master Kong? You devoted a lot of time to the *Book of Changes*, which can be used as an oracle for future events. Can a sage or scholar of occult sciences predict the future?

KZ: One cannot predict the future with certainty. The future is only in the realm of possibility. There are many possible futures, which depend upon decisions and actions in the present. But one who sees present patterns clearly can see the trends and possible outcomes.

JM: So, the *Book of Changes* is more than an oracle for fortune telling.

KZ: Much, much more. Divination is a limited use of one of our most important philosophical treasures.

JM: Please say more.

KZ: What the masters of the *Book of Changes* knew was that life is an expression of a pattern, and that pattern is influenced by decisions made in the world. The life force (we call it *qi*) flows in harmony with *dao*, the way. As humans, we are free to choose whether to follow the signposts that point to the direction of the *dao*. We are also free to choose to disregard this. I taught my students the wisdom of the *Book of Changes* – that the most beneficial situation for all comes with following the signposts. Not slavishly and passively, but choosing the path that contributes to ongoing harmony and life enhancement.

JM: Existentialist philosophers suggest that individual human decisions determine the future that unfolds. We are free to choose, and our choices have consequences.

CJ: Yes, I agree with this.

KZ: I do too. This is at the heart of my teaching. Human conscience and decisions, and choices that are for the community. Beyond selfishness. We choose the kind of human beings we are and the kind of society we create.

JM: In this context then, astrology and the *Book of Changes* and other similar systems are not predictive. They show the patterns of possibility.

CJ: Yes, the gnostic approach is to "know" ... but *we know what IS, not what will be.* What will be ... will flow in unexpected ways from the decisions we make now in the present. We always live in the present.

KZ: So, you agree with the Buddhist idea that the future is an illusion?

CJ: Yes, in this sense I do agree with this. Astrology can show the pattern of one's life, but not a fixed destiny.

JM: We each have a distinct pattern. The more we know of this, the more we are aware of our deep nature and our place in the universe.

BW: The existentialist position, which I like, is that we are free to choose. The more we know our patterns, the more we can make informed choices to remain in harmony with the flow of life.

CJ: This was also the message of the hermetic tradition of the gnostics and the alchemists. There is a pattern of events in the cosmos, which we can choose to follow or disregard. But we disregard it at our peril. We can doom ourselves to dire consequences by our decisions.

JM: This was also a theme in John Milton's *Paradise Lost* ... "sufficient to have stood, yet free to fall." Human beings are free to be in Eden, or to fall from grace.

CJ: Yes, the Bible had the same message as Master Kong and the Chinese ancients. Humans are free, but in the context of universal processes that are beyond human control.

KZ: The *Book of Changes* states that "Human life is conditioned and unfree"; yet we must still find our own individual way, and make our choices and decisions as we go along.

BW: My friend Alan Watts used to say, "The patterns of the *dao* are tendencies in movement, not determinations."

JM: So, as we turn our attention to chaos theory, we are all four agreed that the future cannot be predicted with certainty. But one can have glimpses into future possibilities by learning about present patterns and trends. Thank you, gentlemen.

V.8 Two Worlds: Predictability and Chaos

You will still sleep many hours
here on the beach,
and one clear morning you will find
your boat tied to another shore. – Antonio Machado[1]

We live in two worlds simultaneously – the predictable, routine, dependable *linear world*, and the unpredictable *chaotic world*, full of surprises and upsets. Each world has its own rules, governed by different mathematical principles. The linear world obeys laws of gravity and motion and Newtonian physics we all studied in school. The chaotic world, also called the turbulent world, has its own laws that are not so apparent to us. The study of this domain has intensified in recent decades, especially since the discovery of fractal geometry, the mathematics of chaos. Many people have an aversion to mathematics; if you are amongst them, breathe easily. We are not delving into the scientific intricacies of this subject. Instead, we discuss its psychological implications for people living in this modern era.

In Lewis Carroll's *Through the Looking Glass*, Alice looks at a mirror and ponders what might be on the other side of its reflection. She steps through and finds herself in a completely different world, full of strange events and unexpected surprises.[2] When Alice is on one side of the mirror, she is in her regular, predictable life; when she steps through the looking glass, she enters a completely new realm that seems not to function with the same rules or habits of her regular world.

Briggs and Peat's *Turbulent Universe* utilizes the story of Alice and the looking glass to discuss the two worlds of linear geometry and chaotic dynamics.[3] The first section describes the world on one side of the mirror, showing how conventional order becomes chaos; in the middle section, there is a discussion of the gateway between the two worlds, the mirror function itself; the third section, the other side of the mirror, discusses how chaos can be resolved into linear order and predictability. We refer you to Briggs and Peats' book if you want more detail; it is an accessible way for an interested non-scientist to grapple with very complex scientific concepts and phenomena. In this book, we address elements from chaos theory that relate to psychology, East and West. The central theme is that there are two worlds in which we participate: one linear and predictable (the Newtonian "billiard ball" universe), the other one chaotic and unpredictable (the fractal universe).

Turbulence

The linear world obeys the laws of cause and effect. An action produces a predictable outcome. Flip the light switch and the light comes on. Push down on the accelerator in your automobile, and you go faster. Apply the brake, and you slow down. Eat food when you are hungry, and your hunger disappears. Cause and effect. Predictability.

But within the routine of predictability, life brings us surprises, unexpected events and influences, which are sometimes unsettling, or maybe even catastrophic. They are the many faces of turbulence. In simple terms, *chaos is turbulence*; on a bumpy aircraft flight, you experience chaos in the unexpected knocks and sudden changes. To Jock, this is a horror, and he has joked that he never fully puts his weight down on the seat when he is flying! But a flight attendant friend feels completely positive about turbulence, since this is the time she is required to sit down and gets a break from her service work – it's all in the attitude!

You can witness the world of turbulence in your own kitchen sink. Turn on the tap with a slow stream, and the water will run down as a straight column into the drain hole below; at this slow stream, you are witnessing a linear system. This is called "laminar flow." To see chaos, turn the tap on full. Suddenly, water rushes so quickly that it cannot all get through the drain, and some bounces off the sink, spraying in all directions. Your clothes are wet, the counter is wet, and there are roiling bursts where the stream hits the sink bottom. It all seems very disordered. But – and this is the point – the splashing water is not random. *It is highly ordered, just not strictly predictable*; it is obeying laws of the chaotic dimension.

Another simple example. Throw a stone into a pond, and the surface water will ripple in concentric rings away from the place where the stone enters the water. This is predictable. But if you throw two stones into the pond, the spreading rings can intersect with each other, and what happens at these intersection points is not so predictable; instead, it is turbulent, chaotic. You can observe patterns emerging in the turbulence if you look for them. But you could not have predicted exactly where they would be. Wherever there is intersection between two patterns, producing interference, the setup exists to develop turbulence. Turbulence can be witnessed in our daily world in many places – the movement of billowy clouds across the sky, the flapping of an umbrella in a high wind, the excitement of a phone call that brings unexpected news.

Turbulence involves non-linear activity; as we have seen, the opposite of turbulent is laminar movement. In a kayak on a river, if you are in the laminar flow, the current will carry your boat in a more or less straight line. Where the flow becomes faster and encounters obstacles such as rocks in the stream, the flow changes from laminar to turbulent. For the less experienced, the turbulent flow should be avoided; but, for an experienced kayaker, the chaos is not an enemy. Indeed, it can be a source of excitement to negotiate the sudden twists and knocks that turbulence brings; this is the allure of white water rapids. Indeed, in a kayak, if one knows how to read and use turbulence, one can negotiate a small craft backwards, up the stream against a raging torrent by riding the edges of whirlpools and using the force of the chaos to change direction. We experienced riding whirlpools when we were traveling on the Mekong River in a "cigar boat" with a very skilled pilot who did not avoid swirling water; instead he steered towards whirlpools and rode the edge of them. The result was that he could propel our light craft with sudden bursts of energy. He was using the chaos of the whirlpool to our advantage!

Chaos is Not Disorder
People tend to think of chaos as random, disturbing, and lacking order. Indeed, a conventional synonym for chaos is disorder. "My life is in chaos" generally means that I can't find any order or regularity in my life. But to the scientists who study it, chaos is neither random nor disordered. Chaos obeys rules.

This is an important point to digest: *chaos is not disorder.* There are very subtle and potent ordering principles that underlie such chaotic events as a tornado or a roaring river. These are turbulent and unpredictable, but they are ordered nonetheless. Wherever there is turbulence, chaos is manifesting.

Chaos is unpredictability. Chaos is ordered, but not in ways that can be readily seen. Weather forecasters track chaos, attempting to find the hidden patterns of a storm. There are many parameters of the developing storm systems that can be predicted to a certain point, but ultimately the pattern is so complex, and feeds back on itself to produce "fractal" ordering, that it is impossible to predict. So weather forecasting is at best an engagement with chaos, and the ultimate results cannot be exactly defined in advance.

Human family events are another example of chaotic unpredictability that nonetheless has its own inherent rules and order. An unexpected illness or death can throw the entire family system into disarray, invoking the unpredictability and turbulence of the chaotic order. Somehow people get through these distressing times; hidden forces come into operation that allow them to negotiate the chaos.

Chaos and Equilibrium

Chaos can be seen as distance from equilibrium. Consider a huge boulder balanced precariously at the top of a sheer rock face. At this stage, the rock is in a "distance from equilibrium" condition. A sudden wind could start the rock tumbling, with its ultimate destination indeterminate (other than it will be down there somewhere). If it breaks free, it falls in a turbulent fashion, bouncing and rolling, starting other rock movement. In its collisions, it invites more turbulence. When it finally comes to rest at the bottom, it lodges in a ditch and can go no further; it has achieved equilibrium, and being so massive, is unlikely to move without external assistance. At the top, it was in an unpredictable far-from-equilibrium situation. At the bottom, it is in a quite predictable location.

Intersection and Interference

There would be no turbulence without the intersecting of forces. When there is interference, the possibility of turbulence, chaos and newness arises. A stable linear system can become turbulent through the introduction of a new force. Many young marriages begin peacefully, only to find the birth of the first child to be the beginning of an exhausting period of new events and challenges. Of course, the young couple is thrilled with the new baby, but the whole arrangement is chaotic because the new infant force brings with it so many interruptions to the previously stable system. These are unsettling, but also bring in new possibilities. A mother of two young children blogged:

> Chaos is definitely the new normal in our house. The house is often in shambles with toys and baby stuff everywhere. I'm trying to accept that, but it's not easy.[4]

Musicians and artists can use their understanding of these interferences to advantage. We attended a lecture in New York by jazz trumpeter Wynton Marsalis, who was teaching an audience of mostly children about "challenging the rhythm." He had with him a very accomplished jazz band, who could "change it up" at his direction. To make his point, he instructed the band to play a familiar piece in strict time, with no variation. The piece was on key, clear, and somewhat boring in its predictability. Then, to illustrate, Marsalis instructed the musicians to delay a fraction of a count before playing, to lag a little, and then suddenly catch up to still hit the beat. The band played the same piece with this slight "drag" on the rhythm; the result was that the piece had a textured moodiness to it that was previously lacking. When he told them instead to attack the beat, to land on it with authority, the same piece brightened up and the audience was ready to clap and stomp. Same piece, same basic structure – but the challenges to the rhythm were providing interferences with the staid pattern, bringing life and unexpected enjoyment.

Iteration and Fractal Geometry

To iterate simply means to repeat. If you say, "Do this again and again and again and again," you are iterating on the theme of "again." Mathematicians studying the geometry of chaos utilize iteration to bring the fine-detailed images of chaos into view. When cartoons were first introduced in the movies in the early 20th century, each frame had to be drawn by hand. To show a cartoon character walking, the first frame would have the feet in a particular place. The next frame would be a slightly changed version with a slight advance of one foot, and then a third would have another slight change introduced. In this painstakingly slow fashion, the early cartoons of Mickey Mouse were created by hand. Today, this same process can be done quickly with computers, using iteration. The computer generating program could be given an instruction to redraw the same image with a very slight change, and then iterate this process thousands of times. Now a school child can use a computer to generate a moving cartoon figure. Repetition, iteration, is the key to this.

In the early days of Hollywood, hundreds of extras were required to make up an assembled crowd for a scene. In modern cinema studios, no humans are required at all to depict large groups. Using iteration, a single image of an individual can be multiplied many times, with slight alterations to give the appearance of different people; in this way, crowds of thousands can be generated by a computer in a short time, for the cinematic effect. The key to this is iteration. In this case, it involves a simple computer instruction, repeated many, many, many times (notice the iteration?). Iteration simply means "repeating a pattern or sequence" or "to do again" or "to repeat."

Nature is replete with examples of this kind of iterative dividing at progressively smaller scales. For example consider the branching structure in rivers, plants, and in body organs. One divides into two, which then each divide into two, and so on. Thus you get the structure for the roots and branches of a tree, or the spreading blood vessels in a body organ, or the extraordinary complex interrelationships in the human brain. These patterns are governed by simple principles that result in complex manifestations through iteration. If these iterations feed back on themselves, they can induce chaotic events (as we discuss below, "Feedback and Feedback Loops").

As scientists accumulated the understanding of how natural shapes occur, they began to see the mathematical principles that nature uses.

A "fractal tree" created by iterative division.

James Gleick writes of their fascination with hidden dynamic patterns, as they discovered that "there were forms in nature – not visible forms, but shapes embedded in the fabric of motion – waiting to be revealed."[5]

The structure of these shapes was revealed through a brand of mathematics that describes branching, folding, feedback, and iteration – fractal geometry. Using its principles, a computer artist can produce images that appear just like the natural world. Thus, it is possible to generate a host of virtual landscapes that appear real, yet exist only in the digital world. In this digital art, mountains and canyons and clouds all have this hauntingly realistic appearance because they are generated by the same principles used in nature. The computer-generated characters in movies like *Avatar* can appear so life-like because they are made using fractals.

So, what is a fractal? A fractal is a geometric object with self-similarity (an infinite nesting of structure at all scales). In other words, a fractal can be split off into parts, each of which is a reduced-size copy of the whole. Each part contains the code for the whole. This self-similarity is also a feature of holograms. Each part is isomorphic with each other part, and all are isomorphic with the whole. The same pattern is enunciated at each level.

A fractal is created by executing a simple process repeatedly. For example, a snowflake structure can be created by iteration: it begins with an equilateral triangle and then replaces the middle third of every line segment with a pair of line segments that form an equilateral "bump." Within a few iterations, the distinctive appearance of a snowflake is evident. If the process is continued, the flake will appear increasingly realistic. Amazing and beautiful results from a simple process! This is how nature creates her infinite designs. Wondrous!

Feedback and Feedback Loops

Feedback occurs when a system's action brings a response that acts back on the system; the response becomes a new input into the same system. For example, when you ask a question to your partner, you invite an answer that will provide information as feedback that you can consider and incorporate. Perhaps with the information from your partner, you might change your opinion or point of view. Feedback can thus be shape-shifting.

Not all feedback induces turbulence, but if the feedback occurs suddenly or is introduced repeatedly, the system can become overwhelmed and chaos may be the result. The interference invites a change in the pattern, which then becomes a new feedback to invite a further shift. An example of a turbulence-inducing mechanism is an audio feedback loop. This occurs as you are singing karaoke, delivering your finest version of the song, when all of a sudden, your mellifluous voice is overwhelmed by a huge screech that will not go away until you move the microphone away from the speakers. Experienced singers know that using a microphone in front of a speaker system can bring such trouble. What has happened? The answer lies in the behaviour of the feedback loop.

A microphone is a device that takes the sound waves from your voice and translates them into an electrical impulse, which can be fed into a sound system. As you sing into the microphone, your voice is delivered first to an amplifier, which increases the sound's volume, and then to the speakers. You sing without effort, and the amplifier does the work to boost the volume sufficiently to drive the speakers. However, if you step in front of the speaker, it is likely that within seconds the huge screeching noise will drown out your lovely voice. Why? Because of a growing feedback loop. The microphone is continuously picking up your voice as you sing into it, but if you are in front of the speaker, it also picks up what is coming from the speaker (your amplified voice), and it sends this louder signal (your voice directly into the microphone, plus the amplified voice sounds from the speakers) back to the amplifier, *which further amplifies it.* The much louder sound comes out the speakers, and is added to your gentle voice. The microphone picks up this enhanced sound and delivers it back to the amplifier, but the input now is a larger sound that is delivered back to the amplifier, *which amplifies it again.*

And so on – and in a matter of seconds, the speakers are overwhelmed by the hugely amplified and ever-increasing sounds. This is a feedback loop. If you step away from the speaker or cover the microphone, the whole process is dampened. The horrific screeching sound is the expression of turbulence, of chaos from the iterations of the feedback loop. This audio phenomenon is just one kind of feedback loop. Feedback loops can be used creatively; Jimi Hendrix was hailed by some as a musical genius for his iconoclastic and innovative guitar effects using feedback.

Optical systems can also have feedback loops. For example, you can set up a video feedback loop by aiming a video camera at a television which is connected to its output, to get an image of the camera (and maybe yourself) taking the video. On the screen you will initially see an image of the camera pointing at the television set (it "sees itself seeing"). But then the camera takes a picture of this picture, and sends it back to the television set as an adjusted video input. Each time the new picture appears on the screen, it is changed again by the process of feedback. This is a video feedback loop.

With some adjustments, this setup can be used to generate fractal patterns, the remarkable moving images that appear like magical multicoloured clouds or galaxies. In order to create fractals, the camera's image must be multiplied and recombined so that the images interfere with each other. An easy way to achieve this effect is to overlap the images of two or more video projectors. Or it can be accomplished with changing angles and introducing mirrors. The camera takes an image of what the screen is displaying, which is then delivered to the screen; each time this feedback occurs, there is an influence on the output, and suddenly, the display shows beautiful geometric patterns (fractals) that pulse and mutate with swirling colours and shapes. Once an interference effect is introduced into the feedback loop, the fractals will generate, demonstrating optical turbulence.

Holograms and Holomovement

A hologram is a multidimensional image created by interference patterns generated by a laser light beam. It is a wonder of modern science, developed in the second half of the 20th century. Moviegoers were amazed to see a virtual moving image of Princess Leia stepping out of a robot in an early *Star Wars* movie to make a recorded speech. They weren't simply listening to her words or seeing a two-dimensional video presentation; indeed, the image of the princess was remarkably multidimensional.

Nowadays, holograms are commonplace. They are now frequently seen at science fairs, where you can walk inside a huge virtual image of what is being depicted, walk around inside it, get down underneath it, and see it from all sides. Since this image is created with light effects, one can walk right through it; yet the detail is complete and accurate from every angle. Holograms are now something that people can take for granted; indeed, holographic images are embedded on millions of credit cards worldwide.

The process of creating a hologram has been well described in lay terms, so a short summary is sufficient here.[6] A laser is a coherent light beam (the beam stays straight rather than scatters). When the laser beam is split into two, with one part impinging on a photographic plate directly, and the other part of the beam bounced off a mirror, then arriving at the photographic plate, an interference pattern is generated by the intersecting laser inputs. This generates a pattern that looks like a jumbled mess. But, this apparent randomness actually contains the code for the original subject's image. If a laser beam of the same frequency is later used to illuminate the photographic plate with the messy pattern, a multidimensional image of the original subject will appear in virtual form, true in every detail, from every angle.

The hologram has the property of self-similarity that is a characteristic of fractals – every part contains the information for the whole. If one were to take a small fragment of the photographic plate created as described, it would contain all the information necessary to generate the virtual image of the original subject, albeit with lower resolution if the piece used is small. All the information stored on the hologram is contained in any part of the hologram, although resolution is lower with smaller parts. This self-similarity is related to the concept of isomorphism. The pattern of each piece is the same as the pattern for each other piece, and is the same as the pattern for the whole.

For physicist David Bohm (1917–1992), however, the concept of holograms is too limited, since the virtual holographic image is fixed in time and frozen. Bohm preferred the concept of *holomovement*, which involves a continual interactive process of folding and unfolding. He says that the nature of reality in general, and consciousness in particular, is "a coherent whole, which is never static or complete, but which is an unending process of movement and unfoldment."[7]

Bohm says that the tangible reality of everyday life is a kind of illusion, like a holographic image; he calls this the *explicate order* (meaning "unfolded"). Underlying our usual experience is a deeper order of existence which he calls the *implicate order* (meaning "enfolded"). These two realms are isomorphic with each other; the implicate order is the folded up version, and the explicate order is the unfolded version. The implicate order is hidden from direct view; the explicate order is apparent to the regular senses. Both the implicate and explicate orders exist in time and space; "beneath" both orders is the "ground" which Bohm says is the movement itself. It is, of course, not a physical ground, but rather a fundamental function on which the process depends.[8]

The implicate order is a folding up of the explicate, much like an egg is folded into a cake; the explicate order is the unfolding of the implicate order. Bohm cites the design of a computer as an example to explain his concept – the basic operation of the computer is encoded (enfolded) in the microchip, and the chip displays its activity by images on the screen (explication). These two orders of reality are in constant dynamic relationship with each other in the process of folding (implicating) and unfolding (explicating) in holomovement. Bohm says, "all existence is basically holomovement which manifests in relatively stable form."[9]

Bohm's Ink Drop Experiment, in which he folds and unfolds a sequence of drops of ink in glycerine, is a dramatic model for the implicate order. He demonstrated implicate and explicate by folding an ink drop into glycerine through the process of turning a handle that rotates the container. The ink drop gradually disappeared as it was folded in, trailing off into invisibility. After a number of turns of the device, the ink drop, which was clearly "there" at the beginning, had disappeared; it seemed to have ceased to exist. Yet if the turning was reversed, the ink drop that had vanished gradually reappeared, and in the precise number of counter-turns that had generated its disappearance, it would completely reappear, seemingly reborn in the same position in the glycerine. Somehow, when the ink drop was folded up, it kept track of where it had come from as it spread out through the entire environment. Bohm says that the ink drop had become "nonlocal" but the pattern for the drop still existed in the whole system.[10] This remarkable demonstration shows that physical events such as an ink drop can be folded up and disappear. But they have not ceased to exist, they are merely nonlocal – when they are unfolded again, they can reappear.[11]

If one thinks of the ink blot's disappearance as a kind of 'death', some interesting philosophical possibilities arise. For example, where do people go when they die? Perhaps they become nonlocal. Maybe life occurs in unfolding, when manifestations are local; in death, the manifestations become nonlocal.

Folding, Escher and Chinese Thought

If you take a long piece of white paper (say 12" long by 1" wide) and blacken one side with a pen, leaving the other side unmarked, and then join the paper end to end with scotch tape so that the white side is continuous, and the black side is continuous, you will have a simple structure. If an ant were to walk on the white side of the paper, it could cover the entire white length, and then step over the scotch tape and keep going, walking the white side for as long as it pleased. Another ant could be simultaneously walking on the black side, merrily making its way. Both ants could continue on their respective paths for days and never bump into each other. Indeed, the ant on the white side might not even know that a world of black walking surface even existed. Parallel ant universes!

Now, you can liven things up for these ants considerably if you adjust how you join the paper at the ends. This time, before you tape the ends together, give the piece of paper a half-twist so that at the join the black surface will be juxtaposed to the white surface, and the taped strip will have a curve in it. This is a Moebius strip (named after the mathematician who discovered it), and depicts the strange mathematics of curves and folding. Now, if the ant on the white surface begins to walk in one direction, it will soon reach the joining point, and as it crosses the tape, it will suddenly arrive on the black surface. Same for the ant from the black surface: it begins on the black side but soon ends up on the white surface. If they continue, they can go on (in theory) forever, moving from black to white to black to white. If you could interview them, they would tell you of the miracle they had discovered about how white becomes black becomes white. This is an iterating feedback loop. Walking from the black side to the white side to the black side is repeated over and over. The Dutch artist M.C. Escher (1898–1972),[12] did a drawing of something similar, with ants moving around the intersecting surfaces of a Moebius strip.

Escher was fascinated with this phenomenon of feedback, and looking at his drawings is a mind-bending revelation. One picture shows a tower with a waterfall plunging from the top level, and then the collected water flowing into a moat, which twists and turns at the base of the building and somehow ends up being the feeding water *at the top of the building* for the same waterfall. The bottom becomes the top. Another Escher drawing depicts people going down stairs, then coming to a landing, then after a turn proceeding down more stairs. There are other people going up the stairs facing the descending people. The descending people somehow in the drawing *magically become the ascending people*. Ascent and descent become each other.

Nobel laureate Octavio Paz' poem "The Street" has a twisted loop embedded in the structure of the poem. The one who is followed becomes the one who follows:

A long and silent street.
I walk in blackness and I stumble and fall
and rise, and I walk blind, my feet
stepping on silent stones and dry leaves.
Someone behind me also stepping on stones, leaves:
If I slow down, he slows;
if I run, he runs. I turn: nobody.
Everything dark and doorless.
Turning and turning among these corners
which lead forever to the street
where nobody waits for, nobody follows me,
where I pursue a man who stumbles
and rises and says when he sees me: nobody.[13]

We see a similarity here with the ancient Chinese idea of the interrelationship between heaven and earth; the *Book of Changes* suggests that heaven and earth are linked and somehow become each other, or are folded into each other, or express each other. *Yin* becomes *yang* becomes *yin* becomes *yang*. In the Five Stages of Change, the process repeats (iterates), as each successive stage unfolds into the next; so one could say that one stage is the folded up version of the succeeding stage, which is the unfolding of the previous one. This is also the gestalt cycle in human interaction: contact resolves into withdrawal, which opens the possibility for a new contact. In terms of Alice's two worlds, there is a dynamic relationship between chaos and equilibrium: they fold one into the other, generate each other, and then are resolved into each other. Folding and unfolding, with a half-twist!

The whole universe is moving, folding and unfolding. Realities are generated and then lost from view in this never-ending process of change. To us, this is reminiscent of the notion of "forever flowing constancy" of Daoism, and the concepts of transformation in the *Book of Changes,* which describes a hidden inner world that generates the outer world of appearances. We also link these ideas with Jung's concept of archetypes, ancient patterns that manifest in our everyday world. Indeed, Bohm at times refers to the explicate order as the "manifest order."

In classical Chinese medicine, the meridians can be seen as the implicate (enfolded) order; the body, then, is the explicate (unfolded) order. The concept of folding and unfolding is also expressed in Chinese medicine by the paired ideas of *biao li*. *Biao* is emanation of the life force from within; *li* is intimate structuration of the life force from without, which organizes the body and its deep relationships. *Biao* as manifestation, and *li* as structuring show the dynamic relationship of folding and unfolding between energy and matter. This is the interplay of the heavenly *qi* and the earthly *qi* in the human being.

The process of folding is involved in many complex processes that science is just beginning to understand. In the body, the surface of the human brain and the lining of the small intestine both have the structure of branching and folding, massively increasing the surface area and thus the possibilities for connection and interchange. On a larger scale, according to Steven Hawking the universe is actually finite, but because of the folding of space and time, the possibilities are infinite.[14]

Chaos: Crisis or Opportunity?

Motivational speakers in the West often say that the Chinese word for crisis is composed of "danger and opportunity," as a way of urging us to make the most of situations. Since President John F. Kennedy made this link in a public speech, numerous other political figures in the West have also used the statement.[15] Although this linguistic association is not strictly accurate, it does invite discussion about the Chinese interpretation of crisis. To summarize, the Chinese word for crisis (*wei ji*) involves danger and shares a character with the word "opportunity." In earlier times, *wei ji* represented an emergency situation that was cause for anxiety; in more recent times, it is seen in a more positive light.[16]

The interpretation of crisis relates to our discussion of chaos. As we have seen, chaos simply means unpredictability. Chaos is not disorder; but it is unpredictable. Understandably, people are anxious in face of chaos. Chaos is distance from equilibrium; the greater this distance, the greater the anxiety. But chaos is alive, a source of energy and creativity. If chaos is seen as danger, as the enemy of security, then one wants to control the chaos, to defend against it. But if one sees the chaos as an opportunity for growth and change, chaos is not an enemy; it is an opportunity to embrace.

What do you think? Is crisis only a hardship to endure? Or is it an opportunity for further development? We take the existentialist view and see life as an ever-renewing opportunity for change and learning; so for us, crisis is an opportunity.

Chaos, Satir Work and Maria Gomori

Virginia Satir's work in family therapy was based on a concept of change. Maria Gomori, who is in our view now the most knowledgeable and adept master of Satir's work, has gone beyond Satir's original innovations to synthesize her own distinctive mixture of family therapy, humanism and existentialism. In her book *Personal Alchemy* she writes about the Satir Change Process and characteristically puts her own stamp on the topic. She details the process of movement in family systems from equilibrium, through a period of chaos under the influence of a change agent, to a new integration and equilibrium. Gomori notes the significance of chaos:

> Chaos, because it is unpredictable, creates much anxiety and fear, but it can be positive, even if it doesn't feel that way to the person concerned. It is a high-energy state that can lead to new possibilities and choices. Because there is no change without chaos, we need to find ways to accept the uncertainty and fear that accompanies it.[17]

Maria Gomori is now over 90 years old, and continues to teach her insightful understandings around the globe. A survivor of the Nazi incursion into Hungary and the later Hungarian Revolution, Gomori is adamant that unexpected forces can be teachers if one embraces them rather than fleeing as a victim. She notes that chaos and equilibrium alternate in an ongoing process:

> Since change is ongoing throughout life, every state of equilibrium that we reach leads to another one at a later point ... After becoming accustomed to the challenge of tolerating chaos while on the road to a new equilibrium, we can initiate more changes and continue learning in many aspects of our lives.[18]

Chaos and Relationships

Relationships have alternating episodes of chaos and equilibrium. Coming to know a partner or friend more deeply brings the stability and certainty of knowing the other's likely responses to situations. However, differences continue to be revealed, bringing new interferences, interruptions, and turbulence. We wrote about the chaotic aspects of relationships in our book *The Relationship Garden*, where we devoted a chapter to this topic. The Power Struggle stage of the relationship cycle can bring new growth and possibilities along with the disturbances.[19]

We experienced this repeatedly in working with our editor, Toby, in the preparation of this book. In one instance, after we had worked on a chapter for many days, Toby told us bluntly that he didn't like what we had written, and why. We experienced a sudden shock, since we were kind of in love with this part of the text, and a consequent tension amongst us all. Using the Communication model, we entered the turbulence: we engaged in a dialogue of questions and pondering, to investigate why we saw the same material in such a different fashion. We were tempted (on both sides) to withdraw into defensiveness and blame; however, we recognized that this would simply stop the gestalt movement of our interaction. So we struggled through the chaos and focused our attention on learning more about each other's opinions and points of view. There were surprises and challenges for us all. However, we were intent upon remaining open and seeing the process through to the resolution, to be direct and honest without moralizing. In the midst of this chaotic process of feedback, iteration, and facing the unpredictable, we laboured earnestly with each other to create a piece of writing that had unexpected newness and learning for us all.

Chaos and a Creative Life

Chaos is not disorder, but it is turbulence and it challenges us to face insecurity. If there were no chaos, everything would be still, and there would be no life or creativity or change. Yet we also require some degree of order to maintain a consistency in our lives. It's a balancing act between control and letting go. One is always tempted to retreat into security, to try to find predictability and definite answers when so often, a new unsettling occurs. Creativity needs both predictability and unpredictability. To generate something new, one needs the constraint of applying oneself in a disciplined fashion; yet, at the same time, one must let go of control of the process to allow something new to emerge.

American author Hellen Keller contended with severe challenges her whole life, being struck deaf and blind in early childhood. Yet she maintained a faith in facing the unexpected that is exemplified in her writing:

> Security is mostly a superstition. It does not exist in nature nor do the children of men as a whole experience it. Avoiding danger is no safer in the long run than outright exposure. Life is either a daring adventure, or nothing. To keep our faces toward change and behave like free spirits in the presence of fate is strength undefeatable.[20]

V.9 Cycles

KZ = Confucius (Kong Zi), CJ = Carl Jung, BW = Ben Wong, JM = Jock McKeen

JM: We have just discussed chaos, folding, iteration, and feedback. I think this relates to our ongoing theme about cycles.

KZ: Yes. The Chinese Five Stages of Change begin (and end) with a period of rest, then reactivation, expansion, fruition, distillation of principle, and back to rest, then another expanding spiral of growth again.

CJ: The completion of one turn of a cycle folds in what has been accomplished, and reopens to new possibilities.

BW: The cycles we have described (such as the Dynamic Empathy Model, the gestalt cycle, the Chinese Five Stages) are similar in structure. The stages of such cycles fold into each other. The stages are not mechanical things that simply are replaced by the stage that follows. It is more subtle than this. As each stage develops, it gradually unfolds into the next. One stage becomes the next.

CJ: Would you then say that the previous stage is gone?

BW: Not at all. The previous stage that has seemingly disappeared has folded up into the structure of the next stage and is still invisibly involved in the stage it generated.

KZ: I agree. In the Chinese Five Stages, Wood is still present in Fire, but folded in.

CJ: In this way past is folded into the present, which unfolds into the future.

KZ: Invisibility unfolds into the visible material world (which is then folded up in invisibility).

CJ: In my language, the archetypes are folded up, implicate; they unfold into actuality in the living person.

JM: This is what David Bohm describes as "holomovement."

BW: I propose that when people die, they are not gone; they are folded up. As the ink drop in Bohm's experiment disappears into the glycerine as it is folded in, the drop becomes nonlocal (literally everywhere) and seems to disappear. But it is still there in the invisible relationships. So I think when someone dies, they fold in to the universal and become literally everywhere.

JM: Master Kong and Dr. Jung, in this way, we can talk with you both here, since you are folded up into our experience, but accessible to us.

BW: When friends and loved ones have died I keep them in my heart, and they live in my unfolding in the present ... they are still here, to have input to me through my feelings, and I can pass this on in my interactions with others.

CJ: You can continue to intersect with them, but not in the physical way.

BW: So we are meeting, four men, two deceased, two in the body. Your lives of study, research and dedication are folded up in the present, and as we get to know you, what you were and are unfolds with us.

KZ: Yes, in your terms, we are everywhere, folded up, waiting for contact and interest from someone in the unfolded state such as yourselves.

CJ: Thank you for inviting us to your party!

KZ: We who are not in the body are folded up, and you are unfolding the principles dear to us in your interactions with us.

JM: Yes, you are living in us, and we in you. We, the living, are explicate; you who have passed are implicate.

BW: This is a universal principle of cycles – living and death are just stages that fold and unfold into each other.

JM: Let's go further. Chaos theory indicates that transformation occurs through interaction (called interference in science). So in a dynamic cycle, each stage as it disappears folds into the next one, but it is not gone; it remains to interact with the next stage, albeit nonlocally. This interaction introduces the possibility of chaos and unpredictability.

KZ: This is the movement of life.

BW: Gentlemen, your presence here informs us, intersects with us. We make new patterns of chaos and possibility that we unfold here and anticipate will be folded into future becomings for those that follow us.

KZ: The ancients described the Five Stages of Change in terms of the cycle of the seasons. But everywhere there are cycles. Chinese culture focuses on the family, and we see the cycle of life as some family members become old and slow down, while new children are being born into the family system. As we watch the youngsters grow and develop and see the grandparents finding new life in their play with the children, the cycle of life is palpable.

JM: What are your views on cycles in relation to fate?

CJ: If we can learn to see cycles, we are not trapped by fate.

KZ: Yes, this is the learning of the *Book of Changes*. We cannot change the events of the past or the influences that emerge in the present. But we can learn to see these in their cyclic context and make intelligent decisions about how to proceed, so that we can maximize life and productivity.

BW: I think it is important to underscore that these cycles are not merely repetitions. There is a developmental process where the previous cycle informs the new one, allowing for new possibilities. I think of this as a spiral, since more harmony brings more opportunity.

JM: In psychology, there is much talk of the "cycle of abuse." An individual who was abused as a child is more prone to become an abuser later in life, thus perpetuating the cycle.

BW: I am so uncomfortable with the "voice of doom" that takes this as inevitable. Certainly, I agree that people who have experienced boundary disturbances and who have not had proper parenting will be less equipped to provide appropriate boundaries when they become parents. But this is an issue for learning, not for discouragement.

JM: I have known people who experienced abuse as youngsters who became determined not to do to their future children what their parents were visiting upon them. They applied themselves to learning so that they would not automatically get stuck.

CJ: So this is not a "cycle of abuse." It's a fixation of a cycle. When the interference is addressed, the movement of the cycle can recommence, allowing a spiralling expansion rather than closures and restrictions.

JM: Neuroscience in recent decades says that the human brain is not a fixed entity. It can transform through experience and make new connections – this is called "brain remapping." This fits with our experience that people are not victims of their past; they can learn to be aware of the cycles and tendencies in their lives, and take action to open up new possibilities when they become aware of how they are stuck.

CJ: So with personal development and brain plasticity, the cycles of life can be expanding spirals rather than mere repetitions of limitations. It would seem that with mental reflection we can feed back on our experience, learn from it, and inform the next iteration in our cycle with what came before.

BW: This is the personal choice, through awareness of taking action in life to be more and more in harmony. This is the existential attitude.

KZ: This is also the movement of *dao* towards becoming a wise person, who then can teach.

BW: We can reiterate these cycles in an ever-spiralling fashion, becoming ever more free and ever more responsible.

CJ: And your brain will change, remap.

BW: The present is unfolding into the future, and we have input with our decisions and actions. Awareness means being sensitive to what is possible.

JM: We influence what comes next by taking action, determining what is to be folded up that will inform and influence the unfolding of the next stage. In this way, awareness can also help restart a stalled cycle. The more awareness we have, the more we can have conscious influence.

KZ: This is the meaning of *wu wei,* which is not passive ... it is alert watchfulness for the opportunity to make small choices that facilitate the flow of the cycles.

CJ: And mindfulness meditation?

KZ: Yes.

BW: This is what I have tried to show by saying that a cycle does not return to its place of origin in exactly the same way ... they are spiralling ... larger if the degrees of freedom are enhanced. This is life enhancing.

JM: And life inhibiting if the cycles' spirals contract, becoming smaller, with less freedom.

KZ: This is also Daoist yoga contained in the *Secret of the Golden Flower.*

JM: This is a timely discussion of personal awareness and its effects. The next chapter is on consciousness and the relationship of one's individual mind to the big mind.

V.10
Consciousness and Connection

The dawning realization that we are a fundamentally empathetic species has profound and far-reaching consequences for society.
– Jeremy Rifkin[1]

Being of Two Minds

Many have said that people live in two worlds, one limited, the other vast and timeless. In one they are conscious to varying degrees, but bound in time and space and a limited mortality. The other is mostly unconscious, rooted in the beyond; people experience only fleeting glimpses in dreams and reverie of the vastness of eternity that surrounds them. Buddhists call these "small mind" and "great mind."

Most people live their lives with scarcely any awareness of the second world. Some yearn for it and try in various ways to access it. But for the most part this domain eludes all but the most earnest and graced. Many traditions offer the possibility for people to develop their awareness, to pull back the curtains that impede the view of the vast panorama. The Buddhists contrast the small mind and the great mind:

> How big or how small this world is, depends on the creative faculty of the individual mind. The small mind lives in the world of his ephemeral wants and desires, the great mind in the infinity of the universe and in the constant awareness of that fathomless mystery which gives depth and width to his life and thus prevents him from mistaking his sense world for the ultimate reality.[2]

People think they are separate from each other. But in the two-mind view, this separation is only a feature of small mind; in great mind, each person is part of the whole. Colin Wilson writes,

> Our individuality is a kind of eddy in the sea of mind, a reflection of the total identity of the universal humanity.[3]

Wilson questions whether the personalization of mind is just a habit of thinking:

> I speak of 'my mind' as I speak of 'my back garden'. But in what sense is my back garden really 'mine'? It is full of worms and insects who do not ask my permission to live there. It will continue to exist after I am dead.[4]

One's mind is not a possession, and big mind does not cease with the death of an individual. As the poet Rumi says:

The mind is an ocean ... and so many worlds
Are rolling there, mysterious, dimly seen!
And our bodies? Our body is a cup, floating
On the ocean; soon it will fill, and sink ...
Not even one bubble will show where it went down.[5]

Buddhist teachings aim at liberating oneself from the illusion of separateness, to become aware of the nature of deep mind, which includes everything. Lama Govinda writes of a state of consciousness wherein one embraces "all living beings, which are potentially present and take part in the nature of our mind – nay, who are part of our mind in the deepest sense."[6]

Lama Govinda says personal development is important to prepare the individual for wider vision. The Buddhist view (and ours) is that spiritual development, enhanced consciousness, requires individual work and dedication. Lama Govinda writes:

The highest reality dwells within us ... as long as we have not transformed our consciousness into a receptacle of such a reality we shall not be able to take part in it.[7]

We believe that consciousness is severely limited by defensiveness, inculcated prejudice, and the lack of training to achieve broader perspectives. Transformation in consciousness does not necessitate a particular religious belief or affiliation, or even accepting the universal perspectives offered by many idea systems. Nevertheless, we ourselves are moved to embrace the universal notions that involve humanity in the entire cosmic system. Our home is in the universe.

Our proposal is that each can observe and learn from life and experience, and craft a personal philosophy that has heft and resilience and suppleness – strong enough to embrace the storms of turbulence, gentle enough to sense the most delicate of messages, broad enough to open one's heart to life and other beings. This requires courage, dedication and personal responsibility.

Illusion and Liberation

In Buddhist and Hindu thought, ordinary reality is seen as *maya*, commonly translated as "illusion." Humans are trapped in the erroneous mental representations of reality; meditative practices are aimed to free the individual from the prison of maya. This is done not by destroying *maya* but by seeing through it, to see things as they are, not as they appear to be.

Lama Govinda notes that the Buddhist way is not to deny the world, but to embrace it, to join, but with less attachment:

> As long as we despise the world and merely try to escape from it, we have neither overcome it nor mastered it and are far from having attained liberation. Therefore it is said: "This world is the Buddha-world, within which enlightenment can be found. To search after enlightenment by separating oneself from the world is as foolish as searching for the horn of a hare."[8]

Thought is not reviled, but is a tool, working with in balance with the emotions. Govinda writes,

> The intellect is as necessary for the overcoming of mere emotionality and muddleheadedness as intuition is necessary for overcoming the limitations of the intellect and its discriminations.[9]

He says that the individual, through a dedicated life, can move beyond the habitual limitations of thought and take the leap of faith into the boundless:

> He, however, who has penetrated to the limits of thought, dares to take the leap into the Great Emptiness, the primordial ground of his own boundless being.[10]

Interdependence and Joining

The Buddhist concept of *shunyata* ("emptiness") has been translated as "empty of independent identity." Pico Iyer clarifies this meaning:

> We are all a part of a single body, and to think of "I" and "you," of the right hand's interests being different from the left's, makes no sense at all. It's crazy to impede your neighbor, because he is as intrinsic to your welfare as your thumb is.[11]

Iyer contrasts the Buddhist view of life and being as a network with the Christian, Hindu and Muslim perspectives. The Buddhist approach is human centred, without recourse to a deity that directs the universe.

> But where Buddhism differs from other philosophies is in saying that the architect, the administrator, the guardian of this whole body is not Allah or God or the swarm of deities of the Hindu pantheon; it is a network of which we are part (that is a part of us).[12]

Buddhism is not so much a religion as a practical philosophy that involves individual dedication and effort. Iyer writes:

> Buddhists do not (or need not) seek solutions from outside themselves,

but merely awakening within; the minute we come to see that our destinies or well-being are all mutually dependent ... the rest naturally follows.[13]

Pico Iyer outlines fundamental differences in Christian and Buddhist perspectives. He proposes the Buddhist perspective is more about awakening, while the Christian is about finding redemption from sin. Consequently, Buddhism is concerned with uncovering potential, with "perpetual becoming."[14] The goal is "engagement with what is happening right now ... being wide awake in the middle of confusion and ignorance."[15] Lama Govinda concurs:

> The purpose of Buddhist meditation, therefore, is not merely to sink back into the "uncreated" state, into a state of complete tranquilization with a vacant mind; it is not a regression into the "unconscious" or an exploration of the past. It is a process of transformation, of transcendence, in which we become fully conscious of the present, of the infinite powers and possibilities of the mind, in order to become masters of our destiny by cultivating these qualities which lead to the realization of our timeless nature: to enlightenment.[16]

This focus on awareness and responsibility fits well with our own views. Our goal, too, is not withdrawal from the world but joining in it. The here-and-now approach is central to our way of living and working with people. We believe in full breathing, in being aware of one's senses and environment and responding openly and honestly with feelings and thoughts – to us, this is the way for people to locate themselves, moment to moment. We encourage you to enter the flow of life – breathe, sense, relax, relate, respond, refresh!

Religion and Faith

The word religion comes from the Latin root *religare*, which means "to bind." A religious doctrine involves an adherence to a specific set of tenets so that one belongs to the particular group. Our friend Jack Sproule, a retired Roman Catholic priest, says that religions and beliefs "are what people hold to be true because someone else has experienced it." In contrast, he proposes a faith-based vision that goes beyond doctrinal differences, arising from an earnest life of inner investigation and outward connection. He writes, "Faith is experiencing myself actively on a journey; it is a way of life, of confidence and curiosity." In his career as a parish priest, he always held that human community is more important than any dogma or belief system. He spent much time at The Haven and introduced humanistic ideas into the fellowship of his parish activities, sometimes to the alarm of his more doctrinaire colleagues. He disliked the objectification of the priest as authority; after presenting a sermon, he would often leave the pulpit to sit with his audience and invite direct face-to-face conversations with his parishioners about what he had just said. An ardent scholar of theology, he studied many different religions while continuing to operate within the confines of his chosen Roman Catholic structure. He criticized those who made pursuit of an abstract God more important than human feelings and interaction. Sproule once mused about his studies:

> I am always interested in books concerned with questioning religious significance. I still stub my toe on the word "God."[17]

Sproule sees a place for religions as vehicles to the larger territory of personal faith. He writes:

> Religious traditions can point beyond themselves and their churches toward this larger territory. Each uses its own imagery for description. Christianity for instance, names it and explores it as the "Kingdom of God," a place of becoming fully human, a way of life that is soul making, a place of renewal; similarly, Buddhism points to enhanced dimensions of awareness, rooms where consciousness is enhanced.[18]

Pico Iyer writes of the Buddhist way:

> For the Buddhist ... his first concern is the interior landscape ... faith for him is really self-confidence, and prayer a form of awakening latent energies.[19]

For ourselves, faith is the felt assurance of the continuity of life, an individual experience. We see the value in religions as social organizations to assist people in their spiritual development. But we disagree with those religions and beliefs that exclude others with different ideologies. We believe there are thousands of potential paths to the top of the mountain.

The Kingdom of God

To the Christian fundamentalist, the Kingdom of God is a place beyond the human realm, a location, a heaven to be sought. Elaine Pagels offers an alternative, gnostic perspective that suggests that Jesus was proposing the "kingdom" as a transformed state of consciousness, a new world view of human participation.[20] In the gnostic *Gospel of Thomas* (which does not appear in the regular Bible), Jesus says this:

> The kingdom of the Father is spread out upon the earth, and men do not see it.[21]

In Luke 17:21 Jesus speaks of the kingdom of God. This is variously translated as "The kingdom of God is within you,"[22] or "among you,"[23] or "in the midst of you."[24] The kingdom of God is not somewhere else, some foreign land, but is an interpsychic or intrapsychic space. We suggest that the kingdom is not a place, but rather a state of consciousness that arises when people share their hearts. Stephen Mitchell writes:

> When Jesus talked about the kingdom of God, he was not prophesying about some easy, danger-free perfection that will someday appear. He was talking about a state of being, a way of living at ease among the joys and sorrows of our world ... This state of being is not something alien or mystical. We don't need to earn it. It is already ours.[25]

Jesus said:

> And I will give unto thee the keys of the kingdom of heaven: and whatsoever thou shalt bind on earth shall be bound in heaven: and whatsoever thou shalt loose on earth shall be loosed in heaven. – Matthew 16:19

We see a parallel here between the Christian message and the ancient Chinese view of the interplay of heaven and earth – each dimension is expressed in the other, since they are one system. In the groups we led over the years, we recall many incidents of enhanced awareness that participants described as spiritual experiences. In Matthew 18:20, we read the idea that Christ consciousness can be experienced by groups gathered together in his name:

> For where two or three are gathered together in my name, there am I in the midst of them.[26]

We think this is very compatible with a humanistic view that includes the possibility of spiritual experiences when people open their hearts to each other. Jack Sproule agrees:

> This new consciousness that I believe is emerging cannot be conveyed except by experiencing the connections, the relationships, in short, the community.[27]

Jesus and Awakening

By many accounts, Jesus did not want to be worshiped; instead, he wanted people to discover their original nature. Like Confucius and Buddha, he saw himself as a teacher, to assist people in the way to find harmony in life.[28] In the *Gospel of Thomas*, Jesus said that this self-knowledge is available to all people who seek it, and was not peculiar to him. "When you come to know yourselves, then you will become known, and you will realize that it is you who are the sons of the living Father."[29]

Thomas Merton followed the Christian teachings toward self-discovery and believed in a life of community, of engagement with the world that crossed the usual barriers of nation and religion. He identifies with the words of St. Paul: "It is now not I that live but Christ that lives in me."[30] By this, Merton means that his perspective has been transformed from everyday consciousness to Christ consciousness. His writings address the possibilities for people to awaken to a sense of interconnection that is at once social, political and cosmic. Merton saw that his ideas were compatible with the ideas of Confucianism and Buddhism, and he engaged in dialogues with teachers and devotees from other religions, and with nonreligious people too.

Spanish poet Antonio Machado understood Jesus' message not as salvation, but awakening:

> I love Jesus, who said to us:
> Heaven and earth will pass away.
> When heaven and earth have passed away,
> my word will remain.
> What was your word, Jesus?
> Love? Affection? Forgiveness?
> All your words were
> one word: Wakeup.[31]

A Social Unconscious

To this point in this chapter, we have been considering mainly philosophical and religious perspectives, many of them centuries old. But this is very much a contemporary discussion. In his 2011 book *The Social Animal, New York Times* journalist David Brooks describes a revolution in consciousness in the 21st century, noting that there have been great strides in many academic disciplines to understand human development. He says the unconscious mind is not comprised of primitive vestiges, but rather is the majority of the mind's operation, where most decisions and thought take place. He labels the conscious mind as the "outer mind," which is involved in reason and analysis, and calls the unconscious the "inner mind," which is more involved with passions and perception.[32] Whereas the outer mind focuses on individual concerns, the inner mind is more occupied with relationships and bonding, and "hungers for harmony and connection." We agree with Brooks that people are joined in the unconscious levels in more ways than the conscious recognizes.

> ... below our awareness there are viewpoints and emotions that help guide us as we wander through our lives. These viewpoints and emotions can leap from friend to friend and lover to lover.[33]

Brooks says the unconscious includes the history and deeper meanings of humanity:

> The unconscious is not merely a dark, primitive zone of fear and pain. It is also a place where spiritual states arise and dance from soul to soul. It collects the wisdom of the ages. It contains the soul of the species.[34]

Brooks writes about the changeable patterning of the human brain, concluding that the neural networks embody experience and guide future action. Noting that habits, traits and learning are etched into neural "grooves," he says,

> A brain is the record of a life. The networks of neural connections are the physical manifestation of your habits, personality and predilections. You are the spiritual entity that emerges out of the material networks in your head.[35]

Brooks says that although the unconscious can be chaotic and needs to be controlled, it is very adept at many tasks, and has a natural proclivity to socialize:

> The unconscious is impulsive, emotional, sensitive and unpredictable. It has shortcomings. It needs supervision. But it can be brilliant. It's capable of processing blizzards of data and making daring creative leaps. Most of all, it is also wonderfully gregarious.[36]

We like much of what Brooks writes, but we add into this a stronger emphasis on responsibility. For example, we would restate the above quote in more personal terms, saying that people are impulsive, and also brilliant and gregarious. Often they are not aware – are unconscious – of these qualities, however; we encourage people to become aware, to 'own' these qualities and take responsibility for them. With this proviso, our experience supports many of Brooks' views.

Brooks writes that unconscious sociability is a motivator to relationships. Ben has said that people have a natural inclination to "slide into intimacy"; when they are together for a time, they naturally become closer. Fears of being overwhelmed underlie the defences that people utilize to resist this inclination to intimacy. Thus, we agree with Brooks' view that people are strongly motivated to interact with others, to manifest the joining that is their deep nature. Perhaps, indeed, this is the motivation that drives the cycle of our Dynamic Empathy Model.

> Your unconscious, that inner extrovert, wants you to reach outward and connect. It wants you to achieve communion with work, friend, family, nation, and cause. Your unconscious wants to entangle you in

the thick web of relations that are the essence of human flourishing. It longs and pushes for love, for ... fusion.[37]

Brooks notes the limitations in the current educational system, which is so focused on achievement and developing "hard skills" for students, without developing moral and emotional faculties "down below." Brooks writes,

> Children are coached on how to jump through a thousand scholastic hoops. Yet, by far the most important decisions they will make are about whom to marry and whom to befriend, what to love and what to despise, and how to control impulses. On these matters, they are almost entirely on their own.[38]

We agree that education and child rearing should include a strong emphasis on socialization and skills of interaction. Indeed, our goals in establishing The Haven as a school included our interest in bringing humanistic values into learning. The curriculum at The Haven is focused on communication and relationships skills, to provide a rich array of learning opportunities for people who want to enhance themselves in these ways.

Transformation of Consciousness

Much has been written about the transformation of individual consciousness. For us, this does not go far enough. We maintain that an individual's world is meaningless without linking to the lives of others. Transformation must go beyond individual development into cooperative relationships of mutuality and kindness.

Stephen Mitchell wrote that there is much harmony amongst the teachings of Christianity, the Upanishads, Daoism, Buddhism, Zen, Sufism and Hasidic Judaism.[39]

> When words arise from the deepest kind of spiritual experience, from a heart pure of doctrines and beliefs, they transcend religious boundaries, and can speak to all people, male and female, bond and free ...[40]

In his characteristically pithy way, the Dalai Lama says, "My religion is very simple – my religion is kindness."[41]

We encourage an approach to life that involves *engagement, not withdrawal*. Thus, we counsel against isolating practices, and advocate joining. Be present in all you do, in every action and relationship. People can cultivate an enthusiastic style (literally, this means "being infused with spirit"); with this comes a feeling of robustness and vigour that is well known by many who are deeply involved in their lives. We call this refreshed, positive view "psychic buoyancy." This state can be developed.

Colin Wilson describes consciousness like an automobile tire; if the inflation is insufficient, one is subject to depression and limited consciousness. Wilson says the antidote for this depression is to put full attention onto everything one does:

> The secret is this: that the poor quality of human life – and consciousness – is due to the feebleness of the beam of attention that we direct at the world.[42]

People can learn to develop this beam. Reps said, "Put your mind into what you are doing." We say, breathe, come into your bodily-sensory awareness, touch with intensity, and be fully alive! Then – communicate, share, connect.

We ourselves are still climbing our own mountain, and we have not achieved the summit. We pause on this journey to rest and consider.

Many say the universe is all one, that the world of distinction is illusory. We agree in theory, but our day-to-day life is all we have. So we focus on where we are, and live as fully as we can, moment to moment. It's every minute Zen. Be here now, not in some imagined future-past. We like the Golden Rule of "doing unto others as you would have them do to you." We agree with the Dalai Lama and Jesus in their doctrine of neighbourly kindness to others.

We have struggled with the issue of God, or no-God, throughout our lives. And we still don't have the answer. Religious structures can provide ideas and viewpoints that are useful in our questioning. But ultimately, we find ourselves together, each of us alone, without a God who speaks to us directly. Nevertheless, we are amidst the wonder of a stunningly beautiful universe with coloured morning skies and striking artistic presentations. We are gradually learning to accept. Jock wrote these lines as a younger man

> I yearn to hear God's voice
> And yet I cannot discern any words at all
> I only hear
> a silence ... that roars.[43]

There are no words yet. But the silence is rich and abundant and satisfying, with each other and in the company of friends.

V.11 The Illuminated Heart

KZ = Confucius (Kong Zi), CJ = Carl Jung, BW = Ben Wong, JM = Jock McKeen

BW: A big problem of the modern age is selfishness. Many people have lost the community spirit and succumbed to excessive self-interest.

CJ: The challenge is to become more fully oneself, without being selfish. Then we can have individuation, to become the self fully and be in harmony with the Self, the Universe.

JM: We have discussed your work about this. The individual self is isomorphic with the universal Self, which is the wholeness of the universe.

CJ (smiling): Thank you for your summary.

BW: I have found my individual place in loving another person. Master Kong, what is your perspective on selfishness?

KZ: The opening of the heart is everything. All else relates back to this. We humans have a possibility of connecting with our deeper nature, which is a wellspring from the universe itself. But we become closed over for different reasons, and we lose touch with the inner source. When this occurs, we lose our connection with the universe and we do not live as our deepest humanity.

BW: I understand.

KZ (Confucius' eyes are moist and pained): I know you do understand. It is an unhappy thing to see, yet so common.

BW: In my early career, I said, "It all has to do with loving." But I have been disappointed repeatedly to see that people often do not find loving compelling. They seem to like the superficial excitement that comes with power and domination and quick acquisitions.

KZ: Yes, I have felt this well of sadness also.

BW: I used to think that love overcomes all. But there are darker forces that overshadow the gentle breezes of love. So often, precious moments are lost.

KZ: This is the tragic history of humanity.

JM: How does this loving relate to the *shen* spirits of Chinese medicine?

KZ: The heart, when it is open, has a vast emptiness that permits the spirits of the universe to come and go freely. In this atmosphere, a precious and subtle effect occurs, where the light of the cosmos begins to shine within that person, and that person radiates life and being.

JM: Is this enlightenment?

KZ: In a way. But enlightenment usually involves the clearing of the clouds of the mind, which occurs within the mindspace of a single being. What happens with an open heart is something more extensive than enlightenment. This is illumination.

JM: Please say more.

KZ: This is the illumination from the depths and heights of the universe, which shines through the undefended open being and lights up everything that is surrounding, both physically and nonphysically. A person in illumination is inspiring to others and invites light to shine from them too. The opening of one heart invites other hearts to join, and the illumination intensifies.

CJ: Love as illumination.

BW: In our work, Jock and I experience this in an emotional way, and call this "resonance." When one person experiences a heart opening and shares intimate feelings with others, a light seems to come from that person, and others are also emotionally moved. As they open in response, they begin to shine too. This happened many times in the groups we led. Indeed, this is part of the reason that Jock and I stopped seeing people in private practice, and only worked in groups. The phenomenon of resonance is so life-giving.

CJ: This is wonderful, gentlemen, and I too have witnessed this. But I reluctantly bring up a major area of concern that I had in my intellectual life. This light is insufficient to overwhelm the darkness and the dark forces, which are sometimes very, very potent. I tried to write about this in *Answer to Job*. Even God is subject to the temptations and limitations of the dark forces. The universe is a complex and frightening place.

KZ: The darkness is always there as a temptation.

JM: Is this the attraction of power? We think we can be secure in darkness by gaining power ourselves?

KZ: Yes, I think so. Each individual must choose in each moment whether to open to the light, or succumb to the darkness. We are free, and responsible.

BW: Well, for my part, I believe that if I live my life openly, trying in my own way to show my vulnerability, that is all I can do. This is my loving.

KZ: I am of accord.

CJ: But you do not become powerful or influential through this. It is only your own personality that is made available to connect to others in your field.

BW: This is a personal way of living, not a political one.

JM: Ben, I know you have valued honesty and being open. At times, your honesty is challenging for others. Some people have criticized you, and even reviled you for this. And, Master Kong, I believe something like this occurred for you in your lifetime too.

KZ (sadly): Yes. I wanted so much for a leader to adopt the principle of governing from an open heart. But I never found a ruler who was not prone to use power tactics that resulted in closing the heart. So I thought that I had failed in my overall mission, to help society.

BW: Yes, when I was much younger, I wanted to change the world. I had hoped that a new kind of community could be established in the world where people would share with open hearts.

KZ: Our own personal challenge is to let go of our ambitions to change the world, and accept it as it is.

BW: Now, as an old man, I am content to live honestly with myself and my friends. That's all I can do.

KZ: Ben, you and I tried to change the world. In this, we made our views public. So those who did not want to listen criticized us in different ways.

JM: How do you feel about this now?

KZ: I do not feel bad for myself, or for Ben. We are strong, and we can endure the criticism of others with equanimity. But I do feel sad for those who are less certain of themselves and who can be duped or seduced into unwittingly following the darker paths.

JM: I want to probe this issue of the dark forces more. I have to admit, I am frightened by the topic. When I read Carlos Castaneda's books, I began to sense this dark force. My childhood nightmares were full of dark figures, and I am still afraid of the dark night.

CJ: This issue of darkness and light was such a preoccupation for me. I could be trite and say that there is no light without oppositional darkness.

But the human being's experience of this is fraught with fears and deep psychological disturbances. So much of human motivation is to avoid the dark and to try to find light.

BW: The darkness I face is the darkness in my immediate field, which is in those around me and in myself. I need not fear it if I take ownership of it. So if I don't talk myself into being terrified, I can face my infantile fears (I'm still afraid of the dark too) and embrace those around me. It's only when I think the darkness of others is something separate from me that I get into trouble.

KZ: Yes, I agree. I am the same as everyone else, with the same temptations, and the same weaknesses. So I cannot criticize or condemn the darkness in others, when it is also mine.

JM: Could we say that the heart has an openness to both darkness and light?

KZ: Yes, in the abstract fashion of *yin* and *yang*, the *yin* darkness is the other side of the *yang* light. They are one.

CJ: The darkness is here to test us, for us to wrestle with, to strengthen our resolve. We become stronger lights in facing and embracing darkness.

BW: This is the position of the existentialists also.

KZ: The notion of *ren*, humanity, has this idea of darkness and light in it. We tend to think of it only being positive and light. But both aspects are there, dark and light.

BW: We have to learn to love and accept ourselves and each other in all our aspects. If we can do this, then we are free to choose, to love and live and join.

KZ: I agree, deeply.

JM: Gentlemen, this is the last time we shall appear in the book ... it is very nearly finished. Ben and I thank you with all our hearts. And we look forward to meeting again to continue our discussions!

V.12   From Exile to Harmony

> Man doth not live by bread alone. He lives even more essentially from the nourishing creative flow between himself and another or others.—D.H. Lawrence[1]

Out of Exile

We human beings are lost creatures, rooted deeply in the cosmos, yet estranged from ourselves, alienated from each other and our environment. We live on the surface amidst our apparent differences, rather than in the community of spirit where we are all one. This separation is maintained by fixated concepts and righteous views of reality. Thomas Merton writes of modern humans' exile from themselves and from each other:

> What can we gain by sailing to the moon if we are not able to cross the abyss that separates us from ourselves? This is the most important of all voyages of discovery, and without it, all the rest are not only useless, but disastrous.[2]

The abyss is not just within an individual, but also among people, and between people and the environment. In rediscovering our relationship to nature, we can rest and rejuvenate. This poem "The Peace of Wild Things" by Wendell Berry says so much:

> When despair for the world grows in me
> and I wake in the night at the least sound
> in fear of what my life and my children's lives may be,
> I go and lie down where the wood drake
> rests in his beauty on the water, and the great heron feeds.
> I come into the peace of wild things
> who do not tax their lives with forethought
> of grief. I come into the presence of still water.
> And I feel above me the day-blind stars
> waiting with their light. For a time
> I rest in the grace of the world, and am free.[3]

People are naturally related to each other and to the universe. They lose this connection when they become obsessed with power and control, defensiveness and excessive self-interest. The challenge is to move through and past objectification into a new world of genuine spiritual human relating, to learn to care about ourselves and each other and the earth we all inhabit. We can rediscover communion by connecting heart to heart. The world can be different when we become different, when we learn to move beyond the biases that restrict our vision. We can learn to open ourselves to work in concert with everyone else as stewards of this planet and its creatures, in our little corner of the galaxy. Poet Antonio Machado writes about human beings' responsibility:

> The wind left. And I wept. And I said to myself:
> What have you done with the garden that was entrusted to you?[4]

We say it is time to listen to our deep inner voice, to engage with one another, to contribute more fully. How?

From Morality to Inclusion and Compassion

The challenge for humans today centres around right-wrong morality. As we noted in our discussion of object relations theory, early psychological development takes place within a matrix of good and bad. Sadly, many people do not progress beyond this dualism into a more fully human understanding of self and other.

Whenever people judge anything as good or bad, right or wrong, they limit the possibilities for themselves and others. When I decide that either I am in the wrong, or you are, then there is no further dialogue; there is only the option of maintaining my position and denigrating yours. This moralistic, rigid thinking severely limits further possibilities. Fixated morality keeps people stuck in power and control and blame and victimhood; furthermore, such fixated ego defensive positions hinder the reopening of the self. The higher functions of our brains and our beings become fading possibilities.

Paul Tillich, in his pivotal book *The Courage to Be*, proposed that morality is a common solution to avoid existential anxiety (angst). People become neurotically fixated in order to avoid a deeper issue, namely their fear of annihilation. Accompanying this is the fervent thrust to achieve the ideal self, tolerating immense self-hatred in the process – for most, self-hatred is much preferable to the vulnerability of recognizing one's limitations and embracing them. They would rather feel guilty and bear the symptoms of self-hatred, than be responsible and alone. From this perspective, most people are severely restricted from the life they could have: "Neurosis," said Tillich, "is the way of avoiding nonbeing by avoiding being."[5]

Most people function in this moral bog. They believe what they have been taught is true; they believe that others who do not believe as they do are wrong or bad; they try hard to live up to the ideal self standards of the law and social imperatives. People stuck in this way never question their viewpoints, and do not remain open to other possibilities. If they were to see there is no ultimate "right" or "wrong," only choices and consequences, they could experience an enhanced life of connection and wellbeing.

The challenge for an individual is to grow from self-centred objectification and moralism, through contact and resonance (in which, though we still operate within the framework of right and wrong, we are increasingly willing to acknowledge this to others and be open to other realities) to inclusion (where morality is transcended in imagining the other's world). The development of empathy is not an easy task! Nor is it a linear process; we must be willing to cycle repeatedly through the stages of the Dynamic Empathy Model in order to grow.

This challenge faces people in all regions of the world – to grow past the limiting right/wrong moralistic injunctions, prescriptions and proscriptions of their culture into becoming genuine, participating, ethical beings with a sense of community and communion. People who develop empathy learn to overcome the limitations of their upbringing, to relate to others from different backgrounds, and to become true citizens of the world.

We have often said that one human being cannot harm another human being; in order to hurt another, it is necessary to convert that person into a thing, to objectify the other as inhuman or wrong. The challenge is to transform this dismissive objectification into a curiosity about the life and being of other peoples from other cultures. We are all human beings, with differences, but with a common root of humanity and community. As Thomas Berry puts it, "The universe is a communion of subjects, not a collection of objects." [6]

When people accept cultural diversity and communicate from a heart connection, they can appreciate each other without becoming distracted by the surface differences. We believe this can be achieved by teaching children to be curious and engaged with others. This begins at home, and could be extended into schools and the culture at large. Since most people have been raised in an environment based on objectification and distrust, there is much "unlearning" to do in order to become more compassionate and connected. This has been our goal. Relationships are at the core of the teachings at The Haven. It's never too late to learn, to change your brain and your being. In our experience, enhancement of empathy can occur even in those who are hardened against themselves and life. We have witnessed very disconnected people tune into their caring nature in a supportive atmosphere of openness and sharing.

In her book *Twelve Steps to a Compassionate Life*, theologian Karen Armstrong argues that compassion is hardwired into human brains, yet is opposed by more primitive instincts for selfishness and survival. Armstrong maintains that compassion is no longer a luxury, but a necessity to overcome the challenges of the day. She makes a radical proposal – love your enemy. If the universe is one, your enemy is part of the same wholeness as you. She outlines steps toward emphasizing compassion in one's life and developing the spiritual muscle to enhance one's ability to be compassionate. She affirms her belief that compassion can be revealed by a daily practice of affirming it in face of temptations to selfishness. She proposes that this will have an effect not only in the life of the individual, but in society at large. Armstrong says,

> We want instant transformation and instant enlightenment ... But it takes longer to reorient our minds and hearts; this type of transformation is slow, undramatic, and incremental ... But ... step by step, you will find that you are beginning to see the world, yourself and other people in a different light.[7]

Significance and Reflective Awareness

The individual human life has significance in itself, and each is related to the whole. In his 1941 collaboration with photographer Walker Evans entitled *Let Us Now Praise Famous Men*, James Agee wrote of the nobility in the lives of poor rural people. His writing was accompanied by Evans' stark photographs. We discovered this book around the time we first began to work together, and it has continued to resonate with our belief in the significance of each human life.

> Each is composed of substances identical with the substance of all that surrounds him, both the common objects of his disregard, and the hot centers of stars: All that each person is, and experiences, and shall ever experience, in body and mind, all these things are differing expressions of himself and of one root, and are identical: and not one of these things nor one of these persons is ever quite to be duplicated, nor replaced, nor has it ever quite had precedent: but each is a new and incommunicably tender life, wounded in every breath and almost as hardly killed as easily wounded: sustaining, for a while, without defense, the enormous assaults of the universe.[8]

With awareness and responsibility, people are not doomed to be victims of their past or upbringing, or even of the universe. As individuals distill their understanding of their behavioural tendencies and arrive at clear decisions about what patterns they want to emphasize, their lives can be different. When they take conscious ownership of their patterns, they can choose to emphasize life-enhancing processes (caring relationships, exercise, diet, healthy life style, study and reflection), and reduce their focus on life-inhibiting activities (such as overeating, smoking, compulsive activity, relationship dependency, and addictive behaviours).

When people transform their own lives, this can have ripple effects, sometimes spreading to others they will never personally meet. But it is possible to go further than just personal transformation, progressing into deeper compassion, empathy and inclusion. The poet Rilke writes of human loving as our most significant life's work:

> For one human being to love another: that is the most difficult of all our tasks, the ultimate, the last test and proof, the work for which all other work is but preparation.[9]

Martin Buber asserts that growth occurs in dialogue, not in solitariness:

> For the inmost growth of the self is not accomplished … in man's relation to himself, but in the relation between one and the other … together with the mutuality of acceptance, of affirmation and confirmation.[10]

Throughout our professional careers, we have been dedicated to the exploration of interpersonal connections and communication. In our more private lives, relationships have been personally sustaining, and the topic of our ongoing interest. To us, engagement with others is at the centre of human life and being. The more practiced one can be in relationship, the more one can engage with life – to move deeper into its mysteries and majesties, to celebrate its joys, and not be overwhelmed by setbacks and tragedies.

Relationship Harmony

We have discussed the concept of inclusion as part of our Dynamic Empathy Model and elsewhere in this book. Inclusion is imagining the reality of the other while retaining one's own self-identity at the same time. A genuine dialogue involves a going back and forth, a going over to the side of the other, yet remaining centred in one's own existence. It means broadening one's perspective to include the different viewpoint of the other, without surrendering one's own. It requires an expansion of consciousness, a heart connection, caring and curiosity and adroitness. To become adept at this calls for years of dedicated effort. When two people are committed to being open, honest and curious with each other, they will deepen into this process.

The ancient Chinese believed that the root of an individual's heart reaches to the depths of the universe. When one looks inward and finds genuine personal response, then shares this with another, a spiritual communication is possible. Each person has access to the beauty and music of the universe, which can be shared with others. This reminds us of the line from *Les Misérables*, "To love another person is to see the face of God."

In his commentary on the section of the *Book of Changes* devoted to human fellowship, Confucius says:

> When two people are at one in the inmost hearts,
> They shatter even the strength of iron or of bronze.
> And when two people understand each other in their inmost hearts,
> Their words are sweet and strong, like the fragrance of orchids.[11]

V.13   Final Words

As we close, we pause to reflect. We have distilled and summarized our more than forty years of investigation together. And now, at the end of the process of writing this book, we feel as if we have only begun. We hope you will find some doorways for new explorations yourself, through old ideas refreshed or some new ideas yet to be mined. This passage from T.S. Eliot has always spoken to us about the spiralling cyclic journey of learning:

> We shall not cease from exploration
> And the end of all our exploring
> Will be to arrive where we started
> And know the place for the first time.[1]

The cultures of China and the West are separate in many ways, some obvious, others more subtle. Such different approaches, different politics and different perspectives! Even our view of the night sky is at variance. We have attempted to clarify some of these differences, and to point out the areas where commonness occurs and where links can be made. Prejudice and objectification are diminished by familiarity, with knowledge of each other. Beneath all differences, we are one human community. The access to our communion is through the illumination of the human heart.

We hope this book has brought some messages of communication and possibility. We can join each other in a new vision for a global humanity through understanding and acceptance, one person at a time. Ellery Littleton's poetic rendering of the Chinese *Book of Changes* includes this fitting statement, which offers promise of renewal:

> Old rocks,
> new streams;
> old lives,
> new dreams.
> Yet another untold story
> has begun.[2]

In the process of the creation of this book, we wrote the following words, which we now use as our email signature. This has deep and enduring meaning for us and summarizes our personal view of the illuminated heart:

If we can be positive in a crazy world,
and respond with heart, maybe
we can make a small difference
that ripples …

APPENDICES

Appendix 1:
Further Comments on Key Concepts

We introduced a number of key concepts in Chapter I.5, which have recurred throughout this book. In this appendix we add some further notes on these important ideas.

Further Comments on Isomorphism

The notion of isomorphism (sameness at all levels) was expressed in the hermetic tradition in the words "As above, so below." We might also take the words of the Lord's Prayer "on earth as it is in heaven" as a reflection of this belief. This was a central theme in our book *As It Is In Heaven*; Jock's poems and Ben's comments on them show the direct relationship between an individual's life (in this case, Jock's) and the patterns of nature and the universe that can be revealed through an open heart.[1]

In Chinese philosophy, a dichotomy between *yang* and *yin* is resolved into oneness by the concept that the pattern of heaven and the pattern of earth are one; the physical manifestation on earth is the same pattern as the nonphysical forces of the sky. The *Yi Jing* expounds this central theme. In Kabbalistic writings, the same idea occurs as interpenetrating dimensions of reality, each with an isomorphic structure. In Jungian psychology, the individual self (with a small "s") is isomorphic with the Self (big "S") of the universe, the godness, the ultimate.

This notion is helpful in discussing various "levels" of human existence. A common way of seeing people distinguishes physical, mental, emotional, spiritual and environmental dimensions. Rather than being separate, each of these so-called "levels" is actually the *same* as the other levels; what occurs at one "level" is reflected (expressed) at all the other "levels." The levels are isomorphic with each other. This is a cornerstone to understanding Chinese energy medicine, which embraces the notion of unity of body, mind, spirit and environment.

A friend who is a primary school teacher introduced the concept of isomorphism to her Grade 3 class by giving each pupil a photocopy of a complex geometric drawing that had many enclosed spaces and shapes inside the rectangular outside boundary. The children were instructed to use whatever crayons they wished to colour in the "fill-in-the-blank" drawing. At the end, the children showed their drawings to each other, and were amazed that the same basic picture could appear so differently when the shapes were shaded in unique and individual ways. Each child coloured the same structure with his or her own taste and aesthetics. Although the results looked very different, they were all expressions of the same pattern – they were isomorphs. The teacher laughingly asked, "Which one is best?" The students could grasp that they were all the same, with individual variation; so, none was better than another.

Further Comments on Power and Strength

Concepts related to power and strength include *political* (in a larger sense than simply party politics) and *personal*. To be political is to be involved in the use of power and control; usually there is an investment in a particular outcome. Power and the political involve domination and submission. To be personal requires being revealed and vulnerable, with a willingness to share one's viewpoints and feelings without an investment in controlling the outcome. In the political, the person is not valued; in the personal, humanness is foreground. People who acquire power tend to lose touch with themselves and their authentic nature. As people become more authentic, they manifest strength in being in touch with themselves and others; they possibly have little power, but they are present within themselves. Educational systems tend to emphasize power, as we discussed in *The Relationship Garden*.[2]

From moment to moment, each of us uses both power and strength; both are necessary and important. Power involves closure, and maintains security and predictability; strength is opening, and enhances self-awareness and engagement with others in a feeling way. In power, one de-emphasizes personal feelings and connection; in strength, one is in touch with self and other.

Power is often necessary in order to maintain order. It involves limitation, and inhibition of impulses, and concentration of purpose. For example, in the self-control a child learns in toilet training, the youngster is learning power over his or her impulses. A mature and socialized person requires sensitive facility with the use of power. To operate an automobile, one utilizes myriad controls to be in charge of the vehicle – this is a use of power. For example, a safe driver learns to inhibit random curiosity in order to focus on the road.

Further Comments on Yellow River and Blue Sea Philosophies

The West has focused on the external, visible world and its conquest. China, and much of the rest of the East, has developed a subtle appreciation for invisible patterns of correlation that underlie the phenomenal world. The Blue Sea philosophy gave rise to geometry, and scientific manipulation of space. The Yellow River approach allows for more abstraction; the mathematics of algebra, and numbers themselves, are central to its concern.

The Blue Sea way is logical and linear (considering cause and effect sequence), analytical, and emphasizes *structure*; the form of thought is dominated by causal logic. The Yellow River way is para-logical and circular (considering patterns and cycles), associative, emphasizing *function*.

The Blue Sea way emphasizes the objective world of distinct things; it is analytical, and utilizes the logic of cause and effect. It is objectifying and theoretical. The Yellow River way tends to be subjective, connecting, and utilizes associations between things to see the underlying pattern. There is more emphasis is on the experience itself (a phenomenological approach) and less on theory.

Western science emphasizes the *inductive* approach (proceeding from questions to build up answers that establish theoretical principles). We might call this a Blue Sea or *Socratic* approach. The ancient Chinese favoured the *deductive* approach to thinking (working from principles already established). This is a Yellow River or *Confucian* approach.

When we taught in China, students there asked us very different questions from those their Western counterparts posed. Frequently in a lecture in China, someone, even a noted scholar, would ask, "Why are you telling us this?" Our somewhat churlish response would be, "Because we think you should understand this to get at what we are try-ing to say." However, this question was so commonplace that we eventu-ally reflected upon it, and hit upon a key issue: our way of teaching tends to be Socratic, offering pieces of information, and expecting students to sew the parts together, to synthesize them and see the overall pattern. But Chinese students wanted to be shown the pattern from the begin-ning, and then learn the elements in this context – this is a more Confu-cian approach.

Western students are most accustomed to a Socratic teaching style that uses a process of *inductive logic.* By this process, one gradually builds up general conclusions from careful observation (going from the example to the rule). For example, if you observe a newspaper burning, and then later see a book burning, and then see a paper bag burning, later you draw a general conclusion from your experience that paper burns. This is inductive reasoning and is characteristic of Socrates' method; he encouraged his students to do this, and saw himself as an "intellectual midwife" with his questions. The process of the inductive approach (Socrates) is observation → pattern → tentative hypothesis → theory.

Chinese students are more familiar with the Confucian style, which utilizes *deductive logic*. This approach proceeds in the opposite direction to induction: reasoning is done from the general to the specific (going from the rule to the example). For example, if you already have established that paper burns, and establish that a filing folder is made of paper, then you can conclude that a specific file folder burns. This is deductive reasoning and is characteristic of Confucius' approach; general principles that apply to life and living are used as guidelines in learning new information. To summarize, the process of the deductive approach (Confucius) is theory → hypothesis → observation → confirmation.

Confucius defines the structure of human experience, saying "Here's the way it is, now do something with it." Socrates assigns a method of discovery, but does not give the answer; instead, his admonition is "Find out the way it is." These approaches are characteristic of the Yellow River and Blue Sea ways respectively.

Further Comments on Guru and Master Styles
In the Asian traditions, the original purpose of the guru was as an object of devotion and focus for a dedicated personal effort towards spiritual advancement. The student was not to be passive to the guru, but the active agent of the entire enterprise. Similarly, in the West, the classical Socratic teaching style has been one of encouraging the learning of a student by facilitation, rather than direct orders and instruction.

Although the situation of guru and pupil originated in the East as a relationship that invited personal responsibility and learning, it has often degenerated into an irresponsible form where one person directs the life of another. It has become a power-based relationship, rather than one based on individual choice, personal responsibility and strength. When we refer to the guru style, we are referring to this degenerate form that is unfortunately so widespread. This notion applies equally to power-based teaching methods in the West.

In the guru system, the person's freedom and growth is limited; this is offset by the apparent security to be had by following the "truth" and dictates of the guru. Individual thought is discouraged, and adherence to the politics or the philosophy of the leader is rewarded. Gurus can be found in many social systems (religion, politics, education, the health care system, business and corporate cultures). In "guru medicine" the doctor knows and the patient obeys. In "guru education" students are indoctrinated into the views of the authority. Personal concerns and perspectives are subjugated to the "truth" of the authority, and individual decision making is devalued.

This system is founded upon an assumption of a moral code of "right and wrong." In terms of power and strength, this is a power orientation.

As we have said, we use the term "power" to refer to exertion of control over self or other, and "strength" to refer to a deep quiet experience of being in integrity with oneself that accompanies self-revelation and vulnerability.

When a leader emerges in the guru style, there is power, doctrinaire morality, and weakened immature citizenry. The master style leader shows the inspiration of strength, inviting constituents to participate in community and culture, to develop society and relationships.

Both Confucius and Socrates were probably master style teachers. Their followers, however, often did not understand them, and interpreted them in a guru way, believing that the teachers had the "right" answers. Socrates was killed and his teachings discredited. Confucius' teachings were reduced to moral imperatives. This fate has been repeated many times over the centuries; a leader who has wanted to encourage the populace to be more responsible, has often been reviled for the effort.

Confucius' approach was to point out the structure of experience, as a means of showing people how they could learn to live. He did not believe the structure itself was the final authority; he encouraged people to look into their hearts to find their own personal approach to the structure of the universe. The Confucian method of stating the structure has been abused by guru leaders to direct and control people; people are told this is "right" and they must follow this way without question. Individuals raised in a Confucian system need to interpret the ideas for themselves, rather than take them as rigid doctrine.

The Socratic method is more easily used to enhance a master style. The teaching style of Socrates is unusual for Asian people, because it seeks to discover a structure. In our teaching we have used a more Socratic method, which some Chinese students have found unsettling, especially at the beginning. Our hope is that in both Western and Chinese cultures, people will develop their own ways of learning and communication that encourage growth and strength.

Appendix 2:
Glossary of Chinese Terms

This is a list of Chinese expressions that appear in this book for which the reader might want more information.

A Note on Pinyin and Tones
The tones in the Chinese language provide a formidable challenge and puzzle for Westerners. In Mandarin Chinese, there are four tones: the first tone is a steady high sound, the second is rising pitch, the third is a "scoop the bottom" sound, and the fourth is a descending tone. The same sound uttered with a different tone will have a different meaning. Thus, we include the number following the Pinyin to indicate the tone of the word, to further facilitate understanding. For example, *qi4* (*qi* spoken with a descending tone) indicates "life force" whereas other tones would have different meanings.

Analects of Confucius – see *Lun2 Yu3*.

ba1 gang1 (八綱) are the eight principles for energy diagnosis in CCM. The eight principles are:

- *yin* and *yang* (*yin1-yang2*, 陰陽)
- superficial and internal (*biao3-li3*, 表裡)
- cold and hot (*han2-re4*, 寒熱)
- deficient and excessive (*xu1-shi2*, 虛實)

ba1 gua4 (八卦) are the eight primordial images of the *Yi4 Jing1*, represented by the eight trigrams. They are Heaven (*Qian2*, 乾), Lake/Marsh (*Dui4*, 兌), Fire (*Li2*, 離), Thunder (*Zhen4*, 震), Wind (*Xun4*, 巽), Water (*Kan3*, 坎), Mountain (*Gen4*, 艮), Earth (*Kun1*, 坤). *Yin* is represented by a broken line, and *yang* is represented by a solid line. The lines stacked one above the other in threes make up the eight combinations representing the eight primordial images.

bao1 han2 (包含), inclusion, is the ability to imagine the thoughts, feelings, attitudes and perspectives of another.

biao3 li3 (表裡) is a paired concept in CCM to describe expanding/manifestation (*biao3*) and condensation/structuring (*li3*).

Book of Changes – see *Yi 4 Jing1*.

chan2 (禪) can be translated as "meditation" or "meditative state."

Cold Mountain – See *Han2 Shan1*.

Conception Vessel – see *Ren4 Mai4*.

Confucius – *see Kong3 Zi3*.

Contact – see *lian2 jie1*.

Crisis – see *wei1 ji1*.

dao4 (道) The universe is in a pattern, a flow, called *dao4* (道).

Dao4 De2 Jing1 (道德經) The classical book of Daoist philosophy attributed to *Lao Zi,* made up of poetic chapters that set out the principles of *dao4*.

dao4 and shu4

dao4 (道) and *shu4* (術) as a paired concept relate to the difference between a philosophical approach (*dao*) and a more mechanistic approach (*shu*) in regards to healing and human systems. *Dao4* is holistic, taking in the universal context; *shu4* is more situational, depending upon categorization and parts, and is thus more mechanistic.

Da4 Xue2 (大學), translated as *The Great Learning*, is a Confucian Classic text.

de2 (德) virtue, inner integrity, quality, strength.

di4 (地) earth.

Doctrine of the Mean – see *Zhong1 Yong1*.

Du1 Mai4 (督脈), named the Governor Vessel in English, is a central vessel down the back of the bodymind, said to be the most *yang* vessel. It is paired with the Conception Vessel (*Ren4 Mai4,* 任脈) the *yin* central channel down the front.

Earth – see *di4*.

Eight Primordial Images – see *ba1 gua4*.

Eight Principles – see *ba1 gang1*.

Empathy – see *tong2 li3 xin1*.

Five Stages of Change – see *wu3 xing2*.

Fusion – see *rong2 he2*.

Fu2 Xi1 (伏羲) The Sequence of Earlier Heaven, or the "Primal arrangement" of the trigrams, was attributed to a legendary person of ancient times named *Fu2 Xi1* (伏羲)

Governor Vessel – see *Du1 Mai4.*

gong4 ming2 (共鳴) is the most commonly understood word for resonance. This is somewhat static, a "one time" situation.

The Great Learning – see *Da4 Xue2.*

Han2 Shan1 and *Shi2 De2*
Han Shan (*Han2 Shan1*, 寒山), literally "Cold Mountain," and his friend Shi De (*Shi2 De2*, 拾得) were Chinese Zen recluses who lived at a place called Cold Mountain in the Tiantai range near the city of Suzhou. Han Shan is the laughing monk with a broom who is the reputed author of the *Cold Mountain Poems.*

Heart – see *xin1*

Heaven – see *tian1.*

Huang2 Di4 Nei4 Jing1
The most famous of the ancient classics of CCM is the *Huang2 Di4 Nei4 Jing1* (黃帝內經) translated as *The Yellow Emperor's Classic of Internal Medicine.* See also *Ling2 Shu1 Jing1* and *Su4 Wen4.*

hui2 xiang3 (回響) is a less common idea for resonance that has deeper meanings. The left character emphasizes the sound of echoing, implying a back-and-forth dynamic.

hui2 ying4 (回應) is resonance in the most profound meaning. The left character shows a mouth within a mouth indicating echoing, reverberation, response back and forth. The character *ying4* has a roof that means "broad" and two men together meaning "action" or "motion." And most importantly, *ying4* has the character for *xin1*, heart (心) in the base.

hun2 (魂) is the rising spirit associated with the liver. Literally "cloud-soul," it is also known as spirit soul.

Inclusion – see *bao1 han2.*

jing1 luo4 (經絡) is the meridian pattern comprised of 12 longitudinal channels (*jing1*) and (*luo4*) that are connecting channels for the *jing1.*

jing1 shen2
jing1 (精) *shen2* (神) is essence (*jing1*) and spirit (*shen2*). This paired concept considers the relationship of nonphysical and physical dimensions.

jun1 zi3 (君子) is the Confucian concept of the "superior man," describing an evolved human.

ke4 cycle

In the Five Stages of Change, the *ke4 cycle* (剋環) is the process that counterbalances the *sheng1 cycle* (generative cycle). Sometimes mistranslated as "destructive cycle" its relationship with the *sheng1* cycle is more analogous to a brake to offset the accelerator on an automobile. There is a saying in Chinese that *sheng1* and *ke4* mutually support each other. See *sheng1* cycle.

ke4 ti3 hua4 (客體化), objectification, is making mental representations of the world "out there."

King Wen – see *Zhou1 Wen2 Wang2*.

Kong3 Zi3 (孔子), also known as *Kong 3 Fu1 Zi3* (孔夫子), is the Chinese sage Confucius.

Lao3 Zi3 (老子), the traditional originator of Daoism, was said to be an older contemporary of Confucius.

li3

Note that there are three different words associated with the Pinyin *li3*. Remarkably, these three words are spoken exactly the same with the third tone. However, the characters are different for each, and the meanings are different. This "same sound with different meaning" occurs in English, for example with "need" and "knead." To clarify this distinction, we could speak of the "*li3* of Confucian thought" or the "*li3* of *Zhuang Zi*" or the " *li3* of CCM."

li3 ("The Zhuang Zi li3")

li3 (理) This character which means "cosmic order" or "organic pattern" appears many times in *Zhuang Zi*.

li3 /yi4/ren2 ("The Confucian li3")

These are three key concepts in the Confucian doctrine of rules, awareness and humanity:

- *li3* (禮) rules, etiquette (the *Kong Zi li3* relates to human society patterning)
- *yi4* (義) righteousness, appropriateness
- *ren2* (仁) humanness, benevolence, humaneness

li3 (the li3 of biao3 li3 in CCM)

In the paired concept of *biao3 li3* (表裡) of CCM, *li3* (裡) is the structuring aspect, and *biao3* (表) is the manifestation aspect.

lian2 jie1 (連接), contact, involves awareness of the another as a person, accompanied by reaching out physically, mentally, or emotionally.

Ling2 Shu1 Jing1 (靈樞經) is one of the two parts of the *Nei4 Jing1* (黃帝 內經), *The Inner Canon of Huang Di,* or *The Yellow Emperor's Canon of Internal Medicine. Ling2 Shu1 Jing1 is* known as the *Divine Pivot,* or the *Spiritual Pivot,* or the *Numinous Pivot* in English. The other part is the *Su4 Wen4* (素問) which translates as *Basic Questions.* See *Yellow Emperor's Canon,* see *Su4 Wen4,* see *Huang2 Di4 Nei4 Jing1,* see *Nei4 Jing1.*

Listen – see *ting1.*

lü4 (also written as *lv4*) (慮) is reflection.

Lun2 Yu3 (論語) is a major treatise of Confucian teaching, translated in English as *Analects of Confucius.*

Nei4 Jing1 (內經) is a commonly used shorter expression for *Huang2 Di4 Nei4 Jing1.*

Objectification – see *ke4 ti3 hua4.*

Pattern – see *li3.*

po4 (魄) is the white soul spirit of incarnation, the "animal soul."

qi4 (氣) is life force energy.

ren2 (仁) is humanness (see *li3, yi4, ren2*).

Ren4 Mai4 (任脈) is the Conception Vessel, the *yin* central energy channel down the front of the bodymind. It is paired with the *yang Du1 Mai4,* the Governor Vessel, which runs down the back.

Resonance – see *gong4 ming2,* see *hui2 xiang3,* see *hui2 ying4.*

rong2 he2 (融合) is fusion, which we define as merging or symbiosis in the Dynamic Empathy Model.

ru2 (儒) means "scholar." The classical philosophy of ancient China is sometimes called *ru2* philosophy.

shang4, zhong1, xia4

- *shang4* (上) superior
- *zhong1* (中) mediocre, average
- *xia4* (下) inferior

These characters appear in a familiar saying relating to Chinese medicine: "A superior (*shang4*) doctor deals with the entire country, an average (*zhong1*) doctor deals with the patient, and an inferior (*xia4*) doctor only deals with the symptom."

shen2 (神) is spirit(s). It is probably better translated in the plural, since the Chinese consider not one spirit, but many spirits. See *jing1 shen2*.

sheng1 cycle

The *sheng1* cycle (生環) is the "generative cycle" that involves the progression of the five stages of change from water through wood, into fire, then earth, then metal. In the automobile analogy, *sheng1* would be the accelerator, constrained by the balance cycle (*ke4* cycle) which would be the brake. There is a saying in Chinese that *sheng1* and *ke4* mutually support each other. See *ke4* cycle.

shi2 niu2 (十牛) are the ten Zen Ox pictures, describing the search for self and enlightenment.

si1 (思) thought.

Superior Man – see *jun1 zi3*.

Su4 Wen4 (素問), *Basic Questions,* is one of the two parts of the *Nei4 Jing1* (黃帝內經), *The Inner Canon of Huang Di,* or *The Yellow Emperor's Canon of Internal Medicine.* The other part is the *Ling2 Shu1* (靈樞), known as *The Divine Pivot,* or the *Spiritual Pivot,* or the *Numinous Pivot* in English. See *Ling2 Shu1,* see *Huang2 Di4 Nei4 Jing1,* see *Nei4 Jing1*.

Ten Ox Pictures (Zen Ox Pictures, Ten Bulls) – see *shi2 niu2*.

tian1 (天) heaven.

ting1 (聽) listen. This complex Chinese character which translates superficially as "listening" has a much deeper meaning upon investigation of the parts that make up the word. On the left is the image of an ear above and the character for king below; on the right side above is the character for eyes, a horizontal stroke indicating "undivided" or "one" and the lower right has the symbol for heart. A rough translation of the assembled meaning would be "If you listen actively with one heart, you can be a royal person."

tong2 li3 xin1 (同理心), empathy, empathizing, is contact + resonance + inclusion in our Dynamic Empathy Model. Note the character for the heart (*xin1*) is included in the word.

Virtue – see *de2*.

Wang2 Bi4 (王弼), a scholar said to have lived AD 226–249, wrote a treatise that elucidates the relationship between the primordial images (*ba gua*), and the world of phenomena.

wei1 ji1 (危機) is common translation for crisis that has arisen in modern times. Whereas in previous eras, Chinese people saw crisis as a cause for anxiety, in recent decades this is more seen as an opportunity for change, and hence not necessarily a negative situation. The character *wei1* means danger, and the character *ji1* can mean opportunity.

Wu3 Shen2 (五神) is translated as *The Five Spiritual Aspects.* It sees there are five spiritual aspects, *shen2 (life spirits,* 神*), hun2 (spirit soul,* 魂*), po4 (animal soul,* 魄*), yi4 (purpose, thought,* 意*), and zhi4 (will,* 志*).* In relation to the Five Stages of Change, *shen2* is associated with Fire, *hun2* is associated with Wood, *po4* is associated with Metal, *yi4* is associated with Earth, and *zhi4* is associated with Water.

wu2 wei2 (無爲), action through inaction, watchful engagement.

wu3 xing2 (五行) Five Stages of Change (often incorrectly called "five elements"). The five stages are:

- Wood *Mu4* (木)
- Fire *Huo3* (火)
- Earth *Tu3* (土)
- Metal *Jin1* (金)
- Water *Shui3* (水)

xiao4 (孝) filial piety.

xin1 (心) heart. The Chinese character for heart bears a strong resemblance to the corresponding physical organ. But in Chinese philosophy and medicine, the heart represents much more than the physical entity. Indeed, in considering the various meridian pathways, the heart is distinctive in that there is no radical for flesh (which occurs, for example with the liver, gall bladder, small intestine, and so on). This is indicative of the classical Chinese notion that the heart is more fundamentally a spiritual entity that informs and governs the physical being. The heart is an energy dynamism at the core of each person, an interface between the earthly plane and other, nonphysical dimensions. Human beings who listen to the activity of the heart put themselves into resonance with the forces of nature and the directives from the sky.

Yellow Emperor's Canon of Internal Medicine – see *Huang2 Di4 Nei4 Jing1* (黄帝内经).

yin1 (陰) and ***yang2*** (陽) are descriptive terms to denote the dualisms of the phenomenal world. By convention, *yin* is soft, receptive, feminine, physical, and dark; *yang* is hard, active, masculine, nonphysical, and light.

yi4 (意) purpose, thought.

Yi4 Jing1 (易經), the *Book of Changes* or *Book of Transformations,* is one of the treasures of Chinese culture. Among the oldest of the Chinese classic texts, the written version of this book of wisdom is at least 2200 years old, compiled from an oral tradition that extends back into antiquity.

zang4 fu3 (臟腑) are the meridians, including their associated organ dynamics. The *zang4* (臟) are the six *yin* meridians; the *fu3* (腑) are the six *yang* meridians.

Zen Ox Pictures (10 Bulls) – see *shi2 niu2.*

zhi4 (志) will.

zhi4 (智) know-how, intelligence, wisdom, prudence, talent, capacity.

Zhong1 Yong1 (中庸) is a Confucian text, *The Doctrine of the Mean,* or *The Unwobbling Pivot.*

Zhou1 Wen2 Wang2 (周文王), the founder of the *Zhou* Dynasty, is reputed to be the originator of the sequence of the 64 hexagrams of the *Book of Changes.* The Sequence of Later Heaven – the "Inner World Arrangement" of the trigrams – shows the engineering of the world of phenomena, the unfolding of events in time. Often called King Wen in English, he is generally credited with devising this arrangement over 3000 years ago.

Zhuang1 Zi3 (莊子) is said to have been born around 370 BC, after both Confucius and Lao Zi. He developed the notion of *dao,* advocating non-action in face of nature *(wu wei),* and maintaining personal freedom of body and mind.

NOTES

Foreword

1   McKeen, J. and Wong, B. *A Book About Health and Happiness.* Gabriola Island, BC: Haven Publishing, 2005, pp. 44–65. and *The Relationship Garden.* Gabriola Island, BC: Haven Publishing, 1996, pp. 1–10.
2   Fewster, G. *Ben and Jock: A Biography.* Lantzville, B.C.: Oolichan Books, 2001 and "Introduction" to Wong, B. and McKeen, J. *The New Manual for Life.* Gabriola Island, BC: Haven Publishing, 1998, pp 209–217.

PART I

I.1   Introduction

1   Kipling, Rudyard. "The Ballad of East and West" in Stedman, E.C. (Ed.) *A Victorian Anthology, 1837–1895.* Cambridge: Riverside Press, 1895, New York: Bartleby.com, 2001.
2   Wilhelm, R. *Lectures on the I Ching.* Princeton, NJ: Princeton University Press, 1979, p. xvii.
3   Eber, I. In Wilhelm, R. *Lectures on the I Ching.* Princeton, NJ: Princeton University Press, 1979, p. xvii.
4   Campbell, J. *The Masks of God: Creative Mythology.* New York, NY: Penguin Books, 1976, p. 653.
5   Campbell, Joseph. *An Open Life.* New York, NY: Harper and Row, 1990, p. 68.

I.4   Return of the Flower

1   Kao, F. "China, Chinese Medicine and the Chinese Medical System," *American Journal of Chinese Medicine*, vol. 1, no.1, pp. 23–24.
2   Ibid.
3   Ibid., p. 23.
4   Wong, B. and McKeen, J. *A Book About Health and Happiness.* Gabriola Island, BC: Haven Publishing, 2005, pp 19–34.

I.5   Key Concepts

1   Wong, B. and McKeen, J. *The New Manual for Life.* Gabriola Island, BC: Haven Publishing, 1998, pp. 63–75 and *The Relationship Garden.* Gabriola Island, BC: Haven Publishing, 1996, pp. 46–47.
2   McKeen, J. and Wong, B. *A Book About Health and Happiness.* Gabriola, B.C.: Haven Publishing, 2005, pp. 19–34.
3   Chen, Y.S., Liang, H.H. and Lu, L.Q. (2006). "Psychology of religion in China." *International Journal for the Psychology of Religion*, 16, 153–161.
4   Jing, Q.C. and Fu, X.L. (2001). "Modern Chinese psychology: Its indigenous roots and international influences." *International Journal of Psychology*, 36(6), 408–418.

I.7
The Dynamic Empathy Model

1 Bugental, J. *The Search for Existential Identity*. San Francisco, CA: Jossey-Bass, 1976, p. 274.
2 Wong, B. and McKeen, J. *The New Manual for Life*. Gabriola Island, BC: Haven Press, 1998, p. 218.
3 McKeen, J. and Wong, B. *The Relationship Garden*. Gabriola Island, BC: Haven Publishing, 1996, pp. 50–54; *The New Manual for Life*. Gabriola Island, BC: Haven Publishing, 1998, pp. 171–75; *A Book About Health and Happiness*. Gabriola Island, BC: Haven Publishing, 2005, pp. 145–54.
4 McKeen and Wong, *New Manual for Life*, p. 10.
5 Ibid., p. 12.
6 Ibid., pp. 218–25.
7 *Relationship Garden*, pp. 11–16.
8 Friedman, M. *The Healing Dialogue in Psychotherapy*. Northvale, NJ: Jason Aronson Inc., 1985, p. 201.
9 Kafka, F, in Friedman, M. *Problematic Rebel*. Chicago, IL: University of Chicago Press, 1970, p. 404.

I.8   Professional Puzzles

1 Progoff, I. (trans). *The Cloud of Unknowing*. New York, NY: Dell Publishing, 1983, pp. x–xi.

PART II

II.1   Sigmund Freud

1 Jones, E. *The Life and Work of Sigmund Freud, Vol. 1*. New York, NY: Basic Books, 1953, p. 348.
2 Storr, A. *Freud: A Very Short Introduction*. Oxford, UK: Oxford University Press, 1989, p. 3.
3 Becker, E. *The Denial of Death*. New York, NY: The Free Press, 1973, p. 94.
4 Webster, R. *Why Freud Was Wrong: Sin, Science and Psychoanalysis*. London, UK: The Orwell Press, 2005, p. 12.
5 Storr, A. *Freud: A Very Short Introduction*, p. 14.
6 Freud, S. *The Standard Edition of the Complete Psychological Works of Sigmund Freud, Vol. II*. London, UK: Hogarth Press, 1955, p. 6.
7 Storr, *Freud: A Very Short Introduction*, p. 23.
8 Freud, *Standard Edition, Vol. III*, p. 203.
9 Ibid., *Vol. XI*, p. 83.
10 Ibid., *Vol. VII*, pp. 276–77.
11 Wong, B. and McKeen, J. *The (New) Manual For Life*. Gabriola Island, BC: Haven Publishing, 1998, pp. 320-35.
12 Freud, *Standard Edition, Vol. XXI*, pp. 123–124.
13 Wong, B. and McKeen, J. *The (New) Manual For Life*. pp. 22–30.
14 Ibid., pp. 22–30.
15 Freud, *Standard Edition, Vol. XXIII*, p. 145.

16 Ibid., *Vol. XIX*, p. 26.

17 Progoff, I. *The Death and Rebirth of Psychology*. New York, NY: McGraw-Hill, 1956, p. 155.

18 Ibid., p. 155.

19 Freud, *Standard Edition, Vol. XXIII*, p. 146.

20 McKeen, J. and Wong, B. *The Relationship Garden*. Gabriola Island, BC: Haven Publishing, 1996, pp. 73–81.

21 Freud, *Standard Edition, Vol. XXI*, p. 81.

22 Ibid., pp. 77, 82.

23 Malcolm, J. *Psychoanalysis: The Impossible Profession*. New York, NY: Vintage Books, 1982, p. 6.

24 Storr, *Freud: A Very Short Introduction*, p. 54.

25 Ibid., p. 138.

26 Ibid., p. 153.

II.2   Ego Dynamics

1 Lipton, B. *The Biology of Belief*. Santa Rosa, CA: Elite Books, 2005, pp. 146–47.

2 Ibid, p. 147.

3 Cannon, W.B. "Organization For Physiological Homeostasis." *Physiol Rev.* 1929; 9: 399–431.

4 Freud, A. *The Ego and the Mechanisms of Defense*. New York, NY: International Universities Press, 1966, p. 180.

5 Menninger, K., Mayman, M and Pruyser, P. *The Vital Balance: The Life Process in Mental Health and Illness*. New York, NY: Viking Press, 1963, p. 77.

6 Vaillant, G. *Aging Well: Surprising Guideposts to a Happier Life From the Landmark Harvard Study of Adult Development*. Boston, Little, Brown and Company, 2002.

7 Mitchell, J. A Review of *Aging Well: Surprising Guideposts to a Happier Life From the Landmark Harvard Study of Adult Development*. American Journal of Psychiatry 161:1, January 2004, p. 178, 179.

8 Shenk, Joshua Wolf. "What Makes Us Happy?" in *Atlantic*, Washington, DC, vol 303, no.5, June 2009. p. 44.

9 Ibid, p. 44

10 Ibid, p. 46

11 Ibid, p. 46

12 Ibid, p. 53

13 Wong, B and McKeen, J. *The New Manual for Life*. Gabriola Island, BC: Haven Press, 1998, pp. 63–77 and McKeen, J. and Wong, B. *The Relationship Garden*. Gabriola Island, BC: Haven Publishing, 1996, pp. 63–71.

14 Jung, C.G. *Psychological Reflections: A Jung Anthology [1953] p. 83: Collected Works, vol. 4, The Theory of Psychoanalysis [1913]*, quoted in Bartlett, J. *Familiar Quotations*, Boston, MA: Little, Brown & Co., 1980, p. 755:2.

II.3   Object Relations

1 Bugental, J. *The Search for Existential Identity*. San Francisco, CA: Jossey-Bass, 1976, p. 274.

2 Wong, B. and McKeen, J. *The*

New Manual For Life. Gabriola,
B.C.: Haven Press, 1998, p. 135.

3   In what follows, we draw
extensively on Rinsley, D.B.
"The Developmental Etiology
of Borderline and Narcissistic
Disorders," in *Bulletin of the
Menninger Clinic:* 44(2), 1980,
pp. 127–134. Rinsley provides
comprehensive information
on child development from the
perspective of object relations
theory.

4   Mahler, M.S. et al. *The
Psychological Birth of the
Human Infant: Symbiosis and
Individuation*. New York, NY:
Basic Books, 1975.

5   Ibid.

6   Adapted from Rinsley's chart in
"Developmental Etiology," p. 132.

7   Ibid, pp. 129, 130.

8   Ibid, p. 131.

II.5   A Reps Interlude

1   Reps, P. *Be! New Uses for the
Human Instrument*. New York,
NY: Weatherhill, 1971, p. 10.

2   Ibid., p. 19.

**II.6   Wilhelm Reich and
Approaches to the Body**

1   Reich, W., quoted in Mann, E.,
and Hoffman, E. *The Man Who
Dreamed of Tomorrow: The Life
and Thought of Wilhelm Reich*.
Los Angeles, CA: J.P. Tarcher,
1980, p. 91.

2   Lowen, A. *The Spirituality of the
Body*. New York, NY: Macmillan
Books, 1990, p. 135.

3   Keleman, S. *Sexuality, Self and
Survival*. San Francisco, CA:
Lodestar Press, 1971, p. 23.

4   Sharaf, M. *Fury on Earth: A
Biography of Wilhelm Reich*. New
York, NY: St. Martin's Press/
Marek, 1983, pp. 4–5.

5   Mann, E. and Hoffman, E. *The
Man Who Dreamed of Tomorrow:
The Life and Thought of Wilhelm
Reich*. Los Angeles, CA: J.P.
Tarcher, 1980, pp. 37–39.

6   Wilson, C. *The Quest for Wilhelm
Reich*. London, UK: Granada
Publishing, 1982, p. 19.

7   Rycroft, C. *Reich*. Glasgow, UK:
Fontana/Collins, 1971, p. 79.

8   Ibid., pp. 74–75.

9   Ibid., p. 79.

10   Lowen, *Spirituality of the Body*, p.
21.

11   Ibid., p. 21.

12   Reich, W., quoted in Rosenberg,
J., Rand, M. and Astay, D.
*Body, Self, and Soul: Sustaining
Integration*. Atlanta, GA:
Humanics Ltd.,1985, p. 95.

13   Rycroft, *Reich*, p. 22.

14   Reich, W., quoted in Mann and
Hoffman, *Man Who Dreamed of
Tomorrow*, p. 117.

15   McKeen, J. and Wong, B. *A Book
About Health and Happiness*.
Gabriola Island, BC: Haven
Publishing, 2005, pp. 139–144.

16   Lowen, A. *Pleasure*. New York, NY:
Coward-McCann, Inc., 1970, p. 35.

17   Mann and Hoffman, *Man Who
Dreamed of Tomorrow*, p. 135.

18   Feitis, R. (ed). *Ida Rolf Talks
About Rolfing and Physical
Reality*. New York, NY: Harper &
Row, 1978, p. 124.

19 Ibid., p. 124.
20 Ibid., p. 31.
21 Ibid., p. 69.
22 Ibid., p. 153.
23 Ibid., p. 206.
24 Ibid.
25 Kurtz, R and Prestera, H. *The Body Reveals*. New York, NY: Harper & Row, 1976.
26 Bly, R. *Talking All Morning*. Ann Arbor, MI: University of Michigan Press, 1980, pp. 222–23.

II.8   Alfred Adler

1 Bottome, P. *Alfred Adler: A Biography*. New York, NY: Putnam, 1939, pp. xii–xiii.
2 Wilder, J. "Introduction," to Adler, K. and Deutsch, D. (eds). *Essays in Individual Psychology*. New York, NY: Grove Press, 1959, p. xv.
3 Ellenberger, H. *The Discovery of the Unconscious: The History and Evolution of Dynamic Psychiatry*. New York, NY: Basic Books, 1970, p. 594.
4 Ibid.
5 Adler, A. *Co-operation Between the Sexes*. New York, NY: W.W. Norton & Co., 1978, p. 24.
6 Adler, A. *Social Interest: A Challenge to Mankind*. London, UK: Faber & Faber, 1938, pp. 72–73.
7 Progoff, I. *The Death and Rebirth of Psychology*. New York, NY: McGraw-Hill, 1956, p. 81.
8 Ibid., p. 57.
9 Adler, A. *What Life Should Mean to You*. New York, NY: Putnam 1958 (1931), p. 14.

10 Progoff, *Death and Rebirth of Psychology*, p. 59.
11 Ellenberger, *Discovery of the Unconscious*, pp. 623–25.
12 Ibid., p. 611
13 Adler, A. *The Science of Living*. Garden City, NY: Anchor Books, 1969, p. 12.
14 Ibid., pp. 12–13.
15 Ibid., p. 92.
16 Progoff, *Death and Rebirth of Psychology*, p. 59.
17 Ibid., p. 60.
18 Ibid., p. 50.
19 Ibid.
20 Ibid., pp. 49–50.
21 Friedman, M. *The Healing Dialogue in Psychotherapy*. Northvale, NJ: Jason Aronson Inc., 1985, p. 39.
22 Adler, A., quoted in Ellenberger, *Discovery of the Unconscious*, p. 620.
23 Adler, *Science of Living*, p. 86.
24 Ibid., p. 103.
25 Ibid.
26 Progoff, *Death and Rebirth of Psychology*, p. 90.
27 Adler, *Science of Living*, p. 31.
28 Ellenberger, *Discovery of the Unconscious*, p. 612.
29 Progoff, *Death and Rebirth of Psychology*, pp. 65–66.
30 Ibid., p. 86

II.10   Carl Jung

1 Jung, C.G. *Memories, Dreams, Reflections*. New York, NY: Vintage Books,1965, p. 325.
2 Stevens, A. *Jung: A Very Short Introduction*. Oxford, UK: Oxford University Press, 1994, p. 36.

3   Ellenberger, H. *The Discovery of the Unconscious: The History and Evolution of Dynamic Psychiatry.* New York, NY: Basic Books, 1970, p. 210.

4   Ibid., p. 673.

5   Jung, *Memories, Dreams, Reflections*, p. 110.

6   "Two Essays on Analytical Psychology" in Jung, C.G. *The Collected Works of C.G. Jung, vol. VII.* Princeton, NJ: Princeton University Press, 1967.

7   Stevens, *Jung: A Very Short Introduction*, p. 49.

8   Jung, C.G. in Campbell, J (ed). *The Portable Jung.* New York, NY: Viking Press, 1971, p. 45.

9   Jung, C.G. *Modern Man in Search of a Soul.* New York, NY: Harvest Books, 1933, p. 187.

10 Ibid., p. 187.

11 Jung, C.G. *Psychology and the East.* Princeton, NJ: Princeton University Press, 1978, p. 13.

12 Jung, *Memories, Dreams, Reflections*, p. 4.

13 Jung in Campbell, *Portable Jung*, p. xxi.

14 Serrano, M. *C.G. Jung and Hermann Hesse: A Record of Two Friendships.* New York, NY: Schocken Books, 1966, pp. 84–85.

15 Jung, C.G. *The Collected Works of C.G. Jung, vol. XI.* Princeton, NJ: Princeton University Press, 1967, para. 390.

16 Jung in Campbell, *Portable Jung*, p. 105.

17 Jung, *Collected Works, vol. XI*, para. 144.

18 Jung in Campbell, *The Portable Jung*, pp. 122–23.

19 Ibid., p. 123.

20 Ibid., p. 127.

21 Ibid., p. 99.

22 Jung, *Collected Works, vol. XVI*, para. 317.

23 Jung, *Memories, Dreams, Reflections*, p. 117.

24 Jung, *Collected Works, vol. VIII*, para. 667.

25 Stevens, *Jung: A Very Short Introduction*, p. 120.

26 Jung, C.G. *Psychological Reflections: A New Anthology of his Writings.* London, UK: Routledge and Kegan Paul, 1971, p. 76.

27 Progoff, I. *Jung, Synchronicity, and Human Destiny.* New York, NY: Julian Press, 1973, p. 72.

28 Ibid., p. 152.

29 Ibid., p. 144.

30 Ibid., p. 144.

31 Jung, *Psychology and the East*, p. 6.

32 Ibid., p. 46.

33 Jung, C.G. *Answer to Job.* Princeton, NJ: Princeton University Press, 1973, p. 1067.

34 Jung, *Memories, Dreams, Reflections*, p. x.

35 Ellenberger, *Discovery of the Unconscious*, p. 726.

36 Ibid.

37 Serrano, *C.G. Jung and Hermann Hesse*, p. 57.

38 Jung, *Memories, Dreams, Reflections*, p. 326.

39 Ibid., p. 340.

40 Ibid., p. 342.

41 Ibid., p. 359.

42 Ibid., p. v.

43 Ibid., p. 199.

44 Jung, C.G. *The Red Book: Liber*

Novus. New York, NY: W.W. Norton & Co., 2009, p. 233.

45 Jung, *Memories, Dreams, Reflections*, p. 4.

II.11 Accepting the Unknown

1 Wong, B. and McKeen, J. *In and Out of Our Own Way*. Gabriola Island, BC: Haven Publishing, 1995, p. 153.

2 Ibid., pp. 151–53.

II.12 Existentialism

1 http://workingwithinsight. wordpress.com/2006/08/29/the-tigers-and-the-strawberry-story/

2 Macquarrie, J. *Existentialism*. Harmondsworth, UK: Penguin Books, 1973, p. 18.

3 Flynn, T. *Existentialism: A Very Short Introduction*. Oxford, UK: Oxford University Press, 2006, p. 102.

4 Macquarrie, *Existentialism*, p. 33.

5 Flynn, *Existentialism: A Very Short Introduction*, p. 106.

6 Sartre, J.P. *Existentialism and Humanism*. London, UK: Methuen & Co., 1946, p. 55.

7 Ibid., pp. 55–56.

8 McKeen, J. *Unpublished poem*. 2011.

9 Macquarrie, *Existentialism*, p. 29.

10 Tillich, P. *The Courage to Be*. New Haven, CT: Yale University Press, 1952, p. 40.

11 Sartre, J.P. *Being and Nothingness*. New York, NY: Washington Square Press, 1972, p. 51.

12 Olson, C. "As the Dead Prey Upon Us." http://www. poetryfoundation.org/poem/241034

13 Friedman, M. *To Deny Our Nothingness*. New York, NY: Delta Books, 1967, Dedication page.

14 Sartre, *Existentialism and Humanism*, p. 26.

15 Ibid., p. 28.

16 Ibid., p. 28.

17 Becker, E. *The Denial of Death*. New York, NY: The Free Press, 1973, p. 25.

18 Ibid., pp. 25–26.

19 Ibid., p. 26.

20 Ibid., p. 26.

21 Ibid., p. 26.

22 Pope, A. "An Essay on Man," in *The Norton Anthology of English Literature: Major Authors Edition*. New York, NY: Norton & Co., 1962, p. 770.

23 Becker, *Denial of Death*, p. 26.

24 Tillich, *Courage to Be*, p. 150.

25 Nietzsche, F. *Thus Spoke Zarathustra*. New York, NY: Penguin Books, 1977, p. 41.

26 Heidegger, Martin. *Nietzsches Wort 'Gott ist tot'* (1943) translated as "The Word of Nietzsche: 'God Is Dead,'" in Holzwege, edited and translated by Julian Young and Kenneth Haynes. Cambridge University Press, 2002.

27 Pope, A. "An Essay on Man," in *The Norton Anthology of English Literature: Major Authors Edition*. New York, NY: Norton & Co., 1962, p. 770.

28 Sartre, *Existentialism and Humanism*, p. 28.

29 Ibid., p. 28.

30 Housman, A.E. "Last Poems (1922), XII." http://theotherpages.org/poems/housman1.html

31 Sartre, *Existentialism and Humanism*, p. 34.

32 Camus, A. *The Myth of Sisyphus*. Harmondsworth, UK: Penguin Books, 1975, p. 1.

33 Tillich, P. *Courage to Be*, p. 150.

34 Sartre, *Existentialism and Humanism*, p.55.

35 Kazantzakis, N. *Report to Greco*. New York, NY: Bantam Books, 1966, p. 318.

36 Wong, B. and McKeen, J. *The New Manual for Life*. Gabriola Island, BC: Haven Publishing, 1998, pp 110–115.

37 Wilson, C. *The Philosopher's Stone*. London, UK: Granada Publishing, 1974, p. 112.

38 Kierkegaard, S. *Fear and Trembling and the Sickness Unto Death*. Princeton, NJ: Princeton University Press, 1968, p. 51.

39 Wilson, *Philosopher's Stone*, p. 11.

40 Ibid., p. 12.

41 Tillich, *Courage to Be*, p. 41.

42 Ibid., p. 57.

43 Ibid., p. 58.

44 Ibid., p. 61.

45 Becker, *Denial of Death*, p. 191.

46 Flynn, *Existentialism: A Very Short Introduction*, p. 106.

47 Ibid., p. 106.

48 Sartre, *Existentialism and Humanism*, p. 29.

49 Ibid., p. 29.

50 Flynn, *Existentialism: A Very Short Introduction*, p. 124.

51 Macquarrie, *Existentialism*, p. 185.

52 Ibid., p. 207.

53 Tillich, *Courage to Be*, p. 66.

54 Ibid., p. 66.

55 Ibid., p. 122.

56 Ibid., p. 89.

57 Ibid.

58 Ibid., p. 66.

59 Ibid., p. 91.

60 Ibid., p. 107.

61 Silone, I. *The Seed Beneath the Snow*, trans. Frances Frenaye. New York, NY: Harper & Bros, 1942, p. 299.

62 Camus, *Myth of Sisyphus*, p. 5.

63 Efran, J., Lukens, M, and Lukens, R. *Language, Structure, and Change*. New York, NY: W.W. Norton, 1990, p. 45.

64 Friedman, *To Deny Our Nothingness*, p. 338.

65 Camus, A. *The Plague*. New York, NY: Alfred Knopf, 1948, p. 278.

66 Sartre, *Being and Nothingness*, quoted in Bartlett, J. *Familiar Quotations*. Toronto, ON: Little, Brown and Co., 1980, p. 865.

67 Frankl, V. *Man's Search for Meaning*. New York, NY: Simon and Schuster, 1962, pp. 134–35.

68 Ibid., p. 66.

69 Ibid., p. 134.

70 Kafka, quoted in Friedman, M. *Problematic Rebel*. Chicago, IL: University of Chicago Press, 1970, p. 406.

71 Janouch, G., quoted in Friedman, *Problematic Rebel*, p. 407.

72 Macquarrie, *Existentialism*, p. 212.

73 Friedman, *To Deny Our Nothingness*, p. 123.

74 Bernanos, G. *Diary of a Country Priest*. New York, NY: Macmillan

Co., 1937, p. 108.

75 Tillich, P. *The Shaking of the Foundations*. New York, NY: Charles Scribner's Sons, 1948, p. 163.

76 Friedman, *The Hidden Human Image*. New York, NY: Dell Publishing, 1974. p. 71.

77 Buber, M. *Hasidism and Modern Man*. New York, NY: Harper Torchbooks, 1966, p. 40.

78 Friedman, *Hidden Human Image*, p. 238.

79 Becker, *Denial of Death*, p. 96.

80 May, Angel and Ellenberger (eds). *Existence: A New Dimension in Psychiatry and Psychology*. New York, NY: Basic Books, 1960, p. 36.

81 Rilke, R.M., *Tenth Elegy* in *Duino Elegies and The Sonnets to Orpheus* (A. Poulin, trans). Boston, MA: Houghton Mifflin, 1977, p. 71.

82 Quote has been attributed to Martin Luther, and to Martin Luther King. Source unknown. (See http://de.wikiquote.org/wiki/Martin_Luther).

II.14   Gestalt Therapy

1 Reps, P. *Be! New Uses for the Human Instrument*. New York, NY: Weatherhill, 1971, p. 21.

2 Shepard, R. *Mind Sights: Original Visual Illusions, Ambiguities, and Other Anomalies*. W.H. Freeman & Co, 1990.

3 Clarkson, P., and Mackewn, J. *Fritz Perls*. London, UK: Sage Publications, 1993, p. 7.

4 Latner, J. *The Gestalt Therapy Book*. New York, NY: Bantam Books, 1974, p. 30.

5 Hunt, M. *The Story of Psychology*. New York, NY: Doubleday, 1993, p. 290.

6 Gaines, J. *Fritz Perls Here and Now*. San Francisco, CA: Celestial Arts, 1979, p. 267.

7 Clarkson and Mackewn, *Fritz Perls*, pp. 184–85.

8 Polster, E., and Polster, M. *Gestalt Therapy Integrated*. New York, NY: Brunner/Mazel, 1973.

9 Ibid., p. 7.

10 Ibid., pp. 13–14.

11 Ibid., p. 17.

12 Ibid.

13 Ibid., p. 20.

14 Wheeler, G. *Gestalt Reconsidered*. New York, NY: Gardner Press, 1991, pp. 85–93.

15 As noted, Wheeler summarizes the evolution of the Experience Cycle. The association to the Chinese Five Stages is our own addition, as is the notion of the stages overlapping. We use the same five-stage dynamic approach in our Dynamic Empathy Model, which we outlined in Chapter I.7. The Experience Cycle diagram we used as a beginning is here: Wheeler, G. *Gestalt Reconsidered*. New York, NY: Gardner Press, 1991, p. 89.

16 Kepner, J. *Body Process: Working With the Body in Psychotherapy*. San Francisco, CA: Jossey-Bass, 1987, p. 91.

17 Polster and Polster, *Gestalt Therapy Integrated*, pp. 70–71.

18 McKeen, J. and Wong, B. *A Book*

About Health and Happiness. Gabriola Island, BC: Haven Publishing, 2005, pp. 35–43.

19 Kepner, *Body Process*, p. 195.

20 Polster and Polster, *Gestalt Therapy Integrated*, p. 234.

21 Ibid., p. 99.

22 Ibid.

23 Ibid., p. 101.

24 Ibid., p. 102.

25 Perls, F., Hefferline, R and Goodman, P. *Gestalt Therapy.* New York, NY: Julian Press, 1951, p. 248.

26 Kepner, *Body Process*, p. 65.

27 Ibid., p. 65

28 Polster and Polster, *Gestalt Therapy Integrated*, p. 82.

29 Ibid., p. 87.

30 Ibid., p. 89.

31 Kepner, *Body Process*, pp. 1–2.

32 Ibid., p. 49.

33 Ibid.

34 Ibid., p. 51.

35 Ibid., p. 53.

36 Ibid., p. 214.

37 Ibid.

38 Ibid., pp. 214–15.

39 Ibid., p. 140.

40 Ibid., p. 142.

41 Ibid.

42 Ibid., p. 312.

43 Perls, F. *Gestalt Therapy Verbatim.* Lafayette, CA: Real People Press, 1969, p. 120.

44 Wilson, C. *The Philosopher's Stone.* London, UK: Granada Publishing, 1974, p. 159.

45 Ibid., p. 159.

46 Reps, *Be! New Uses for the Human Instrument*, p. 66.

II.16
A Psychology of Dialogue

1 Rogers, C. *Client-Centered Therapy, Its Current Practice, Implications and Theory.* Boston, MA: Houghton Mifflin, 1951, p. 172.

2 Friedman, M. *The Hidden Human Image.* New York, NY: Delta Books, 1974, p. 81.

3 May, R., Angel, E. and Ellenberger, H. (eds). *Existence.* New York, NY: Basic Books, 1958, p. 36.

4 Ibid., p. 19.

5 Buber, M. (W. Kaufman, trans) *I and Thou.* New York, NY: Scribner's, 1970, p. 53.

6 Ibid.

7 Ibid., p. 54.

8 Ibid., p. 56.

9 Ibid., p. 54.

10 Buber, M. *The Knowledge of Man: A Philosophy of the Interhuman.* New York, NY: Harper & Row, 1965.

11 Hycner, R., and Jacobs, L. *The Healing Relationship in Gestalt Therapy: A Dialogic/Self Psychology Approach.* Highland, NY: Gestalt Journal Press, 1995, p. 65. Although Hycner and Jacobs are listed as co-authors, they wrote many of the chapters independently. Thus, when a quotation is cited from a chapter that is clearly written by one of them, we have noted that individual as the author.

12 Ibid., p. 5.

13 Ibid.

14 Polster, E., and Polster, M. *Gestalt Therapy Integrated*. New York, NY: Brunner/Mazel, 1973, pp. 102–103.

15 Hycner and Jacobs, *Healing Relationship in Gestalt Therapy*, p. 5.

16 Ibid., p. 8.

17 Ibid., p. 9.

18 Ibid.

19 Ibid.

20 Buber, *I and Thou*, p. 85.

21 Perls, F. *Gestalt Therapy Verbatim*. Lafayette, CA: Real People Press, 1969, p. 6.

22 Friedman, M. *The Healing Dialogue in Psychotherapy*. Northvale, NJ: Jason Aronson Inc., 1985, pp. 88–89.

23 Ibid., p. 90.

24 Ibid., p. 89.

25 Polster and Polster, *Gestalt Therapy Integrated*, p. 99.

26 Ibid., p. 99.

27 Ibid.

28 Ibid.

29 Buber, M. (R.G. Smith, trans). *Between Man and Man*. New York, NY; Macmillan, 1965, p. 22.

30 Hycner and Jacobs, *Healing Relationship in Gestalt Therapy*, p. 15.

31 Ibid., p. 22.

32 Ibid., p. 20.

33 Ibid., p. 63.

34 Friedman, *Healing Dialogue in Psychotherapy*, p. 5.

35 Rogers, C. *On Becoming a Person. A Therapist's View of Psychotherapy*. Boston, MA: Houghton Mifflin, 1961.

36 Ibid., p. 35.

37 Ibid., pp. 201–203.

38 Ibid., p. 90.

39 Guntrip, H. *Schizoid Phenomena, Object-Relations and the Self*. New York, NY: International Universities Press, 1969, p. 353.

40 Ibid.

41 McKeen, J. and Wong, B. *The Relationship Garden*. Gabriola Island, BC: Haven Publishing, 1996.

42 Rilke, R.M. (M.D. Herter, trans). *Letters to a Young Poet*. New York, NY: W.W. Norton & Co., 1962, p. 59.

PART III

III.1
The Place of the Yellow River

1   McKeen, J. *As It Is In Heaven*. Gabriola Island, B.C.: Haven Publishing, 1992, pp. 33–35.

III.3   The Book of Changes

1   Govinda, A. *The Inner Structure of the I Ching: The Book of Transformations*. San Francisco, CA: Wheelwright Press, 1981, p. xiii.

2   Progoff, I. *Jung, Synchronicity and Human Destiny*. New York, NY: Julian Press, 1973, pp. 24–45.

3   Larre, C., Schatz, J., De La Vallee, E. *Survey of Traditional Chinese Medicine*. Paris, France: Ricci Institute, 1986, p. 7.

4   Wilhelm, R. (trans). *The I Ching, or Book of Changes*. Princeton,

NJ: Princeton University Press, 1950, p. 235.

5   John Blofeld's "Introduction" in Govinda, A. *The Inner Structure of the I Ching: The Book of Transformations*. San Francisco, CA: Wheelwright Press, 1981, pp. xiv–xv.

6   Wilhelm, R. (trans). *The I Ching, or Book of Changes*. Princeton, · NJ: Princeton University Press, 1950, pp. 266–267.

7   Ibid., pp. 262–272.

8   McKeen, J. "Wellspring," in McKeen, J. and Wong, B. *As It Is in Heaven*. Gabriola Island, BC: Haven Publishing, 1993, p. 170.

9   Wilhelm, H. *Change: Eight Lectures on the I Ching*. New York, NY: Harper Torchbooks, 1960, p. 88.

10 Ibid., p. 87.

11 Ibid.

12 Ibid., p. 87.

13 Ibid., p. 94.

14 Ibid., pp. 94–95.

15 Kwan, T. *A Study of the Book of Changes*. Rome, Italy: Vatican Library, 1987, p. 52.

16 Ibid., p. 53.

17 Ibid., p. 146.

18 Feng, Gia-Fu and English, J. *Tao Te Ching*. New York, NY: Vintage Books, 1972, Chapter 25.

III.5   Confucius

1   Chan, W. *A Source Book in Chinese Philosophy*. Princeton, NJ: Princeton University Press, 1963, p. 15.

2   Ibid., p. 3.

3   McQuarrie, J. *Existentialism*, Penguin Books, London, 1972, p. 38.

4   Jaspers, K. *The Origin and Goal of History*, trans. Michael Bullock. New Haven and London, 1953, p. 2

5   Cleary, T. *The Essential Confucius*. San Francisco, CA: HarperSanFrancisco, 1992, p. 6.

6   Ibid., p. 7.

7   Larre, C. *The Way of Heaven*. Cambridge, UK: Monkey Press, 1994, p. 95.

8   Wilhelm, R. *Confucius and Confucianism*. New York, NY: Harcourt Brace Jovanovich, 1931, p. 92.

9   Ibid., p. 147.

10 Pound, E. (trans). *Confucius: The Unwobbling Pivot, The Great Digest, The Analects*. New York, NY: New Directions, 1950, p. 198. Many of the quotations in this section on Confucius were translated by Ezra Pound, whose poetic, penetrating and iconoclastic style helps to overcome the ponderous inclinations in the generally accepted translations of these texts. In this case, we have taken liberties with Pound's translation for *Lun Yun* 11.4 to propose our own.

11 *Lun Yu* IV.10 in Pound, *Confucius*, p. 207.

12 *Lun Yu* IV.16 in Pound, *Confucius*, p. 207.

13 Watts, A. *Tao: The Watercourse Way*. New York, NY: Pantheon Books, 1975, pp. 82–83.

14 *Li Chi* 32 in Watts, *Watercourse Way*, p. 83.

15 Ibid.

16 Ware, J.R. (trans). *The Sayings of Confucius*. New York, NY: New American Library 1955, p. 110.

17 *Lun Yu* V.15 in Waley, A. (trans). *The Analects*, Changsha, China: Foreign Languages Press, 1999, pp. 45–47.

18 Watts, *Watercourse Way*, p. 83.

19 Chan, *Source Book in Chinese Philosophy*, p. 84.

20 Wilhelm, *Confucius and Confucianism*, p. 163–64.

21 *Da Xue* I.1 in Pound, *Confucius*, p. 27.

22 *Da Xue* I.2 in Pound, *Confucius*, p. 29.

23 *Zengzi's Comment* X.7 in Pound, *Confucius*, p. 73.

24 *Da Xue* XI.8 in Pound, *Confucius*, p. 73.

25 *Da Xue* I.4 in Chan, *Source Book in Chinese Philosophy*, p. 86.

26 Pound, *Confucius*, p. 197.

27 Chan, *Source Book in Chinese Philosophy*, p. 95.

28 *Zhong Yong* I.1 in Pound, *Confucius*, p. 99.

29 *Zhong Yong, Zi Se Zi's 3rd Thesis* in Pound, *Confucius*, p. 173.

30 Ibid., p. 179.

31 Ibid., p. 173.

32 Ibid., pp. 173–175.

33 *Zhong Yong* XXIII in Pound, *Confucius*, p. 175.

34 *Zhong Yong* XX.21 in Pound, *Confucius*, p. 171.

35 *Zhong Yong* XXIV. This translation by James Legge is more accessible to us than some others. <http://ctext.org/liji/zhong-yong>

36 Pound, *Confucius*, p. 197.

37 *Zhong Yong* XX.4 in Pound, *Confucius*, p. 147.

38 *Zhong Yong* XX.10 in Chan, *Source Book in Chinese Philosophy*, p. 105. We have slightly altered Chan's translation to make this text more accessible.

39 Wong, B. and McKeen, J. *The New Manual For Life*. Gabriola Island, BC: Haven Publishing, 1998, pp. 143–150.

40 Wilhelm, R. *Confucius and Confucianism*. New York, NY: Harcourt Brace Jovanovich, 1931, p. 154.

41 Ibid., pp. 155–56.

42 Ibid., p. 156.

III.7 Daoism

1 Frye, N. *The Great Code: The Bible and Literature*. Toronto, ON: Academic Press Canada, 1982, p. xviii.

2 Wing, R.L. *The Tao of Power*. London, UK: Thorsons, 1988, chapter 14.

3 Watts, A. *Tao: The Watercourse Way*. New York, NY: Pantheon Books, 1975, p. 40.

4 Ibid., p. 48.

5 Ibid., p. 46.

6 Ibid., p. 15. This *li* (理) discussed by Watts is a different word than *li* (禮) commonly associated with Confucius' related concepts of *li/yi/ren*, or the *li* (裡) of *biao li*. Remarkably, these three words are spoken

exactly the same, with the third tone. However, as we show here, the characters are different for these three, and the meanings are different. Something similar occurs in spoken English, for example with "need" and "knead" (different meanings for same sound). Confucius' emphasis is on societal orderedness and thus he more commonly utilizes the character *li* (禮), whereas Zhuang Zi relates to a cosmic patterning expressed in nature expressed by *li* (理), and CCM relates to the energy dynamics in the bodymind expressed in the paired *biao* (表, emanation) and *li* (裡, structuring). To clarify this distinction, we could speak of the "*li* of Confucian thought" or the "*li* of Zhuang Zi" or "the *li* of CCM."

7 Feng, Gia-Fu and English, J. Chapter 1, *Tao Te Ching*. New York, NY: Vintage Books, 1972. Pages not numbered.

8 Ibid., Chapter 14.

9 Ibid., Chapter 16.

10 de Bary, W.T. (ed). *Sources of Chinese Tradition, vol. I*. New York, NY: Columbia University Press, 1960, p. 62.

11 Ibid., p. 63.

12 This quote is a summary of Zhuang Zi's perspective. Wang Bo says it is not Zhuang Zi's writing, but it is a good overview of his thought. (Personal correspondence, 2007).

13 Palmer, M. (trans). *The Book of Chuang Tzu*. London, UK: Penguin Books, 1996, p. 106.

14 Wang Rongpei (trans) *Zhuangzi I*. Beijing, China: Foreign Languages Press, 1999, pp. 39, 41.

15 Ibid., p. 45.

16 Ibid.

17 Muzhi, Yang. "Preface" in *Library of Chinese Classics: Zhuangzi I*. Changsha, China: Foreign Languages Press, 1999, p. 16.

18 de Bary, *Sources of Chinese Tradition, vol. I*, p. 70.

19 Feng, Gia-Fu and English, J. *Chuang Tsu: Inner Chapters*. New York, NY: Vintage Books, 1974, p. vii.

20 Chan, Wing-Tsit. *A Source Book in Chinese Philosophy*. Princeton, NJ: Princeton University Press, 1963, p. 178.

21 Merton, T. *The Way of Chuang Tzu*. New York, NY: New Directions, 1965, p. 24.

22 Watts, *Watercourse Way*, p. 76.

23 Ibid.

III.9   Buddhism and Zen

1 Waley, A. (trans) *The Analects of Confucius*. New York, NY: Vintage Books, 1938, p. 155.

2 Keown, D. *Buddhism: A Very Short Introduction*. Oxford, UK: Oxford University Press, 1996, p. 76.

3 Ibid., p. 76.

4 Watts, A. *The Way of Zen*. New York, NY: Vintage Books, 1957, p. 190.

5 Ibid., p. 3

6 Watts, A. *The Spirit of Zen*. New York, NY: Grove Press, 1958, p. 24.

7   Ibid., p. 25.

8   Watts, *Way of Zen*, p. 29.

9   Ibid., p. 39.

10 Ibid., p. 43.

11 Watts, *Spirit of Zen*, p. 49.

12 Wong, B. and McKeen, J. *In and Out of Our Own Way*. Gabriola Island, BC: Haven Publishing, 1995, p. 154.

13 Watts, *Way of Zen*, p. 119.

14 Ibid., p. 118.

15 Ibid., p. 119.

16 Ibid., p. 125.

17 Ibid., p. 126.

18 Ibid., p. 136.

19 Ibid., p. 146.

20 Ibid., p. 147.

21 Ibid., p. 21.

22 Ibid., p. 19–20.

23 Pirsig, R. *Zen and the Art of Motorcycle Maintenance*. New York, NY: Bantam Books, 1975, p. 136–37.

24 Ellenberger, H. *The Discovery of the Unconscious: The History and Evolution of Dynamic Psychiatry*. New York, NY: Basic Books, 1970, p. 670.

25 Trevor, M.H. (trans). *The Ox and His Herdsman: A Chinese Zen Text*. Tokyo, Japan: Hokudseido Press, 1969. Reps, P. *Zen Flesh, Zen Bones: A Collection of Zen and Pre-Zen Writings*. Tokyo, Japan: Charles Tuttle Co., 1937, pp. 168–87.

26 Trevor, *Ox and His Herdsman*, p. 5.

27 Red Pine (trans) *The Collected Songs of Cold Mountain*. Port Townsend, WA: Copper Canyon Press, 1983.

28 Snyder, G. (trans). *Cold Mountain Poems: Twenty-Four Poems by Han-Shan*. Portland, OR: Press-22, 1970.

29 Watson, B. (trans). *Cold Mountain: 100 Poems by the T'ang Poet Han-shan*. New York, NY: Columbia University Press, 1970, p. 10.

30 Snyder, *Cold Mountain Poems*.

31 Ibid.

32 Watson, *Cold Mountain*, p. 100.

III.10   Sky Flat Mountain

1   McKeen, J. *As It Is In Heaven*. Gabriola Island, B.C.: Haven Publishing, 1992, pp. 49–53.

PART IV

IV.2
Classical Chinese Medicine

1   Larre, C., Schatz, J., De la Vallée, E. *Survey of Traditional Chinese Medicine*. Paris, France: Ricci Institute, 1986, p. 8.

2   Wong, B. and McKeen, J. *A Book About Health and Happiness*. Gabriola Island, BC: Haven Publishing, 2005, pp 19–34.

3   Tao Yuan-Ming, "Two Drinking Songs" in Bly, R. *News of the Universe: Poems of Twofold Consciousness*. San Francisco, CA: Sierra Club Books, 1980, p. 270.

4   Larre et al., *Survey of Traditional Chinese Medicine*, p. 158.

5   Ibid., p. 158.

6 Porkert, M. *The Theoretical Foundations of Chinese Medicine: Systems of Correspondence.* Cambridge, MA: MIT Press, 1974.

7 Goleman, D. *Working With Emotional Intelligence.* New York, NY: Bantam Books, 1998, p. 33.

8 Wong, B. and McKeen, J. *The New Manual for Life.* Gabriola Island, BC: Haven Publishing, 1998, pp 219–220.

9 Ibid., pp 209–217.

IV.4
Spiritual Dimensions in Chinese Medicine

1 *Hamlet* 1:5 in Shakespeare, W. *The Complete Works of William Shakespeare.* London, UK: Oxford University Press, 1954, p. 878.

2 Larre, C., and Rochat de la Vallée, E. *Rooted in Spirit: The Heart of Chinese Medicine.* Barrytown, NY: Station Hill Press, 1995, p. x.

3 Ibid., p. xii.

4 Ibid.

5 Ibid., p. xiii.

6 Ibid., p. xii.

7 Larre, C. *The Way of Heaven: Neijing Suwen Chapters 1 and 2.* Cambridge, UK: Monkey Press, 1994, p. 54.

8 Larre, C., and Rochat de la Vallée, E. *The Heart in Ling Shu Chapter 8.* Cambridge, UK: Monkey Press, 1991, pp. 57–62.

9 Larre, C., and Rochat de la Vallée, E. *The Secret Treatise of the Spiritual Orchid: Su Wen Chapter 8.* Cambridge, UK: Monkey Press, 1992, pp. 33–139.

10 Larre and Rochat de la Vallée, *Rooted in Spirit*, p. xii.

11 Firebrace, P, in Larre and Rochat de la Vallée, *The Heart in Ling Shu Chapter 8*, p. vi.

12 Wilhelm, R. (trans). *The Secret of the Golden Flower.* New York, NY: Harcourt Brace Jovanovich, 1962.

13 Ibid., p. 90.

14 Govinda, A. *Creative Meditation and Multi-Dimensional Consciousness.* Wheaton, IL: Theosophical Publishing House, 1976, p. 190.

15 Ibid., p. 221.

16 Pound, E. "Canto LXXXI" in *Ezra Pound: Selected Cantos.* New York, NY: New Directions, 1970, p. 83.

IV.5   A Remarkable Meeting

1 Wong, B, and McKeen, J. Originally published in *Shen*, Issue 26, Fall 2000.

PART V

V.1   Self and Community

1 Hycner, R., and Jacobs, L. *The Healing Relationship in Gestalt Therapy: A Dialogic/Self Psychology Approach.* Highland, NY: Gestalt Journal Press, 1995, p. 98.

2 Hillman, J., and Ventura, M. *We've Had a Hundred Years of Psychotherapy – And the World's*

Getting Worse. San Francisco, CA: HarperSanFrancisco, 1992.

3   Whitaker, Carl. Personal Correspondence.

4   Hillman and Ventura, *We've Had a Hundred Years*, p. 6.

5   Ibid., p. 6.

6   Ibid., p. 5.

7   Ibid., p. 40.

8   Ibid.

9   Ibid., p. 12.

10 Wilhelm, R. (trans). *The I Ching, or Book of Changes*. Princeton, NJ: Princeton University Press, 1950, p. 17.

11 Buber, M. *Hasidism and Modern Man*. New York, NY: Harper & Row, 1958, p. 163.

12 Hillman and Ventura, *We've Had a Hundred Years*, p. 17.

13 Hillman, J. *The Soul's Code: In Search of Character and Calling*. New York, NY: Random House, 1996, p. 4.

14 Hillman and Ventura, *We've Had a Hundred Years*, p. 29

15 Auden, W.H., quoted in Hillman, *Soul's Code*, p. xi.

16 Hillman, J. *Soul's Code*, p. 6.

17 Ibid., p. 4.

18 Ibid., p. 8.

19 Ibid., p. 5.

20 Hillman and Ventura, *We've Had a Hundred Years*, p. 63.

21 Ibid., p. 68.

22 Ibid., p. 52.

23 Ibid.

24 Ibid., p. 130.

25 Ibid., p. 154.

26 Ibid., pp. 128–29.

27 Ibid.

V.3   Patterns and Processes

1   Shakespeare, W. *The Tempest*, Act IV scene 1, in *The Complete Works of William Shakespeare*. London, UK: Oxford University Press, 1954, p. 17.

2   *Dao De Jing*, verse 25. Watts, A. *Psychotherapy East and West*. New York, NY: Ballantine Books, 1961, p. 204.

3   Watts, *Psychotherapy East and West*, p. 203.

4   Levenson, E. *The Fallacy of Understanding*. New York, NY: Basic Books, 1972, p. 33.

5   Bly, R. (ed). *The Soul is Here For Its Own Joy: Sacred Poems from Many Cultures*. Hopewell, NJ: Ecco Press, 1995, p. 84.

6   Wong, B. and McKeen, J. *The New Manual for Life*. Gabriola Island, BC: Haven Publishing, 1998, pp. 240–46.

7   Levenson, E. *The Purloined Self: Interpersonal Perspectives in Psychoanalysis*. New York, NY: W.A. White Institute, 1991, p. 20.

8   Ibid., p. 20.

9   Levenson, *The Fallacy of Understanding*, p. 188.

10 Ibid., p. 189.

11 Levenson, *The Purloined Self*, pp. 102–3.

12 McGuire, M. *Reflections on the Path: Zen Training in Everyday Life*. Victoria, BC: Vancouver Island Zen Sangha, 2008, p. 62.

13 Ibid., p. 49.

V.5   The Problem of "I"

1   Lawrence, D.H. *Fantasia of the Unconscious*. Harmondsworth, UK: Penguin Books, 1971, p. 25.

2   Wei Wu Wei. *Ask the Awakened*. Toronto, ON: Little, Brown and Co., 1963, p. 1.

3   Wilhelm, Richard. *Lectures on the I Ching*. Princeton, N.J.: Princeton University Press, 1979, p. xvii.

4   Blackmore, S. *Consciousness: A Very Short Introduction*. Oxford, UK: Oxford University Press, 2005, p. 67.

5   Ibid., p. 68.

6   Ibid., pp. 68–69.

7   Ibid., p. 69.

8   Fewster, G. *Don't Let Your Kids Be Normal*. Salt Spring, B.C.: Centre for Child Honouring, 2010, p. 209.

9   Fewster, G. Personal correspondence.

10 Hunt, M. *The Story of Psychology*. New York, NY: Doubleday, 1993, pp. 368–70.

11 Fewster, *Don't Let Your Kids Be Normal*, p. 204.

12 Ibid., p. 211.

13 Rinsley, D.B. "The Developmental Etiology of Borderline and Narcissistic Disorders," in *Bulletin of the Menninger Clinic*: 44(2), 1980, pp. 127–134.

14 Fewster, *Don't Let Your Kids Be Normal*, p. 169.

15 Ibid., p. 212.

16 Ibid., p. 341.

17 McKeen, J. and Wong, B. *The Relationship Garden*. Gabriola Island, BC: Haven Publishing, 1996, p. 195.

18 Buber, M. *The Knowledge of Man: A Philosophy of the Interhuman*. New York, NY: Harper & Row, 1965, p. 85.

19 Hycner, R., and Jacobs, L. *The Healing Relationship in Gestalt Therapy: A Dialogic/Self Psychology Approach*. Highland, NY: Gestalt Journal Press, 1995, p. 52.

20 Hillman, J., and Ventura, M. *We've Had a Hundred Years of Psychotherapy – And the World's Getting Worse*. San Francisco, CA: HarperSanFrancisco, 1992, p. 140.

21 Parfit, D., quoted in MacFarquhar, L. "How to Be Good," *The New Yorker*, Sept. 5, 2011, p. 44.

22 Ibid., p. 44.

23 McKeen, J. and Wong, B. *A Book About Health and Happiness*. Gabriola Island, BC: Haven Publishing, 2005, pp. 107–121.

24 Wong, B. and McKeen, J. *The New Manual for Life*. Gabriola Island, BC: Haven Publishing, 1998, pp. 103–109.

25 McGuire, M. *Reflections on the Path: Zen Training in Everyday Life*. Victoria, BC: Vancouver Island Zen Sangha, 2008, p. 60.

V.6
Paul Reps: A Modern Zen Master

1   Reps, P. *Zen Flesh, Zen Bones: A Collection of Zen and Pre-Zen*

Writings. Tokyo, Japan: Charles Tuttle Co., 1937, p. 13.

2   Portions of this section on Paul Reps originally appeared in a eulogy by the authors: McKeen, J. and Wong, B.R. "Paul Reps – A Remembrance," *Journal of Humanistic Psychology*, vol. 31, no. 2, Spring 1991, pp. 44–48.

V.8
Two Worlds:
Predictability and Chaos

1   Bly, R. (ed). *Times Alone: Selected Poems of Antonio Machado*. Middletown, CT: Wesleyan University Press, 1983, p. 29.

2   Carroll, L. *The Annotated Alice*. Harmondsworth, UK: Penguin Books, 1970, p. 184.

3   Briggs, J. and Peat, F.D. *Turbulent Mirror: An Illustrated Guide to Chaos Theory and the Science of Wholeness*. New York, NY: Harper & Row, 1989.

4   Lilley, C. "Deep Breaths: When Chaos is the New Normal." <http://is.gd/RpxLX8>

5   Gleick, J. *Chaos*. New York, NY: Penguin Books, 1987, p. 118.

6   Talbot, M. *The Holographic Universe*. New York, NY: HarperCollins, 1991, pp. 14–18.

7   Bohm, D. *Wholeness and the Implicate Order*. London, UK: ARK Paperbacks, 1983, p. ix.

8   Bohm, D., interviewed in Wilber, K. (ed). *The Holographic Paradigm and Other Paradoxes*. London, UK: Shambhala, 1982, p. 51.

9   Ibid., p. 51.

10 Ibid., pp. 46–48.

11 Ibid., pp. 46–49.

12 The Official M.C. Escher website features many of his pictures: <www.mcescher.com>

13 Paz, O. *Octavio Paz: Selected Poems*. New York, NY: New Directions, 1984, pp. 2–3.

14 Hawking, S. *A Brief History of Time*. New York, NY: Bantam Books, 1988.

15 Remarks by President Kennedy at the Convocation of the *United Negro College Fund*, Indianapolis, IN, April 12, 1959.

16 The word for crisis is *wei ji*. This not a classical Chinese concept or word. One of its earliest appearances was in a translation of Karl Marx's *Das Kapital*, where it was used to signify the inevitable and doomed end result of the economic patterns of capitalism. A crisis was an emergency that was cause for panic and anxiety, a negative thing. In the past 25 years, with China's changing attitude to economics, a new, more positive, interpretation of this word has come into usage. The attitude of recent decades in China sees crisis as an opportunity and a turning point. The character *wei* means danger; the character *ji* has several meanings, including "crucial point when something begins or changes." The two characters *wei ji* now are interpreted as "a moment of opportunity." This

all turns on the character *ji* which appears in two words, one meaning opportunity (*ji hui*) and one meaning crisis (*wei ji*). So, it is not true that crisis and opportunity are the same word in Chinese. But the two words share a common character, *ji,* which means a crucial point. An expression currently used in China (*wei ji ji joan ji*) means "A crisis is or can be a point of turning." So, crisis can be an optimum moment for change if the challenges are met; then the crisis can be seen as a turning point to bring a higher level of equilibrium.

17   Gomori, M. and Adaskin, E. *Personal Alchemy: The Art of Satir Family Reconstruction.* Kowloon, Hong Kong: 2008, p. 70.

18   Ibid., p. 71.

19   McKeen, J. and Wong, B. *The Relationship Garden.* Gabriola Island, BC: Haven Publishing, 1996, pp. 67–68, and pp. 92–100.

20   Keller, H. *Let Us Have Faith.* New York, NY: Doubleday, 1941.

V.10
Consciousness and Connection

1   Rifkin, J. *The Empathetic Civilization: The Race to Global Consciousness in a World in Crisis.* Los Angeles, CA: Jeremy P. Tarcher, 2010, p. 1.

2   Govinda, A. *Creative Meditation and Multi-Dimensional Consciousness.* Wheaton, IL: Theosophical Publishing House, 1976, p. 22.

3   Wilson, C. *The Mind Parasites.* Oakland, CA: Oneiric Press, 1972, p. 79.

4   Ibid., p. 40.

5   Bly, R. (ed). *The Soul is Here For Its Own Joy: Sacred Poems from Many Cultures.* Hopewell, NJ: Ecco Press, 1995, p. 236.

6   Govinda, *Creative Meditation,* p. 19.

7   Govinda, A. *The Psychological Attitude of Early Buddhist Philosophy.* New York, NY: Samuel Weiser, 1974, p. 29.

8   Govinda, *Creative Meditation,* p. 19.

9   Ibid., p. 21.

10   Ibid., p. 19.

11   Iyer, P. *The Open Road: The Global Journey of the Fourteenth Dalai Lama.* New York, NY: Alfred A. Knopf, 2008, p. 86.

12   Ibid., p. 87.

13   Ibid.

14   Ibid., p. 155.

15   Ibid., p. 40.

16   Govinda, *Creative Meditation,* p. 102.

17   Jack Sproule, personal correspondence.

18   McKeen, J. and Wong, B. *The Relationship Garden.* Gabriola Island, BC: Haven Publishing, 1996, p. xvi.

19   Iyer, *Open Road,* p. 159.

20   Pagels, E. *The Gnostic Gospels.* New York, NY: Vintage Books, 1981. p. 155.

21   The Gospel of Thomas, Saying

113, in Robinson, J. (ed). *The Nag Hammadi Library in English*. San Francisco, CA: Harper & Row, 1988, p. 138.

22 Luke 17:21 in *Holy Bible*. Guelph, ON: Gideons International, p. 929.

23 Luke 17:21 in *The New English Bible*. Cambridge, UK: Cambridge University Press, 1970.

24 Luke 17:21 in *The Holy Bible, Revised Standard Version*. New York, NY: Thomas Nelson & Sons, 1946, p. 824.

25 Mitchell, S. *The Gospel According to Jesus*. New York, NY: HarperCollins, 1991, p. 11.

26 Matthew 18:20. *The Holy Bible, Revised Standard Version*. New York, NY: Thomas Nelson & Sons, 1952, p 773.

27 Jack Sproule, personal correspondence.

28 Armstrong, K. *A History of God*. New York, NY: Alfred Knopf, 1994, pp. 81–83.

29 The Gospel of Thomas, Saying 3, in Robinson, *Nag Hammadi Library in English*, p. 126.

30 McDonnell, T. (ed). *A Thomas Merton Reader*. Garden City, NY: Image Books, 1974, p. 482.

31 Machado, A. In Bly, R. (trans). *Times Alone: Selected Poems of Antonio Machado*. Middletown, CT, Wesleyan University Press, 1983, p. 109.

32 Brooks, D. *The Social Animal: The Hidden Sources of Love, Character and Achievement*. New York, NY: Random House, 2011, p. xi.

33 Ibid., p. xvii.

34 Ibid.

35 Ibid., p. 49.

36 Ibid., p. xviii.

37 Ibid.

38 Ibid., p. xiv.

39 Mitchell, S. *The Gospel According to Jesus*, p. 9.

40 Ibid.

41 H.H. Dalai Lama. <http://www.wildnesswithin.com/dalai.html>

42 Wilson, *The Mind Parasites*, p. 103.

43 McKeen, J. "Words (Palabras)" in McKeen, J. and Wong, B. *As It Is in Heaven*. Gabriola Island, BC: Haven Publishing, 1993, p. 167.

V.12   From Exile to Harmony

1 Lawrence, D.H. *Fantasia of the Unconscious and Psychoanalysis and the Unconscious*. Harmondsworth, England: Penguin Books, 1971, p. 246.

2 Merton, Thomas. *The Wisdom of the Desert*. New York: New Directions, 1960, p. 11.

3 Murray, J. (ed). *Poems to Live by in Uncertain Times*. Boston, MA: Beacon Press, 2001, p. 43.

4 Machado, A. In Bly, R. (ed). *The Soul is Here For Its Own Joy: Sacred Poems from Many Cultures*. Hopewell, NJ: Ecco Press, 1995, p. 42.

5 Tillich, P. *The Courage to Be*. New Haven, CT: Yale University Press, 1952, p. 66.

6 Swimme, B., and Berry, T. *The Universe Story*. San Francisco, CA: HarperSanFrancisco, 1992, p. 243.

7 Armstrong, K. *Twelve Steps to a Compassionate Life*. London, UK: The Bodley Head, 2011, p. 20.

8 Agee, J., Evans, W. *Let Us Now Praise Famous Men*. Boston, MA: Houghton Mifflin Co., 1988.

9 Rilke, R.M. (M.D. Herter, trans). *Letters to a Young Poet*. New York, NY: W.W. Norton & Co., 1962, pp. 53–54.

10 Buber, M. *The Knowledge of Man: A Philosophy of the Interhuman*. New York, NY: Harper & Row, 1965, p. 71.

11 Wilhelm, R. (trans). *The I Ching, or Book of Changes*. Princeton, NJ: Princeton University Press, 1950, p. 59.

V.13   Final Words

1 Eliot, T.S. *The Complete Poems and Plays of T.S. Eliot*. London, UK: Faber and Faber, 1969, p. 197.

2 Littleton, E. "Before Completion" in *Old Rocks, New Streams*. Victoria, B.C.: Ellery Littleton, 1993, Poem #64.

APPENDICES

Appendix 1

1 McKeen, J. and Wong, B. *As It Is in Heaven*. Gabriola Island, BC: Haven Publishing, 1993.

2 McKeen, J. and Wong, B. *The Relationship Garden*. Gabriola Island, BC: Haven Publishing, 1996, pp. 46–47.

Bennet Wong MD, FRCP(c), DLitt received his psychiatric training at the Menninger School of Psychiatry. Jock McKeen MD, LicAc(UK), DLitt studied at the College of Chinese Acupuncture, Oxford, England. In 1983 they founded The Haven Institute.

In over 40 years of professional association together, they have presented at conferences and workshops around the world. They have travelled and taught extensively in Asia and Europe, as well as Russia, Africa and South America. They bring an ease with cross-cultural approaches to their work and as consultants to many agencies, corporations and groups, they have a wide experience in working with people in a variety of contexts.

They have derived the core of their approach from the intense investigation of their own relationship, as well as their experiences with their clients. In their unique, personable way, they create an atmosphere of intimacy and trust in which each person is able to transform in his or her own fashion.

In 2004, The Haven Foundation was established, a federally recognized Canadian non-profit charity. Wong and McKeen and their three sons passed the ownership of The Haven Institute into The Haven Foundation so that the facility and their work could continue in perpetuity. Both men are now Emeritus Faculty of The Haven Institute. In 2012, they were awarded honorary doctorates by Vancouver Island University.

THE HAVEN

The Haven is a not-for-profit charitable organization located on beautiful Gabriola Island, BC, Canada. Celebrating its 30th anniversary in 2013, The Haven offers group-based programs that encourage personal, relational, and professional growth. People leave these programs with skills to be fully alive, have healthy relationships and communicate effectively.

Visit The Haven's websites to find out more:

www.haven.ca
www.couplesalive.com

☏ (1) 250 247 9211 or toll free 1 877 247 9238
✉ info@haven.ca

Made in the USA
Charleston, SC
03 October 2012